Wordsmith

Essentials of College English

Wordsmith
Essentials of
College English

Pamela Arlov
Macon State College

Nick Arlov
Central Georgia Technical College

PEARSON

Prentice Hall

Upper Saddle River, New Jersey 07458

Library of Congress Cataloging-in-Publication Data

Arlov, Pamela.
    Wordsmith : essentials of college English / Pamela Arlov, Nick Arlov.
        p. cm.
Includes index.
    ISBN 0-13-048894-1
    1. English language—Rhetoric. 2. Report writing. 3. English
language—Grammar—Handbooks, manuals, etc. I. Arlov, Nick. II. Title.
    PE1408 .A695 2003
    808'.042—dc22

                                                        2003018286

Senior Acquisitions Editor: Craig Campanella
Editor-in-Chief: Leah Jewell
Executive Managing Editor: Ann Marie McCarthy
Editorial Assistant: Joan Polk
Senior Marketing Manager: Rachel Falk
Marketing Assistant: Adam Laitman
Production Editor: Fran Russello
Manufacturing Buyer: Brian Mackey
Cover Designer: Bruce Kenselaar
Cover Photo: © Getty Images
Composition/Full-Service Project Management: Pine Tree Composition, Inc./
    Karen Berry
Printer/Binder: RR Donnelley & Sons
Cover Printer: Phoenix Color Corp.

Credits and acknowledgments borrowed from other sources and reproduced, with permission, in this textbook appear on pages 489–490.

Pearson Education LTD., London
Pearson Education Singapore, Pte. Ltd
Pearson Education Canada, Ltd
Pearson Education-Japan
Pearson Education Australia PTY,
    Limited
Pearson Education North Asia Ltd.
Pearson Educación de Mexico, S.A.
    de C.V.
Pearson Education Malaysia, Pte. Ltd
Pearson Education, Upper Saddle
    River, New Jersey

10 9 8 7 6 5 4 3 2 1
ISBN: 0-13-048894-1
AIE ISBN: 0-13-049265-5

Contents

Chapter 7   Essays, Essay Exams, and Summary Reports   81

Chapter 8   Communication Beyond the Classroom: Oral Presentations and E-Mail   111

Chapter 22   Misplaced and Dangling Modifiers

Chapter 23   Parallel Structure

Chapter 24   Capital Letters

Chapter 25   Words Commonly Confused

Chapter 26   Word Choice

Chapter 27   Commas

Preface
To the Instructor

Thank you for choosing *Wordsmith: Essentials of College English* as your textbook.

Like you, we are teachers of writing. Like you, we struggle to find the best way of teaching a subject that, on its surface, seems as simple as touching pen to paper. Yet writing is remarkably complex, incorporating the personality and experience of each writer and each reader. It requires adherence to agreed-upon rules of grammar, punctuation, and form. It is, in fact, a craft that might be best taught to a small group of students in a series of unhurried sessions and individual conferences over an extended period of time. But reality is the fifty-minute hour, the class of twenty or more, the term that is measured in weeks. How best to handle that reality?

Most writing instructors constantly refine their teaching methods, striving to make difficult concepts clear and tedious details interesting. Most of all, they try to ignite the spark that will help students see writing as a meaningful, life-enriching activity. A good textbook should reinforce those efforts.

The authors have spent considerable time trying to analyze what a good textbook should do, above and beyond presenting information in a given field. Here is what we have come up with: The book should be orderly and user-friendly, with a flexible format. Explanations should be clear and supported by numerous exercises and examples. The book should contain much more than is strictly necessary: it should be a smorgasbord, not just a meal. Finally, if it includes a little bit of fun, so much the better. We have written *Wordsmith* with those principles in mind.

Some Features of *Wordsmith: Essentials of College Communication*

- A direct, conversational, student-friendly approach is used through-out.
- The book is written on an adult level that appeals to both nontraditional students and traditional-age students.
- Lighthearted chapter openings encourage a positive and playful approach to learning.
- A flexible three-part layout allows you the freedom to mix and match writing chapters, grammar chapters, and readings as you wish.

Although each of you will use the book in a different way and adapt it to your own students' needs, the following overview of each section may give you some ideas. Also, check the Instructor's Guide in the back of the textbook for ideas on using a text and model syllabi.

Part 1   Essentials of Composition

Part 1, Essentials of Composition, takes the paragraph as its primary focus. The book begins with an overview of the writing process (Chapter 1), followed by a chapter on prewriting (Chapter 2). Chapters 3, 4, and 5 guide the student through the writing of the paragraph and address four principles of effective writing,: direction, support, unity, and coherence. Chapter 6 addresses revising, proofreading, and formatting.

The section continues with Chapter 7, Essays, Essay Exams, and Summary Reports" and concludes with "Communication Beyond the Classroom: Oral Presentations and E-Mail."

Special Features of Part 1   Essentials of Composition

- A student paragraph is presented in all drafts and stages along with a transcript of a student writing group's discussion of the work in progress. (Chapter 1)

- A section "For Right-Brained Writers" gives tips for students who tend to think in terms of "the whole" rather than in terms of a step-by-step process. (Chapter 1)

- The five steps in the writing process are presented in the order in which most writers address them: prewriting, planning, drafting, revising, and proofreading.

- One entire chapter and numerous exercises are devoted to writing a topic sentence and planning the paragraph. (Chapter 3)

- Topics for paragraph and journal writing provide a basis for assignments and encourage further practice.

- A chapter on essays, essay exams, and summary reports prepares students for the types of assignments they will encounter throughout their college career.

- A chapter on e-mail and oral presentations prepares students to communicate both in the classroom and in the workplace.

Part 2   Essentials of Grammar

Part 2, Essentials of Grammar, can be used in a variety of ways. It can be used along with direct, in-class instruction, in a lab setting, as a supplement to lab assignments, or for independent study. It also works well for instructors who want to combine methods by addressing more difficult topics in class, while assigning easier material or material that is clearly "review" for independent study.

In the grammar chapters, explanations are clear, and each topic is taken one skill at a time, with numerous practice exercises for each skill. At the end of each chapter are review exercises in increasing order of difficulty, ending with a paragraph-length editing exercise.

Special Features of Part 2   Essentials of Grammar

- Explanations are clear, logical, and user-friendly.

- Step-by-step, easy-to-understand presentation is suitable for classroom discussion or independent study.

- An abundance of practice exercises allows instructors to assign as much or as little as they wish, without having to hunt for supplemental exercises.

- Text boxes—"Real-world Writing," "Grammar Alert!" and "Punctuation Pointers"—add liveliness and interest.
- Practice exercises allow immediate review of each skill, while review exercises at the end of each chapter allow practice on increasing levels of difficulty.

Part 3   Essential Readings for Writers

Part 3, Essential Readings for Writers, offers essays by professional writers. These essays model writing at its best: entertaining, challenging, and thought-provoking. Each reading is followed by a comprehension exercise that includes questions about content, questions about the writer's techniques, and related topics for discussion and writing. Diversity in authorship, subject matter, and rhetorical method is emphasized.

Special Features of Part 3   Essential Readings for Writers

- High-interest readings provide professional models, reinforce reading skills, and serve as springboards for discussion and assignments.
- Questions help students understand both the content of the essays and the writer's techniques.
- Suggested topics for writing connect students' writing to ideas they have explored in the readings.

Supplements

Instructor's Edition. The IE for *Wordsmith: Essentials of College English* contains in-text answers to help instructors best prepare for class and a 26-page built-in instructor's guide bound directly into the back. Written by Pam and Nick Arlov, the Instructor's Guide provides sample syllabi, teaching tips, and additional chapter-specific assignments. Free to adoptors. ISBN: 0-13-049265-5.

Instructor's Resource Manual. The Instructor's Resource Manual contains additional sample syllabi and two chapter tests for each of the 30 chapters in the text. For each chapter there is one short answer and one multiple-choice test for instructors to choose from. There is also a grammar pretest and posttest. All are ready for easy duplication. Free to adoptors. ISBN: 0-13-049266-3.

Companion Website™ (www.prenhall.com/arlov). Free to students, the companion website for *Wordsmith: Essentials of College English* provides chapter learning objectives that help students organize key concepts, online quizzes, which include instant scoring and coaching, dynamic web links that provide a valuable source of supplemental information, and built-in routing that gives students the ability to forward essay responses and graded quizzes to their instructors.

PH WORDS. An internet-based, course management program, PH WORDS gives English instructors the ability to measure and track students' mastery of the elements of writing from the writing process, to patterns of development, to grammar. Covering over 100 topics, PH WORDS allows students to work on their specific areas of weakness, freeing up class time for instructors. Sold at a discount when packaged with *Wordsmith: Essentials of College English.* Visit www.prenhall.com/phwords for more information. Package ISBN: 0-13-104619-5.

The Prentice Hall Writing Skills Test Bank. Written as a source of extra tests for instructors, this printed test bank includes over 50 additional quizzes for instructors to give students. Covering the writing process, patterns of development and grammar, the Prentice Hall Writing Skills Test Bank offers two quizzes for each skill—one multiple choice and one short answer. It can be used with any Prentice Hall writing text. Free to adoptors. (0-13-111628-2)

The New American Webster Handy College Dictionary. Available free to students when packaged with *Wordsmith,* this dictionary has over 1.5 million Signet copies in print and over 115,000 definitions, including current phrases, slang, and scientific terms. It offers more than 1,500 new words, with over 200 not found in any other competing dictionary and features boxed inserts on etymologies and language. Package ISBN: 0-13-113504-X.

The Prentice Hall ESL Workbook. Available free to students when packaged with *Wordsmith,* this 138-page workbook is divided into seven major units, providing explanations and exercises in the most challenging grammar topics for non-native speakers. With over 80 exercise sets, this guide provides ample instruction and practice in nouns, articles, verbs, modifiers, pronouns, prepositions, and sentence structure. ISBN: 0-13-092323-0.

The Prentice Hall Grammar Workbook. Available free when packaged with *Wordsmith,* this 21-chapter workbook is a comprehensive source of instruction and practice for students who need additional grammar, punctuation, and mechanics instruction. Each chapter provides ample explanation, examples, and exercise sets. ISBN: 0-13-092321-4.

The Prentice Hall TASP Writing Study Guide. Available free to students when packaged with *Wordsmith,* this guide prepares students for the writing portion of the Texas Academic Skills Program test. In addition, it familiarizes the reader with the elements of the test and provides strategies for success. There are exercises for each part of the exam, and then a full-length practice test with answer key so students can gauge their own progress. ISBN: 0-13-041585-5.

The Prentice Hall Florida Exit Test Study Guide for Writing. Free when packaged with *Wordsmith,* this guide is designed to prepare students for the writing section of the Florida Exit test. It also acquaints readers with the parts of the test and provides strategies for success. ISBN: 0-13-111652-5.

Research Navigator™. Research Navigator™ is the one-stop research solution—complete with extensive help on the research process and three exclusive databases including EBSCO's ContentSelect Academic Journal Database, The New York Times Search by Subject Archive, and Best of the Web Link Library. Take a tour on the web at http://www.researchnavigator.com. Your students get FREE ACCESS to Research Navigator™ when you package Along These Lines with our exclusive Evaluating Online Resources: English 2004 guide.

To order any of these supplements, please contact your local Prentice Hall sales representative, or contact customer service at 1-800-526-0485.

Acknowledgments

We could not have written this book without the help, support, and collaboration of a great many people. We thank the staff at Prentice Hall, including Craig Campanella, Senior Editor, English, who has vision and a knack for seeing the big picture; Joan Polk, Editorial Assistant, who is knowledgeable, helpful, and truly a class act; Christy D. Schaack, Media Editor, who worked tirelessly on the *Wordsmith* Web sites; Rachel Falk, Marketing Manager, who always has just the right words. We also thank the incomparable Karen Berry of Pine Tree Composition, Production Editor; Jeanne Tibbetts of Pine Tree Composition, Pager; Elizabeth Morgan, Development Editor; Michael Farmer, Permissions Specialist; and Carolyn

Ingalls, Copyeditor. Profound thanks go to Deborah Brooks and Kurt Norlin of LaurelTech Integrated Publishing Services for lending their expertise to this project.

In addition, we thank the reviewers, whose comments helped to shape this book: Candace R. Ready, Piedmont Technical College; Debbie L. Noland, State Fair Community College; Elsie M. Burnett, Cedar Valley Community College; Michelle Dijak, Delta College; Judy D. Covington, Trident Technical College; Dennis Keen, Spokane Community College; Joyce Cheney, Santa Monica College; Shirley Hart Berry, Cape Fear Community College; and Patrick Haas, Glendale Community College.

We also thank our favorite muse, Ruby S. Acres, for inspiring us to do our best.

Pamela and Nick Arlov

Dear Instructors—

Writing well is perhaps the single most important skill needed to be successful in college. At Prentice Hall, our mission is to publish the highest quality writing textbooks to provide the instruction and practice needed for students to become the best writers they can be.

In a course where accuracy is crucial to success, we also realize it can be frustrating when a textbook contains errors that might distract students from the ultimate goal—becoming a better writer.

We are committed to providing the best and most accurate textbooks for students and instructors alike. To that end, we have done more than ever before to ensure that *Wordsmith: Essentials of College English* is as error-free as possible.

In addition to our standard three rounds of copyediting and proofreading, we hired an independent company, Laurel Technical Services, to perform a three-step accuracy check on this text. LaurelTech has checked for any remaining typographical errors, completed every exercise to make sure the answers provided were correct, and worked with the author to guarantee every explanation is as clear as possible.

Since 1993, LaurelTech's editorial team has assisted textbook publishers with over one hundred titles in the college market alone. The company's services include accuracy checking, revising, copyediting, proofreading, and the writing of original material for both textbooks and supplements. LaurelTech has a reputation for working closely with authors to help make texts as error-free as possible. We are very excited to have this wonderful company on board with us.

We take the accuracy of our textbooks very seriously. If you see something in this text that you believe to be an error, I ask you to please contact me at craig_campanella@prenhall.com.

Thank you for using Prentice Hall textbooks.

Sincerely,

Craig Campanella
Senior Editor, English
Prentice Hall
1 Lake Street–Suite 4F
Upper Saddle River, NJ 07458

Preface
To the Student

A Look at the Future

You open your e-mail and read a message from the human resources director at the company you hope to work for. You have been called back for a second interview. As you think back on the interview process, from the preparation of your resumé and letter of application to the final handshake, you realize that interviewing is entirely a process of communication. At the second interview, you'll meet and talk with several of the people you'll be working with if you are hired. Again, strong communication skills will help you. If your prospective coworkers like you and what you have to say, you'll have a better chance at the job.

As you reply to the e-mail, you feel confident. Your college experience and your own effort have prepared you for this moment. You take a moment to proofread your e-mail, and then you press the "send" button.

No Time like the Present

The ability to communicate well is not the only skill you need in college and in the workplace, but it's one of the more important ones. In the classroom and beyond, the people who do well are most often those who think logically, who consider all the possibilities, and who communicate clearly. Writing can help you develop those skills.

In the college classroom, those who stand out also tend to be good writers and speakers. They write clearly, they state their ideas completely, and they don't embarrass themselves with poor grammar or misspelled words.

Perhaps, like most people, you feel that there's room for improvement in your communication skills. Maybe you feel that your grammar is not up to par, or maybe you're just never sure where to put commas. Or perhaps you go blank when you see an empty page in front of you, waiting to be filled.

But there's good news. The ability to communicate is not a talent bestowed by fate; rather, it is a skill, like driving a car, playing a harmonica, or designing a web page on the computer. It is built through your own hard work and improved by practice.

How can you improve your communication skills? You're in the right place, enrolled in a writing course, and you are holding the right object in your hand—this textbook. But the real key is not the course, the textbook, or even your instructor. The key is you. If you take guitar lessons but never practice, how well will you play? Or think of weight training—if you buy a book about it but never exercise your muscles, how much change will occur? You have a book on writing and a "personal trainer"— your instructor—ready to help you. If you work at improving your communication skills, you will amaze yourself.

There's no time like the present to shape your future.

How This Textbook Can Help

This textbook is designed to help you on your journey to becoming the writer you want to be, the writer your future demands. Read on to find out how each section can help you develop your writing skills.

Part 1, Essentials of Composition, gives you an overview of the writing process and provides step-by-step instructions for writing a paragraph, the basic building block for any longer piece of writing. It introduces the five-paragraph essay, a flexible tool that can be your admission ticket to the academic world. Shrunk down a bit, the essay format can be used to answer a question on an essay test. Expanded a bit, it can be used to write a research paper, a term paper, or even a master's thesis. Communications skills that you use beyond the classrooms, such as writing e-mail messages and speaking in public, are also addressed in this section of the book.

Part 2, Essentials of Grammar, provides wide coverage of grammar and punctuation. Some of the concepts covered are probably review for you, whereas others are new. The chapters are user-friendly and take a step-by-step approach, so that you can work with them in class or on your own.

Feel free to use the chapters in this section as a reference. If you aren't sure of a comma rule, look it up in the chapter on commas. If you aren't sure of your subject-verb agreement, check it out in the subject-verb agreement chapter. You will gain knowledge as you improve your writing.

You can also the chapters as a way to improve your grammar. If your instructor marks several sentence fragments on your paper, don't wait until the topic is covered in class; instead, work through the chapter on your own so that you can correct the problem *now*.

Part 3, Essential Readings for Writers, contains readings from professional writers. You will notice differences between the journalistic writing of these professionals and the academic form you are encouraged to use. Topic sentences are not always placed at the beginning of each paragraph. The language is often informal. But these are merely differences of *audience*—writing in the academic world is expected to be more formal than journalistic essays written for a general audience. You will see similarities, too. The essays have the same qualities you are encouraged to incorporate in your paragraphs: direction, unity, coherence, and support.

Good readers make good writers. The more you read, the better your writing will become.

Just the Beginning

Writing is hard work. But it is also worthwhile. The more you write, the better you will become, all your life long. Whatever your major, whatever your vocation, writing can serve you well. May this book mark just the beginning of your journey as a writer.

Part 1
Essentials of Composition

1

The Writing Process

prewrite PLAN draft PLAN REVISE proofread DRAFT plan PREWRITE plan DRAFT revise PROOFREAD prewrite DRAFT revise REVISE plan PREWRITE proofread PLAN REVISE plan REVISE plan PROOFREAD plan PROOFREAD prewrite PLAN plan PREWRITE plan DRAFT

The Writing Process

Writing is not a single act, but a process composed of several steps. As with most processes—shooting a basketball, riding a motorcycle, reading a book—writing is sometimes easier to do than to analyze. When people try to analyze how they write, their descriptions of the process are uniquely their own. Yet from a sea of individual accounts, the same steps emerge.

One writer, Marina, described the process this way:

> When I get an assignment, I don't usually start right away. I have to think about it for a while before I get started because ideas don't come to me right away. After I have given it a little thought, I usually jot down some ideas or make a short outline. Sometimes, though, I just start writing. After I finish with my rough draft, I sometimes ask someone to look at it and to give me ideas, or I look at it myself to see what needs fixing. I am my own worst critic. I always find something—places where I have gone off the subject or where I could put in some more detail. When I have fixed the problems, I give it one last

reading to find errors in spelling and grammar. Then I'm ready to turn it in.

Though everyone approaches writing a little differently, most of us follow a process similar to the one just described. Though the writer in the preceding example may not be aware of it, she is following all of the steps in the *writing process*: prewriting, planning, drafting, revising, and proofreading.

Prewriting

"I have to think about it for a while . . ."

Prewriting covers a range of activity from casually thinking about your topic to going through a **prewriting exercise** to get your thoughts on paper. You will probably find yourself doing some form of prewriting throughout the writing process. When you are sitting at a traffic light and the perfect example to illustrate your point pops into your head, you are prewriting. When you realize that your paragraph isn't working the way you wanted it to work and you stop to list ideas or to try another approach, you are returning to the prewriting stage. Prewriting *is* thinking, and the more thought you put into your paper, the stronger it will be.

Planning

"I usually jot down some ideas or make a short outline."

A well-planned paragraph is easier for you to write and easier for your readers to read. Your plan may include a *topic sentence*, your statement of the main idea. Because it states the main idea, the topic sentence is the cornerstone of your paragraph. Besides a topic sentence, your planning will probably also include an informal outline. Don't be afraid that planning will waste your time. Careful planning—or lack of it—always shows in the final draft.

Drafting

"I just start writing."

Writing a draft of your paragraph is sometimes a quick process, with ideas flowing faster than you can get them down on paper. At other times, the process is slow and difficult. If you get stuck during the drafting process, don't quit in frustration. The creative process is still at work. *Write through* the problem, or, if necessary, return to the planning or prewriting stage.

As you draft your paragraph, you should not worry about grammar, spelling, or punctuation. Concentrate on ideas, and save the proofreading for later.

Revising

| "I look at it . . . to see what needs fixing."

In its Latin roots, the word *revising* means "seeing again." Revising is difficult because it is hard to see your work with the eyes of a reader. Writers often see what they *meant* to say rather than what they really said. Sometimes it helps to put your draft aside for a day or so before trying to revise it. With twenty-four hours between writing and revising, you will see your paper more clearly. It is also helpful to ask someone else to look at your work—perhaps a friend, classmate, or relative. Ask the person to focus on the *content* of your paper rather than on grammar, spelling, or punctuation. Ask which ideas are clear and which ones need more explanation. Also, ask how well your examples illustrate your points. A reader's comments can help you see your paper in a new light.

One word of advice—if you don't know how to use a computer, learn. Writing multiple drafts of your paragraph is much easier on a computer. Once you learn to write on a computer, the essays, term papers, and reports that you are assigned in college will look much less intimidating.

Proofreading

| "I give it one last reading to find errors in spelling and grammar."

Proofreading is the final polish that you put on your paragraph. When you proofread, consider such matters as grammar, spelling, and word choice. Replace vague words with specific words, and take out words that are not carrying their weight. Look at connections, making sure that ideas flow smoothly from one sentence to the next. Because the stages of the writing process overlap, you will have probably done some minor proofreading as your paragraph has taken shape. Before the final proofreading, set your paragraph aside for a while—a couple of hours or a couple of days. Then proofread it once more to give it a final polish.

An Important Point

If you go through the writing process expecting the steps to fall in order, like the steps involved in changing the oil in your car, you may think the process is not working. However, writing a paragraph is not a sequential process. It is a repetitive process, more like driving a car than changing its oil.

If you take a two-hundred-mile trip, the steps you follow might be described as "Turn on the ignition. Put the car in drive. Accelerate. Brake. Put the car in park. Turn off the ignition." Yet the process is not that simple. During a two-hundred-mile drive, you repeat each step not once but several times, and you may even stop for rest or fuel.

The same principle holds in writing a paragraph. You may list the steps as "prewrite, plan, draft, revise, proofread," but the process is not that simple. You may find yourself correcting a spelling mistake or changing the order of the paragraphs as you write the first draft. Sometimes you repeat a step several times. You may even stop for rest or fuel, just as you might when driving a car. Eventually, both processes will get you where you want to go.

EXERCISE 1   THE WRITING PROCESS

Fill in the blanks in the sentences that follow to review your knowledge of the writing process.

1. The five steps in the writing process are ___prewriting___, ___planning___, ___drafting___, ___revising___, and ___proofreading___.

2. The "thinking step" in the writing process is called ___prewriting___.

3. The part of the writing process that involves correcting grammar and punctuation is called ___proofreading___.

4. Major changes would most likely be made during the ___revising___ step in the writing process.

5. True or false? The steps in the writing process often overlap. (T) F

The Writing Process: Rodrigo's Paragraph

The next section of the chapter follows the development of the paragraph of one writer, Rodrigo, from start to finish. In writing his paragraph, Rodrigo went through several forms of prewriting, made two different outlines, conferred with his instructor and members of his writing group, and wrote two rough drafts. (Only the first is shown here, since the final draft reflects all of the changes Rodrigo made.) Before turning in his final draft, Rodrigo also proofread the paragraph once from top to bottom and twice from bottom to top. Then he asked a member of his writing group to look over the final draft for any mistakes he had overlooked.

The steps that Rodrigo goes through are steps that you will take as you learn the writing process. You will also share some of his frustrations. But like Rodrigo, you will probably find that what seems difficult at first is attainable, one step at a time.

Rodrigo's Assignment

Rodrigo's instructor handed out a list of three paragraph topics. Rodrigo chose to write on this one: "Write about a person who has made a difference in your life."

Rodrigo's instructor suggested that the students try one or more forms of prewriting, then make an outline. Earlier, the class had been divided into writing groups of four or five people who would help one another during the term. The instructor suggested that the writing groups meet to discuss each student's outline. Then, students would write rough drafts to bring to individual writing conferences with the instructor.

Rodrigo's Prewriting

In class, Rodrigo did a form of prewriting called *freewriting*. (For more information on freewriting and other forms of prewriting, see Chapter 2.) In this prewriting, Rodrigo did not worry about grammar or spelling but focused on gathering ideas. Rodrigo's prewriting is reproduced here without correction.

Rodrigo's Freewriting

My family has made a difference in my life. Without my mothers love and support, there is no telling where I would be today. My little brother makes a difference, too. I know he is always watching me and copying whatever I do, so I try to be a good role model. Stan, my supervisor at work, is a jerk and a hypocrite and I really hate him. As much as I hate to give him any credit, he is the reason I am in college. I guess I should write about my mother. She has always loved and supported me and even when I have done things she has not approved of, she has always given me her support. She goes to work everyday so that we can have food on the table and clothes on our backs, and I will always be grateful.

Rodrigo's instructor returned his prewriting with a note: "I am intrigued by the jerk. Try a focused freewriting on Stan." Focused freewriting is a technique in which the writer does a freewriting focused on a single aspect of a previous freewriting. Rodrigo's focused freewriting appears next, followed by a rough draft based on the focused freewriting.

Rodrigo's Focused Freewriting

Stan, my supervisor at the home improvement center where I work, is a total jerk. I used to get along with him okay, until the day I found out how he really was. He always acted nice to my face, but one day I overheard him tell the manager not to promote me from the stockroom to the customer service area. He said — exact words, I'll never forget — "Rod's a good kid, but he's never going anywhere. He has absolutely no ambition." I thought, "How does he know? What does he know about me except what he sees in that crummy stockroom?" It really got to me, and somehow I had to prove him wrong, so I enrolled in college. I do have ambition, but I guess it was on hold. The truth is, I really wasn't going anywhere. I had been out of highschool for three years, and just worked at the Home Place. I don't guess I ever showed much enthusiasm for the job. I don't like Stan, but I guess the truth is that he did me a favor.

Rodrigo's Rough Draft

It's hard to admit that someone you don't even like has changed your life for the better, but in my case, it's true. I work in the warehouse at a home-improvement store that sells lumber, appliances, kitchen and bathroom fixtures, and hardware of all types. Work in the warehouse is tough, physical work, which I don't mind but it can get old. When I had a chance to be promoted to the customer-service area of the store, I applied. I had been at the store since even before I graduated from high school, so I had some seniority, but that's not all that they consider in promotions. One day, I was on my way back to the break room, and I heard my boss discussing promotions with the store manager. I was not deliberately listening, but when I heard my name, I stopped in the hall. I heard Stan say, "Rod's a good kid, but he's never going anywhere. He has absolutely no ambition." I thought, "How does he know? What does he know about me except what he sees in that crummy stockroom?" It really got to me, and somehow I had to prove him wrong, so I enrolled in college. I do have ambition, but I guess it was on hold. The truth is, I really wasn't going anywhere. I had been out of highschool for three years, and just worked at the Home Place. I don't guess I ever showed much enthusiasm for the job. I don't like Stan, but I guess the truth is that he did me a favor.

Rodrigo's Writing Group Meets

Next, Rodrigo met with his writing group. A transcript of the portion of the session dealing with Rodrigo's outline appears here.

Transcript: Writing Group Session, Wednesday, September 12

Jamesha: Okay, who's the first victim? Lu?

Lu: No thanks. Rod, you go.

Rodrigo: Okay, I don't mind.

(Rodrigo passes out copies of his prewriting and rough draft, and the group reads silently.)

Lu: I like it.

Rodrigo: No, Lu, you like that you didn't have to go first.

(Laughter.)

Andrew: I like it, too. And I agree that writing about a jerk is more interesting than writing about your mother. Mothers are great, but they're so *nice*.

Rodrigo: Yeah, I didn't want to write about Stan because I still don't like him, but I have to admit, it's more interesting.

Jamesha: One thing, though. You spend a lot of time giving background about where you work and the appliances and so on. Are you sure we need that?

Rodrigo: I don't know. I just wanted to sort of set the stage.

Jamesha: Maybe you can do it in just a sentence or so.

Andrew: I agree with Jamesha. I'd rather hear more about the jerk.

Rodrigo: Maybe you're right. I really don't go into much detail about him or about how my life has changed for the better. I just say I'm in college.

Lu: Yes, and I hate to point it out, but look— the last part of your paragraph is exactly like your prewriting. Talk about lazy!

(Laughter.)

Rodrigo: Hey, why mess with perfection? Okay, I'll spice it up a little. Anything else, other than "change the entire paragraph"?

(Laughter.)

Andrew: No, it looks good to me.

Lu: Me, too.

Rodrigo: Thanks, everybody. You've been a big help.

Rodrigo's Final Draft, after Proofreading

Rodrigo wrote a second rough draft. Then, he met with his instructor for a conference before writing his final draft. Rodrigo's final draft follows.

Rude Awakening

It's hard to admit that a total jerk changed my life for the better, but it's true. I had always thought that Stan, my supervisor at the home improvement store, liked me and my work. But one day, I overheard him talking to the store manager about me. He said, "Rod's a nice kid, but he's never going anywhere. He has absolutely no ambition." I

was angry, but more than that, I was determined to
prove him wrong. I do have ambition, but I have to
admit that it had been on hold. I decided to change
my ways. At first, I started paying more attention
to the way I dressed for work. I tried to take
initiative, see what needed to be done, and do it
before I was asked. Then, I began to fantasize that
one day I would be Stan's boss. I realized how
unlikely that fantasy was without a college degree,
so I signed up for classes. One day, when Stan asked
me to work overtime, I casually told him I had a
class I could not miss. I loved the look of surprise
on his face. Now, I can see that my negative image
at work is turning into a positive one. Best of all,
my self-image is improving. I have higher ambitions
than just the petty revenge of being Stan's boss. As
for Stan, I still don't like him, but his negative
assessment of me gave me the rude awakening I needed
to turn my life around.

Rodrigo's Approach to Writing—and Yours

Rodrigo's final draft is the product of many hours of thought and work,
and is at least partly a result of his willingness to listen to the advice and
comments of others.

Writing is a process of trial and error, and sometimes it can feel like
mostly error. Even experienced writers often find writing difficult, often
wondering each time they write whether they have anything worthwhile
to say or the ability to say it. If you fear writing, even if you dislike it, you
are not alone. But writing is a skill that improves with practice, and if you
give it daily serious effort, you will amaze yourself.

Journal Writing: Jump-Starting the Writing Process

One way to give yourself the practice you need to become a better writer
is through journal writing. Journals are "daily writings"—the word
journal comes from *jour*, the French word for *day*. A journal usually contains informal writings on a variety of subjects.

How can a journal make you a better writer? Different activities improve writing in different ways. Reading enriches your vocabulary, sparks your imagination, and allows you to see how other writers express themselves. The study of grammar helps you understand and use the standard English that is expected of writers. But even reading and the study of grammar won't help you with *fluency*—the ability to put words onto the page. Only practice of the kind that you get in journal writing can help you develop fluency.

A journal also allows you to experiment with the techniques you are learning in your writing class. In a journal, the only form of writing you should avoid is "diary mode." An "I-got-up-I-fed-the-dog-I-went-to-school" format makes for dull writing and even duller reading. Write about issues that matter to you. Tell your dreams. Describe your grandfather's tool shed. Work toward detailed writing that follows a logical pattern.

Whether you receive credit for it in class or not, make journal writing a habit. Unlike some writing assignments, which may involve researching, writing, revising, and revising again, a journal entry should take less than an hour of your time. Even that may seem like a lot of time to invest, but practice is the only thing that is *guaranteed* to make you a better writer. Courses and texts are of limited value without time spent alone with a word processor or pen and paper. If you think, "Practice won't matter. I'll never be a good writer," ask yourself this: how good a driver would you be if the only driving you had done was in a driver education course? You *can* be a better writer. Daily writing in your journal will start you on your way.

Journal Topics

1. What are some reasons for keeping a journal or diary?
2. If you could spend a week anywhere, where would you go?
3. Should people who move to the United States from other countries make special efforts to preserve their native culture as they begin to live in a different culture?
4. Among the popular athletes and entertainers of today, whom do you consider to be a good role model? Why?
5. Are you frugal, or are you a spendthrift? Give specific examples.
6. What are some of the advantages and disadvantages of cell phones?
7. What part of the newspaper do you read first? Why?
8. Which modern convenience would you most hate to do without?
9. What is your recipe for success in life?
10. Do you enjoy following politics? Why or why not?

11. If you could have one skill that you do not now possess, what would it be?

12. Are today's schools doing a good job? Explain.

13. How do you cope with stress?

14. What job would you absolutely refuse to take?

15. What is your favorite season? Why?

Using the Writing Process

Writing Assignment 1   Writing and You

During your lifetime, you have had many experiences with writing. Some may have been positive. You may have enjoyed writing in a journal or diary, or may have experimented with creative writing. Perhaps you had a teacher who encouraged you or an assignment that inspired you and brought out your best. Other experiences may have been negative—you may have received a poor grade on an assignment or had a teacher who never seemed pleased with your writing. All of these experiences contributed to your attitude toward writing. Your assignment is to use the steps in the writing process to write a paragraph describing your attitudes toward writing.

Step 1: Prewrite. Jot down a few of the words that come to mind when you think of writing. Think of any significant experiences you have had that have shaped your attitude toward writing. Consider your writing habits. Are you organized? Do you procrastinate?

Step 2: Plan. Look over your prewriting. Try to sum up your attitude toward writing in a single word or phrase, and then construct an opening sentence for your paragraph using that word or phrase. Use one of the following sentences, filling in the blank with your word or phrase, or construct your own sentence.

My attitude toward writing is_____.

When I think about writing, I feel _____.

My feelings about writing have always been _____ ones.

Once you have constructed an opening sentence, decide how to organize your paragraph. A couple of possibilities follow.

1. One approach you might take is a historical approach, describing the influences that have shaped your writing. Use chronological (time) order.

2. Another possible choice is a step-by-step approach, describing what you do and how you feel as you go through a writing assignment.

Finally, complete the planning stage by making an outline that briefly lists the points you plan to make in support of your opening sentence.

Step 3: Draft. Write out a rough draft of your paragraph. Focus on expressing your ideas rather than on grammar and punctuation.

Step 4: Revise. Read over your rough draft. Have you left out anything important? Is each idea clearly expressed? Does the paragraph flow smoothly? Is the sequence of ideas logical and effective? If possible, ask a classmate to look over your rough draft with the same questions in mind. Then revise your paragraph, incorporating any necessary changes.

Step 5: Proofread. Check your paragraph for mistakes in spelling, grammar, or punctuation. Look at each sentence individually. Then proofread once more. You have now completed all the steps in the writing process.

Writing Assignment 2   The Road to Your College Education

In this assignment, you will write a paragraph that reflects on the path that has brought you to college.

Step 1: Prewrite. Consider the forces in your life that brought you to college. Is college something that has always been planned for you, a logical next step in your education? Or did you come by a different path, trying out the world of work or raising your own children first? Is there a person or an event that inspired you to further your education?

Step 2: Plan. As you plan your paragraph, consider your method of organization. You may want to place the factors in order of importance, or you may wish to organize your paragraph chronologically, from past to present.

Step 3: Draft. Write out a rough draft of your paragraph. Focus on expressing your ideas rather than on grammar and punctuation.

Step 4: Revise. Read over your rough draft. Have you left out anything important? Is each idea clearly expressed? Does the paragraph flow smoothly? Is the sequence of ideas logical and effective? If possible, ask a classmate to look over your rough draft with the same questions in mind. Then revise your paragraph, incorporating any necessary changes.

Step 5: Proofread. Check your paragraph for mistakes in spelling, grammar, or punctuation. Look at each sentence individually. Then proofread once more. You have now completed all the steps in the writing process.

2

Preparing to Write

> Writing is easy. All you do is stare at a blank sheet of paper until drops of blood form on your forehead.
>
> —Gene Fowler

As the quotation above suggests, writing *isn't* always easy. Many writers develop "writer's block" when they are confronted with a blank sheet of paper or a blank computer screen. They fear that they will not be able to think of anything to say, or that if they do find something to say, it will be wrong. Writer's block happens to almost everyone at one time or another. It is not an indication of poor writing ability. In fact, writers who get writer's block are usually those who care most about how they present themselves.

One of the best defenses against writer's block is preparation. Care in finding your topic and exploring that topic through prewriting will help you lay the groundwork for a strong paragraph or essay and will also help you avoid writer's block.

Finding a Topic

The first step in preparing to write is finding a topic. Fortunately, academic assignments usually provide you with guidelines. Very rarely will an instructor tell you to "just write about anything." Instead, you may be given a list of one or more topics to explore. You may even be given a structured assignment with specific objectives to work toward. Your approach will depend on the nature of the assignment. If you are given a general topic, you will need to narrow it through prewriting to find a focus. If you are given a more structured assignment, you will need to analyze and understand it, and then prewrite to generate ideas.

Narrowing a Topic

If you are assigned a broad topic, narrowing the topic through prewriting is the next logical step. A *broad topic* is too large to develop in a single paragraph; however, it has many possible subtopics waiting to be discovered and developed. For example, a topic such as "college" is broad and can be narrowed to many possible subtopics: choosing a college, adjusting to college life, participating in extracurricular activities, and many more. The exercises that follow will help you distinguish a subtopic from a broad topic and will help you recognize subtopics that arise in your prewriting.

EXERCISE 1   DISTINGUISHING BROAD TOPICS FROM SUBTOPICS

Each numbered item contains three subtopics and one broad topic. Put an *S* beside the subtopics and a *B* beside the broad topic.

1. __B__ Money

    __S__ How to save money on clothing

    __S__ Paying yourself first: developing a savings plan

    __S__ Managing credit card debt

2. __S__ Air fare nightmare

    __S__ A favorite vacation spot

    __B__ Travel

    __S__ Travel games to keep children entertained

3. __S__ Safe and effective weight training

    __S__ Stretching

    __S__ The benefits of yoga

    __B__ Exercise

4. __S__ Caring for your car's engine

    __B__ Automobiles

    __S__ What cars reveal about their owners

    __S__ How to buy a used car

5. __S__ Managing diabetes

    __B__ Coping with chronic health conditions

    __S__ Eating to lower cholesterol

    __S__ Managing a child's asthma

EXERCISE 2   NARROWING A TOPIC

For each topic, list at least three potential subtopics that could be developed into individual paragraphs. The first one is done for you.

Answers will vary; sample answers are provided.

1. Self-improvement

    Losing weight through exercise

    Becoming a more effective speaker

    Becoming more organized

2. Recreation

    Hiking as a hobby

    Outdoor games for people with physical disabilities

    My volleyball disaster

3. Addictions

    Internet addiction: a twenty-first century disorder

    Nicotine patches for smoking cessation

    Using drug education to prevent addiction

4. Relationships with people

    How to cultivate good relationships with coworkers

    Why close relationships are important to good health

    The risks and rewards of online relationships

5. Music

    The new popularity of "roots music"

    Internet radio

    My harmonica

Analyzing and Understanding an Assignment

If you are given a structured assignment rather than a broad topic, the narrowing has at least partially been done for you, and a focus has been provided. The next task is to analyze the assignment to make sure that you understand it.

Understanding an assignment may seem too simple to mention, but it is an essential first step. In the novel *Bridget Jones' Diary,* the main character is invited to what she thinks is a costume party. Arriving in a skimpy bunny costume, complete with ears, tail, and fishnet stockings, Bridget at first endures the smirks and stares of more soberly dressed partygoers, but then leaves in embarrassment. It does not matter how charming she is or how cute she looks in her costume, because her approach was wrong from the start. She didn't understand her assignment—to come to the party dressed in everyday clothes.

By the same token, it will not matter how convincing or well written a paper is if the writer has misunderstood the assignment. Analyzing an assignment prevents embarrassing misunderstandings and ensures an approach that is right from the start.

Look at the following assignment, taken from the end of this chapter:

> Write a paragraph discussing the qualities of an effective teacher (or if you prefer, qualities of an ineffective teacher). As you prewrite, think of the best (or worst) teachers you have ever had so that you can use specific examples.

The assignment is just two sentences long and not at all complex. Still, a writer who does not bother to analyze the assignment can easily misread it. It is essential, for instance, to note that the assignment itself is in the first sentence while the second sentence refers to prewriting to generate examples. It's also important to notice the word *or,* which implies a choice between two alternatives.

EXERCISE 3   ANALYZING AN ASSIGNMENT

Look at the following responses to the assignment. Only two are direct and exact responses. The others are the academic equivalent of Bridget Jones' bunny suit: they make it all too clear that the assignment was not understood. Read the responses, and put a check beside the two that directly respond to the assignment. Put an ✗ beside those that do not. Be prepared to explain how the two assignments that you checked fulfill the assignment and why the others do not. The assignment is repeated for easy reference.

Write a paragraph discussing the qualities of an effective teacher (or if you prefer, qualities of an ineffective teacher). As you prewrite, think of the best (or worst) teachers you have ever had so that you can use specific examples.

✗ Antoine writes a paper called "Third Grade Horror," describing how his life was nearly ruined by Ms. Morgan, the meanest teacher at Brookdale Elementary. He supports with a detailed example of how Ms. Morgan humiliated tardy students by making them stand with their noses in a circle on the chalkboard.

(Antoine's paper does not directly respond to the assignment. His focus is not on "qualities of an ineffective teacher" but on his bad experience with one specific teacher.)

✔ Sarita writes that patience is an essential quality of a good teacher. She uses the example of her high school math instructor, who patiently answered the same questions over and over. She mentions a sense of humor as another essential quality, describing a history teacher who kept students entertained with funny stories about historical figures.

(Sarita's paper fulfills the assignment by mentioning two essential qualities of a good teacher and giving specific examples.)

✗ Ashley writes about why she wants to be a teacher.

(Ashley's paper does not directly respond to the assignment. Ashley gives reasons for wanting to be a teacher but does not provide characteristics of an effective or ineffective teacher.)

✗ Derrick writes a paragraph contrasting the characteristics of good and bad teachers. He uses specific examples from his own experience to support his ideas.

(Derrick's paper responds to the assignment. However, Derrick goes beyond the boundaries of the assignment by including both effective and ineffective teachers. The first sentence of the assignment clearly says "or." Derrick should check with his instructor before modifying a topic.)

✔   Javon writes that bad teachers are lazy and mean-spirited. He uses specific examples to support his ideas.

(Javon fulfills the assignment by mentioning two qualities of bad teachers and giving specific examples.)

✗   Glenda writes that student evaluations of teachers at the college she attends should be made available to students, so that they can choose the good teachers and avoid the bad.

(Glenda's paper does not directly respond to the assignment. Glenda's focus is on availability of student evaluations rather than on characteristics of effective or ineffective teachers.)

Careful reading of an assignment, then, is the essential first step. As you consider your assignment, questions may come to mind. Your instructor will welcome the opportunity to clarify the assignment for you, and your question will probably provoke other questions from your classmates. People sometimes hold back questions for fear of sounding stupid or uninformed. The paradox is that in school and in the world of business, it's usually not the person who has all the answers who gets the job done. It's the person who asks the right questions.

Once you are sure you understand the assignment, you are ready for the next step, prewriting.

Prewriting

Prewriting is the act of sorting out your thoughts and finding out what you have to say. Most often, you discover that you have more to say about a subject than you thought, that you know more than you imagined. Occasionally the opposite happens, and you find that you have less to say than you initially thought. In either case, using one or more prewriting methods can help you discover what you know about a topic.

Prewriting Methods

There is no "right" or "wrong" way to prewrite. Instead, there are various methods to choose from. The goal of all the methods is the same: to help you get ideas on paper. At this point in the writing process, it is not the quality of ideas that counts, but the quantity.

When you are ready to prewrite, sit at the computer or in a comfortable spot with pen and paper. Relax your mind and body, and remind yourself that prewriting is a playful, creative exercise and that it is okay to write down anything that comes to mind. As for the part of your mind that automatically jumps in to criticize what you think and say, tell it to take a hike. Your purpose in prewriting is to put down every thought on your topic, *no matter how silly or ridiculous it seems*. Later, you can discard what is not usable. But while you are prewriting, there is no good or bad, no right or wrong.

Some of the methods may feel awkward at first, but try them all. One will be right for you.

Brainstorming

Brainstorming, a listing technique, is one of the easiest prewriting techniques. To brainstorm, take a few minutes to list whatever comes to mind on your topic. Your purpose is not to censor or come up with the "right" items for your list, but to generate ideas.

Example

Here's how one writer, Jamal, approached a brainstorming exercise on the topic "Describe a situation that was stressful for you."

Job interview

sweaty palms when I shook interviewer's hand

talked too much out of nervousness

office was hot — worried about deodorant failure

chair had one short leg, kept me off balance

interviewer seemed bored, like he had already decided

worried I was overdressed in tie & jacket

cluttered office, papers piled everywhere

nearly fell over when he asked when I could start

When Jamal looked at his prewriting, he was not sure he could use it all, but he knew he had captured some of the vivid memories of his job interview.

EXERCISE 4   BRAINSTORMING

Read and understand the following sample assignments, and then brainstorm on one of the topics to find ideas for a possible paragraph.

Answers will vary.

1. Discuss the way you handled a situation that was stressful for you.
2. What characteristics do you find annoying in a classmate?
3. Think of a place that you would describe as "comfortable." Describe and explain the characteristics that make it a comfortable place.
4. Explain the steps involved in a task that you do well.
5. Is it better to stay in one job for one's entire career or to move from job to job?

Freewriting

Freewriting is nonstop writing on a topic for a set time. The point of freewriting is that your flow of words never ceases; your pen never stops moving. If you have nothing to say, repeat your last thought again and again until a new thought replaces it. Do not worry about spelling, about clarity, or about whether your thoughts are logically connected. Just write.

If you are using a computer, try turning your monitor off or adjusting the contrast button at the bottom of your screen until the words are no longer visible and your screen is completely dark. This form of freewriting, called "invisible writing," may seem strange at first. Soon, though, your fingers—and your thoughts—will fly.

Example

Elena did the following freewriting when her instructor asked the class to write on the general topic "grades."

Grades are the way a teacher lets you know how you are doing. Really, they are just feedback, but they take on more importance to students. I stress out about my grades. Partly because they are important to my parents, who always tell me I can do better when I bring home bad grades. On the other hand, if you look at it from a long-term point of view, who cares? Do you know what grades your doctor got in medical school? For that matter, have you ever seen your professor's college *transcript? The grades you make aren't what's important in the long run, it's how much you learn and how well you do your job. And what about people who cheat? They may make good grades, but what have they learned? Also, what is the definition of good grades? Who has achieved more, a math genius who aces every test without studying or the person who really struggles and manages to pull a C out of the course? Grades are not as important as my parents think they are.*

When Elena looked over her freewriting, she noticed that her focus seemed to be on whether grades are important and valid.

EXERCISE 5   **FREEWRITING**

Freewrite on one of the following questions, and then see if you have a focus for a paragraph.

Answers will vary.

1. Are grades important?
2. What is your favorite memory?
3. Is it wise or foolish for the average person to own a gun?
4. Are you easily amused or easily bored?
5. What can you tell about a person from the car he or she drives?

Clustering

Clustering is a technique designed to boost your creativity by stimulating both hemispheres of the brain. The left hemisphere, or "left brain," is used in logical tasks that move in 1-2-3 order. When you count to ten, write a sentence, or make an outline, you use your left brain. Your right brain, on the other hand, specializes in tasks involving visual images and intuition. Since clustering involves both listing (a left-brain task) and drawing (a right-brain task), it allows you to tap both your logical side and your creative side.

To cluster, begin with a circled word: your topic. From there, map out ideas. Some people group ideas when they cluster, with smaller clusters branching out from larger ones. When this type of cluster is finished, it resembles a diagram of a molecule in a biology textbook. Other people branch ideas from the central word like quills on a porcupine.

What your diagram looks like does not matter. In clustering, what matters is that you get your thoughts on paper, using both images and words.

Look at the following examples of clustering.

Example

Glenn did his "porcupine" cluster on the topic "road rage."

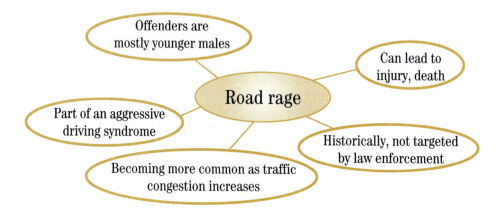

Example

Here, Molly's "molecule" cluster is on the topic "How have your eating habits changed since you have been in college?"

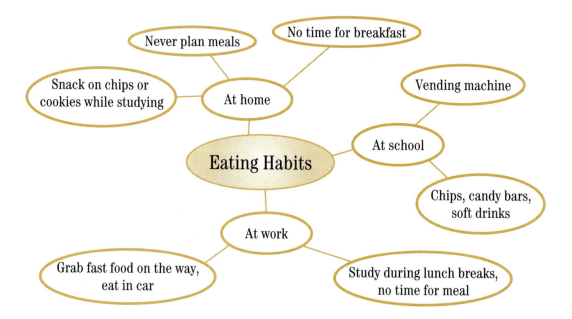

EXERCISE 6   **CLUSTERING**

Draw a cluster diagram using one of the following topics.

Answers will vary.

1. Discuss some of the problems created by junk mail—either the postal variety or spam, the e-mail version of junk mail.
2. Write a paragraph about your favorite way to exercise.
3. Describe the benefits or the disadvantages of television.
4. Discuss the advantages or the disadvantages of any form of transportation.
5. Describe some ways to discourage drug and alcohol abuse.

Outlining

Outlining is often the last step in the prewriting process. Once you have used one of the other prewriting methods, making an outline will take you one step further in the writing process. Forget about the formal outline with its Roman numerals, ABCs, and 123s. A short paragraph calls for a short outline. Your outline may be just a few words jotted on a page, or it may include a topic sentence and a brief listing of supporting ideas. Following is Hisa's outline of a paragraph describing the advantages and disadvantages of taking an online class.

```
Topic Sentence: The online class I took last
semester had a few advantages and a few serious
drawbacks.

Advantages:
  Convenient—I could sign on anytime, even at
     midnight. I could spend a few minutes or a
     few hours working on the class, depending on
     the amount of time I had. Did not have to
     dress—could go to class in my underwear.

Disadvantages:
  Impersonal—No classmates to joke with, only
     e-mail communication with instructor.
  Inconvenient—In a regular class, you can ask a
     question and get an immediate answer. In an
     online class, you ask by e-mail and get your
```

```
          answer within 24 hours. The instructor
          replied quickly, but it was still slower than
          in a regular class.
        Too easy to put off—With no regular class
          meetings, it was easy to put off the work or
          let something else take priority.

     Summary Sentence: My online class was convenient,
  but the drawbacks would make me think twice before
  taking another class online.
```

EXERCISE 7   OUTLINING

Choose one of your practice prewriting topics and make an outline for a paragraph.

Answers will vary.

Writing Assignments

Following are three writing assignments that ask you to write about yourself or about others. For each assignment, answer the question in a paragraph of about 250 words. Use the "Steps for Writing a Paragraph" at the end of this chapter to guide you through the writing process.

Writing Assignment 1   The Challenge of College

Every task has its challenges. Some challenges are physical, and some are mental. Some tasks may challenge the emotions or test the limits of a person's ability to organize and to handle time wisely. Write a paragraph describing the single biggest challenge you face in attending college.

Writing Assignment 2   Effective Teachers

Write a paragraph discussing the qualities of an effective teacher (or if you prefer, qualities of an ineffective teacher). As you prewrite, think of the best (or worst) teachers you have ever had so that you can use specific examples.

Writing Assignment 3   Heroes

Heroes come in all shapes. They may be male or female. They may be involved in a profession that often calls for heroic acts, such as medicine or firefighting, or they may be in a profession in which heroism would not be expected. Heroes may be public figures who are heroes to many, or they may be people who are heroes only to their own families. Write a paragraph telling who your hero is and why.

Steps for Writing a Paragraph

Follow the step-by-step procedures outlined here to ensure that your paragraph is the best that you can make it.

Step 1: Read the assignment and make sure that you understand it completely. Note any restrictions or limitations on the assignment and any requirements detailing length or format.

Step 2: Prewrite by thinking about your topic and by using one of the prewriting strategies described in this chapter. Be thorough.

Step 3: Outline by writing your topic sentence and a list of the major details you will use to support it.

Step 4: Write a rough draft of your paragraph. Don't stop to revise or check spelling at this stage. Just get your thoughts on paper.

Step 5: Revise your paragraph. Use the following checklist to help with revising.
- ✔ Does the topic sentence prepare the reader for the content of the paragraph?
- ✔ Are support sentences specific and clear?
- ✔ Do you include examples, details, and explanations?
- ✔ Is enough support provided so that the reader gets a clear picture?
- ✔ Do you avoid repetition of ideas?
- ✔ Does your paragraph end on a final note?

Step 6: Proofread your work at least three times. Read once from the top down to check for continuity and transitional words and to make sure that your sentences flow smoothly. Proofread a second time from the bottom up, reading each sentence as if it were an exercise in a grammar book. Sometimes, you miss errors reading from the top down because the ideas sweep you along from one sentence to the next. Reading from the bottom up, there is no continuity between sentences, and it is easier to spot errors in verb use, sentence structure, or pronouns. Your third proofreading will be a check for misspelled words, comma errors, and word usage. Once you have completed the third proofreading, put your paragraph aside for a while. Later, you may want to proofread again, or you may want to let someone else look over your paper.

3

Writing a Paragraph: The Topic Sentence

> **A Silly Riddle**
>
> How is a topic sentence like a compass?
>
> a. It always points to magnetic north.
> b. It's useful on a hiking expedition.
> c. It shows exactly where you are headed.

The riddle in the box above may be silly, but the comparison it makes is valid. A topic sentence *is* like a compass. It shows your reader exactly where your paragraph is headed, and it also helps to keep you on track as you write your paragraph. It gives **direction** to your paragraph.

Direction is one of four characteristics of effective writing that you will read about in this text and will learn to develop in your own writing. Before exploring the topic sentence further, look at the four characteristics of effective writing introduced in the next section.

Introducing the Four Characteristics of Effective Writing

In college and in your career, you will be called upon to write many types of papers, but no matter how varied the subject matter, all of them will contain paragraphs. No matter what type of composition you write, the four principles of *direction, support, unity,* and *coherence* will help you to communicate clearly and effectively with your reader.

Direction, Support, Unity, and Coherence

1. **Direction** means that the paragraph has a strong topic sentence that states the main idea and sets the course that the paragraph will follow.
2. **Support** means that the paragraph contains specific and detailed discussion of the idea stated in the topic sentence.
3. **Unity** means that the paragraph makes one main point and sticks to that point.
4. **Coherence** means that the ideas in the paragraph are logically connected and easy for the reader to follow.

Direction: Shaping the Topic Sentence of a Paragraph

The first step to take with any piece of writing is to find your direction—your focus. As you recall from Chapter 2, choosing a topic, narrowing a topic, and prewriting are preliminary steps that help determine the direction of your paragraph. With the writing of the topic sentence, the direction of a paragraph becomes explicit. A topic sentence clearly tells the reader exactly where the paragraph is headed.

Writing a Topic Sentence

A topic sentence does two things. First of all, it tells the **general topic** of the paragraph. Second, it makes a **specific point about the topic**. In other words, the topic sentence states the main idea of the paragraph.

Example

                topic   specific point about the topic

✔ <u>Walking to work instead of driving</u> <u>has had unexpected benefits.</u>

             topic   specific point about the topic

✔ <u>Effective communication</u> <u>is an essential skill in the workplace.</u>

          topic   specific point about the topic

✔ My friend Isaac has a negative attitude about our school.

EXERCISE 1   ANALYZING TOPIC SENTENCES

In each of the following topic sentences, underline the topic and double-underline the specific point that the writer is making about the topic.

1. Mushrooms are delicious in almost any meat or vegetable dish.
2. Housecleaning is a demanding chore.
3. The crowds at hockey games are often rude and unruly.
4. Morning is the perfect time to exercise.
5. UFO sightings usually can be explained rationally.

EXERCISE 2   COMPLETING TOPIC SENTENCES

Complete the following topic sentences. Beside the word or words that you add, indicate whether you have added a topic (T) or a point about the topic (P).

Answers will vary. Sample answers are provided.

1. Patience _is necessary in training a puppy (P)_ .
2. _A backpack (T)_ is something no college student should be without.
3. _My mother (T)_ is the person who inspires me most.
4. _Driving in a large city (T)_ can be dangerous.
5. Taking a class in time management _has helped me become more productive (P)_

Avoiding Topic Sentences That Are Too Broad or Too Narrow

Problems in narrowing the topic may result in a topic sentence that is *too broad* or *too narrow*. A topic sentence that is **too broad** outlines more territory than a paragraph can comfortably cover. A topic sentence that is **too narrow** draws the boundaries of the paragraph uncomfortably small, usually by focusing on some fact that would make a good supporting detail but that does not lend itself to development.

Look at the following sample topic sentences on the subject "holidays":

✗   Around the world, holidays are celebrated by people of many cultures.

The topic sentence is too broad. It promises more than one paragraph can deliver. There are too many holidays and too many cultures to fit into just one paragraph.

✗   Thanksgiving always falls on the fourth Thursday in November.

Although the preceding sentence might work as a supporting point in a paragraph, it is too narrow to be a topic sentence. A topic sentence that is too narrow is a dead-end statement, usually a simple statement of fact that does not invite exploration. A good topic sentence should open a door to discussion.

✔   Americans celebrate New Year's Day with customs that symbolize a new beginning.

This topic sentence is neither too broad nor too narrow. In support of this topic sentence, the writer can give examples of New Year's customs that symbolize beginnings. For example, the writer might discuss the custom of making a new start with New Year's resolutions, the custom of offering a toast to the New Year at midnight on December 31, and the custom of eating greens and black-eyed peas on New Year's Day for money and luck.

EXERCISE 3   ANALYZING TOPIC SENTENCES

Each of the following sets of sentences contains one topic sentence that is too broad, one that is too narrow, and one that would make a good topic sentence for a paragraph. In the blank to the left of each sentence, label it TB (too broad), TN (too narrow), or TS (topic sentence).

Set 1

___TN___   a.   My cat, Pirby, is a long-haired Persian.

___TB___   b.   Throughout the history of the world, cats and people have had a complex relationship.

___TS___   c.   In horror films, cats often represent evil.

Set 2

____TB____   a.   Dating back thousands of years, cheese-making is an ancient and a fascinating process.

____TN____   b.   My dad's favorite cheese smells like old socks.

____TS____   c.   Cheeses are a wonderful blend of flavor and nutrition.

Set 3

____TB____   a.   Dictionaries are helpful.

____TN____   b.   The *Oxford Dictionary of the English Language* is a multivolume work.

____TS____   c.   In addition to a word's meaning, a dictionary can provide an abundance of useful information.

Set 4

____TB____   a.   The construction of a house is a coordinated effort requiring a number of people with unique skills.

____TN____   b.   People who build houses employ carpenters.

____TS____   c.   When choosing between wood siding and vinyl siding, a homeowner must consider cost, appearance, and durability.

Set 5

____TB____   a.   There is much information on the Internet.

____TS____   b.   Successful Internet research requires persistence.

____TN____   c.   I received no e-mail today.

EXERCISE 4   ANALYZING TOPIC SENTENCES

Each of the following sets of sentences contains one topic sentence that is too broad, one that is too narrow, and one that would make a good topic sentence for a paragraph. In the blank to the left of each sentence, label it TB (too broad), TN (too narrow), or TS (topic sentence).

Set 1

____TB____   a.   Banks are a vital part of our country's economic system.

____TN____   b.   First National Bank charges a $20.00 fee for a returned check.

____TS____   c.   Banking online offers an easy way to pay bills and keep up with transactions.

Set 2

____TN____   **a.** I was angry when I noticed that someone had put a small dent in the door of my car.

____TS____   **b.** Anger can often be used in positive ways.

____TB____   **c.** Anger is an emotion that everyone feels at one time or another.

Set 3

____TS____   **a.** Drinking coffee is a ritual that I enjoy every day.

____TB____   **b.** Coffee has been a popular beverage for hundreds of years.

____TN____   **c.** A cup of coffee costs $2.50 at the Cuppa Joe.

Set 4

____TN____   **a.** The sign above the numeral seven on a computer keyboard is called an ampersand.

____TB____   **b.** In only a few decades, computers have revolutionized business worldwide.

____TS____   **c.** For many students, a computer is a necessity.

Set 5

____TB____   **a.** Birds are fascinating creatures.

____TN____   **b.** My sister's pet canary is named Tweety.

____TS____   **c.** A bird feeder in the backyard can provide hours of entertainment.

EXERCISE 5   WRITING TOPIC SENTENCES

Alone or in groups, write a topic sentence for three of the five following topics. Before you write the topic sentence, prewrite to decide how you want to approach the topic.

Answers will vary. Sample answers are provided.

1. sports in college

    College basketball games are more exciting than professional games.

    _____

2. clothing fads

    The first time I wore platform shoes, I learned that following fashion trends can

    be dangerous.

3. individual responsibility to the environment

   Recycling at home and at work is one way that an individual can be environ-

   mentally responsible.

4. dangerous driving habits

   Drivers who are in a hurry often drive dangerously.

5. the role of exercise in health

   Regular aerobic exercise builds cardiovascular health.

EXERCISE 6   WRITING TOPIC SENTENCES

Alone or in groups, write a topic sentence in answer to three of the five following questions. Make sure that the topic sentence directly answers the question.

Answers will vary. Sample answers are provided.

1. Do you believe that athletes, movie stars, or others in the public eye have a responsibility to be role models for youth?

   The job of role model is one that athletes should take seriously.

2. What one quality of your personality or character are you most grateful for?

   I am grateful for my optimistic nature.

3. What are the advantages or disadvantages of tattoos, piercings, and other forms of "body art"?

   Tattoos and body piercings can damage one's health and create a negative im-

   pression in the workplace.

4. Should driving while talking on a cell phone be illegal?

   Driving while talking on a cell phone should be illegal.

5. Is there any job that you would absolutely refuse to take?

   Unless I were starving, I would never work as a preschool teacher.

Where Should a Topic Sentence Go?

If you look carefully at paragraphs that appear in textbooks, essays, and news stories, you will see that a topic sentence may appear anywhere in a paragraph. However, the most common position for a topic sentence is at or near the beginning of a paragraph. Placing the topic sentence at the beginning of a paragraph lets your reader know exactly where the paragraph is going and gives the impression that you have thought about the organization of your paragraph. And you *will* have thought about it. The very act of constructing a topic sentence places your focus on the main idea of your paragraph and helps to keep you on track in supporting that idea.

Topic Sentence First

Placing the topic sentence first is often your best choice. A topic sentence at the beginning of the paragraph conveys your main idea and provides a clear, strong opening for the paragraph.

```
                    Lots of Trouble

    The parking lots on this campus are a student's
nightmare. In the north parking lot, the speed
bumps are bone-jarring mountains of asphalt. Anyone
driving more than five miles an hour has his teeth
loosened and his car's suspension ruined, all at
the same time. In the parking lot to the west of
the campus, the lines separating the parking spaces
are so faded that many drivers ignore them entirely
and end up taking two spaces and risking a parking
ticket. In addition, the lines are too close
together and are painted straight instead of on the
diagonal, making the spaces almost impossible for
larger cars to maneuver into. The small lot toward
the center of campus is pockmarked with large, deep
potholes. The pothole problem is not a new one—
campus legend has it that back in the 1970's, a
Volkswagen Beetle entered that lot and was never
seen again. The east parking lot is in the best
condition, but it is half a mile from the classroom
buildings and the library, and the walk from the
```

campus back to the lot is entirely uphill. A
student choosing a place to park has to choose
among huge speed bumps, deep potholes, tight
parking spaces, or a long walk uphill at the
end of the day—not much of a choice at all.

Topic Sentence after Introductory Sentence

Sometimes, you may need to include background material before you
state the main point of your paragraph. In these instances, condense the
background material to one sentence, and let that sentence open your
paragraph. After your introductory sentence, state the topic sentence.

Presumed Guilty

Employers have a right to protect themselves from
employee theft. **However, the large retail store
where I used to work goes to insulting lengths to
make sure employees stay honest.** When I applied for
my job, I had to agree to a credit check, even
though I was not borrowing money. In fact, it was
my employer who borrowed money, by holding my first
paycheck until I left. I had worked there a year,
but I was paid no interest on my money. In addition,
I was not allowed to bring my purse on the premises.
Instead, I had to carry my belongings in a clear
plastic container so that the contents were readily
visible to anyone who wanted to look. As I worked
my register, I was watched constantly by security
personnel through the cameras in the ceiling. I
realize that stores have to take measures to protect
their property. However, it seems to me that if they
want employees they can trust, they should start by
making employees feel trusted.

EXERCISE 7 **RECOGNIZING TOPIC SENTENCES**

One of the following paragraphs has a topic sentence at the beginning of the
paragraph, while the other has a topic sentence after an introductory sentence.
Underline the topic sentence in each paragraph.

Paragraph A

<pre>   Born to Be Wild</pre>

Researchers are beginning to believe that a person's willingness to take chances is at least partially due to a "thrill-seeking gene" that drives some people to seek out risk. While some people read the warning labels on a nighttime cold medicine and decide that taking it is just not worth the risk, others line up for the chance to bungee-jump off a bridge, tethered at the ankles by what looks like an oversized rubber band. As some parents try to persuade fearful children to have their picture taken with Santa, others hold their breath as their youngsters gleefully plummet thirteen stories on an amusement park ride. If geneticists are right, parents of risk-takers should make sure their family's health insurance policies are up to date. One day their children will forgo in-line skating in favor of riskier delights, such as parasailing, parachuting, and motocross. As researchers are discovering, those who court disaster for the fun of it can't help it— they're born to be wild.

Paragraph B

<pre>   How to Fail a Class</pre>

After a disastrous first term in college, I am back, determined to succeed. The only thing I learned well during that first term was how to fail a class. To successfully fail a class, a student must realize that he has a strike against him from the start because professors usually want their students to pass. Therefore, the student must make his apathy clear by missing classes, falling asleep during lectures, and not completing assigned readings. These tactics dampen the concern of most professors, but if the professor expresses concern, the student can simply say, "I'm sorry, Professor, but I am just not interested in history (or math, or whatever applies). It bores me." That will

squelch any lingering sympathy the professor might
be harboring. Naturally, a person who really wants
to fail should never study for tests, and if by
some fluke he should happen to pass a test, he
should not show up for any of the others. If, by
midterm, all efforts at failure have failed, it's
time to analyze what is going wrong. Perhaps the
student is becoming interested in lectures or class
activities, or perhaps, out of boredom, he actually
finds himself picking up the textbook and reading.
If so, he must either stop attending classes
entirely or face the fact, as I did, that he is
just not cut out for failure.

Writing Assignments

Choose one of the three writing assignments that follow, and write a paragraph. Follow the shortened version of "Steps for Writing a Paragraph" below. (A complete version of "Steps for Writing a Paragraph" can be found on pages 27–28.) Make sure that your paragraph has a strong topic sentence that mentions the main idea of the paragraph.

Steps for Writing a Paragraph

Step 1: Read the assignment and make sure that you understand it completely.

Step 2: Prewrite using one of the prewriting strategies described in Chapter 2.

Step 3: Outline by writing your topic sentence and a list of the major details you will use to support it.

Step 4: Write a rough draft of your paragraph.

Step 5: Revise your paragraph. Use the following checklist to help with revising.
  ✔ Does the topic sentence prepare the reader for the content of the paragraph?
  ✔ Are support sentences specific and clear?
  ✔ Do you include examples, details, and explanations?

✔ Is enough support provided so that the reader gets a clear picture?

✔ Do you avoid repetition of ideas?

✔ Does your paragraph end on a final note?

Step 6: Proofread your work at least three times. Proofread the first time from the top down, then once from the bottom up, reading each sentence as if it were an exercise in a grammar book. Your third proofreading will be a check for misspelled words, comma errors, and word usage.

Writing Assignment 1   An Hour's Conversation

Imagine that you could have an hour's conversation with anyone, living or dead. The person may be a historical figure, a celebrity, or a relative, and you may ask anything you want and discuss any topic you desire. Whom would you choose, and what would you talk about? Write a paragraph to answer the question.

In this paragraph, the topic sentence should introduce both the person you have chosen and the situation. Using a word such as "if" will establish the situation as hypothetical.

Writing Assignment 2   Scholarly Success

Ambitious students have different ideas about how to get ahead in school. Some believe in hours of study every day, while others swear that choosing the right classes and the right teachers is the key. What are the keys to academic success? Prewrite to generate ideas; then write a topic sentence that directly answers the question. Support the topic sentence in a well-developed paragraph.

Writing Assignment 3   Student Activities

At every college, student clubs and organizations provide extracurricular activities and learning experiences for students. Write a paragraph discussing the advantages or the disadvantages of joining such organizations.

4

Writing a Paragraph: Support

In the box above, the second ad is the clear winner. The writer has a "certain something" that would appeal to many potential mates. But the success of the ad rests on more than just the writer's attributes or even his lottery winnings. It rests on his specific description of himself. On the other hand, who is the writer of the first ad? It is not clear whether he is seventeen or seventy, or whether his "many interests" include scuba diving and snowboarding or shuffleboard and exotic butterflies. Though each ad contains thirty-four words, the second writer manages to pack in much more detail than the first. Specific support is one of the keys to good writing. Before looking at paragraph support, review the four principles of effective writing that follow. The highlighted principle, support, is the focus of this chapter.

Four Characteristics of Effective Writing

Direction, Support, Unity, and Coherence

1. **Direction** means that the paragraph has a strong topic sentence that states the main idea and sets the course that the paragraph will follow.
2. **Support** means that the paragraph contains specific and detailed discussion of the idea stated in the topic sentence.
3. **Unity** means that the paragraph makes one main point and sticks to that point.
4. **Coherence** means that the ideas in the paragraph are logically connected and easy for the reader to follow.

Support: Using Specific Detail

A strong topic sentence, unity, and smooth transitions can give a paragraph structure and style. Only support can bring it to life. Without specific details, a paragraph will remain on a broad, general level. What is it like to read a paragraph without specific details? Imagine watching a movie, television show, or video that never shows a close-up but instead maintains a camera distance of ten feet from every character. You would probably feel detached and uninvolved. Readers feel the same way when a writer never gets close enough to the subject to describe it in detail.

The Difference Between Topic Sentences and Supporting Sentences

A topic sentence provides direction—the road map for a paragraph—but supporting sentences supply the scenery. While topic sentences are broad and general, large enough to encompass the entire paragraph, supporting sentences are specific, giving details and examples. The following exercise provides practice in distinguishing topic sentences from supporting details.

EXERCISE 1   **DISTINGUISHING TOPIC SENTENCES FROM SUPPORTING DETAILS**

Each numbered item contains three supporting details and one topic sentence. Write *SD* beside each of the three details and *TS* beside the topic sentence.

1. _**SD**_ a. Absorbed in careers and families, many people may feel they no longer have much in common with old schoolmates.

   _**SD**_ b. People who have recently divorced, gained weight, or lost a job may not feel like facing former classmates.

   _**SD**_ c. Students who were not popular in high school don't want to see the bullies who called them "nerd," "geek," or "pizza face."

   _**TS**_ d. Some people avoid high school reunions.

2. _**SD**_ a. Plaques that say "I love my job; it's the work I hate" or "Take your petty problem somewhere else" are generally not welcome in the workplace.

   _**TS**_ b. Some offices put restrictions on the appearance of employees' work areas.

   _**SD**_ c. In some offices, even children's artwork and family photographs are forbidden.

   _**SD**_ d. Some offices restrict clutter and require employees to clear their desks of papers and work paraphernalia by the end of the day.

3. _**TS**_ a. Even among the young and healthy, memory is often unreliable.

   _**SD**_ b. Many people recognize faces but have trouble remembering names.

   _**SD**_ c. Some people actually develop "memories" of events they have heard about but never experienced.

   _**SD**_ d. "Tip-of-the-tongue syndrome," a sudden inability to recall a familiar word, is another common memory problem.

4. _**SD**_ a. Consumers can compare prices and read product reviews of anything from cars to computers.

   _**SD**_ b. Online libraries, encyclopedias, and periodicals provide a resource for researchers.

   _**SD**_ c. In addition to news from all over the world, news sites feature celebrity gossip, stock quotes, and weather.

   _**TS**_ d. An Internet connection offers access to a world of information.

5. ___SD___ a. A shutterbug takes his camera everywhere he goes, from family gatherings to sporting events.

   ___SD___ b. He is seldom in a picture because he is usually behind the camera.

   ___TS___ c. A camera buff, also known as a shutterbug, is easy to spot.

   ___SD___ d. It may be difficult to have a conversation with a shutterbug because his attention is often on the camera.

Recognizing Specific Detail

One of the most difficult tasks a writer faces is providing strong, specific supporting details. If a writer provides only vague, sketchy details, the picture presented to the reader will be fuzzy and out of focus. As details become sharper and more specific, the picture becomes clear. The following exercise will give you practice in recognizing sharp, clear detail.

EXERCISE 2   RECOGNIZING SPECIFIC DETAILS

Each of the following topic sentences is supported by three details. Place a check (✔) beside the two details that are sharp and specific. Place an ✘ beside the detail that needs to be more specific. Then, in the space provided, rewrite the vague sentence to make the supporting detail more specific.

Rewritten sentences will vary. Sample answers are provided.

1. The restaurant staff sent out clear signals that it was closing time.

   ___✔___ a. The server brought our check and wished us a good evening.

   ___✔___ b. Staff members began to turn chairs upside down on neighboring tables.

   ___✘___ c. The cashier performed duties normally connected with closing.

   The cashier counted the money in the register and placed it in a zippered bank bag.

2. The apartment complex was not a pleasant place to live.

   ___✘___ a. The pool looked unfit to swim in.

   ___✔___ b. Buildings had broken windows, torn screens, and peeling paint.

   ___✔___ c. The grounds were overrun with weeds and littered with cans, fast-food wrappers, and cigarette butts.

The pool was covered in green scum and littered with dead insects.

3. The mall is too crowded on weekends.

   ___✔___ a. In the parking lot, drivers desperately circle the lot for parking spaces or park illegally on the grass.

   ___✔___ b. In clothing stores, people stand elbow to elbow and wait in lines to enter dressing rooms.

   ___✘___ c. The food court is extremely crowded.

   Lines at the food court stretch ten to twenty people deep, and finding a free

   table is often impossible.

4. Major league sporting events are too expensive for the average person to attend.

   ___✔___ a. For a family of four, tickets to a major league baseball game can cost as much as a week's groceries.

   ___✘___ b. Stadium food is expensive.

   ___✔___ c. Buying a program and a t-shirt for the kids can easily add another $25.00 to the tab.

   A soft drink, a hot dog, and a bag of popcorn costs as much as a restaurant

   meal.

5. It was evident that the man had been driving drunk.

   ___✘___ a. The way he came into the parking lot was the first clue.

   ___✔___ b. He got out of his car, staggered, and almost fell.

   ___✔___ c. When he came closer, I could see his red, unfocused eyes and smell the alcohol on his breath.

   As he made a wide turn into the parking lot, his tire hit the curb, and he nar-

   rowly missed a light pole.

Steps in Making Details Specific

Writing in rich, colorful detail does not come naturally to most people. However, since writing is a craft that can be learned, writing colorful and specific detail also can be learned.

To make details specific, start small. Don't expect to produce vivid paragraphs on the first try. Instead, add detail as you revise. Find vague words and replace them with more specific words or phrases. Weed out sentences that are not carrying their weight, and replace them with vibrant, detailed sentences. Finally, use words that convey ideas to readers through sight, hearing, taste, touch, or smell.

Making Words Specific

Sometimes, a simple change in word choice can make all the difference. You paint a clearer picture for your reader when you use specific words and phrases: *Great-Aunt Hetty* instead of *a relative*; *five hours of study* instead of *a lot of work*; *Sid's Bread Basket Café* instead of *a restaurant*; *ambled* instead of *walked*; *the students in my math class* instead of *everybody*; or *an empty plastic cup, a digital camera, and a small green notebook* instead of *things*.

Using a Thesaurus

A **thesaurus,** or dictionary of synonyms, can help you choose the best word for the situation. But shades of meaning vary, so don't just choose a synonym at random. If you are not sure of a word's exact meaning, check your dictionary.

Adding Relevant Detail

Consider the following sentence:

✗ Before Audrey entered the *building,* she made sure that she had *everything she needed.*

Different readers will interpret this sentence in different ways. What kind of building did Audrey enter? What items did she need? Specific detail would serve two purposes: it would clearly convey the writer's meaning, and it would capture the reader's interest. Consider the following revisions.

✔ Before Audrey entered the *Shop-n-Save,* she made sure that she had *her checkbook and her grocery list.*

✔ Before Audrey entered the *bank,* she made sure that she had *her ski mask and her gun.*

✔ Before Audrey entered the *First Presbyterian Church,* she made sure that she had *her Bible and her notes for the sermon she would deliver.*

Notice how the detail not only provides specific information but also helps to characterize Audrey. How does your impression of her change with each example?

EXERCISE 3   PROVIDING SPECIFIC DETAILS

Create new impressions of Audrey by varying the place that she enters and the items that she carries.

Answers will vary. Sample answers are provided

1. Before Audrey entered the __restaurant__, she made sure that she had __her uniform and her comfortable shoes__.

2. Before Audrey entered the __murky water__, she made sure that she had __a full tank of oxygen and her spear gun__.

3. Before Audrey entered the __deserted parking garage__, she made sure that she had __her car keys and her pepper spray__.

4. Before Audrey entered the __hunting preserve__, she made sure that she had __her rifle and her orange safety vest__.

5. Before Audrey entered the __boardroom__, she made sure that she had __her glasses and a copy of her speech__.

EXERCISE 4   CHOOSING SPECIFIC DETAILS

From the three choices for each of the following sentences, pick the most specific word or phrase to fill in the blank.

1. After trying to balance her checkbook for twenty minutes, Marina angrily picked up _____ and threw it across the room.
   a. some defective equipment
   (b.) her broken calculator
   c. a small machine

2. Because he had _____, Jerry wore his baseball glove and watched carefully for foul balls.

    a. a good seat

    b. a prime position within the stadium

    c. a seat next to the third base line

3. Frank told his friend that his fast new inkjet printer _____.

    a. worked just fine

    b. was featured in a recent publication

    c. printed 12 pages per minute

4. The new science fiction movie was laughable because the aliens _____.

    a. looked like fuzzy, overripe peaches

    b. looked ridiculous

    c. were round

5. Lilly is a small, white cat with a bad habit of _____ rolls of paper towels.

    a. messing with

    b. shredding

    c. ruining

6. The carpenter pored over the blueprints in front of him and realized that he had just _____.

    a. installed cabinets on the wrong side of the kitchen

    b. made a big mistake

    c. wasted many hours

7. Hank paid $100 for the rare book, but he was disappointed when it arrived in the mail. The book _____.

    a. was not as advertised

    b. was not signed by the author as the seller had claimed

    c. lacked one important feature

8. The frozen Belgian waffles _____.

    a. were unappetizing

    b. did not look good

    c. had a sour odor and crumbled easily

9. After Frank lost money following a hot stock tip from a friend, he said he could get better results _____.

    a. by another method

    b. by blindfolding himself and throwing a dart at the *Wall Street Journal*

    c. by following someone else's advice

10. Michael said that his parents' taste in music was great, if a person liked _____.

    a. that kind of thing

    b. bland pop music

    (c.) oldies by the Jackson Five and Boy George

Making Verbs Specific

Verbs bring life and movement to writing. Vague, poorly chosen verbs add nothing to your writing, or worse, drag it down. Well-chosen verbs leap off the page, adding power and energy to your writing. To choose effective verbs, reject the easy choice and look for powerful verbs that express your meaning exactly.

Examples

✗ Kevin *moved* toward the finish line, panting with exertion.

✔ Kevin *sprinted* toward the finish line, panting with exertion.

✗ The angry customer *took* the bill from the server's hand.

✔ The angry customer *snatched* the bill from the server's hand.

EXERCISE 5   USING EFFECTIVE VERBS

Cross out the italicized verb in each of the following sentences, and replace it with a verb that more effectively conveys the sense of the sentence.

Answers will vary. Sample answers are provided.

1. Four strips of bacon *were* in the pan, giving off a tempting aroma as they browned.

    sizzled

2. The onlookers gasped as the parachutist *came* toward the earth, then cheered in relief as the chute finally opened.

    plummeted

3. The new magnetic bullet train *moved* down the tracks at an amazing 250 miles an hour.

    sped

4. The angry man *placed* his fist on the table.

   <u>slammed</u>

5. Silently and carefully, the cat *walked* close to its prey.

   <u>crept</u>

6. The punk rock band played as the audience *called out* its approval.

   <u>roared</u>

7. The two dieters *glanced* intently at the restaurant's dessert buffet.

   <u>stared</u>

8. Nailing on the last piece of wood, Ignatius *reacted* as the hammer landed on his thumb.

   <u>yowled</u>

9. Huge and majestic, the cruise ship *moved* away from the dock toward the open sea.

   <u>glided</u>

10. The football team *came* onto the field for the championship game.

    <u>charged</u>

Making Sentences Specific

Sentences with specific language are sentences with power. As you write, strive for forceful verbs and vivid phrases, and as you revise, look for opportunities to make vague language more specific. Look at the following examples to see how much stronger a sentence becomes when specific words replace vague words.

Example 1

Vague word choice:

✗ *After the weather turned,* the umpires delayed the baseball game.

Specific word choice:

✔ *After lightning struck the field,* the umpires delayed the baseball game.

Vague word choice:

✗ David's briefcase *was large* and filled with *many useless items.*

Specific word choice:

✔ David's *swollen* briefcase contained *a torn map, a used toothbrush, several dog-eared books, a broken ruler, and two dead calculators.*

Vague word choice:

✗   The bird sat in the birdbath while the cat *waited underneath*.

Specific word choice:

✔   The bird sat in the birdbath while the cat *crouched below, preparing to pounce*.

EXERCISE 6   USING SPECIFIC LANGUAGE

Rewrite each of the following sentences, replacing the vague terms in italics with language that is more specific.

Answers will vary. Sample answers are provided.

1. Spiros quit *a lucrative job* to follow his dream of opening *a small business*.

    Spiros quit a six-figure job as head of an advertising agency to follow his dream

    of opening a catering shop.

2. At the neighborhood picnic, my hungry neighbor *consumed a great deal of food in a short amount of time*.

    At the neighborhood picnic, my hungry neighbor ate two plates of fried chicken

    and half an apple pie in ten minutes.

3. Two firefighters received *awards* for *heroic behavior*.

    Two firefighters received commendations from the mayor for rescuing five chil-

    dren from a burning apartment building.

4. *The couple* went out *for an evening of entertainment*.

    Hannah and Joe ate dinner at Antonio's and then played miniature golf.

5. *One of the players* was put on the disabled list because of *an injury*.

    Rodriguez was put on the disabled list because of a broken collarbone.

6. When Jenna saw a man *behaving strangely* in the mall parking lot, she *took appropriate action*.

    When Jenna saw a man hiding behind a car in the mall parking lot, she re-

    ported him to a security guard.

7. The *smell* from *the restaurant* tantalized Francine.

    The smell of pizza from Pop's Pizza Palace tantalized Francine.

8. The *expensive car* looked *terrible*.

   The new Mercedes was caked with mud and had one broken headlight.

   _____

9. *The organization* sent volunteers and staff members to help after the *disaster*.

   The Red Cross sent volunteers and staff members to help after the flood.

   _____

10. John's *pet* was reluctant to take the *piece of food* I offered her.

    John's iguana was reluctant to take the dead cricket I offered her.

    _____

EXERCISE 7   RECOGNIZING A WELL-SUPPORTED PARAGRAPH

One of the following paragraphs is well supported with specific details and examples, while the other is poorly supported with vague, general sentences. Read each paragraph; then answer the questions at the end of the exercise.

Paragraph A

From ancient to modern times, long hair on men has been both a badge of honor and a source of confusion. In ancient Greece, the Spartans wore long hair to symbolize their membership in the ruling warrior class. Long-haired men, they believed, were clearly warriors because one could not toil in the fields and wear long hair. However, enemy Persian soldiers became confused—and greatly underestimated their Spartan enemies—at the sight of the Spartans combing their long locks of hair, preparing for battle. More recently, youthful rebels and Vietnam war protesters of the 1960s wore long, flowing hair to show their rejection of society's values. Long hair was also a way to distinguish themselves from military personnel, whose hair was kept short. Pride in long hair was reflected in the lyrics of songs such as "Hair," which glorified "a head with hair, long beautiful hair." However, older, more conventional people claimed they could no longer tell the sexes apart, and songs such as "Are You a Boy or Are You a Girl?" reflected that confusion. When long hair on

men is not the norm, it can be a source of pride
for those who wear it and a source of bewilderment
for those who don't.

Paragraph B

From ancient to modern times, long hair on men
has been both a badge of honor and a source of
confusion. Ancient Spartan soldiers wore long hair
to symbolize their position in society. Long-haired
men, they believed, were clearly warriors and not
workers in a field. However, enemy Persian soldiers
became confused at the sight of long-haired Spartan
soldiers. In the modern era, youthful rebels and
war protesters of the 1960s wore long hair to show
their rejection of society's values. For obvious
reasons, long hair was also a way to distinguish
themselves from military personnel. Pride in long
hair was reflected in the lyrics of songs of the
time. However, older, more conventional people
claimed they could no longer tell the sexes apart,
and other songs reflected that confusion. When long
hair on men is not the norm, it can be a source of
pride for those who wear it and bewilderment for
those who don't.

■ Questions

Fill in the blanks of each of the following questions.

1. Paragraph _____B_____ is less specific.

2. Paragraph _____A_____ is more specific. Three specific details from the
   paragraph are

   Answers will vary. Possibilities include "the Spartans combing their long locks

   of hair, preparing for battle"; "Vietnam war protesters of the 1960s wore long,

   flowing hair"; and "songs such as 'Hair,' which glorified 'a head with hair, long

   beautiful hair.'"

EXERCISE 8   PROVIDING SPECIFIC SUPPORT

For each of the following topic sentences, provide two sentences that give specific
details.

Answers will vary. Sample answers are provided.

1. The toy store window was filled with games and sports equipment.

   In one side of the window, a table was stacked with board games such as checkers, Parcheesi, Monopoly, and Chinese Checkers. On the other side, hockey masks and sticks, tennis rackets, cycling helmets, and skis were artfully displayed.

2. When a test is announced, it is a good idea to begin preparing immediately.

   First, begin reviewing the portions of your notes and your text that you will be tested on. Next, make up and answer sample test questions on the material that is emphasized.

3. Television is often a waste of time.

   It is often easy for me to leave homework undone as one hour of television watching turns into two or three. In addition, sleazy talk shows or reruns of *The Three Stooges* do little to improve my mind.

4. Strong communication skills are an asset on any job.

   People who speak confidently and in a friendly manner inspire confidence in clients and coworkers. Strong writing skills in reports and e-mails are likely to be noticed by supervisors.

5. Mental stress often causes physical symptoms.

   "Tension headaches" are the result of shoulder and neck muscles tensing in response to mental stress. Insomnia is often due to worry over a dreaded event such as an exam or a job interview.

Using Sense Impressions

Imagine sitting outside on a bench on a beautiful day. You see the brilliant blue sky, feel the warm sun on your face and the rough surface of the bench against your hand. You hear the voice of a friend asking you, "How do we know that the sky is really blue?"

If you are like most people, the question would astonish you. You would probably blurt something on the order of, "Well, we're looking at it, aren't we?"

"We're looking at it" is exactly right. For most people, seeing is believing. Every scrap of information that people receive about the world around them is obtained through the senses—sight, hearing, smell, touch, and taste. Good writers often present ideas in the same way that we perceive them: in terms of the senses.

EXERCISE 9   **IDENTIFYING SENSORY DESCRIPTIONS**

In each of the following sentences, underline the words that suggest sense impressions and identify above each underlined item the sense or senses (sight, hearing, touch, taste, or smell) used in the description.

Answers may vary slightly.

1.   The loan officer <u>banged</u> her <u>heavy</u> ceramic coffee cup like a <u>gavel</u> and told Alan that his loan application had been rejected.
         hearing   *touch*   *sight*

2.   <u>Shining</u> in <u>rainbow colors</u>, a <u>slick</u> coating of oil lay on the <u>murky</u> water.
       sight   *sight*   *touch*   *sight*

3.   The <u>sweet</u>, <u>gummy</u> candy stuck to the roof of Annie's mouth.
        taste   *touch*

4.   The <u>green</u> beans tasted <u>salty</u> and slightly <u>burned</u>.
       sight   *taste*   *taste*

5.   The <u>sharp, pungent</u> odor of ammonia drifted into the classroom from the hall, where the cleaning crew was working.
         smell

6.   A <u>cold</u> wind <u>knifed</u> through Manuel's <u>thin</u> jacket.
       touch   *touch*   *touch*

7.   The kitten's <u>sweet</u>, <u>milky</u> breath greeted Brenda even before she opened her eyes.
            smell   *smell (since Brenda is smelling, not tasting, the kitten's breath)*

8.   The <u>cold</u>, <u>fizzy</u> cola <u>bubbled</u> over the side of the glass as Mike poured it from the can.
       touch sight   *sight*

9.   In the back of the room, a <u>crackling</u> candy wrapper unfolded as Adam tried to focus on the test.
                hearing

10.   A <u>slippery</u> ice cube fell from the tray and <u>skimmed</u> across the floor.
      touch   *sight*

EXERCISE 10   **IDENTIFYING SENSORY DESCRIPTIONS**

Write a sentence that describes each of the numbered words in sensory terms (terms relating to sight, hearing, smell, touch, or taste). Underline those terms. Then label the terms as words of sight, hearing, smell, touch, or taste, as you did in the previous exercise. The first one is done for you.

Answers will vary. Sample answers are provided.

1. photograph

   sight   *sight*   *sight*   *sight*
   The <u>old</u>, <u>black and white</u> photograph was <u>cracked</u> and <u>faded</u>.

   _____

2. bottle

           sight   *hearing*
   The <u>empty brown</u> bottle rolled across the cement floor with a <u>hollow sound</u>.

   _____

3. tree

      touch   *touch*
   The <u>rough</u> bark of the tree <u>scraped</u> against Mandy's skin as she climbed to a

   low branch.

4. eyes

                         touch   *touch*   *sight*
   The doll's eyes, as <u>hard as two marbles</u>, were ringed by <u>bristly, brown</u> eyelashes.

   _____

5. snow

      touch
   <u>Icy, wet</u> flakes of snow fell on Heather's upturned face.

   _____

6. horn

      hearing   *hearing*
   The <u>loud</u>, urgent <u>blare</u> of a horn sounded behind Danny as the light changed.

   _____

7. perfume

                              smell   *smell*
   The woman next to me on the bus <u>reeked</u> of an overpowering <u>floral</u> perfume.

   _____

8. house

sight   *hearing*
The <u>old, unpainted</u> house <u>creaked and groaned</u> as the hurricane gained strength.

_____

9. socks

touch   *touch*   *touch*
The <u>fuzzy woolen</u> socks kept Nan's feet <u>warm</u> in the <u>coldest</u> weather.

_____

10. roar

hearing
Sleeping in his tent, Ken was awakened by the <u>loud, deep-throated</u> roar of a

grizzly bear.

Writing Assignments

The following writing assignments will help you apply the paragraph writing techniques you learned in this chapter. Choose an assignment and complete it, following the steps for writing a paragraph listed at the end of Chapter 2 (pp. 27–28). Focus on providing detailed and effective support.

Writing Assignment 1   Adding Details

The following paragraph needs supporting details. After each point listed, write at least two sentences of supporting detail.

Answers will vary. Sample answers are provided.

        Keeping my two nephews one Saturday afternoon has shown me how hard it is to keep up with two active children. Instead of playing the quiet games I had planned, my nephews raced through my apartment, creating chaos.

Michael, the eight-year old, decided that my sofa was a battleship and the pillows on it were torpedoes. Meanwhile, six-year-old Dion began to chase my cat through halls, over beds, and under tables.

Allowing my nephews to make their own peanut butter and jelly sandwiches for lunch turned out to be a disaster.

Using his spoon as a catapult, Michael flipped a large glob of jelly at Dion, and a food fight began. Before it was over, jelly and peanut butter dotted the two children, the table, the floor, the walls and even the family dog.

Worst of all, my nephews seemed to fight and bicker constantly.

They fought over their toys with fierce cries of "Mine!" and "Give it here!" They also called each other names, pinching and punching one another when they thought I was not looking.

When my sister finally came to pick them up, I waved goodbye with a sense of relief, wondering whether all children were as tiring as my two rowdy nephews.

Writing Assignment 2   Quick on the Draw

Can you create a description so accurate that a reader can draw what you are describing even though you never name the object?

Part 1: In Class or at Home. Choose an object close at hand—a wristwatch you are wearing, a clock on the wall, one of the shoes you are wearing, or some other small item—and describe it in terms of the senses. Try to choose an object that is small enough so that you can get down to the fine detail. Look at the object closely. Then investigate it with your other senses. Listen to it—tap on it, or pick it up and shake it to see if it makes a noise. Touch it. Is it rough, smooth, warm, cold? Smell it. Is the smell strong? Faint? Pleasant? Unpleasant? Tasting the object may not be wise, especially if you are describing your shoe.

Next, write a paragraph describing the item in terms of the senses. Include very specific detail about the object. Try to make your description so specific that a reader not only could guess what it is from the description but also could draw the object in detail from your description.

Part 2: In Class. Trade paragraphs with a classmate. From your classmate's paragraph, draw a picture of the object your classmate has described. When you have finished your drawing, show it to your classmate and see how close you came to the object described in the paragraph.

This exercise is not intended to reveal your artistic abilities but rather the difficulty of conveying ideas exactly. If your description was a good one, your classmate's drawing of your object should contain some of the details that make your object stand out from others of its kind—the broken shoelace on your sneaker or the exact number of keys on your key ring, for example. As you look at your classmate's drawing, try to analyze the major differences between your paragraph and the drawing to see where the communication process may have broken down.

Writing Assignment 3   Photographic Memory

Find a photograph that brings back a memory for you. Perhaps it is a childhood birthday photo, with you blowing out candles on a frosted cake. Maybe it was taken at a wedding or a family reunion. Whatever the occasion, the photograph should evoke a specific memory that you will reconstruct for your reader. If you choose a candid photo showing people in action rather than a posed shot, it may be easier for you to describe what is going on.

The topic sentence for this paragraph will be a simple mention of the photograph you have chosen: "An old photograph of my sister, taken the day she received her first pair of in-line skates, brings back memories for me." In the paragraph, describe the scene and the memories it brings back for you.

Writing Assignment 4   A Picture of Virtue

Describe an incident that illustrates one of the following virtues: courage, kindness, or generosity. Perhaps you saw someone stand up to a bully instead of giving in (courage), including someone who was left out (kindness), or giving something—help, time, or money—to someone who needed it (generosity). These are just a few of the possibilities; feel free to choose any illustration that comes to mind. Prewrite to get all the details down; then write a draft showing a complete picture of the incident that illustrates the virtue you are writing about. Sample topic sentences may look something like this:

Last week, in the elementary school where I serve as a teacher's aide, I witnessed an act of pure courage.

My brother's kindness was evident in his treatment of a stray dog that showed up at our house.

A complete stranger showed me generosity when I was stranded in an unfamiliar town.

5

Writing a Paragraph: Unity and Coherence

Unity COHERENCE *unity* **coherence**
UNITY coherence **unity** **Coherence**
unity *COHERENCE* unity UNITY
coherence **unity** *coherence* ***unity***

Unity and coherence go hand in hand to make your paragraph flow seamlessly from one sentence to the next. Before looking at these principles, review the following four principles of effective writing. The highlighted principles, unity and coherence, are the focus of this chapter.

Four Characteristics of Effective Writing

Direction, Support, Unity, and Coherence

1. **Direction** means that the paragraph has a strong topic sentence that states the main idea and sets the course that the paragraph will follow.

2. **Support** means that the paragraph contains specific and detailed discussion of the idea stated in the topic sentence.

3. **Unity** means that the paragraph makes one main point and sticks to that point.

4. **Coherence** means that the ideas in the paragraph are logically connected and easy for the reader to follow.

Unity: Sticking to the Point

Every topic sentence is a promise to the reader, a promise that you will discuss the idea expressed in that sentence and no other. If your topic sentence is "It is true that the best things in life are free," then you will discuss the good things in life that do not carry a price tag. You will not discuss the joys of driving your lime-green Volkswagen Beetle to an expensive restaurant on a beautiful fall day, since Volkswagens and food both cost money. The fall day, however, is free, so leaves, cool breezes, and blue skies may figure prominently in your paragraph, as may other free things such as the love of family and friends or the satisfaction of spending time to help someone else. Your paragraph will have unity because it sticks to its topic and to the specific point that you make about that topic.

EXERCISE 1   RECOGNIZING PROBLEMS IN UNITY

A list of possible supporting points follows each of the topic sentences in the exercise. In each group, circle the letter of the point that breaks the unity of the paragraph.

1. Topic sentence: Vacations are best when they provide excitement.
   a. Rides and roller coasters are a thrill for children and adults who vacation at a theme park.
   b. A cruise ship offers the excitement of a floating hotel that provides entertainment, food, and activities around the clock.
   c. Staying at home and catching up on chores is a practical way to vacation.
2. Topic sentence: I decided to cut back on watching television for several reasons.
   a. I was becoming a "couch potato," lazy and out of shape.
   b. Many television programs are informative and educational.
   c. Television was keeping me from more important activities, such as studying.
3. Topic sentence: Dogs are becoming valuable in health care.
   a. Dogs can be fierce protectors of families and property.
   b. Dogs can be trained to assist people who have lost their mobility or their vision.
   c. With their keen sense of smell, some dogs can be trained to sniff out cancer.
4. Topic sentence: Wearing uniforms to work or school has several advantages.
   a. Uniforms eliminate time-consuming decisions about what to wear.
   b. The sameness of uniforms can become boring.
   c. Uniforms eliminate the pressure that some people feel to wear expensive, name-brand clothing.

5. Topic sentence: Chocolate is a popular treat for several reasons.

  a. Chocolate contains chemicals that induce a feeling of well-being.

  b. The rich, creamy taste of chocolate is delicious.

  (c.) Chocolate contains fats and sugars, which can be harmful in excess.

EXERCISE 2   RECOGNIZING PROBLEMS IN UNITY

A list of possible supporting points follows each of the topic sentences in the exercise. In each group, circle the letter of the point that breaks the unity of the paragraph.

1. Topic sentence: On the job, a firefighter protects lives and property.

  a. Firefighters often risk their lives to halt the spread of flames or to rescue people trapped in a fire.

  (b.) Firefighters' long hours require them to buy groceries and prepare meals in the station house.

  c. Often, firefighters are first to assist at the scene of an accident.

2. Topic sentence: Aliens on the popular *Star Trek* television series often mirror and exaggerate one human characteristic.

  a. The Ferengi care only about business and profit.

  b. Vulcans believe every situation can be solved with logic.

  (c.) Andorians have blue skin.

3. Topic sentence: My sister Lauren is the brainy one in our family.

  a. Lauren received several scholarship offers.

  b. She made a near-perfect score on the math portion of the SAT.

  (c.) Unfortunately, Lauren does not have enough common sense to fill an eyedropper.

4. Topic sentence: Concrete is one of today's most popular building materials.

  a. Most modern buildings are constructed, at least partially, of concrete.

  b. Because of its strength, concrete allows builders to build multistory buildings.

  (c.) Concrete was invented by the ancient Romans.

5. Topic sentence: Most computer experts agree that the compact disk is taking the place of the floppy disk as an information storage device.

  a. The information on a floppy disk begins to degenerate after a few years, but a compact disk will store information indefinitely.

  b. It would take more than a dozen floppy discs to load a popular word processing program into a computer, but one compact disc provides more than enough storage capacity for the same job.

  (c.) A floppy disk is smaller and more easily stored or carried than a compact disk.

EXERCISE 3   RECOGNIZING PROBLEMS IN PARAGRAPH UNITY

In the following paragraph, find the topic sentence and underline the topic and the specific point that is made about that topic. Then find the two sentences that break the unity of the paragraph. If you have trouble, go back and look at the topic sentence to see the specific point that is made about the topic. Then read the paragraph again to see which sentences do not support the topic sentence.

> [1]<u>My methods for wiping out ants</u> <u>never seem to work</u>. [2]When I see ants marching in a line through my kitchen in search of food, I put down ant baits, which contain poison that ants carry back to the nest. [3]Ants live in hives that are centered around a queen whose sole job is to lay eggs. [4]The poison may kill some of the ants, but there always seem to be more ants to replace them. [5]I have also tried pouring boiling water over the anthills in my yard. [6]Carrying pots of boiling water from the house to the yard is extremely dangerous and could result in serious burns if I tripped on the way out. [7]Even boiling water does not deter the ants for long. [8]The entrance to the ants' nest collapses under the weight of the boiling water, but the next day, a new entrance pops up and ants are back in business. [9]Ants are almost impossible to eradicate, and my battle with them is never completely won.

Numbers of the sentences that break the unity of the paragraph: ___3___, ___6___.

Coherence: Connecting Ideas

If your writing does not have **coherence,** then the sentences in your paragraph are like a pile of loose bricks: there is little connection between them. Coherence is the mortar you use to make your paragraph a brick wall, with solid and strong connections between ideas. To achieve coherence, first make sure that your ideas are logically related and well thought out. Then use **transitional expressions** to cement the connections between those ideas in the most effective way possible.

Using Transitional Expressions

As a writer, not only must you express an idea clearly, but you must also keep your reader oriented in time and space and aware of relationships between ideas. **Transitional expressions** can help you juggle these multiple tasks without detracting from the ideas you express. Ideally, these words and phrases should do their job in the background, as guideposts that show the path of your logic. Following is a list of transitional words and expressions, organized by their function within the sentence.

Some Common Transitional Words and Expressions

* Transitions of Time

after	as	before	during	first	yet
immediately	later	meanwhile	now	often	then
previously	suddenly	temporarily	while	when	next
since	ever since	until	till	whenever	

* Transitions of Space

above	around	behind	beside	between
by	down	in	on	next to
over	toward	under	near	

* Transitions of Addition

also	another	first	furthermore
in addition	next	finally	

* Transitions of Importance

as important	just as important	equally important	major
most important	essential	primary	significant

---

* Transitions of Contrast

although	but	even though	however	in contrast
instead	in spite of	nevertheless	on the other hand	yet

---

* Transitions of Cause and Effect

as a result	because	so	consequently
a consequence of	since	therefore	thus

---

* Transitions of Illustration or Example

for example	for instance	including	such as

EXERCISE 4   PROVIDING EFFECTIVE TRANSITIONS

In the following paragraph, provide the indicated type of transition in each blank.

Answers will vary. Sample answers are provided.

¹ __When__ (time signal) she arrived home after a long day at work, Terri wanted nothing more than a quiet dinner and an evening at home. ²__However__ (contrast signal), as soon as she heard the doorbell, she knew her peace was about to be shattered by her next-door neighbor, Doris. ³__Ever since__ (time signal) Terri had moved in three months before, Doris had become increasingly more intrusive. ⁴Almost every evening, Terri answered the insistently ringing doorbell to find Doris standing ____on____ (space signal) her porch. ⁵__Because__ (cause-effect signal) Terri was kindhearted and afraid that Doris might be lonely, she did not discourage the visits at first. ⁶Soon, though, she began to make excuses to her neighbor, __such as__ (example signal) "I am about to leave" or "I'm really busy right now." ⁷__However__ (contrast signal), Doris would

pay no attention, saying, "I'll just take a minute of your time," and pushing past Terri uninvited. [8]On this particular day, Terri did not feel like seeing Doris, __but__ (contrast signal) she did not feel like having a confrontation either. [9]__So__ (cause-effect signal) she sneaked to the window, feeling like a thief in her own home, and peeked out to confirm that it was Doris. [10]__Then__ (time signal) she waited quietly for her lonely neighbor to give up and go home.

Writing Assignments

Choose one of the following assignments and follow the steps in the writing process to complete the assignment. Pay special attention to the unity and coherence of your composition. Ask yourself whether your composition is about a single idea, whether it flows smoothly, and whether you have used transitions effectively.

Writing Assignment 1   A Significant Meeting

Prewrite. Your paragraph will describe the moment you met someone significant in your life. The "someone" may be a friend, a significant other, a child, or even a pet. The relationship may be new or old, but the focus of your prewriting and of your paragraph should be on the moment of meeting. Prewrite, using your favorite prewriting method.

Plan. As you plan your paragraph, decide which details from your prewriting you will discard and which you will keep. Write a topic sentence that tells where your paragraph is going. Your topic sentence should be the most general sentence in the paragraph. In other words, write, "When I met Hannah, I never imagined that we would be good friends," rather than "Hannah greeted me in a voice that sounded as harsh as sandpaper on wood." In other words, save the specific support for the body of the paragraph.

Draft. Write the first draft of your paragraph. Use chronological order to relate the event. Reinforce the coherence of your paragraph with appropriate transitional words that show sequence and transition of time.

Revise. As you revise your paragraph, pay particular attention to coherence and unity. Check coherence first. Does your paragraph flow smoothly? Have you used appropriate transitional words where necessary? Next, check the unity of your paragraph. Make sure that everything in your paragraph relates to the topic sentence.

Proofread. Proofread your paper, checking carefully for errors in spelling, grammar, and punctuation. Trade paragraphs with a fellow student to check for errors that may have been missed on the first proofreading.

Writing Assignment 2   Public and Private

Human beings are complex creatures, and the face that a person presents to the world is often different from the face he or she displays in private. How is your public image different from your private self? Write a paragraph describing in detail the differences between your public self and your private self.

Coherence check:	Does your paragraph flow smoothly?
	Do you use transitions of contrast where appropriate?
Unity check:	Do all sentences support the topic sentence?

Writing Assignment 3   Five-Finger Discount

Most large stores are tough on shoplifting. They install sophisticated equipment to monitor their sales floors, hire security personnel to prevent theft, and prosecute shoplifters who are caught. In spite of these measures, a small percentage of shoppers still choose to take a "five-finger discount" rather than paying for their goods. Write a paragraph discussing some of the reasons that people shoplift.

Coherence check:	Does your paragraph flow smoothly?
	Do you use transitions of contrast where appropriate?
Unity check:	Do all sentences support the topic sentence?

6

Revising, Proofreading, and Formatting

proofreading *revising* formatting
REVISING **formatting** revising
PROOFREADING *formatting*
FORMATTING **proofreading**
REVISING *proofreading* **revising**

For many writers, **revising, proofreading,** and **formatting** are an afterthought. However, these steps in the writing process assure that your document says what you want it to say and has a professional appearance. **Revising** helps you to capture your ideas more clearly and accurately, **proofreading** helps to eliminate errors and ensure accuracy, and proper **formatting** gives your document a professional appearance.

Revising

Revising your document helps you to ensure that it says what you want it to say in the way you want to say it. Revising helps you do justice to your ideas and get your message across.

In conversation, messages are received through give-and-take. You make a statement, your listener asks a question, and eventually, understanding is reached. But writing does not offer the same opportunity for response. Your readers cannot ask questions if they do not understand. Therefore, you have to anticipate questions and clarify possible misunderstandings before you present the finished work.

The word *revise* combines the Latin root meaning *to see* with the prefix meaning *again*. In its most literal sense, *to revise* means *to see again*. "Seeing again" is the essence of good revision. The difficult part is distancing yourself far enough from the work to see it with new eyes. When the work is fresh from your pen or word processor, you often see what you *meant* to say rather than what is actually on the page.

To see your work again, you need to create a space, a mental distance, between yourself and the work. You can best achieve this mental distance with time. Lay the writing aside for at least a twenty-four-hour period. When you return to it, words that aren't precise, sentences that aren't clear, and explanations that don't really explain will be easier to spot.

If you do not have twenty-four hours to lay the work aside, it may help to have someone else look at it. Ask your reader to focus on content and to ask questions about any point that does not seem clear. The written word carries no facial expression, no gesture, and no tone of voice, so it is more open to misinterpretation than face-to-face communication. Discussing work with a reader can help to close the gap between what you *think* you said and what your reader actually sees.

In addition to letting a work "cool" before revising and enlisting the help of a reader, you can also check your paragraph point by point to make sure that it fulfills the purpose you had in mind. There is nothing mysterious about this procedure. It works like the diagnostic test a mechanic might perform to evaluate a car, checking all major systems to make sure that they are working as they should. The following revision checklist will help you to go through your paragraph, part by part, to make sure each part is doing the job you intended it to do.

Checklist for Paragraph Revision

The Topic Sentence

✔ Does the paragraph have a topic sentence that clearly states the main idea of the entire paragraph?

✔ Is the topic sentence the first or second sentence in the paragraph?

The Supporting Sentences

✔ Does each sentence of the paragraph support the topic sentence?

✔ Do your examples and explanations provide *specific* detail to support the topic sentence?

✔ Is each point you raise adequately explained and supported?

The Closing Sentence

✔ Is the last sentence satisfying and final-sounding?

✔ Does the last sentence serve as a summary or closing sentence for the *entire* paragraph?

Checking Coherence

✔ Is the order of ideas clear and logical?

✔ Are transitional words used effectively?

EXERCISE 1   **DISTINGUISHING A REVISION FROM A ROUGH DRAFT**

Read the two versions of the paragraph "Saving Earth's Resources." Using the preceding checklist for revision as your guide, decide which version is the revision and which is the rough draft.

Version 1

Saving Earth's Resources

[1]One common way of saving resources is recycling. [2]Schools and office buildings provide containers for recycling of aluminum cans and paper. [3]At home, people can separate newspaper and plastic and aluminum containers from the rest of the trash and make a monthly trip to a recycling center if municipal trash pickup does not provide a recycling service. [4]Limiting the use of automobiles can save precious fuel. [5]Americans have a love affair with the automobile, and who can blame them? [6]I remember my first car and how carefully I would polish it and care for it. [7]Finally, Americans can save energy by controlling the heat and air conditioning in homes and offices. [8]With little inconvenience, it is possible to help conserve the earth's resources and, in many cases, save a dollar or two as well.

Version 2

Saving Earth's Resources

[1]Americans are heavy users of the earth's resources, but there are ways to preserve those resources for future generations. [2]One common way of

saving resources is recycling. [3]Schools and office buildings provide containers for recycling of aluminum cans and paper. [4]At home, people can separate newspaper and plastic and aluminum containers from the rest of the trash and make a monthly trip to a recycling center if municipal trash pickup does not provide a recycling service. [5]Another way to save fuel is to limit the use of automobiles. [6]In large cities where traffic is heavy and public transportation is extensive, many people elect to save money and fuel by not owning a car. [7]But even in areas where the family car is a necessity, people can make one trip do the job of several by carpooling, coordinating errands, and taking care of errands such as grocery shopping on the way home from work or school. [8]Finally, Americans can save energy by controlling the heat and air conditioning in homes and offices. [9]In summer, 72° is a reasonable and comfortable indoor temperature, and in winter, heavier clothing can keep most people comfortable with the thermostat turned to 68°. [10]With very little inconvenience, it is possible for an ordinary person to help conserve the earth's resources.

The revised version of the paragraph is Version ___2___.

EXERCISE 2   REVISING A PARAGRAPH

Go back to the unrevised version of "Saving Earth's Resources" and fill in the blanks to answer the following questions.

1. A topic sentence should appear before sentence ___1___.

2. A transitional word or expression is needed as the writer moves to a new major point in sentence ___4___.

3. Two sentences that do not support the topic sentence are sentence ___5___ and sentence ___6___.

4. More support is needed to fully make the writer's point after sentence ___7___.

Proofreading

Think about the last time you saw a misspelling in a newspaper. The minute you saw it, your thoughts moved away from the story itself and focused on the error. Similarly, errors in your writing take a reader's focus away from your ideas and put emphasis on grammar, spelling, or punctuation. Naturally, you want the ideas to stand in the foreground while grammar, spelling, and punctuation remain in the background. Proofreading, then, is an essential last step. It is a chore; however, it is a necessary chore.

After you have completed the final revision of your work, proofread it at least twice, once from the top down and once from the bottom up. If you have a special problem area, such as comma splices or subject-verb agreement, do at least one extra proofreading focused on those areas.

Proofreading is the job that is never done. No matter how thorough you are, some little error seems to escape your notice. Then, just as you are turning in your beautifully written or word-processed manuscript, the error pops out at you as if it were written in neon. Therefore, the more thorough your approach to proofreading, the better. The techniques outlined in the following sections will help to ensure thorough proofreading.

The Top-down Technique

The first proofreading should go from the top of the page down. As you proofread from the top down, check to make sure that the connections between ideas are smooth and solid and that the sentences and paragraphs flow smoothly into one another. Check for parallel structure, clear pronoun reference, and appropriate transitional expressions. After correcting any problems you find in the top-down proofreading, move to the second type of proofreading, the bottom-up proofreading.

The Bottom-up Technique

The bottom-up proofreading technique is more labor-intensive and more focused than the top-down proofreading. When you read from the bottom up, you are no longer reading your paragraph as a single piece of writing but as disconnected sentences that do *not* flow into one another. You are focusing on a single sentence, so you can look at it closely, as if it were a sentence in a grammar exercise. Read it, correct any errors you find, and then move back to the next sentence.

The Targeting Technique

If you have a "favorite error"—one that you seem to make more often than any other—try proofreading one more time to target that error. Following are some common errors and shortcuts to finding those errors. As you become more experienced, you will find yourself devising your own strategies to target your problem areas.

Subject-verb agreement. Check each subject-verb sequence. Look for present-tense verb forms and make sure that they agree with their subjects.

Comma splices and run-ons. Target long sentences; they are more likely to be run-ons. Target commas to see whether there is a sentence on both sides of the comma; if so, you have a comma splice.

Other comma errors. Target each comma, and question its reason for being there. If you aren't sure why it is there, maybe it doesn't belong.

Pronoun agreement. Look for the plural pronouns *they* and *their*, and make sure that they have a plural, not a singular, antecedent.

Sentence fragments. Using the bottom-up technique, read each sentence to see if it could stand on its own.

Proofreading the Word-Processed Paragraph

Spelling and grammar checkers can be helpful in proofreading, but they are no substitute for knowledge and judgment. A spelling or grammar checker can find possible errors and suggest possible solutions. However, it is up to you to decide what, if anything, is wrong and how to fix it.

Even when you use spelling and grammar checkers, you should do at least two separate proofreadings. The following sentence may illustrate the need for proofreading:

Weather or knot ewe use a spelling checker, you knead too proofread.

Whether to proofread onscreen or to print out a hard copy to proofread is a personal choice. Some writers find it easier to scroll up and down on the computer screen, viewing the paragraph in small segments. Others prefer to hold the printed copy in their hands. Find out what works for you, and proceed accordingly.

Group Exercise 1   Proofreading a Paragraph   Feeling confident? Go solo!

'Each of the ten sentences in the following paragraph contains an error. Form a small proofreading team with two or three of your classmates. Pooling your knowledge, see how many errors you can identify and correct.

Distracted Driving

[1]Laws in some places prevent the use of cell phones on the highway, however, it would be impossible to regulate all of the other crazy and distracting things that drivers do. [2]Some acts are just to ordinary to be banned. [3]For instance, their is no way to legislate against sneezing, changing the radio station, or fumbling for sunglasses while driving. [4]Other actions that go along with driving is too economically important to ban. [5]The drive-thru restaurant industry would certainly lobby against any proposal to make eating in cars illegal. [6]Countless hamburgers, chicken sandwich, and tacos would remain unsold. [7]If drivers could not munch them as they sped down the interstate or crawled through rush-hour traffic. [8]Finally, some drivers activities are so bizarre that no one would think to legislate against them. [9]Who would write a law banning a person from shaving while they are driving to work? [10]Or reading while driving. [11]Laws against using cell phones while driving may be beneficial they will cut accidents to some extent. [12]Drivers will always find activities that distract him or her from driving.

Corrections

Answers may vary slightly.

1.	highway; however	7.	unsold if drivers
2.	too	8.	drivers'
3.	there	9.	while he is driving
4.	are	10.	work or reading
5.	drive-through	11.	beneficial; they
6.	sandwiches	12.	that distract them

Formatting

You have heard it all your life: First impressions count. The document you hand to your instructor, the resumé you hand to a prospective employer, or the letter you send to the editor of a newspaper has the ability to present a positive first impression or a negative one. When an instructor sees a paper that is typed or clearly and neatly handwritten, with no smudges, crossovers, or dog-eared edges, the instructor expects that paper to be a good one, written as carefully as it was prepared. On the other hand, a hastily scrawled document smudged with eraser marks or heavily laden with White-Out suggests that the writer did not take the time to create a good impression—or to write a good paper.

Manuscript format is so important that entire books have been written about it. An instructor who asks you to use MLA style, APA style, or Chicago style is referring to styles outlined in books published by the Modern Language Association, the American Psychological Association, and the University of Chicago.

If you are given instructions for formatting a document, follow those instructions carefully. If you have no specific instructions, use the guidelines in the following section. They will help you to format a document effectively, whether that document is written in class or out of class, by hand or on a computer.

Handwritten Documents

Paragraphs and Essays

For handwritten paragraphs and essays, use lined white 8½ × 11-inch paper and blue or black ink. Write on one side of the paper only, and leave wide margins.

In the upper right-hand corner of the page, put your name and the date. If you wish, include your instructor's name and the name of the class for which you are preparing the assignment. Center your title, if any, on the first line of the paper, but do not underline the title or put it in quotation marks. Indent each paragraph five spaces, or about three-quarters of an inch. In a handwritten document, do not skip lines unless your instructor specifically requests that you do so. If you make an error, draw a single line through the error and rewrite your correction above the crossed-out error. Put a single paper clip, not a staple, in the upper left corner to join the pages.

Essay Tests

When you take an essay test, you may be required to use a "blue book" or to write on the test itself. If you are allowed to use your own paper, use lined paper and write on one side only.

Answers to questions on essay tests should be written in blue or black ink. Since time is too limited for a rough draft, take a moment to organize your thoughts, and then answer the question. Indent each paragraph that you write five spaces (three-quarters of an inch to one inch). Just as in any paragraph or essay, state your main idea first.

If you misspell a word or make a mistake, cross through it with a single line. Be sure to write clearly and legibly, and if your handwriting is difficult to read, try printing instead.

Computer-Generated Documents

Formatting the Document

Choose a font and a font size that are easily readable, such as Times New Roman in a 12-point size. Do not use a bold or an italic font.

Margins should be one inch all around. One-inch margins are the default in most word-processing software, so you probably will not have to set the margins at all. Double-space the text. Leave the right edge ragged rather than justifying it. (To justify means to line up in a straight edge, like a newspaper column.) A ragged right edge is the default setting on most computers.

Page Layout

Put your name and the date in the upper right corner of the page. Other information, such as the name of your instructor or the class for which you are preparing the assignment, is optional. Center the title, and indent each paragraph with a single tab as shown in the following example. A title page is not necessary unless your instructor asks for one.

Derek Smith

April 1, 2004

Format Reform

I am ashamed to say that I used to be a format abuser. I used strange fonts such as Adolescence and Space Toaster. I tried to make my papers look longer by using two-inch margins with 14-point font. At my lowest point, I turned in a report on lime-green paper printed in 15-point Star Trek font. A caring instructor saw that I had a problem, and helped me to turn my formatting around. Now, I know how to format a document perfectly.

The first step in preparing a document is formatting. Margins should be set at one inch all around—left, right, top, and bottom. The text should

Printing and Presenting Your Document

When the document has been revised and proofread, print it on good quality 8½ × 11 white paper. To hold the pages together, place a single paper clip in the upper left corner. Do not staple your document or put it in a report cover.

Writing Assignments

Choose one of the following assignments and follow the steps in the writing process to write a finished composition. Be sure to revise, proofread, and format your document so that the paper you turn in is a polished composition.

Writing Assignment 1   A Recommendation

Imagine that you have applied for a job and been asked to write a letter of recommendation for yourself. Although you have many qualities that might make you valuable in the workplace, your recommendation will focus on the three most important qualities that will make you an asset on the job.

Consider this assignment carefully. The first ideas that pop into your head may not be the most important qualities. Maybe you are always on time, but so are most other wage earners. Perhaps being on time is really a part of something larger, such as your dependability. Or perhaps it's not as important as some of your other traits, such as creativity or willingness to tackle jobs you have never done before.

Your recommendation may be written in the third person ("Lakeshia is a natural leader") or in the first person ("My enthusiasm makes me a natural salesperson"). It may be written in letter form or as a single paragraph. In either case, you should begin with a topic sentence that states the main idea of your paragraph or letter and a summary sentence that sums it up.

Writing Assignment 2   A Special Day

Some days, such as holidays, birthdays, and anniversaries, have special significance. Aside from those days, what other day is a special day for you? For some people, Fridays are special because they mark the end of the workweek and the beginning of the weekend. Other people value their Saturday shopping trips or nights out, their Sunday church attendance or family meals. Write a paragraph that answers the question, "What ordinary day is special to you, and why?"

Writing Assignment 3   Simplify, Simplify

In today's complex world, many people say that they would like to simplify their lives. If you could, would you simplify your life? Write a paragraph describing the steps you would take to simplify your life.

7

Essays, Essay Exams, and Summary Reports

T This ticket entitles those who have mastered
I the essay to write effectively in any
C subject area, to express themselves
K in a way that their professors will
E respect, and to modify the essay format
T for career and academic writing.

You are about to meet a form of writing that can help you in the academic world and beyond. When you master the fundamentals of the essay, you master a form of writing that can be used to express an opinion, analyze a poem, or compare two methods of government. Shrunk down a bit, the essay format can be used to answer a question on an essay test or an employment application. Expanded a bit, it can be used to write a research paper, a term paper, or a report. Even this textbook is, in many ways, an expansion of the essay format. This chapter focuses first on essays, then on essay exams.

Writing an Essay

This chapter uses the five-paragraph essay as a model. Once you learn to write a five-paragraph essay, you can modify the essay form and length to suit your purpose for writing.

A diagram of the five-paragraph essay appears on page 82. Study it to get a "mental map" of the five-paragraph essay; then use it for planning and checking your own essays.

Essay Diagram and Revision Checklist

Introduction

- The first sentence gets the reader's attention.
- The indroduction provides background and introduces the subject.
- The thesis statement comes last (main idea) and may list the points of development

---

First Body Paragraph

- The topic sentence states the first thesis point that will be developed.
- Support sentences give specific examples, information, and an explanation of the topic sentence.
- A summary sentence (optional) sums up the entire paragraph.

Second Body Paragraph

- The topic sentence states the next thesis point that will be developed.
- Support sentences give specific examples, information, and an explanation of the topic sentence.
- A summary sentence (optional) sums up the entire paragraph.

Third Body Paragraph

- The topic sentence states the third thesis point that will be developed.
- Support sentences give specific examples, information, and an explanation of the topic sentence.
- A summary sentence (optional) sums up the entire paragraph.

Conclusion

- The first sentence of the conclusion is a broad, thesis-level statement. It may restate the thesis.
- The last sentance of the conclusion is satisfying and final-sounding.

Here's how a five-paragraph essay looks:

First comes an **introduction** that catches the reader's attention, provides background, introduces the subject, and states the **thesis,** or the main idea of the essay.

Next there are three **body paragraphs:** Each discusses one point of your thesis. The topic sentence of each body paragraph tells which thesis point will be developed in that paragraph.

The essay ends with a **conclusion** that sums up the points you have made and lets your reader know that you have ended the essay.

EXERCISE 1   RECOGNIZING ELEMENTS OF AN ESSAY

Read the sample essay carefully as you follow the directions in this exercise.

Answers will vary slightly.

1. Underline and label the essay's thesis statement.
2. Underline and label each body paragraph's topic sentence.
3. Underline and label each body paragraph's summary sentence.
4. Underline and label one transitional expression in each body paragraph.
5. Underline and label a supporting detail in each body paragraph.
6. Underline and label the thesis restatement in the conclusion.

Superstition in Today's World

Superstition would seem to have no place in our modern, technological world. Today, people look for scientific proof of everything, including the existence of God. <u>Yet even in modern times, superstition plays a surprisingly large role in sports, business, and personal matters</u>.

Thesis statement

<u>Superstition is a mainstay of professional athletics</u>. Athletes have lucky jerseys, tennis shoes, and socks. Sometimes these garments are worn well beyond the point of good hygiene for as long as

Topic sentence

the player's luck holds. Some athletes have rituals

that they follow for good luck. Some touch or kiss a

Supporting detail

religious medal or lucky amulet. Others go through

elaborate ritualistic motions. Some baseball

Transitional expression

players, for example, repeatedly adjust gloves,

sleeves, or caps, or perform motions in a prescribed

sequence. Athletes may look silly performing these

superstitious rituals, but they don't care. They

Summary sentence

believe that the rituals improve their performance

and would feel strange without them.

Topic sentence

    Superstition also plays a part in the business

world, where common sense and the dollar sign

usually prevail. Because the number thirteen is

considered unlucky, many hotels and office

Transitional expression

buildings do not have a thirteenth floor. Instead,

the elevator goes from the twelfth floor to the

fourteenth floor, sparing hotel guests or office

occupants from having to sleep or work on an

Supporting detail

"unlucky" floor. Many businesses report that

employee absenteeism rises on Friday the 13th, a

Summary sentence

day considered unlucky by many. In the buttoned-

down world of business, superstition is still

firmly entrenched.

Topic sentence

    Personal superstitions are a complex maze of the

lucky and the unlucky. Some people believe that bad

luck is brought on by breaking a mirror, walking

under a ladder, or having a black cat cross their path. *Four-leaf clovers, crickets chirping in the house, and the number seven are widely considered lucky.* Some things are lucky under some circumstances and unlucky under others. Finding a penny is usually considered lucky, but a penny lying "tails up" should be left alone. *Similarly,* the company of a stray dog is lucky, but a howling dog is said to foreshadow doom. *Through good luck and bad, superstitions endure.*

Even in this age of technology, superstitions permeate every area of life, from sports to business to everyday life. Superstitions probably do no harm, and they may actually help by giving people an illusion of control in an uncertain world.

[margin annotations: Supporting detail, Transitional expression, Summary sentence, Thesis restatement]

TOPICS FOR ESSAY WRITING

Essay Assignment 1: Lucky You?

Do you consider yourself a lucky person? Perhaps you are always the person who wins the door prize or spots the five-dollar bill on the sidewalk. Maybe you have never won anything, but consider yourself lucky in your relationships with others. Maybe you are unlucky, with a little cloud of doom that follows you around like a lost puppy. Or, like most people, you may be extremely lucky in some aspects of your life, and not so lucky in others.

Write an essay about your luck—or the lack of it. First, brainstorm to generate a list of areas in which you are lucky or unlucky. Look at your list, and decide what you want to include. Since you will have three body paragraphs, you may want to write about three areas of your life where you are lucky or three where you are unlucky. It's also permissible to write about your good luck in one or two aspects of your life and your bad luck in another. Alternatively, you may have so much good or bad luck in one area that you want to devote your entire essay to it. The choice is yours.

Essay Assignment 2: Be There or Be Square

Every school has an attendance policy, and most colleges require a student to attend a certain percentage of classes to be eligible for a passing grade. Some people argue that at the college level, there should be no attendance requirement: if students can pass with just occasional attendance, then they should be allowed to do so.

Do you believe that attendance policies in college classes should be abolished? Write an essay giving reasons for your belief.

How to proceed:

Step 1: Prewriting. Prewrite to generate reasons for and against abolishing attendance policies. Look at both sides of the question. Even if you believe you know which side of the question you support, it is wise to be aware of arguments for the opposing side.

Step 2: Planning. Look carefully at both sides of the issue and decide which side has the most compelling evidence. Is it the side you intend to take in your essay? If so, choose the strongest reasons in support of your argument. If not, take extra time to consider the examples and details you use in support of your argument to make sure that your essay is convincing.

As a second step in planning, draft your thesis statement and the topic sentence of each paragraph.

Step 3: Drafting. Drafting your essay using a computer will ensure ease of revision later. Follow your outline as you draft. If you have trouble writing your introduction, write the rest of the essay and come back to the introduction later. Sometimes introductions are easier to write when you know exactly what you are introducing.

Step 4: Revising. Lay your essay aside for a day; then come back to it and revise it. Focus on making ideas clear and providing specific details and examples. Use the Essay Diagram and Revision Checklist on page 82 as a guideline for revision.

Step 5: Proofreading. If you are writing your essay on a computer, use the spelling checker, consulting a dictionary if necessary to make sure you have the correct word. The grammar checker should be used with a little more caution, if at all. Grammar checkers on computers so often present wrong choices that it's essential to know more grammar than the machine does before trying to use one.

Proofread your essay carefully. Read once from the top down to check for continuity and transitional words and to make sure that your sentences flow smoothly. Proofread a second time from the bottom up, reading each sentence as if it were an exercise in a grammar book. Your third proofreading will be a sweep for misspelled words, comma errors, and word usage. Once you have completed the third proofreading, put your essay aside for a while. Later, you may want to proofread again.

Essay Assignment 3: My Generation

Most people identify themselves with a particular generation, and often, generations have been given names that reflect their characteristics. At the beginning of the twentieth century, the "Lost Generation" of the 1920s and 1930s felt alienated from society. People who came of age in the 1940s have been called "The Greatest Generation" in reference to their hard work, patriotism, and moral fiber. Their children, who came of age during the Vietnam War, are called "Baby Boomers" because of the huge increase in the birthrate (the "baby boom") that occurred after World War II. Children of the Baby Boomers were considered an unpredictable and unknown quantity, "Generation X." The children of Generation Xers are sometimes called "Generation Y."

Think about your own generation, and make a list of its characteristics. These questions will get you started: Is your generation politically involved or not? Optimistic or pessimistic? Filled with alienated loners or with people-loving volunteers? What name would you give your generation if you could name it?

Once you have done some prewriting and thinking about your generation, write an essay that describes the major characteristics of your generation. Give specific examples that illustrate each characteristic.

When you have written your essay, use the Essay Diagram and Revision Checklist on page 82 as a guideline for revision.

Taking Essay Exams

Essay exams require an ability to interpret questions and to organize and present information. Strong preparation, good writing skills, and use of strategies tailored to the essay exam can put you on the road to success.

Preparing for the Exam

Preparation for any exam begins long before that last-minute cram session the night before the test. It begins with strong study habits. For busy students, the short-term goal of passing tests and making good grades can sometimes obscure the real goal of learning the material. However, if you approach every class with the objective of learning the subject matter and understanding the important theories, facts, and events that make up the subject matter, passing tests will be a natural part of the process. Following are some time-tested ways to make the material in any class your own.

1. **Read the textbook.** Before you go to class, be sure to read the textbook's version of the material that will be covered in that day's class. Read actively, underlining or highlighting important concepts and writing marginal questions where there is material you do not fully understand.

2. **Listen and take notes.** In class, listen carefully and take good notes. Taking good notes does not necessarily mean taking down every word your professor utters. Some classes, such as history or psychology, focus on the presentation of facts and theories and require extensive note-taking. In these classes, professors often help by writing important material on the board, providing handouts, or vocally stressing material that is essential to know. In other classes, such as mathematics, the focus is on the application of ideas, and the notes taken, though still important, are more concise.

3. **Review.** Review your notes as soon after class as possible. The brain quickly loses new material unless the learning is reinforced. As you review, anticipate possible test questions. For example, if two major theories in the field conflict in important ways, you might be asked to contrast (or to compare and contrast) those theories. If your instructor has provided you with a list of any kind, be prepared to reproduce that list on a test. Think like a teacher. What would you ask if you were testing students on the subject matter?

4. **Have a Study Plan**. As the test approaches, plan your study sessions for the test. Plan at least one study session with other members of the class. They may have picked up on something that you have not, and vice versa.

   It is also important to plan study sessions alone, giving yourself time to absorb and rehearse the material in your own way.

   If you are preparing for an essay test, be sure to include essay test "rehearsals" in your group study plan and your solo study plan. The first step in rehearsing for an essay test is to make up your own questions. From your notes, from the book, and from hints that your instructor may have dropped in class, choose several topics that are likely to appear on the test. Think up likely questions on those topics and likely ways those questions will be asked. If you have studied two conflicting views of a topic, a contrast question may be in order. If your notes contain a section headed "Three major characteristics of a wetland," anticipate a question that asks you to list and explain those characteristics.

As you formulate your questions, also plan how you will answer them, and make a brief outline to use as a study guide.

As the test approaches, you may want to plan one timed session in which you write out answers to essay questions that you have made up from the material. In your practice essay test session and during the actual test, follow the guidelines in the next section for taking essay tests.

Taking the Exam

On the day of the exam, you are prepared, but your task has not ended yet. Good test-taking strategy is essential to turning in your best possible performance. The following section contains tips for approaching essay exams and answering essay questions.

1. **Look over the entire test.** Before you begin, look at the test as a whole, and read directions and notations carefully. Directions such as "answer five of the eight questions," "answer in a short paragraph," or "answer in blue or black ink" are important to note. Once you have looked at the general directions, check the questions. Are they all the same point value, or do they vary? You'll want to spend more time on a thirty-point question than on a ten-point one, and you may want to answer the high-point-value questions first.

   As you look over the questions themselves, it may help you to jot easily forgotten names, dates, or concepts in the margins to ensure that the information is readily available when you answer the questions.

   This brief survey of the test should take no more than a minute or two, but it is an important step that should not be omitted.

2. **Read and understand the question.** As you approach each specific question, look carefully at what it asks you to do. You may want to underline key words and phrases such as "compare and contrast," "explain," and "give an example."

3. **Answer the question.** Essay exams require full and complete answers, but since the exams are timed, your answers must also be precise. Some specific strategies for answering questions follow.

   Plan briefly. On an essay exam, you will have no time to write a rough draft. Keep your planning to a brief list of the points you intend to cover.

   Write legibly. When you're in a hurry, it's easy for the most legible handwriting to deteriorate into a scrawl. Slow down just a bit to keep your handwriting legible. If your handwriting is indecipherable even on a good day, print instead.

Get to the point. An answer to an essay question does not require an introduction. Start with your topic sentence or thesis.

Answer the question directly. Make sure that your thesis statement or topic sentence answers the question directly and completely. One way to do this is by rephrasing the question. This technique ensures that all the key words from the question appear in your answer. The following examples show typical questions and answers that begin by rephrasing the question.

> **Q:** List and explain the four steps in the scientific method.
> **A:** The four steps in the scientific method are observation, formulation of a hypothesis, prediction, and experimentation. The first step, observation, involves observing a particular phenomenon, usually over a period of time. In the second step, the scientist constructs a hypothesis that explains something about the phenomenon. In the third step, the hypothesis is then used to make a prediction about the phenomenon, an "educated guess" that the scientist must prove through the fourth step, experimentation. The experiment must be set up so that it can be repeated by the same scientist or by others to verify the results. If the experiment confirms the prediction consistently, the hypothesis becomes a theory, an assumption about the way the phenomenon works.

> **Q:** Discuss the functions of the public baths in ancient Rome.
> **A:** The public baths in Ancient Rome had two main functions. The first was hygiene. Like modern Americans, ancient Romans valued cleanliness and considered hygiene important. Since it was rare for a private household to have running water, most Romans made daily trips to the baths to ensure personal cleanliness. The second function of the Roman bathhouses was a social function. Bathhouses served as a meeting place, and many a business deal was born at the public baths. At the bathhouse, all portions of society intersected. The price of admission to the public baths was so low that the poorest Romans could afford to enter and take their baths beside the wealthiest members of Roman society.

Use key terms. Every subject area has its own terminology, sometimes called *jargon*. If your instructor has introduced special terms, know how to use them, and include them in your answers on the test. Speaking the language of a particular field is an integral part of learning that field.

Don't tell everything you know. Sometimes it's tempting to throw in a little extra information that does not directly relate to the question. After all, you studied it; you know it; so why not show it off? Don't succumb to that temptation. Stick to information and examples that directly support the question.

Use specific supporting details and examples. On an essay test, specific details and examples help to convince your reader that you know the answer, not just in a general way, but down to the last detail.

4. **Keep one eye on the clock.** As you finish each question, check the clock to make sure you are on track. If time is tight, keep your answers brief and answer the questions you are sure of first.

5. **Proofread.** Spelling and grammar *do* count on essay exams. Even if your instructor does not specifically mark off for errors, errors detract from the effectiveness of an answer. As you proofread, mark through errors with a single line, and print the correction neatly above the crossed-out word or phrase.

EXERCISE 2   ANSWERING ESSAY QUESTIONS

Read and study the following textbook excerpt. Then answer the essay question that follows, referring to the text as needed. Although this exercise is "open-book," your answers should be in your own words rather than in the words of the text.

Healthy and Dysfunctional Relationships
by Cara DiMarco

from *Moving Through Life Transitions with Power and Purpose* (Prentice Hall, 2000)

What is a healthy relationship? A healthy relationship is one in which your individuality is strengthened by your connection with another person. A healthy relationship allows room for you to grow; to express yourself; to have differing opinions; to be open, vulnerable, scared, affectionate, excited, and sad; and to be accepted as a worthwhile person regardless of whether someone is pleased with your behavior. In this kind of relationship, you are not asked to give up any integral part of yourself—your feelings, independent thoughts and beliefs, or your way of being in the world.

In healthy relationships, power is not used to dominate; rather, each person uses his or her own personal power and is able to do the things he or she deems important and valuable. In addition, each individual provides support and encouragement for the other person, doing what is possible and reasonable to help the other feel personally empowered.

A dysfunctional relationship is one in which aspects of the above are not possible. There may be bullying, intimidation, some form of abuse—verbal, emotional, physical, or sexual—or threats and coercion used to control the other person.

In a dysfunctional relationship there is room for only agreement, not individuality and differences. Your uniqueness is devalued; your worth is in question. You come out of interactions feeling less than you did going into them. These relationships consistently and chronically seem to suck out your life energy. They take your strengths and the best of you and belittle them, leaving you no room for growth, acceptance, love, or caring. In a dysfunctional relationship you are under siege, held hostage emotionally in a psychological war zone, never knowing when you're going to catch another piece of emotional shrapnel. You're diminished and devalued by the connection, and who you are as an individual is in danger because of the destructiveness of the relationship. There is no room to be freely yourself, to freely express yourself. Love is not possible because control, domination, and disruption take precedence over caring emotions.

How do you know if a relationship is healthy or unhealthy? How do you determine whether a relationship merely has challenges, struggling points, and issues to be discussed, negotiated, and resolved—or is truly unhealthy and perhaps needs to be terminated?

One good gauge is to look at the level of respect and regard for one another that is present in the relationship. There can be massive disagreements about choices in career, how you spend your leisure time, finances, political issues, child-rearing concerns, what you find funny, choice of friends, choice of areas to live—and still a relationship can be healthy.

What allows substantial differences to exist within a healthy relationship is the level of respect accorded each person's individuality, preferences, opinions, beliefs, and choices. I don't need to agree with you or see things eye-to-eye in order to have a healthy relationship with you. I do need to respect you and not denigrate you for your differing opinions. In healthy relationships communication is always a possibility, even when it doesn't result in agreement. It might very well result in choosing to agree to disagree. In healthy relationships both partners are seen for who they are, for their uniqueness, and for their abilities and strengths. They are able to be heard for their values, opinions, preferences, wants, and joys, and acknowledged for the unique contributions they bring to the relationship.

Healthy relationships allow each partner to affect the other without damage. Healthy relationships exist on a continuum—what might feel healthy, satisfying, and appropriate for one person may be entirely different for another. Despite disagreement and disappointments, in healthy relationships no deep damage is done to a person's self-esteem, sense of self, dignity, or self-worth.

Unhealthy or dysfunctional relationships are just the opposite. In them the partners are not seen as who they truly are; they are not heard; their opinions are drowned out; someone is bullied into submission; dominance prevails; and blame, shame, and punitive behavior are the major forms of communication rather than acceptance, appreciation, and celebration of the other person.

In dysfunctional relationships each person feels diminished and less valued because of the connection; his or her human worth and dignity are in question. Rather than experiencing normal disagreements and disappointments, the partners feel damaged and deeply wounded by the interactions.

In my private psychology practice, individuals often ask me, "How come I seem to keep attracting or being attracted to partners who aren't good for me?" Part of what causes this is that we are drawn to situations that have components or familiar aspects of painful situations in our childhood that we did not have the power to change. In an effort to grow and attain mastery over events that we didn't have mastery over as children, in our adult life we unconsciously seek partners who embody at least some of the characteristics of important people who were the source of pain that we couldn't alleviate earlier in life.

Rather than being a source of doom ("Oh great, no matter what I do, I'm going to attract people who ignore me just as my father did"), this is actually a positive drive to solve what was unsolvable in childhood. Unfortunately, even if you do manage to pick a partner who exhibits that trait and even if you do manage to do things differently as an adult, this still won't heal that early childhood wound. The only way to really heal that childhood wound is to obtain personal counseling, write in a journal, join a support group, or do something that actually works at healing the initial wound. Trying to heal old wounds through your day-to-day adult life never seems to work.

Knowing this, how can you tell if you are attracted to someone as part of attempting to heal old wounds? What I often hear from individuals in my practice and women in the Transitions to Success program is that they don't realize that they have picked a partner with characteristics from their past until they are entrenched in the relationship.

One good way to try to spot this pattern early in a relationship is to examine your excitement level. A young woman in my practice was once talking about the young men in her life, whom she referred to as "boys." She was feeling a great deal of agony over one young man because he was distant, evasive, and did not call her when he said he would. She said, "But he's so exciting. I always feel like I'm living on the edge." So I said to her, "It sounds like he's an excitement boy." And she said, "That's it—he really is an excitement boy."

Then she went on to describe a female friend who had been dating a young man. The two women went over to watch videos at his house, and as the evening progressed they grew cold and hungry. The young man brought them blankets, bowls of macaroni and cheese, and big mugs of coffee; and as she finished relating the story, she said, "I didn't know there were boys out there that did the same things that I did for people, that like to care for other people." I said to her, "So he's a love boy, a boy who likes to nurture and love other people." So that became our code phrase for looking at her relationships—was her current date an excitement boy or a love boy.

Part of what we learned together in exploring her choice of partners is that it is perfectly okay to pick an excitement partner if what you want is excitement and to live on the edge emotionally, feeling sweeping lows and soaring highs. All of that can be a wonderful adrenaline rush; just don't expect love partner behavior out of that person. An excitement partner probably isn't going to bring you a steaming bowl of macaroni and cheese or, upon learning you have a miserable cold, come over with chicken soup and videos.

So whatever you want to choose in the moment, choose it freely and enjoy it; but don't expect a love partner to be an excitement partner, and don't expect an excitement partner to be a love partner. The kind of person who loves you steadily and well probably isn't going to take you to never-ending peaks of ecstasy and pits of despair.

Part of what creates dysfunctional relationships is that someone looks at an excitement partner and believes it is possible to turn that person into a love partner. If you hang out with an excitement partner and just enjoy the excitement until it becomes hurtful or disruptive, you can have a lot of enjoyment. But what usually creates the excitement is that something about the excitement partner vaguely reminds you of some significant trait an important adult possessed—an adult who created childhood pain for you. Much of the excitement comes from the opportunity to grapple with the issue again, to struggle with a partner who is not accessible, who is preoccupied with other things, or who has a substance abuse problem. And while the partner might be entertaining for two weeks or two months, he probably isn't going to turn out to be a love partner anywhere in the near future. The person is not going to emerge as someone who can love you back with an equal and answering force.

It's perfectly acceptable to choose an excitement partner and enjoy the emotional rush. Just be conscious that you are doing it and don't get too attached to be able to let go when the relationship no longer works. If you don't feel ready to settle down with someone who loves you solidly and well, that's fine; just don't bemoan the fact that you can't turn an excitement partner into a love partner. They are two very different species, and while sometimes excitement partners grow into people who can nurture and love deeply, it's usually a gradual process that won't occur in the course of a brief relationship no matter how wonderful you are.

■ Essay Questions on "Healthy and Dysfunctional Relationships"

Please answer each of the following questions in a paragraph. Answer completely and thoroughly, following this chapter's guidelines on taking essay exams.

Answers will vary. Sample answers are provided.

1. Discuss the ways in which healthy and dysfunctional relationships differ in terms of use of power.

   In a healthy relationship, power is used for personal growth and for completion of personal projects. It is also used to help out the other partner and to make that partner feel empowered. In other words, power is used for the good of both parties. In a dysfunctional relationship, however, power is used to dominate a partner. Sometimes this domination is emotional or verbal, sometimes physical or sexual. Instead of feeling empowered, the partner feels demeaned and constantly off balance. In a dysfunctional relationship, power is used to control another person.

2. How are personal differences and differences of opinion handled in a healthy relationship? In an unhealthy relationship?

   In a healthy relationship, personal differences and differences of opinion are accepted. Each person is an individual, and personal differences do not stand in the way of love, communication, or respect. In a dysfunctional relationship, there is no room for individuality or for disagreement. The dominated partner feels devalued and diminished, and, because there is no room for free expression, is in danger of losing his or her identity.

3. Define the terms "excitement partner" and "love partner," and discuss what a person might expect from each type of partner in a relationship.

   An excitement partner is one who makes the adrenaline flow and the heart beat faster. An excitement partner is fun and stimulating. However, the excitement partner is also undependable, and the highs of being with him are offset

by lows when he is not there when his partner needs him. A person going into a
relationship with an excitement partner should expect a short-term fling, not
an enduring relationship. A love partner, on the other hand, is steady, and his
love does not fluctuate every time the wind changes. A person entering a relationship with a love partner may be able to form an enduring relationship with
a partner who is there in good times and in bad.

Writing a Summary Report

A **summary report** condenses and presents information, often from a single source. When you write a summary, your goal is to present information from an essay, an article, or a book so that your reader understands
the main points. At the end of your report, if the assignment calls for it,
write a brief evaluation of the essay, article, or book.

The following section shows you the steps in summarizing an article.

Five Steps in Writing an Article Summary

Step 1: Choose a Topic and Find Sources of Information

Your instructor may assign a topic or an area of investigation or may ask
you to choose your own topic. Articles on your topic may be found in periodicals, in databases, or on Internet sites. An overview of each type of
information source follows.

Periodicals are publications such as newspapers, magazines, and
scholarly journals that are published on a regular basis—daily, monthly,
or quarterly, for example.

Subscription and CD-ROM Databases

Periodical articles are also available through subscription databases or
CD-ROM databases. Most college libraries subscribe to databases such as
ABI/INFORM, Academic Search Premier, and Research Library. These
databases may contain full-text articles from journals, newspapers, or

magazines, or they may contain article abstracts. **Full-text articles** are complete articles, exactly as originally published. **Article abstracts** are summaries intended to help you decide whether a particular article is appropriate for your purposes. If it is, you will need to find and read the original article in the periodical in which it originally appeared.

Internet Sources

Some websites may contain articles previously published in print sources; others may contain articles written for and published on the Internet. Internet sources vary widely in quality, and it is up to you to evaluate the credibility of each site you visit.

■ What Does the Suffix ■ of an Internet Site Mean?

An Internet site's suffix can tell you a bit about the person or group behind the site. Here's a key to decoding Internet suffixes.

.org: A nonprofit organization
.edu: A college or university
.gov: A U.S. government site
.com: A business or a private individual

Step 2: Evaluate Sources and Choose Your Article

Once you have found articles on your chosen topic, evaluate them to make sure that they are suitable for your summary. Use the following list of criteria for evaluation to find suitable articles.

- **Length.** If an article summary covers all the major points in the article, it will probably be 25 to 50 percent as long as the actual article. Therefore, if you are assigned a five-hundred-word summary, choose an article of approximately one thousand to two thousand words.

- **Readability.** Expect to find unfamiliar terminology and new concepts in any article that you choose. After all, the purpose of research is to learn something new. However, some articles are written for experts in the field and may be hard for a layperson to understand. Choose an article that you can comprehend fully.

- **Publication date.** A publication date helps you to evaluate the timeliness of the source. In fields where change is rapid, such as medicine or computer technology, finding up-to-date sources is essential.

- **Author.** Is the author an authority in the field? If not—if the author is a journalist, for example—does the author consult and quote credible, authoritative sources? These questions help you evaluate the authority and credibility of your source.

◼ Advice for Online Researchers ◼

Get Ready to Go Online

Research used to mean poring through stacks of books and periodicals. Today, it usually means sitting in front of a computer screen. Even print sources must be located through online catalogs, indexes to periodicals, and databases. Even if you are comfortable using a computer, these resources may seem alien to you at first. If you need help, do not hesitate to ask for it.

Find a Friend

Find someone in class who will agree to be your research partner. You don't need an expert, nor do you need someone who is working on the same topic. All you need is someone who is willing to go through the process with you. The two of you can work side by side and handle the rough spots together.

Ask a Librarian

Librarians are experts in finding information, and they are there to help. Explain your project and the kind of information you are looking for, and a librarian will point you in the right direction.

Print the Information

When you find useful articles online, print them so that you will not have to find them again. Documentation of online sources requires that you note the database you are using and the date you accessed the information.

Be Patient

Be patient with yourself and with the process of finding information—it always takes longer than you think it will.

Step 3: Read the Article and Take Notes

Before taking any notes, read your article through once or twice. Then, highlighter in hand, look for the following information:

- **Main and major ideas.** Read through the article, highlighting main and major ideas. Remember, main ideas often are found at the beginning of an article and are repeated at the end. Major ideas are often stated at the beginning of a paragraph or after a headline, and they are often supported by examples. Don't worry if this step takes more than one reading.

- **Examples and supporting details.** Once you have found the main and major ideas, go back and highlight the supporting details and examples that most directly support those ideas. A summary contains a minimum of the detail that fleshes out the main ideas, so be selective and choose only necessary and important details.

- **Information for the Works Cited list.** The final step in taking notes from your source is to write down the information you will need for your Works Cited list. In a summary of a single article, you have only one work to cite, but it is important to cite it correctly. A list of information needed for your Works Cited list follows.

For all sources
- Author
- Title of article
- Title of the magazine, journal, or newspaper in which the article was published
- Date of publication
- Volume and issue number of periodical, if available
- Page numbers

For online sources, note the following additional information:
- Date of access
- The URL (Universal Resource Locator, or complete web address) of an article from a website
- The name of the database for articles accessed from subscription databases through a college (or other) library, and the name of that library.

Step 4: Draft Your Paper

Drafting a summary report is similar to drafting an essay. Your draft should contain the following elements:

- **Introduction.** The introduction includes the author's name, the title of the article, and the central idea of the article.
- **Body paragraphs.** The body paragraphs outline the most important points in the article. The topic sentence of each body paragraph should state the idea that the paragraph will develop. Including occasional references to the author makes it perfectly clear to the reader that you are still discussing the ideas of another person rather than your own ideas.

    The body paragraph itself will paraphrase the author's ideas; that is, you will state the ideas in your own words. Quoting the author is also permissible, but use quotations sparingly. Most of the summary should be in your own words.

    One of the most difficult tasks of writing a summary is to put an author's ideas in your own words. When you **paraphrase,** you capture an idea using your own sentence structure and your own words. Here are some pointers to help you when you paraphrase:
    - It's always permissible to repeat key terms. If the author uses the term "geriatric medicine," there's no need to rephrase it as "medical care of old people."
    - Unusual phrasings should be reworded. If the author refers to a spider web as "a spider's gossamer trap," a paraphrase should simply call it a spider web.
    - The sentence structure of a paraphrase should vary from that of the original material.
- **Conclusion.** The conclusion sums up the author's ideas and presents your evaluation of or reaction to the article. Placing your evaluation in the conclusion is a way of clearly separating your reaction to the article from the summary. If your evaluation is lengthy, you may place it in a final body paragraph before beginning the conclusion.

Step 5: Format, Proofread, and Cite Your Source

The final draft of your paper will include proper formatting and a Works Cited page. Use the documentation style recommended by your instructor, or follow the brief guide to MLA style that appears later in this chapter. Your instructor may also ask you to provide a copy of the article you are summarizing.

A Brief Guide to MLA (Modern Language Association) Style

The following section outlines some of the basic principles of MLA style. For complete information on MLA style, consult the *MLA Handbook for Writers of Research Papers*, available in most college libraries and bookstores.

Formatting Your Paper

- Double-space the paper, including the Works Cited page.
- Use one-inch margins.
- Indent paragraphs one-half inch.
- Do not use a title page. Instead, put your name, your instructor's name, your course name, and the date at the top of the first page, each on a separate line, each line flush with the left margin. Center the title above the first paragraph. This material, like the rest of your paper, should be double-spaced.

The Works Cited List

The Works Cited list is double-spaced and alphabetized according to the last name of the author. The first line of each entry begins at the left margin; subsequent lines are indented one-half inch. Sample Works Cited entries appear below and in the model summary report that appears later in the chapter.

Magazine Article

```
Pinker, Steven. "The Blank Slate." Discover October
     2002: 34-40.
```

Newspaper Article

> Hummer, Steven. "Surviving the Sweet Science" Atlanta Journal-Constitution 13 October 2002: E-9.

Article on a Website

> Dunleavy, M. P. "Twenty Ways to Save on a Shoestring." MSN/Money. 29 Dec. 2001. 16 October 2002. <http://moneycentral.msn.com/articles/smartbuy/basics/8677.asp.>

Article Accessed from an Online Database

If you access a periodical or an encyclopedia article from an online database, provide information about the database from which you received it, the library where you accessed it (if applicable), and the date of access. If your college is part of a larger university system that has a systemwide set of databases, reference that systemwide set of databases rather than the individual library.

> Zimbardo, Phillip G. "Time to Take Our Time." Psychology Today 35: 2 Mar/Apr 2002 Psychology and Behavioral Sciences Collection. EbscoHost. 10 October 2002. Metro College Library.
>
> Jackson, Carol D., and R. Jon Leffingwell. "The Role of Instructors in Creating Math Anxiety in Students from Kindergarten through College." Mathematics Teacher 92.7 (1999). ERIC. EbscoHost. 2 May 2003. GALILEO.

A Model Summary Report

For his summary report, Miguel chose an article about reasons for obesity and overweight in the United States. The article, along with Miguel's highlighting and annotations, appears here, followed by the final draft of his summary report.

Why We're So Fat
Paul Raeburn, Julie Forster, Dean Foust, and Diane Brady

introductory anecdote

When McDonald's Corp. shareholders met in May on the corporate campus adjoining Hamburger University in Oak Brook, Ill., CEO Jack M. Greenberg expected an angry crowd. Sales were stagnant. The company's earnings had declined for six consecutive quarters. And 2001 was the company's worst year ever for profits. Yet Greenberg didn't field a single query on the company's finances. Where is the diet plate? someone asked. What about a veggie burger? asked another. Greenberg replied that the company is testing veggie burgers in Canada. And a veggie wrap is being offered in New York—but it isn't selling. "We would love to find the right product we can sell a lot of," he said. Indeed, the company's sagging profits might be a sign of the nation's growing concern about nutrition: Americans are getting fatter at an alarming rate, and some of them are worried enough, perhaps, to skip those trips to the Golden Arches.

background data

Obesity is, by far, the nation's leading health problem. A report in the Oct. 9 Journal of the American Medical Assn. found that 30.5% of Americans are obese, up from 22.9% a decade ago. And 64.5%, or nearly two-thirds, are overweight. The researchers also found that 15% of children aged 6 to 19 are overweight. More than vanity is at stake: Obesity raises the risk of heart disease, cancer, diabetes, high blood pressure, angina, and lung disease, among other ailments. It accounts for about 300,000 deaths a year, second only to tobacco.

main idea

A growing number of health experts say this alarming rise in obesity is the consequence of an unhealthy environment that encourages overeating and discourages physical activity. High-calorie, artery-clogging foods are cheap and plentiful. Healthy foods can sometimes be hard to find. And children are surrounded by increasing amounts of junk-food advertising. The food industry spends an estimated $33 billion a year on ads and promotions. "When you have $33 billion of marketing aimed at you, challenging you to eat more at all times, it's difficult not to eat too much," says Marion Nestle, chair of the nutrition and food studies department at New York University and author of *Food Politics*, published earlier this year.

background — shared responsibility

That's not to say the food industry and its ads are solely to blame for the fattening of America. Nestle acknowledges that people choose to eat what they eat. "Is it a matter of personal responsibility? Ultimately, it is," she says. But diets and public-health campaigns, which focus on changing individuals' behavior, have failed spectacularly. That's why the search for a cure for the epidemic has shifted to the environment—especially regarding children. "You can argue that adults are personally responsible. With kids, that's a harder argument to make," she says.

main idea restated

The idea that obesity is partly the consequence of an unhealthy environment is a relatively new one—but its time has arrived. In July, Senators Bill Frist (R-Tennessee), Jeff Bingaman (D-New Mexico), and Christopher J. Dodd (D-Connecticut) introduced a bill to foster better nutrition and more physical activity, especially among children and minorities. Food activists and attorneys with experience in tobacco litigation met recently to devise strategies to recover some of the $117 billion spent on obesity-related illnesses. And the surest sign the anti-obesity campaign is starting to work is the wave of new health programs from foodmakers. Many companies—from PepsiCo Inc., with its Get Active, Stay Active program, to McDonald's, with its just-announced yogurt and sweetened-fruit menu for kids—are rushing to show their concern for the nation's health.

the case against responsibility of foodmakers/ environment

The food and restaurant industries stiffen at charges that foodmakers are partly responsible for the rise in obesity. "We have a long record of giving people choices," says Richard M. Detwiler, a Pepsi spokesman. Diet Pepsi was introduced in 1964, he notes, and Frito-Lay has offered low-fat products for a decade. "We recognize it's a problem. We've brought on consultants who are helping us to improve our products to make them healthier." One of ConAgra Foods Inc.'s best-known brands is Healthy Choice, which was launched in 1988 after former CEO Charles M. "Mike" Harper had a heart attack and began searching for healthier foods. "We have a responsibility for providing information about what is in our foods," says Timothy P. McMahon, a ConAgra senior vice-president. But, he says, "people have a right to choose how they want to eat." Or, as analyst Eric Katzman of Deutsche Bank puts it: "The last time I looked, I didn't see a food executive stuffing a high-calorie, high-fat food product into somebody's mouth."

major point — economics of food.

support for major point

To understand the rise in obesity, it's useful to look at the economics of food. The U.S. food industry produces enough to supply each of us with 3,800 calories a day. That's one-third more than what most men need and nearly double the needs of most women. Supply exceeds demand. Prices fall. And Americans eat more. With the exception of a spike during the oil shock in the 1970s, food prices have dropped by an average of 0.2% a year since World War II, according to the Bureau of Labor Statistics. At the same time, the average American's food intake, which was 1,826 calories a day in the late 1970s, rose nearly 10%, to 2,002, by the mid-1990s.

major point — supersizing

And serving sizes have ballooned. According to the Agriculture Dept., muffins that weighed an average of 1.5 ounces in 1957 now average half a pound each. Fast-food hamburgers have swollen from an ounce of meat to six ounces or more. An eight-ounce bottle of soda is now a monstrous one-quart tumbler. And the original order of McDonald's fries, at 200 calories, pales next to today's 610-calorie supersize fries. McDonald's would not discuss portion sizes, but spokesman Walt Riker said in a statement: "You can find plenty of nutritious and balanced options" at McDonald's, including salads.

support — examples of supersizing

supersizing in entire industry

McDonald's doesn't deserve all the blame, though—supersizing is going on all over the fast-food industry. From 1970 to 1998, the average per-person consumption of soda in the U.S. climbed from 22.2 gallons per year to 56 gallons. That may sound impossible, but not to soft-drink executives. As one former Coca-Cola Co. exec says: "Have you ever seen how many 32-ounce Big Gulps a teenage boy can drink on a summer day?"

major point — fast food in schools.

Another concern is that fast foods increasingly are showing up in schools. At the start of the 1990s, only 2% of U.S. schools offered brand-name fast food. That grew to 13% by the middle of the decade. Products from Pizza Hut Inc., Taco Bell Corp., and others are now sold in schools. It's a win-win situation for everyone but kids, say critics: Franchisers sell more products and schools make more money because the price markup on fast foods is far higher than it is on federally subsidized school meals. The losers are the schoolchildren, who are eating food that seldom meets USDA nutritional guidelines.

support

School districts also are making money selling soft drinks to their students. Pepsi and Coke compete for what are called "pouring rights" in schools—meaning one company signs a contract giving it the exclusive rights to the district's thirsty young mouths. Vending machines and company logos are positioned around the schools, and school districts often get a higher payback if the students drink more. A study in 2000 by the CDC found that 49.9% of school districts have signed contracts with soft-drink makers.

major point — television

Television is just as crucial a factor in the rise of obesity in children, critics say. In 1987, an average of 225 commercials were shown during Saturday morning cartoon hours. By the mid-1990s,

support — TV ads

that had jumped to 997, NYU's Nestle says. Roughly two-thirds of those commercials promote "foods of dubious nutritional value," Nestle says—presweetened cereals, candy, and fast foods. "I think marketing to kids is unconscionable," she adds.

support—inactivity caused by TV

The captive power of TV is contributing to another piece of the unhealthy environment: the drop in physical activity, especially among children. In 1989, kids watched an estimated 22 hours of TV a week, Nestle says. TV viewing has declined slightly since then, but combined with video games and PCs, children aged 2 to 18 now spend an average of 38 hours per week sitting in front of a flickering screen, she says.

possible solution

Food companies are starting to address these concerns. Kenneth H. Cooper, the founder of Cooper Aerobics Center in Dallas and a prime mover behind the exercise boom of the 1970s and 1980s, has signed on with PepsiCo to evaluate the nutritional content of Pepsi products. "We want to modify some of the foods and make them good foods," he says.

possible solution

And Coca-Cola is undertaking a children's exercise program. This fall, it will launch "Step with It!"—which challenges kids to take at least 10,000 steps a day. Coke hopes to reach some 50,000 students and 5,000 teachers in 2002.

possible solution

Solving the obesity epidemic is, on one level, quite easy. Kelly D. Brownell, director of the Yale Center for Eating & Weight Disorders, offers this prescription: "Do four simple things: Eat less junk. Eat more fruits and vegetables. Control your portion sizes. And exercise." To make that happen, however, the environment in which Americans live and eat must be changed, he says: "First of all, you get the unhealthy things out of schools."

effects of possible solutions

Changing the environment could sharply cut America's health costs. And if it's done by shifting to healthier foods, it doesn't have to cripple the industry. That's a lesson McDonald's, Coke, Pepsi, and others may be starting to learn.

Reyes 1

Miguel Reyes

English 1101

Dr. Gilbert

8 March 2004

Article Summary: "Why We're So Fat"

In their article, "Why We're So Fat," Paul Raeburn, Julie Forster, Dean Foust, and Diane Brady point to a new theory of why people become overweight. In the past, overweight was considered strictly a personal responsibility. The authors do not deny that people are ultimately responsible for what they eat. However, they also suggest that an environment in which fast food is plentiful, cheap, and widely advertised can also contribute to overweight.

Obesity has become the number one health problem in the United States, rising from about 22 percent ten years ago to 30 percent today. The problem is becoming the focus of attention nationwide. Nutritionist Marion Nestle of New York University points to the fast food industry's yearly advertising expenditure of thirty-three billion dollars as part of the problem. The U. S. Senate is looking at measures to encourage better nutrition and exercise. Lawyers, encouraged by the success of tobacco lawsuits, are eyeing the food industry as a possible target. Even food companies are starting programs and offering menu choices to promote good health.

The authors discuss several factors that may account for the recent increase in obesity. First of all, food is abundant, and food prices have fallen in almost ever year since World War II. In addition, portions have become larger and "supersizing" has become common in the fast-food industry. McDonald's supersize fries, for example, have more than three times the calories of the original 200-calorie order of fries.

Reyes 2

Fast foods are also now available in a place once closed to them: the public schools. Taco Bell, Pizza Hut, and Pepsi now market their products in schools, resulting in menus that fall short of USDA guidelines for good nutrition.

According to the authors, television contributes to the obesity epidemic in two ways. First of all, the marketing of sugary cereals, candy, and fast foods during Saturday morning cartoons makes children want to eat those foods. In addition, spending an average of 38 hours per week sitting inactively in front of a television or computer can contribute to childhood obesity.

What are the solutions to widespread obesity in the Unites States? The article quotes Kelly D. Brownell of the Yale Center for Eating and Weight Disorders, who suggests increasing exercise and eating more healthy foods and fewer unhealthy ones. Brownell warns, however, that such changes will not work unless the environment is changed also, for example, by providing healthier menus in schools.

Food companies are becoming part of the solution, with Pepsi planning to overhaul the nutritional content of some of its products. Coca-Cola is launching a children's exercise program called "Step with It!" Such measures could cut health costs in the U.S. while allowing the food industry to remain profitable.

I found "Why We're So Fat" informative and helpful. I now understand how the pressures of advertising, the abundance of unhealthy food, and supersize portions contribute to obesity. The article also provided encouragement that the problem is being noticed and that solutions are at hand.

Reyes 3

Centered

Works Cited

First line is flush with left margin; any subsequent lines are indented one-half inch.

Raeburn, Paul, Julie Forster, Dean Foust, and Diane Brady. "Why We're

So Fat." Business Week 21 October 2002: 112–15

SUMMARY REPORT ASSIGNMENTS

Summary Report Assignment 1: Summarizing an Article about Your Career or Major

Write a summary of an article that deals with some aspect of your chosen career or major. The article may be one about job opportunities in your field, or it may focus on a particular issue central to your field. Follow the step-by-step process outlined in this chapter to find your article, evaluate it, read it to find the main ideas, and write your summary.

Summary Report Assignment 2: Summarizing an Article That Solves a Problem

Write a summary of an article that helps you solve a problem in your life. Whether you are trying to find ways to save more money, impress an interviewer, organize your time, choose an automobile, or eat more nutritiously, dozens of articles await you in the library or on the Internet. Because articles of this type vary widely in length, be sure to choose an article substantial enough to lend itself to summarizing. Follow the step-by-step process outlined in this chapter to find your article, evaluate it, read it to find the main ideas, and write your summary.

Summary Report Assignment 3: Summarizing an Article That Explores a Social Issue

Write a summary of an article that explores a current social problem. You will find articles on homelessness, drug abuse, domestic violence, school violence, and many more issues of current concern in the library or on the Internet. Articles may vary in length, so be sure to choose an article substantial enough to lend itself to summarizing. Follow the step-by-step process outlined in this chapter to find your article, evaluate it, read it to find the main ideas, and write your summary.

8

Communication Beyond the Classroom: Oral Presentations and E-Mail

> Be sincere; be brief; be seated.
> —Franklin Delano Roosevelt's
> advice on public speaking

Franklin D. Roosevelt's advice on public speaking applies equally well to both subjects of this chapter. Whether you are giving a presentation or sending an e-mail, the advice is worth considering. "Be sincere" suggests having a purpose and a sincere desire to communicate a specific message. "Be brief" suggests getting the message across in as few words as possible—condensing it to its essence. "Be seated" suggests a no-frills approach: once the message has been delivered, you don't add any unrelated material that might waste the person's time—you are finished.

Oral presentations and e-mail are, by their very nature, different from the paragraphs and essays you have been writing. Paragraphs and essays are intended to communicate a specific idea in a permanent form. E-mail and oral communication, on the other hand, are less permanent. E-mail is designed to be tossed in the electronic trash can almost as soon as it is read. Words, unless they are recorded, last only as long as the listener's memory of them. However, the impression that your words make is a lasting one. Even a short e-mail message speaks volumes about your ability to communicate, and the ability to speak well has the power to carry you further in life and in your career than any other single ability.

Oral Presentations

In college classes, in the workplace, and in life, the time will come when you are asked to "say a few words." The occasion may be as simple as being called on to answer a question in class or to give your opinion on an issue. Or you may be asked to give a prepared speech or make a presentation. Whatever the occasion, you want to be ready.

Impromptu Speeches and Prepared Speeches

Impromptu speeches are unrehearsed speeches. An impromptu speech might be the informal remarks that you make on the first day of class when your instructor asks class members to introduce themselves. It might be the brief talk that you give in a meeting at work when you are asked about a project you are working on. In these instances, the speech is informal—you may not even be asked to stand up, and you may not say more than a few sentences. Nevertheless, those few words constitute an impromptu speech. It is *impromptu* because it was not prepared in advance. It is a speech because you are in a group, you have the floor, and all eyes are on you.

Prepared speeches are planned speeches. Delivering a prepared report at a club meeting, speaking on an assigned topic in class, or giving a Power-Point presentation to a group of fellow employees are examples of prepared speeches. Prepared speeches are planned in advance and rehearsed thoroughly, and visual aids may be used to supplement the speech.

Impromptu Speeches

Impromptu speeches are unprepared speeches. However, with practice, you can make even an unprepared speech sparkle. Read the "Seven Habits of Effective Impromptu Speakers" that follow for hints on delivering an effective impromptu speech. Remember as you read that habits are developed gradually and acquired over time. Don't expect to acquire them instantly. Instead, look for opportunities to practice and to develop these habits.

Seven Habits of Effective Impromptu Speakers

1. **Pausing to prepare.** A brief pause before beginning gives an effective speaker a moment to gather her thoughts and to begin with poise. In addition, a pause gives the audience time to shift its attention from the last person who spoke and focus on the speaker. An effective impromptu speaker also learns to steal a few moments of preparation time whenever she can. If others are speaking and she expects to be called on, she gathers her thoughts as others speak. However, an effective speaker is also an effective listener, so she never completely tunes out those who are speaking. Instead, she listens to pick up ideas for her own remarks.

2. **Speaking to be heard.** Speaking loudly enough to be heard and enunciating words clearly is an essential speaking skill. Mumbling and muttering can make a speaker seem less than confident and can frustrate audiences who have trouble understanding the speaker's message. Clear, easily audible speech gives a speaker the appearance of confidence and ensures that the audience hears the message.

3. **Using standard English.** An effective speaker knows that speaking to a general audience requires language that everyone can accept and understand. Therefore, realizing that standard English is acceptable for all business and academic uses, he avoids slang and uses careful grammar.

4. **Eliminating filler words and sounds.** Words such as "well" and "you know" and sounds such as "um" and "ah" creep into almost everyone's speech occasionally. An effective speaker tries to become aware of these "fillers" and to reduce these sounds in his own speech.

5. **Making eye contact.** An effective speaker knows that eye contact is the way to make a real connection with her audience. When a speaker pauses briefly to glance into the eyes of an audience member, she makes her message personal.

6. **Taming the butterflies.** For most people, there is no way to avoid that feeling of "butterflies in the stomach," that nervousness that comes along with public speaking. Effective speakers learn to channel nervous energy into an energetic presentation. They also learn to focus on the message and the audience instead of on their own performance.

7. **Taking an interest.** Effective speakers have something to say partly because they know what is going on in the world and in their communities. They read newspapers and magazines, so they know something about national and international events, about what their city council is voting on, or about why so many citizens oppose the new road

project. Because they have interests that go beyond school or the job, they can talk about fly fishing or yoga or about how to find the best car stereo equipment at the best price.

Assignments for Timed Impromptu Speaking

Speech time for all assignments: 30 seconds to one minute.

The instructor or a designated student will time the speaker. At thirty seconds, the timer will hold one finger up to show that the speaker has spoken for the required amount of time. At one minute, the timer will hold two fingers up to let the speaker know that time is up. At one minute fifteen seconds, the timer holds three fingers up, showing that the speaker has gone overtime and must conclude.

Assignment 1   Speaker's Choice

A speaker is called on at random to speak on his or her choice of the following topics.

a. If your life were a color, what color would it be, and why?
b. If you could eat only one food for the rest of your life, what would it be, and why?
c. Are you an introvert or an extravert? How do you know?
d. What do you like or dislike most about traveling by car?
e. If you were given a choice of a weekend at a hot, sunny beach or on a cold, snowy mountain, which would you choose, and why?

Assignment 2   Fortune Cookie

Place fortune cookies or quotations in a bowl. The person speaking will choose one at random and tell how the fortune or quotation applies to his or her life.

Assignment 3   Paired Partners

Each speaker is assigned a partner. Each partner writes a question for the other partner. Just before the speech, the speaker is given the question to answer in an impromptu speech. Questions should not be too personal and should be relatively easy to answer.

Prepared Speeches

While impromptu speeches reflect a speaker's ability to think on his or her feet, prepared speeches offer the opportunity to carefully construct a speech and to rehearse it to ensure a smooth delivery. A prepared speech will eventually be spoken, but it is first written. Therefore, in preparing your speech, you can rely on the steps in the writing process, modified to suit an oral presentation rather than a written one.

Using the Writing Process to Prepare a Speech

Prewrite

First, prewrite to generate ideas for your speech, just as you would if you were writing a paragraph or an essay.

Plan

Next, plan your speech. Like an essay, it will have an introduction, a body, and a conclusion. One old formula for speaking goes like this:

1. Tell them what you are going to tell them.
2. Tell them.
3. Tell them what you told them.

Though the formula is usually presented humorously, it's a workable formula for a speech. The first step, "Tell them what you are going to tell them," is a preview of the speech. This preview takes the form of a statement of the main idea and maybe even a brief outline of the points.

The second step, "Tell them," is the body of the speech. Here, the important information is presented in detail.

The third step, "Tell them what you told them," is a summary conclusion that reviews the major points, restates the main idea, and ends on a strong, final-sounding note.

When you use this formula, your speech will have an introduction that presents your idea, a body that goes into detail about your idea, and a conclusion that restates or summarizes your idea. Although you should always have a strong opening and a strong closing, don't be afraid to vary from the preview-style opening or the summary conclusion if your topic or the purpose of your speech leads you in another direction.

Draft

Draft your speech from beginning to end, as if you were writing a paper. Although it is considered bad form to read a speech to an audience, you will need a complete draft of the speech for your practice sessions.

Revise

The revision stage of speechwriting involves reading your speech multiple times to see how it sounds. First, read through the speech to make sure that you feel comfortable saying the words. Speech patterns are often different from writing patterns. Sentences are shorter and simpler. Revise to make sure that the speech conforms to your own speech patterns. If it does not, you will feel uncomfortable, and your delivery will reflect your discomfort. Also, time your speech to make sure it fits within time limitations, if any.

Proofread

Proofreading also takes a slightly different form when you are preparing a speech. As with a written document, weed out grammatical errors, wordy expressions, slang, and clichés.

Other proofreading items become less important. Spelling does not matter in a prepared speech. However, if your speech contains difficult or technical vocabulary or words that are commonly mispronounced, check the pronunciation of those words in a dictionary (some online dictionaries will even pronounce the word for you), and practice pronouncing the words until you can say them smoothly and with no hesitation.

Punctuation marks will not matter; no one will ever see them. However, your audience will *hear* the pauses in your speech. Effective speakers know how to make good use of pauses. Is there a point you would like to emphasize? Pause before you make that point. The momentary silence will catch the attention of your listeners, allowing you to make your important point effectively.

Practicing and Polishing Your Speech

After you construct your speech using the steps in the writing process, take the time to practice and polish your speech. During this phase of preparation, you will incorporate gestures, vocal variety, and eye contact into your speech.

✷ Twenty Everyday Words That Are Often Mispronounced

accept	*say* ak SEPT	*not* uh SEPT
asked	*say* ASKT	*not* AST or AXT
asterisk	*say* ASS ter isk	*not* ASS ter ick
athlete	*say* ATH-leet	*not* ATH-uh-leet
business	*say* BIZ ness	*not* BID ness or BIN ess
doctoral	*say* DOC tor al	*not* doc TOR ee al
drowned	*say* DROWND	*not* DROWN ded
environment	*say* en VIRE uhn ment	*not* en VIRE o ment
escape	*say* es CAPE	*not* eck SCAPE
especially	*say* es PESH uh ly	*not* eck SPESH uh ly
height	*say* HITE	*not* HITE th
interesting	*say* INT tres ting	*not* INNA resting
library	*say* LIE brerry	*not* LIE berry
mirror	*say* MEER ur	*not* MEER
nuclear	*say* NEW clee ur	*not* NEW cu lar
often	*say* OFF un	*not* OFF ten
picture	*say* PIK cher	*not* PITCH er
probably	*say* PROB uh bly	*not* PROLLY *or* PROBLY
sherbet	*say* SHER bit	*not* SHER bert
supposedly	*say* suh POSE ed ly	*not* suh POSE a bly

Practice

An old joke involves a tourist in New York City looking for Carnegie Hall, where only top musicians and performers appear. He stops a native New Yorker and says, "How do you get to Carnegie Hall?" The New Yorker, hurrying on his way, throws a one-word answer over his shoulder: "Practice!"

"Practice" may not be the answer that the tourist was seeking, but it is the answer for anyone who wants to deliver an effective prepared speech. Practice is important to ensure a smooth delivery with very little reliance on notes. The first thing to do is practice your speech by reading it out loud. If your speech has a particular time limit, be sure to time the speech for the first few practices to make sure you are within the limits.

Once you have rehearsed your speech a few times by reading it, make a brief outline of your speech on 8½ × 11 paper or on large index cards. These are the notes you will take with you to the lectern when you give your speech.

If you use 8½ × 11 paper, type your outline in large type, or print it in letters large enough to see without straining. The advantage of using a piece of paper is that you will need only one sheet. The disadvantage is that paper is light and can easily be blown from the lectern by a gust of air or an accidental movement. Index cards, on the other hand, are heavy enough to remain in place on a lectern. However, you may need more than one card. Use large index cards—3 × 5 cards are too small to read and handle easily.

Practice your speech, using the outline as a guide. If you forget some parts, insert key words as reminders, and practice again until you are getting all the key points in.

You may wonder why you are not advised to memorize the speech and take the entire text to the lectern with you, referring to it as needed. Although some speakers use this method, it is not the best method. Memory can be tricky. When you memorize, each word in your speech becomes a link in a chain. If one link—a single word—is lost, then everything that comes after it can also be lost. Then you spend long, agonizing moments looking through the text of your speech to find your place. However, if you remember ideas rather than specific words, then you can vary the wording of your speech without losing the entire idea. A speech that is not memorized will also seem fresher and more spontaneous that a memorized speech.

Whatever you do, don't read your speech to the audience. A speaker who reads a speech usually loses contact with the audience. His eyes are on the speech, not on audience members, so the connection created by eye contact is lost. In addition, a speaker who reads a speech tends to make fewer gestures, so part of the visual element that helps establish a connection with the audience is also lost.

Gestures

As you practice your speech, you will also want to practice the body language and gestures you will use.

When you stand up to speak, your message reaches the members of the audience through their eyes as well as through their ears. Therefore, your posture and gestures should reflect the confidence that the audience will hear in your voice as you deliver your well-rehearsed speech.

Avoid gestures that close off or protect the body. Hunching the shoulders, crossing the arms, clutching the hands together, or putting the hands in pockets can make a speaker seem defensive and nervous. Pointing at or turning your back on an audience may be interpreted as hostile or rude.

Open gestures, on the other hand, welcome and embrace an audience. Incorporating gestures that take the hands and arms slightly away from the body makes your audience feel included. When you are not gesturing, keeping your hands loosely at your sides makes you appear open and relaxed. Maintaining an erect posture makes you appear more confident and allows your breath and your voice to flow freely.

Vocal Variety

As you practice, try varying the tone and pitch of your voice. Decide where you will pause and where you will make your voice louder or softer to make a point. Vocal variety and use of effective pauses help to make your speech come alive.

Visual Aids

The first rule of using a visual aid is to use it only if it is relevant and necessary to the speech. If it is, decide exactly how you will incorporate it into the speech. The minute you show a visual aid, you should refer to it or explain it; otherwise, the audience will be curious and will be distracted from the content of your speech. As you practice your speech, practice using your visual aid.

With visual aids, be prepared for disaster and have a backup plan. The card trick you performed perfectly at home may turn into a game of "fifty-two pickup" when you try it in front of an audience. An extra deck in your pocket can save the day. Electrical or battery-operated equipment may decide not to function at the crucial moment, so check batteries and equipment beforehand.

Conquering Nervousness

Nervousness when speaking in public is normal—even professional speakers and actors often feel nervous before going onstage.

Nervousness affects both the mind and the body. Mental effects may include worry about your performance or self-criticism as you speak. Physically, you may be aware of tense muscles or sweaty palms. Therefore, any plan to defeat nervousness must address both the mental and the physical symptoms. The best defense against the mental symptom of performance anxiety is strong preparation and practice. The more you rehearse, the less anxious you should feel. In addition, self-criticism is often prompted by an inward focus. The more conscious you are of your performance, the more nervous and self-critical you may feel. The cure is to focus outward on your audience and on the message itself.

Releasing physical tension before your speech can also help you to feel more relaxed. Before the speech, talk and laugh with members of the class or audience, or take a brisk walk down the hall. If you are the next speaker and want to quickly release tension as you wait in your seat, take slow breaths that push your stomach (not your chest) in and out, or press the heels of your hands together for a few seconds with steady, intense pressure, then release.

Assignments for Prepared Speeches

Speech time: Four to five minutes

The instructor or a designated student will time. At four minutes, the timer will hold one finger up to show that the speaker has spoken for the required amount of time. At five minutes, the timer will hold two fingers up to let the speaker know that time is up. At five minutes thirty seconds, the timer holds three fingers up, showing that the speaker has gone overtime and must conclude.

Assignment 1   Introducing Yourself

This assignment allows you to speak about a topic you know very well—yourself. Since you have only five minutes, you will not have time to cover your entire life, and a bare-bones sketch of your life—where you were born, where you went to school, where you have worked—may not have enough detail to interest the audience. Instead, narrow your focus to two or three aspects of your life that interest you and that tell your audience who you are. You are a student, but what else? Are you are a goal-oriented person, a parent, a fry cook, a dreamer, a reader, a music lover? Think of some terms that apply to you—no more than three—and provide details, examples, or brief stories that help your audience understand you as a tennis player, a computer enthusiast, a student, or whatever terms you choose.

Assignment 2   Show Them How

Your task in this speech is to describe a process that you know well. Examples include cooking a meal, hitting a golf ball, doing a magic trick, applying makeup, changing the oil in a car, or studying for a test.

A good way to organize a speech about a process is to describe the items that will be needed, discuss the steps in the process, and end with encouraging words that remind listeners of the value of the process and that encourage them to try it—or if the process is a common one, to try it your way.

In this speech, you may decide to use visual aids. However, before you bring any visual aids, clear them with your instructor, since some items (alcohol, live animals, weapons) may not be permitted on campus or in the classroom. If your visual aids are permitted, you may use them either to demonstrate a part of the process (a deck of cards to show a magic trick) or to demonstrate the finished product (a loaf of bread to show the result of the process of baking bread). Practice using them when you rehearse your speech so that you will use them smoothly and effectively.

Assignment 3   Consumer Research

Research and report on a consumer product or issue. You may be dreaming of a new car and decide to do research in *Consumer Reports* to find the best car in your price range. You may be in the market for a new pair of athletic shoes and decide to search the Internet to see what features you should look for in an athletic shoe. You may wonder which restaurant has the best buffet, the best burritos, or the best fries, and decide to conduct on-site research by visiting local restaurants. The method of research is up to you, but your research and your speech should center on a question about something that can be purchased.

Writing E-Mail Messages

E-mail seems so informal that some people say that no rules are needed. Yet anyone who uses e-mail regularly can think of a few dos and don'ts such as "Never write in all capital letters" or "Always include a subject line." More important than the need for rules is the fact that e-mail, like any other form of writing, represents you. It is your electronic emissary to a reader who forms an impression of your personality and your communication skills from that e-mail. E-mail is an informal mode of communication, but an effective e-mail message, like any other effective piece of writing, requires planning, skill, and attention to any rules that apply, including rules of grammar, spelling, and punctuation.

Appropriate Use of E-Mail

In academic and business settings, e-mail has a specific purpose. Class listservs, bulletin boards, and e-mail systems are used to conduct class business. In the business world, e-mail has replaced the memorandum as the favored method of in-house communication. Yet in every class and in every business, there is at least one person who periodically e-mails jokes, cookie recipes, or offers of free kittens to the entire group. No matter how funny the joke, how delicious the cookies, or how cute the kittens, such mass mailings are not appropriate in academic and business settings. They waste time and distract people from the legitimate communications that are being sent. In addition, they may violate school or company policy.

---

* Emoticons

Emoticons are *icons* or symbols that express *emotion* in an e-mail. Viewed sideways, they look like faces. They are made with keyboard symbols and used for fun (but are best left out of business e-mail).

Smiling	:)	Winking	;)
Sad	: (	Crying	:'(
Undecided, skeptical	:\	Laughing	:D
Surprised	:O	Frowning	>:(

Parts of an E-Mail Message

E-mail messages contain a "from" address, a "to" address, a subject line, a salutation, a body, a closing, and sometimes a signature line. They may also have attachments that contain separate documents. Each part plays an important role in getting your message across.

The "From" Address

The "from" address, or return address, is the sender's e-mail address. It looks something like this: jandrews@readymail.com. This address automatically appears on any e-mail you send. If you have a school or business e-mail account, you may be required to use your name or first initial and the first few letters of your last name. With personal e-mail accounts, the name you use may be your own name or a nickname that you make up. The choice is yours, but you should choose carefully. How seriously will an instructor or a potential employer take an e-mail from "sweetcheeks" or "bungeeboy"? Consider whom you will be contacting with your e-mail account, and choose your e-mail name accordingly.

The "To" Address

The "to" address is the recipient's address, the e-mail address of the person to whom you are writing. The complete "to" address will look something like this: jjones@collegemail.edu or Keisha_Rutherford@ companymail.com. Be sure to type the address accurately, or the e-mail will be returned to you as undeliverable.

The Subject Line

The subject line indicates the topic of your e-mail. Like the title of a composition, it should sum up the main idea of your message. "Today's Absence," "Essay 2," and "Quarterly Sales Report" are subject lines that concisely reflect the content of the e-mail.

A subject line should never leave your reader guessing. Never intentionally send an e-mail with a blank subject line (although accidental blank subject lines happen to almost everyone). Vague subject lines such as "Guess what?" "Did you know . . ." "Ha Ha," or "Info 4 U" are fine among friends, but not in academic or professional situations.

The Salutation

In an e-mail, the usual salutation is simply the person's name followed by a comma. "Dear" followed by the person's name is acceptable but is less often used. Address the person by whatever name you would use if the two of you were face to face:

Leo,

Dr. Smith,

Dear Angela,

Ms. Bell,

Don't leave out the salutation. People like to be called by their names, and adding a salutation makes your message more personal. If you are e-mailing a group of people, a salutation is still appropriate:

Classmates,

Colleagues,

Friends,

Fellow Committee Members,

A salutation gives your e-mail a personal touch and lets readers know immediately whether they are being addressed individually or as part of a group.

The Body

The body of your e-mail contains your message. E-mail messages should be cordial, yet get to the point quickly. However, since a bare-bones message can seem abrupt, a final sentence that ends the letter on a cordial note is a welcome touch. If you cannot think of a cordial closing sentence, try a simple "thank you."

Fellow Study Group Members,

This is a reminder that our study group will meet in the library tomorrow at 2:00 p.m. to discuss Chapter 12.

I look forward to seeing you tomorrow.

Antwan

The Closing

The close of your e-mail should simply be your name. Depending on your level of familiarity with the person you are writing to, use your first name alone or your first and last name. No "sincerely" or "yours truly" is needed in e-mail.

The Signature File

Some e-mail programs allow you to put in a signature file that is automatically sent with each e-mail. The signature file may contain your name, your title (if any), and contact information such as telephone, fax, or address.

Attachments

Sending an e-mail **attachment** means sending an exact copy of one of the files on your computer. The attachment is not a part of the e-mail; instead, it "hitches a ride" with the e-mail and is opened separately. Check the "help" section of your e-mail program for specific directions on sending attachments.

Any multipage message or any report that needs to be in a specific format should be placed in an attachment. For example, if you send your English instructor an essay via e-mail, send it as an attachment to preserve the formatting. Otherwise, the font, the paragraphing and indentations, and any underlining or italics you incorporated may be lost. Similarly, if you are sending a report that contains charts, tables, or numbered lists, send it as an attachment.

When you send an attachment, include a short, explanatory e-mail. No one likes to receive a blank message with only an attachment.

Dr. Salkowski,

My second essay is attached.

Thank you.

Bryan

E-Mail Etiquette

Even informal methods of communication develop their own etiquette, and e-mail is no exception. Following are some of the rules of courtesy that have evolved among e-mail users.

1. **Don't shout.** Writing in ALL CAPS is considered shouting and is probably the easiest way to offend the recipient. Even a single capitalized word should be avoided. For emphasis, use an *asterisk* before and after the word, or if your e-mail program permits, use italics or underlining.

   Examples

   ✘ PLEASE SEND YOUR NOMINATIONS TO ME BY WEDNESDAY.

   Use of all capital letters is considered shouting.

   ✘ PLEASE send your nominations to me by Wednesday.

   Even a single capitalized word should be avoided.

✔ *Please* send your nominations to me by Wednesday.

Emphasis can be conveyed politely with the use of asterisks.

✔ Please send your nominations to me by Wednesday.

A message with no words emphasized is simple and direct.

2. **Be concise but not abrupt.** Short sentences and paragraphs make an e-mail message easier to read. In fact, a one-sentence paragraph, unacceptable in most written documents, is perfectly acceptable in e-mail. However, a message that is too brief can seem abrupt to the point of rudeness.

Examples

Text of Original Message:

Would you mind lending Ashley Kauffman, the new purchasing agent, a copy of your employee manual? I have ordered one for her, but she needs to read through it as soon as possible.

Sample Answers:

✗ No answer at all.

Some people leave e-mails such as this unanswered, assuming that the writer will understand that the message has been received and the request has been fulfilled. However, e-mail etiquette requires the courtesy of a reply.

✗ OK

This answer gets the message across, but it is too abrupt.

✔ I'll deliver it to her right away.

This reply, short but courteous, is all that is needed.

3. **Answer immediately.** Users of e-mail expect fast answers. Same-day answers are desirable but not always possible. The end of the next business or school day is the longest you should normally wait to answer e-mail.

4. **Answer above the original message.** When replying to an e-mail, you want to make sure that your reply, not the original message, is visible to the recipient. If you answer underneath the original message, the recipient will see his or her own message and have to scroll down for your answer.

The following example shows a reply below the original message. Shonda, who wrote the original message, has to wade through her own message to get to Kelly's reply.

Original Message:

Kelly,

Can you tell me what we did in English class today? I had car trouble and did not get to campus until 10:00 a.m.

Also, may I borrow your notes tomorrow?

Shonda

----Reply

Shonda,

We discussed the topic sentences we wrote for homework last night. Everyone's sentences were put up on the overhead and we critiqued them. It was actually fun—sorry you missed it!

For tomorrow, bring in a rough draft of your paragraph and begin the exercises in Chapter 18.

We did not take many notes yesterday, but you are welcome to what I have.

See ya!

Kelly

The best way to avoid the problem is to reply above the original message. This method preserves the entire original message in case the person receiving your reply wants to refer to it, and it puts your reply exactly where it should be: immediately visible to the recipient of the message.

In the following message, the first thing Celia will see is Josh's reply to her.

----Reply

Celia,

Definitely. Save me a seat. I am coming straight from work and may be a few minutes late, but I will see you there.

Josh

Original Message:

Josh,

A bunch of us from class are going to sit together at the lecture on AIDS tomorrow night. Afterwards, we are going to the Green Door to have some pizza and pool our notes for the extra credit paper.

If you plan to go, would you like to meet us at the lecture and go with us afterward? It will be Matt, Arlethia, José, and a few others.

Celia

Some sources advise deleting all but the portion of the message relevant to your answer, placing that portion in brackets < >, and replying below that portion. That method is also acceptable.

In the following message, Celia sees her question first. Josh's reply immediately follows.

Portion of Original Message:

< would you like to meet us at the lecture and go with us afterward?>

----Reply

Celia,

Definitely. Save me a seat. I am coming straight from work and may be a few minutes late, but I will see you there.

Josh

5. **Don't "flame" the recipient.** Angry, insulting replies to electronic messages are called *flames*. With e-mail, it's all too easy to write an angry message and to hit the "send" button quickly. Once the "send" button is clicked, the message cannot be recalled. If you are tempted to send a flame, do yourself the favor of waiting twenty-four hours before you hit "send."

EXERCISE 1   CRITIQUING E-MAIL MESSAGES

Critique each of the following numbered e-mail messages, using the lines provided beneath each section of the e-mail to critique individual sections. Some sections may be acceptable as they are; others may need changes. An example follows.

Example E-Mail Message

FROM: sugarbear@pooh.net

The e-mail address is not appropriate for an academic or a business situation.

TO: abrainerd@mycollege.edu

Acceptable.

SUBJECT: My Absences in Math 1111

Acceptable, gives the basic information needed.

SALUTATION: Dr. Brainerd,

Acceptable. Addresses the person as the writer would address him or her face-to-face.

BODY: I have been sick for the past week. I would appreciate it if you would send my assignments.

Acceptable. Explains the situation and politely requests assignments.

CLOSING:

No closing. Since the "from" address is "sugarbear@pooh.net," the professor may not know who sent the e-mail.

E-Mail Message 1

Answers may vary slightly.

FROM: dsingleta@usacollege.edu

 Acceptable.

TO: Astronomy Club (Note: Many e-mail systems contain an address book feature that allows addresses of large groups such as clubs to be entered just one time. On subsequent messages, a key word or phrase, such as "Astronomy Club," is entered to automatically send the message to all group members. Assume here that an address book feature has been used.)

 Acceptable.

SUBJECT: (blank)

 No subject line.

SALUTATION: Fellow Astronomy Club Members,

 Acceptable.

BODY: As you know, the Leonid meteor shower is expected to be visible in our area of the country next Monday around 4:00 a.m. Dr. Isaac has agreed to meet us out here and to allow us to use the Astronomy Department's telescopes for viewing.

If it rains or is cloudy, the viewing in canceled. Otherwise, I hope to see you all at 4:00 a.m. on Monday.

 Acceptable.

CLOSING: (blank)

 No closing.

E-Mail Message 2

FROM: dfarrell@webnet.com

 Acceptable.

TO: allemployees@bigcompany.net

 Acceptable.

SUBJECT: Puppies

Subject does not relate to business.

SALUTATION: Colleagues,

Acceptable.

BODY: A stray dog has taken up residence in my yard, and a few weeks ago she surprised me with a litter of puppies. They are about ready to go to new homes now, and I'd rather place them with my friends here at BigCompany than any-where else. They are tan and white, mixed breed puppies. I am not sure if they are male or female.

If you are interested, send an e-mail or call me at extension 4205.

Thanks.

The message does not relate to company business and will be viewed as a

waste of employees' time.

CLOSING: Don

Acceptable.

SIGNATURE FILE: Donald A. Farrell
            Associate Vice President in Charge of Recycling

Acceptable.

E-Mail Message 3

FROM: 2cute4u@egotrip.net

Acceptable only for messages to friends, not for business or academic use.

TO: ksmith@university.edu

Acceptable.

SUBJECT: Yikes!

Subject line does not adequately convey the content of the message.

SALUTATION: Hello Ms. Smith,

Acceptable.

BODY: How are you today? I am not so hot. I woke up this morning and I was like, "Whoa! Is my midterm paper due TODAY???!!!!" Well, you can guess that I just don't have it, and I would like to ask you, please, please, for an extension. I have, actually, now that I think about it, not been feeling so well lately. I probably have the flu, and that always affects my memory.

Thanks in advance for your understanding.

The writer uses poor grammar and punctuation and "shouts," using all caps.

In addition, the message rambles and is unconvincing.

CLOSING: Holly

Acceptable.

E-Mail Message 4

FROM: ellen1342@snailex.com

Acceptable.

TO: samason@speedmail.com

Acceptable.

SUBJECT: MEETING ON NOVEMBER 23?

All caps denote "shouting."

SALUTATION: SARITA,

All caps denote "shouting."

BODY: IS OUR COMMUNITY IMPROVEMENT GROUP MEETING NEXT WEEK? NEXT WEDNESDAY IS THE DAY BEFORE THANKSGIVING, AND A LOT OF OUR MEMBERS MAY BE OUT OF TOWN. THANKS.

All caps denote "shouting."

CLOSING: ELLEN

All caps denote "shouting."

E-Mail Message 5

FROM: smoothmoves@allmail.com

Unless this person owns a fleet of moving vans, the name "smoothmoves" may

be inappropriate for business and academic use.

TO: gsackem@bestco.com

Acceptable.

SUBJECT: George Anderson's Resumé

Acceptable.

ATTACHMENT: Resumé.doc

SALUTATION: Dear Ms. Sackem,

Acceptable.

BODY: As you requested, I am sending my resumé attached to this e-mail.

As I told you during my interview on Tuesday, I may be younger than most of the managers you hire, but I am a serious, goal-oriented person with a firm sense of purpose.

Thank you for your consideration of my resumé, and I hope to hear from you soon.

Acceptable. Polite, well-written, and likely to impress a prospective employer.

CLOSING: Respectfully,
George Anderson

Acceptable.

SIGNATURE FILE: "The Babe Magnet"
smoothmoves@allmail.com
(555) 555-5683

Conveys an impression that contradicts the businesslike tone of the letter.

Using the forms provided at the end of this section, write an e-mail appropriate to two of the following scenarios.

E-Mail Message 1: Message to an Instructor. Instructions: Write a message to your instructor (instructorsname@yourcollege.edu), explaining a two-day absence and inquiring about assignments.

E-Mail Message 2: Sending a Transcript to a Prospective Employer. Write an e-mail message to Marquita Nesmith (mnesmith@apexlabs.com), the human resources director of Apex Laboratories, where you have applied for the position of Safety Procedures Director. You interviewed on Monday, but you have not yet been told whether the job is yours. You are attaching the unofficial college transcript that she requested. You are also letting her know that the official copy is on the way.

E-Mail Message 3: Message to a State Representative. Write an e-mail message to Rep. Giselle Fowler (gfowler@state.gov), your representative in the state legislature. A vote is scheduled on a bill that, if it becomes law, will raise the legal driving age in your state to eighteen. Give your reasons for supporting or opposing the bill, and tell Rep. Fowler how you would like her to vote on the bill.

E-Mail Message 4: Message to a Campus Organization. In your capacity as treasurer, write an e-mail message to the members of the Campus Volunteers, reminding all members that club dues of $10.00 are payable by the next meeting. You have entered the twenty club members' e-mail addresses into the address book feature of your e-mail, so all you need to put on the address line is "Volunteers."

E-Mail Message 5: Request for Extension. Write an e-mail message to your instructor (instructorsname@yourcollege.edu), requesting an extension on the deadline for a paper due on Friday. Give your reasons for needing an extension.

E-Mail Assignment Form

FROM: _____

TO: _____

SUBJECT: _____

ATTACHMENT: _____

SALUTATION: _____

BODY: _____

_____

_____

_____

_____

_____

CLOSING: _____

SIGNATURE FILE: _____

E-Mail Assignment Form

FROM: _____

TO: _____

SUBJECT: _____

ATTACHMENT: _____

SALUTATION: _____

BODY: _____

_____

_____

_____

_____

_____

CLOSING: _____

SIGNATURE FILE: _____

Part 2
Essentials of Grammar

In Part 2 of your Instructor's Edition, sample answers are provided for all Practice and Review Exercises. On many questions, more than one answer is possible, so answers may vary.

9

Parts of Speech

Nouns
Pronouns
Verbs
Adverbs
Adjectives
Prepositions
Conjunctions
Interjections

Words in the English language are divided according to function into categories called **parts of speech.** The way a word is used determines its part of speech. Some words can take on more than one role:

✔ Benita is always in need of **cash.** (**Cash** is used as a noun. It represents a thing.)

✔ I **cash** my paycheck at the bank down the street. (**Cash** is used as a verb. It describes an action.)

✔ A **cash** reward was offered for information leading to the arrest of the criminal. (**Cash** is used as an adjective. It gives information about the kind of reward.)

Parts of speech are not necessarily single words. Phrases and clauses can also function as parts of speech.

✔ Darryl **will be leaving** tomorrow. (The phrase **will be leaving** acts as a verb and describes an action.)

✔ **Dressed in a red hat and mittens,** Lilly was easy to spot. (The phrase **dressed in a red hat and mittens** acts as an adjective describing Lilly.)

This chapter provides a brief overview of the different parts of speech and their functions. Don't be discouraged by the wide scope of this chapter. It is intended only as a starting point, a reference to help you as you go through other chapters. For example, if you have trouble with subject-verb agreement, it may help you to identify not only verbs and nouns but also prepositions and prepositional phrases. This chapter will help you in identifying parts of speech and understanding their function within a sentence.

Nouns

A **noun** names a person, place, thing, or idea. **Catherine, Atlanta, soup,** and **justice** are nouns. Nouns that give the specific, proper name of a person, place, or thing are called **proper nouns** and are always capitalized. **Toyota, Jemal,** and **Oregon** are examples of proper nouns. Nouns that give the general, common name of a person, place, or thing are called **common nouns.** These nouns are capitalized only if they begin a sentence. **Car, lawyer,** and **city** are examples of common nouns.

PRACTICE 1   IDENTIFYING NOUNS

Underline the two nouns in each sentence.

1. The <u>hitchhiker</u> carried a worn leather <u>backpack</u>.
2. The <u>cheese</u> was covered with dark green <u>mold</u>.
3. <u>Yashika</u> quickly pulled out of the <u>driveway</u>.
4. The <u>lawyer</u> said that <u>justice</u> had not been done.
5. The <u>Internet</u> is often called the information <u>highway</u>.

PRACTICE 2   IDENTIFYING COMMON AND PROPER NOUNS

Underline the nouns in each sentence. Label common nouns C and proper nouns P.

1. <u>Sam</u> drank a <u>Pepsi</u> while he waited.
       P   P

2. I was not sure whether to take <u>aspirin</u> or <u>Tylenol</u>.
                                        C   P

      C   C

3. <u>Patience</u> is said to be a <u>virtue</u>.

        C   C

4. The <u>turtle</u> retreated into its <u>shell</u>.

        P   C

5. On <u>Tuesday</u>, I applied for a new <u>job</u>.

Pronouns

Pronouns are words that stand for or replace nouns. There are many different kinds of pronouns, but they all perform the same basic function. **She, everyone, both, it,** and **who** are just a small sample of the many pronouns you use every day.

The noun that the pronoun stands for is called the **antecedent** of the pronoun.

> Raj works the night shift at a convenience store. **He** goes to school during the day. (**He** is a pronoun that stands for Raj, its antecedent.)

> Lisa passed **her** nursing boards with flying colors. (**Her** is a pronoun that stands for Lisa, its antecedent.)

Even if a pronoun has no visible antecedent, it is still used in place of a noun or nouns.

> **Everyone** in the class passed the midterm exam. (**Everyone** is a pronoun, used instead of listing the name of every person in the class.)

> **Who** ate the last Oreo cookie? (**Who** is a pronoun, used to designate the unknown eater of the last Oreo.)

PRACTICE 3   **IDENTIFYING PRONOUNS AND THEIR ANTECEDENTS**

Each of the following sentences contains a pronoun and its antecedent. Underline the pronoun once, and underline its antecedent twice.

1. The <u>car</u> ran quietly for many miles until <u>it</u> began to backfire.
2. <u>Joe</u> wiped jelly from the corner of <u>his</u> mouth.
3. <u>Sara</u> found a calico cat in the parking lot of the video rental store. <u>She</u> decided to call the cat Rewind.
4. The <u>house painter</u> got into trouble last week. <u>He</u> painted the wrong house.
5. <u>Natalie</u> decided not place an ad in <u>her</u> local newspaper.

Types of Pronouns

There are several different types of pronouns, including **personal pronouns, relative pronouns,** and **indefinite pronouns.**

Personal Pronouns

Personal pronouns can refer to people or things and can be **first-person, second-person,** or **third-person.**
First-person pronouns refer to a person or persons speaking:

I, me, my, mine, we, us, our, ours

Second-person pronouns refer to a person spoken to:

you, your, yours

Third person pronouns refer to a person, place, thing or idea spoken about:

he, him, his, she, her, hers, it, its, they, them, their, theirs

PRACTICE 4   IDENTIFYING PERSONAL PRONOUNS

Underline the personal pronoun in each of the following sentences.

1. I do not understand how the stock market works.
2. Have you filled the car with gas?
3. After the accident, Burton said that he felt happy to be alive.
4. Natalie says that she can't resist glazed doughnuts.
5. The machine works simply, yet it costs a fortune to operate.

Relative Pronouns

Relative pronouns are used to begin a type of subordinate clause called a **relative clause.** In this function, they often connect, or *relate,* information to their antecedents within a sentence. The relative pronouns are **who, whom, whose, which,** and **that.**

relative clause
✔ The questions that Julio missed were the easiest ones on the exam.

The relative clause *that Julio missed* provides information about the noun *questions*. Without the clause, the sentence reads, "The questions were the easiest ones on the exam." The clause tells *which questions* were the easiest ones on the exam.

relative clause
✔ The accident, which injured two workers, could have been prevented with proper safety procedures. (For an explanation of the use of commas with relative clauses, see Chapter 20.)

The relative clause *which injured two workers* provides information about the noun *accident*.

relative clause
✔ The troop member who sells the most cookies receives an award.

The relative clause *who sells the most cookies* provides information about the noun *member*.

PRACTICE 5   IDENTIFYING RELATIVE CLAUSES AND THE WORDS THEY MODIFY

Underline the relative clause in each of the following sentences. Circle the relative pronoun and draw an arrow to its antecedent.

1. The headache that had plagued Monica for two days was finally gone.
2. The barber, who never had time for a haircut, looked unkempt.
3. The car, which ran a red light, was painted cherry red.
4. The worker who had fixed the broken assembly line received praise from the supervisor.
5. The newspaper that Miriam was searching for lay in the thick, wet grass behind a juniper bush.

Indefinite Pronouns

Indefinite pronouns refer to an unspecified person or group of people. Some indefinite pronouns are always singular, some are always plural, and others are singular or plural, depending on the context.

The Indefinite Pronouns

Singular Indefinite Pronouns

each	everybody	anyone	anything
either	somebody	everyone	everything
neither	nobody	someone	something
anybody	one	no one	nothing

Plural Indefinite Pronouns

both	few	many	several

Indefinite Pronouns That May Be Singular or Plural

any	all	more	most
none	some		

✔ Something has been bothering Erin lately.

✔ Few of the water samples were uncontaminated.

✔ Some of the pizzas have anchovies on them.

✔ All of the gasoline has evaporated from the can.

PRACTICE 6   IDENTIFYING INDEFINITE PRONOUNS

Underline the indefinite pronouns in the following sentences.

1. Something bothered Hal, but he wasn't able to identify it.
2. Most of us will avoid the opportunity to speak in public.
3. All of the sandwiches had the same defect—no mustard.
4. Everybody needs fresh water, food, and air; the rest is luxury.
5. Anyone who has read a movie critic's review will agree that it's better to judge the film personally.

Verbs

A **verb** shows the action or state of being of the noun or pronoun that serves as the subject of a sentence.

✔ The ball **bounced** into the underbrush.

The verb *bounced* shows the action of the subject *ball*.

✔ Many resources for research **are** available on the Internet.

The verb *are* shows the existence, or being, of the subject *resources*.
 Verbs may be expressed as a single word, like *bounced* or *are*. They may also be expressed as phrases.

✔ Girl Scouts **have been selling** cookies in front of the grocery store all day.

✔ The bus **will be leaving** at 10:15.

PRACTICE 7   IDENTIFYING VERBS

Underline the verb in each of the following sentences.

1. Jake <u>rolled</u> the greasy tire across the clean garage floor.
2. Often, polar bears <u>will rub</u> uneaten food across their faces.
3. New computer components seldom <u>work</u> properly without the addition of drivers.
4. Of all the arts, music <u>touches</u> the heart most easily.
5. The kitten <u>had been climbing</u> the pine tree in the yard.

The Principal Parts of Verbs

Each verb has four **principal parts:** present, past, past participle, and present participle. The following chart shows principal parts of selected regular and irregular verbs. See Chapter 12 for more information on the principal parts of irregular verbs.

Principal Parts of Selected Regular Verbs

Present	Past	Past Participle	Present Participle
ask	asked	(have) asked	(are) asking
carry	carried	(have) carried	(are) carrying
depend	depended	(have) depended	(are) depending

Present	Past	Past Participle	Present Participle
hunt	hunted	(have) hunted	(are) hunting
pretend	pretended	(have) pretended	(are) pretending
walk	walked	(have) walked	(are) walking

Principal Parts of Selected Irregular Verbs

Present	Past	Past Participle	Present Participle
am, are, is (to be)	was, were	(have) been	(are) being
become	became	(have) become	(are) becoming
begin	began	(have) begun	(are) beginning
catch	caught	(have) caught	(are) catching
choose	chose	(have) chosen	(are) choosing
come	came	(have) come	(are) coming
cut	cut	(have) cut	(are) cutting
feel	felt	(have) felt	(are) feeling
get	got	(have) gotten	(are) getting
give	gave	(have) given	(are) giving
go	went	(have) gone	(are) going
grow	grew	(have) grown	(are) growing
know	knew	(have) known	(are) knowing
lay	laid	(have) laid	(are) laying
lie	lay	(have) lain	(are) lying
put	put	(have) put	(are) putting
ride	rode	(have) ridden	(are) riding
see	saw	(have) seen	(are) seeing
take	took	(have) taken	(are) taking
throw	threw	(have) thrown	(are) throwing
write	wrote	(have) written	(are) writing

Verb Tenses

Verb tenses give the English language its sense of time, its sense of *when* events occur. The following timeline shows six verb tenses, and the chart that follows the timeline briefly explains how each tense is used. See Chapter 13 for a more thorough explanation of verb tenses.

Verb Tense Timeline

past	present	future
I walked	I walk	I will walk

past ◊← - - - * - - - - - - - * - - - - - - * - - - - - - * - - - - - - - - - - * - - - * - - - - - →◊ future

I had walked	I have walked	I will have walked
past perfect	present perfect	future perfect

*	*	*
I was walking	I am walking	I will be walking
past progressive	present progressive	future progresive

Verb Tense Chart

◊◊◊	Furthest in the past; happened before another past action.	past perfect had + -ed verb (past participle)	I *had walked* up the stairs, and I was out of breath.
◊◊	In the past; happened before now.	past -ed verb form (past)	I *walked* all the way around the nature trail.
◊◊	In the past; happened before now.	past progressive was, were + -ing verb	I *was walking* around the trail when I saw her.
◊•	In progress during a past time.	present perfect have or has + -ed (past participle) verb form	I *have walked* every day for the last month. He *has walked* a mile already.
•	Happens regularly or often, or is happening now.	present base verb form or base verb + -s	I *walk* at least five miles a week. She *walks* quickly.
•	Happening now.	present progressive am, are, is + -ing verb	I *am walking* as fast as I can.
◊	Happens in the future but before another future event.	future perfect will have + -ed (past participle) verb form	By the time you join me on the track, I *will have walked* at least two miles.
◊◊	Happens at some time in the future.	future will + base verb	I *will walk* with you tomorrow if we both have time.
◊◊	In progress at a future time.	future progressive will be + -ing verb	I *will be walking* with you tomorrow at noon.

Adverbs

An **adverb** modifies a verb, an adjective, or another adverb and tells *when, where,* or *how (in what manner or to what degree)*. Although this section of the book examines only single-word adverbs, an adverb can be a word, a phrase, or a clause.

✔ We can rest *later.* (Modifies the verb *rest* and tells *when*)

✔ Anna felt *extremely* confident about her interview. (Modifies the adjective *confident* and tells *to what degree*)

✔ The motorcycle approached *rapidly.* (Modifies the verb *approached* and tells *how–in what manner*)

✔ Weeds have *almost* completely taken over the yard. (Modifies the adverb *completely* and tells *to what degree*)

PRACTICE 8   IDENTIFYING ADVERBS AND THE WORDS THEY MODIFY

Draw an arrow from each italicized adverb to the verb, adverb, or adjective it modifies.

1. The phone rang *abruptly* and made Brian jump.
2. Christopher chewed the orange noodles *cautiously.*
3. The faulty transistor worked *intermittently.*
4. In the days before modern anesthetics, dental treatments were often *extremely* painful.
5. *Very* slowly, the chicken pecked its way across the road.

Adjectives

An **adjective** modifies a noun or pronoun. It tells what kind, how many, or which one. Possessive nouns and pronouns (Dr. Smith's, her, its) and the articles *a, an,* and *the* also function as adjectives.

✔ The **blue** car belongs to Rico. (Tells *which one.*)

✔ **Rico's** car is in the shop for repairs. (Tells *which one.*)

✔ **Several** students spent the weekend doing research. (Tells *how many.*)

✔ **Spinach** pizza is surprisingly good. (Tells *what kind.*)

PRACTICE 9   IDENTIFYING ADJECTIVES AND THE WORDS THEY MODIFY

Underline the two single-word adjectives in each sentence. (Disregard the articles *a*, *an*, and *the*.) Draw an arrow from each adjective to the noun or pronoun it modifies.

1. The young pitcher gave his coach an uncertain look.
2. A steady hand is always welcome in an unexpected emergency.
3. The tornado devastated the small community in a few minutes.
4. A good film needs an intelligent script.
5. A large, oily blob rested on the surface of the lake.

Prepositions

Prepositions are often short words like *of, to, by, for,* or *from*. They are often words of location, such as *behind, beside, beneath, beyond,* or *below*. Following is a list of common prepositions.

Frequently Used Prepositions

about	beneath	in	to
above	beside	into	toward
across	between	like	under
after	beyond	near	underneath
along	by	next to	until
along with	down	of	up
around	during	off	upon
at	except	on	with
before	for	outside	within
behind	from	over	without

Recognizing Prepositional Phrases

Prepositional phrases begin with a preposition and end with a noun or pronoun that is the **object** of the preposition. Prepositional phrases often, but not always, express ideas about location or time: *to the house, in an hour, by next week, above the trees*.

•   **Prepositional phrases always *begin* with a preposition.** One way to spot prepositional phrases is to look for prepositions. Every prepositional phrase begins with a preposition. Familiarizing yourself with the preceding list of prepositions will help you to recognize prepositions when you see them.

- **Prepositional phrases always *end* with a noun or pronoun.** The object of a preposition, always a noun or pronoun, comes at the end of a prepositional phrase: of *them*, beside the *laundromat*, with *her*, to *Rome and Paris*, within a *year*.

- **Prepositional phrases often have a three-word structure.** Prepositional phrases frequently have a three-word structure: preposition, article (*a, an* or *the*), noun. Thus phrases like *of an armadillo, under a rock*, and *with a glance* become easy to recognize. But prepositional phrases can also be stretched with modifiers and compound objects: *of Ann's sharp tongue and her frequent mood fluctuations.* More often, though, the three-word pattern prevails.

PRACTICE 10   IDENTIFYING PREPOSITIONAL PHRASES

Underline the prepositional phrases in each sentence.

1. Martha's dog buried Leonard's keys under four inches of topsoil.
2. Exhausted by the heat, the dog found a cool, shady spot under the house.
3. My computer monitor crackles when I turn it on in the morning.
4. In the driveway, a small calico kitten played with a shiny beetle.
5. Erin's office chair has the annoying habit of squeaking as she leans into the backrest.

Conjunctions

Conjunctions, or joining words, connect words, phrases, or clauses, and often show the relationship between the ideas they join. There are four types of conjunctions: *coordinating* (FANBOYS) *conjunctions, correlative conjunctions, subordinating conjunctions,* and *conjunctive adverbs.*

Coordinating Conjunctions (FANBOYS Conjunctions)

Coordinating conjunctions are used to join words, phrases, and clauses. The nonsense word FANBOYS is an easy way to remember the seven coordinating conjunctions: **for, and, nor, but, or, yet, so.**

---

* FANBOYS Conjunctions

for   and   nor   but   or   yet   so

✔ A sticky liquid had been spilled on the mouse *and* the keyboard.

✔ Anna went to get her umbrella, *for* it had started to rain.

✔ Spiders are often considered pests, *but* many are actually beneficial to humans.

Correlative Conjunctions

Correlative conjunctions are used in pairs to join words, phrases, or clauses. Some commonly used correlative conjunctions are shown in the following box.

---

* Correlative Conjunctions

| both . . . and | either . . . or |
| neither . . . nor | not only . . . but also |

✔ The ancient Roman coin was *both* beautiful *and* rare.

✔ The senator said she was *neither* in favor of the proposed law *nor* opposed to it.

✔ Kendrick *not only* works a full-time job, *but* he *also* goes to school at night.

PRACTICE 11   IDENTIFYING CONJUNCTIONS

Underline the FANBOYS conjunction or the paired correlative conjunctions in each of the following sentences.

1. Beth entered the discount store with forty dollars, <u>but</u> she left with just five.
2. After an oil change <u>and</u> a new a set of tires, Michael was ready for the trip.
3. <u>Neither</u> the hot sun <u>nor</u> the high humidity kept Raul from walking around the twelve-mile nature trail.

4.   The documentary was entertaining, <u>yet</u> I cannot remember its title.

5.   One would expect to see <u>both</u> pens <u>and</u> paper in a stationery store.

Subordinating Conjunctions

While coordinating and correlative conjunctions join relatively equal elements, subordinating conjunctions (also called **dependent words** or **dependent conjunctions**) put one of the elements in a position of lesser importance—a subordinate position. And while there are only seven coordinating conjunctions and only a few correlative conjunctions, there are many subordinating conjunctions. A partial list follows.

* Subordinating Conjunctions (Dependent Words)		
after	even though	what
although	if	whatever
as	once	when
as if	since	whenever
as long as	so that	where
as soon as	that	wherever
as though	though	which
because	unless	while
before	until	who

Subordinating conjunctions join subordinate or dependent clauses to sentences.

✔   Even though he was reluctant, Luis agreed to the plan.

✔   Work seems to run smoothly whenever Rashae is on duty.

Conjunctive Adverbs

Conjunctive adverbs (also referred to as *transitional expressions*) are used to join clauses of equal importance. They also serve as transitional words that show relationships between ideas. A partial list of conjunctive adverbs follows.

---

* Conjunctive Adverbs (Transitional Expressions)

accordingly	furthermore	nevertheless
also	however	of course
as a result	in addition	on the other hand
besides	in fact	then
finally	instead	therefore
for example	meanwhile	thus
for instance	namely	

PRACTICE 12   IDENTIFYING SUBORDINATING CONJUNCTIONS AND CONJUNCTIVE ADVERBS

Underline the subordinating conjunction or the conjunctive adverb in each of the following sentences.

1. The open bottle of orange juice has sat in the sun so long <u>that</u> I am sure it is spoiled.
2. <u>Before</u> he cut the lawn, Ralph checked the level of the blade on the mower.
3. <u>When</u> land is developed, there may be a lack of space to plant new trees.
4. Shannon joined a yoga class <u>because</u> she wanted to improve her flexibility.
5. The newspaper printed the unfavorable article about the senator's family <u>even though</u> the senator threatened a lawsuit.

Interjections

Interjections are words or phrases that convey surprise or strong emotion. They are often used with exclamation points: Oh! Yikes! Whoa! Good grief!

In academic writing, there is little need for interjections or for exclamation points. Interjections are more often used in conversation and in casual written communication.

PRACTICE 13   IDENTIFYING INTERJECTIONS

Underline the interjections in the following sentences.

1. <u>Wow</u>! This is a good hamburger.
2. <u>Good grief</u>! The puppy has chewed my new tennis shoes.

3. <u>Oh!</u> I didn't know that I was going 85 miles per hour, Officer.
4. <u>Whoa!</u> Look at the size of the fish that Jessie caught!
5. <u>Ouch!</u> This kitten's claws are sharp!

REVIEW EXERCISE 1   IDENTIFYING PARTS OF SPEECH

In each of the following sentences, the same word is used as two different parts of speech. For each use of the word, tell whether it is a noun, a verb, or an adjective.

1. <u>verb</u> / <u>noun</u>   Renaldo will *cash* his paycheck so that he will have *cash* for groceries and gas.
2. <u>verb</u> / <u>adjective</u> Alfreda *spent* a few minutes spraying oven cleaner into her oven, then threw the *spent* can away.
3. <u>noun</u> / <u>verb</u>   Ben wanted to ask Emily to the *dance,* but he had a shameful secret: he could not *dance.*
4. <u>noun</u> / <u>verb</u>   When his plane developed engine trouble, the pilot looked for flat, open *land* where he could *land.*
5. <u>adjective</u>/ <u>noun</u>   John opened the *glove* compartment of his car. To his surprise, he actually found a *glove* inside.

REVIEW EXERCISE 2   IDENTIFYING PARTS OF SPEECH

In each of the following sentences, the same word is used as two different parts of speech. For each use of the word, tell whether it is a noun, a verb, or an adjective.

1. <u>noun</u> / <u>verb</u>   "I guess my children are not old enough to appreciate a *play,*" said Jill. "Instead of watching, they *play* in the aisle of the theater."
2. <u>verb</u> / <u>adjective</u> "Just *press* through the crowd and show your *press* pass at the door," the editor told the cub reporter.
3. <u>adjective</u>/ <u>noun</u>   Juanita found a white *sand* dollar half-buried in the *sand* on the beach.
4. <u>verb</u> / <u>noun</u>   Ava and Paul usually *walk* every evening, but it rained on Tuesday, so they could not go for their *walk.*
5. <u>noun</u> / <u>verb</u>   The bugs flew near the *light,* but they would not *light* on anything long enough for Karen to swat them.

REVIEW EXERCISE 3   IDENTIFYING PARTS OF SPEECH

In the space to the left, identify the part of speech of the italicized words in each sentence.

1. <u>adjective</u> / <u>adverb</u> Wilbur had a *disturbing* thought: What if everyone he owed money to *suddenly* demanded payment?

2. <u>noun</u> / <u>pronoun</u> The *trouble* with these steamy Georgia nights is that *I* can't sleep with the window open.

3. <u>conjunction</u> / <u>preposition</u> The tires *and* the battery cost Jason half *of* his weekly paycheck.

4. <u>subordinating conjunction</u> / <u>conjunctive adverb</u> The car, *which* costs a fortune to operate, is difficult to control in quick turns; *nevertheless,* it is exciting to drive.

5. <u>verb</u> / <u>verb</u> The driver of the wagon *lost* control when the horse *panicked* and bolted forward.

REVIEW EXERCISE 4 IDENTIFYING PARTS OF SPEECH

In the space to the left, identify the part of speech of the italicized words in each sentence.

1. <u>noun</u> / <u>adjective</u> Historically, small *automobiles* have always used less gasoline than *large* models.

2. <u>subordinating conjunction</u> / <u>pronoun</u> *Since* I arrived, I can't seem to find *my* glasses or my wallet.

3. <u>noun</u> / <u>conjunction</u> In the *evening,* Trey is taking a time management course, *but* he can't find enough time to study.

4. <u>interjection</u> / <u>adjective</u> *Wow!* That movie was so *realistic* that I covered my eyes when the alligator bit the hero's leg.

5. <u>verb</u> / <u>verb</u> The airplane *dove* at such a steep angle that Marcia *clutched* her seat's armrests in alarm.

REVIEW EXERCISE 5 USING PARTS OF SPEECH

Write a sentence using each of the italicized words as directed in each numbered item.

1. *computer*—use as a noun

   John's moldy bologna sandwich rested on top of his *computer* for two weeks.

2. *computer*—use as an adjective

   The latest *computer* hardware was too expensive, so Carlotta decided to buy used equipment.

3. *baby*—use as an adjective

   At the *baby* shower, Wanda received blankets, booties, and clothing for her child.

4. *baby*—use as a noun

   As soon as he saw Santa Claus, the *baby* began to cry.

5. *sleep*—use as a noun

   Sleep came easily to Nick, who worked fourteen hours a day.

6. *sleep*—use as a verb

   The cat *sleeps* on a high shelf in the closet, away from the household noise and activity.

7. *glass*—use as an adjective

   The *glass* slipper sat untouched because the princess found its style revolting.

8. *glass*—use as a noun

   John dropped the *glass* and watched it break against the tile floor.

9. *fund*—use as a noun

   The *fund* was nearly drained because the finance committee neglected to keep tabs on the spending.

10. *fund*—use as a verb

    The government *funded* research proving that young pigs are happiest when they sleep on a waterbed.

10

Verbs and Subjects

If there were no verbs or subjects, the top two items on the list of traditional journalist's questions would be eliminated. Verbs tell *what* was done, while subjects tell *who or what* the sentence is about.

A **verb** carries the **action** of the sentence, if any, and directs that action to and from the other words in the sentence. Some verbs, called **linking verbs,** connect related words in a sentence.

Action and Linking Verbs

Verbs work in two ways within a sentence. They show the **action,** physical or mental, of the subject of the sentence, or they **link** the subject with other words in the sentence.

Action Verbs

Action verbs show physical or mental action performed by a subject. Look at the following action verbs in bold print.

✔ Ron **pulled** the brass handle of the heavy, ornate door. (physical action)

✔ Harold **wondered** whether he **had driven** past his exit. (mental action, physical action)

✔ Lou Anna **summoned** the nerve to ask her boss for a raise. (mental action)

PRACTICE 1   IDENTIFYING ACTION VERBS

Find the action verb in each of the following sentences, and underline it twice.

1. The dog <u>barked</u> loudly at the intruder.
2. The unmarked police car <u>followed</u> the suspect at a discreet distance.
3. Jeremy <u>listened</u> carefully to the speaker's words.
4. Professor Bivins <u>approached</u> the lectern, shuffling his papers.
5. Clarice <u>dropped</u> four months' worth of bank statements on the branch manager's desk.

Linking Verbs

A **linking verb** *links* its subject with an adjective, a noun, or a pronoun that tells more about that subject. The most common linking verb in English is the verb *to be,* in all its various forms: *is, are, was, were, has been, will be, could have been,* and so on. Look at the following examples to see how the verb *to be* functions as a linking verb.

✔ The accountant's office **is** tiny and overcrowded.

The verb **is** links the subject, *office,* with *tiny* and *overcrowded,* adjectives that describe the subject.

✔ Li **has been** a good student throughout his freshman year.

The verb **has been** links the subject, Li, with a noun, *student,* that tells more about him.

Other common linking verbs include the verbs *to seem, to appear, to grow,* and *to become.* Verbs of the senses, such as *to smell, to taste, to look,* and *to feel,* can be action or linking verbs depending on how they are used.

Examples

L The store *manager* **seems** *unfriendly*. (The linking verb, *seems*, links the subject with an adjective that describes it.)

L Myra's *hair* **looked** *terrible*. (*Looked* is used as a linking verb—Myra's hair is performing no action)

A Ernesto **looked** at the dent in the front fender of his car. (*Looked* is used as an action verb—Ernesto is performing a physical action.)

L The potato *salad* **smelled** *bad*. (*Smelled* is used as a linking verb—the potato salad is performing no action.)

A Janice **smelled** the aroma of grilling hot dogs. (*Smelled* is used as an action verb. Janice is performing a physical action.)

The Linking Verb Test

To tell whether a verb is a linking verb, see if you can substitute *is* or *was* in its place. If the substitution works, the verb is a linking verb.

Examples

? Lee **felt** nervous about his upcoming job interview.

To see whether *felt* is used as a linking verb, try the linking verb test, substituting *was* for *felt*.

L Lee ~~felt~~ **was** nervous about his upcoming job interview. *(linking verb)*

The substitution makes sense; therefore, *felt* is used here as a linking verb.

? Dan **felt** someone brush against him in the crowd; then he realized his wallet was missing.

To see whether *felt* is used as a linking verb, try the linking verb test, substituting *was* for *felt*.

A Dan ~~felt~~ **was** someone brush against him; then he realized his wallet was missing. *(action verb)*

The substitution does not makes sense; therefore, *felt* is used as an action verb.

? The crowd **grew** larger with every passing minute.

L The crowd ~~grew~~ **was** larger with every passing minute.

The substitution makes sense; therefore, *grew* is used here as a linking verb.

? As their business **grew** and word of their success spread, the Saunders brothers became minor celebrities in the small town.

A As their business ~~grew~~ **was** and word of their success spread, the Saunders brothers became minor celebrities in the small town.

The substitution does not makes sense; therefore, *grew* is used as an action verb.

PRACTICE 2   IDENTIFYING ACTION AND LINKING VERBS

In the blank to the left of each numbered item, write **A** if the verb in bold type is an action verb, **L** if it is a linking verb.

   L   **1.** One of Jaime's front teeth **is** slightly crooked.

   A   **2.** David thought he **smelled** gas, but he could not find the source.

   L   **3.** Jemal **looks** thinner than he did last year.

   A   **4.** Todd **devotes** two hours a day to practicing the trombone.

   A   **5.** Since she was the first to arrive home, Kim **prepared** dinner.

   A   **6.** The salesperson **asked** Arthur how much he could afford to pay monthly.

   L   **7.** The crab cakes **tasted** slightly fishy.

   A   **8.** Leandro **tasted** the stew and nodded approvingly.

   A   **9.** Alison **wrote** confidently as her paper began to take shape.

   A   **10.** The maintenance crew **worked** quickly and competently.

Helping Verbs and Compound Verbs

The verb of a sentence is not necessarily a single word. Some verbs consist of more than one word. That is, they include a *main verb* and one or more *helping verbs.* Some subjects have more than one verb. When a subject has more than one verb, that verb is called a *compound verb.*

Helping Verbs

Some verbs include a main verb and one or more **helping verbs.** Thus you will see verbs expressed as phrases such as *had gone, will be given,* or *have been seen.* Adverbs such as *not, never,* or *always* are not considered part of the verb. Therefore, in the sentence *"Liver has never been Hal's favorite food,"* the verb is *"has been,"* not *"has never been."*

✔ Carlotta <u>has been working</u> in an accounting office since graduation.

✔ Kevin <u>had</u> not <u>expected</u> the computer course to be so interesting.

✔ The store <u>will be receiving</u> a shipment of safety goggles from the warehouse tomorrow.

PRACTICE 3   IDENTIFYING COMPLETE VERBS

Underline the complete verb (verb + helping verb) in each of the following sentences.

1. Dr. Freedman <u>has been practicing</u> medicine for almost thirty years.
2. The school's advising center <u>will be opening</u> early tomorrow for fall registration.
3. A moth <u>was flying</u> dangerously close to the candle's flame.
4. The moon, a huge orange disk, <u>had risen</u> just above the horizon.
5. I <u>am</u> not <u>working</u> past five o'clock today.

Compound Verbs

Sometimes a subject has more than one verb, as in the sentence *John <u>sat</u> at the kitchen table and <u>read</u> his mail.* Such verbs are called **compound verbs.**

✔ Music <u>blared</u> from the car's open windows and <u>reverberated</u> through the quiet neighborhood.

✔ The cashier <u>counted</u> his money and <u>locked</u> his cash drawer.

✔ At the Italian restaurant, Harold <u>ordered</u> calamari but <u>did</u> not <u>realize</u> that it was squid.

PRACTICE 4   IDENTIFYING COMPOUND VERBS

Underline the compound verb in each of the following sentences.

1. At the interview, Karen <u>wore</u> conservative clothing and <u>used</u> careful grammar.
2. The car <u>screeched</u> to a halt and <u>backed</u> into a parking space.

3. The dry cleaning shop <u>opens</u> at 7:00 A.M. and <u>closes</u> at 6:00 P.M.
4. The members of the aerobics class <u>danced</u> and <u>sweated</u> to the sound of loud rock music.
5. Ronald <u>pulled</u> another tissue from the box and <u>blew</u> his nose loudly.

Infinitives and *-ing* Verbs

Some forms of verbs can never act as a main verb in a sentence. **Infinitives** (to + verb) are never used as the main verb in a sentence.

✗   The career counselor advised us <u>to accept</u> any invitation to interview for a job.

The underlined phrase *to accept* is an infinitive and cannot be the main verb of the sentence. The verb in this sentence is *advised.*

✗   No one wanted <u>to volunteer</u> for the midnight shift.

The underlined phrase *to volunteer* is an infinitive, not the verb of the sentence. The verb in this sentence is *wanted.*

In addition, any verb form ending in *-ing* cannot act as a verb in a sentence unless a helping verb precedes it.

✗   Andy's small dog lagged behind, <u>stopping</u> occasionally to smell a tree.

Stopping cannot be the verb because a helping verb does not precede it. The verb in this sentence is *lagged.*

✗   The sound of the <u>dripping</u> faucet set Katie's nerves on edge.

Dripping cannot be the verb because a helping verb does not precede it. The verb in this sentence is *set.*

✔   To save money, Brian <u>had been using</u> his heater only on the coldest nights.

The verb in this sentence is *had been using* (helping verb + main verb).

✔   Tracie <u>has been working</u> at the hospital for nearly two years.

The verb in this sentence is <u>has been working</u> (helping verb + main verb).

PRACTICE 5   IDENTIFYING VERBS

Underline the verbs in each sentence twice. Do not underline infinitives or *-ing* verb forms.

1. Running excitedly from the car, the children <u>greeted</u> their grandparents.
2. The game show host <u>smiled</u> constantly to show off his brilliant white teeth.
3. Sunning themselves on a broad, flat rock, two brown turtles <u>sat</u> contentedly.
4. Someone <u>had left</u> a paperback book lying on the bench beside the walking path.
5. Jodie <u>spoke</u> to the group about her petition to abolish soft-drink machines on campus and even <u>convinced</u> one or two people to sign it.
6. During the summer, Keiko <u>plans</u> to visit her parents in Japan.
7. To keep anyone from hitting his new truck, Ben <u>parked</u> it in a deserted area of the parking lot.
8. The magazine cover <u>showed</u> a picture of a koala bear sleeping in a tree.
9. My sister, a maternity ward nurse, <u>says</u> that more babies <u>are born</u> during a full moon.
10. The city <u>planned</u> to tear down the aging housing project.

Subjects of Verbs

A **subject** of a verb is what the sentence is about. It is usually a noun or a pronoun. It is probably not the only noun or pronoun in the sentence, but it is the only one that enjoys such a direct grammatical connection to its verb. If you ask, "Who or what _____?" and put the verb in the blank, the answer to your question will always be the subject of the sentence. Note: Be sure the words "who or what" are stated *before* the verb, or you will find the object rather than the subject.

✔ The photograph on Ann's desk <u>showed</u> a red-haired man and two freckled children.

Who or what showed? The <u>photograph</u> showed. *Photograph* is the subject of the verb *showed*.

✔ The hot chili <u>burned</u> Brad's tongue.

Who or what burned? <u>Chili</u> burned. *Chili* is the subject of the verb *burned.*

✔ Edward and Rhonda <u>planted</u> tomatoes and squash in their backyard garden.

Who or what planted? <u>Edward and Rhonda</u> planted. *Edward and Rhonda* is the compound subject of the verb *planted.*

✔ Carefully, Marcus <u>punched</u> numbers into the calculator and <u>entered</u> information on his federal tax form.

Who or what punched? <u>Marcus</u> punched. Who or what entered? <u>Marcus</u> entered. *Marcus* is the subject of the compound verb *punched* and *entered.*

✔ Carefully, Marcus <u>punched</u> numbers into the calculator while Teresa <u>entered</u> information on their federal tax form.

Who or what punched? <u>Marcus</u> punched. *Marcus* is the subject of the verb *punched.* Who or what entered? <u>Teresa</u> entered. *Teresa* is the subject of the verb *entered.*

PRACTICE 6   IDENTIFYING VERBS AND SUBJECTS

Find the verb in each sentence and underline it twice. Then find the subject by asking "Who or what _____?" Underline the subject once.

1. From the depths of someone's backpack, a cell <u>phone</u> <u>rang</u>.
2. The <u>elevator</u> slowly <u>came</u> to a stop on the first floor.
3. The grainy, black-and-white <u>video</u> <u>showed</u> the robber entering the store.
4. The tennis <u>ball</u> <u>bounced</u> just once before the <u>dog</u> <u>caught</u> it in his mouth.
5. The lawnmower's <u>engine</u> <u>coughed</u> once, then <u>purred</u> to life.

Subjects and Prepositional Phrases

In many sentences, prepositional phrases intervene between subject and verb, as in the following example.

The <u>surface</u> *of the window* <u>was covered</u> with frost.

When we pick out the subject of the verb by asking "What was covered with frost?" it is tempting to say, "The window was covered." But *window* cannot be the subject of the verb in this sentence. Grammatically, it already has a job: it is the object of the preposition. The subject of this sentence is *surface*.

To avoid mistakes in picking out the subject of the sentence, cross out prepositional phrases before picking out subject and verb.

Recognizing Prepositional Phrases

To recognize prepositional phrases, learn to recognize their pattern. Prepositional phrases always begin with a preposition and end with a noun or pronoun. Often, they have a three-word structure, with the middle word being *a*, *an*, or *the*. More detail is provided in the sections that follow.

- **Prepositional phrases always *begin* with a preposition.** Prepositions are often short words like *of, to, by, for*, or *from*. They are also often words of location, such as *behind, beside, beneath, beyond*, or *below*. Following is a list of common prepositions.

---

* Frequently Used Prepositions

about	beneath	in	to
above	beside	into	toward
across	between	like	under
after	beyond	near	underneath
along	by	next to	until
along with	down	of	up
around	during	off	upon
at	except	on	with
before	for	outside	within
behind	from	over	without

- **Prepositional phrases always *end* with a noun or pronoun.** The object of a preposition, always a noun or pronoun, comes at the end of a prepositional phrase: of the *ceiling*, beside the *restaurant*, with *us*, to *Rita and Dean*, within four *months*.

- **Prepositional phrases often have a three-word structure.** Often, prepositional phrases have a three-word structure: preposition, article (*a, an,* or *the*), noun. Thus phrases like *of an airplane, under the bleachers,* and *with a frown* become easy to recognize. But prepositional phrases can also be stretched with modifiers and compound objects: Everyone made fun *of Sam's extra-distance, glow-in-the dark, Super-Flight golf balls and his tasseled, monogrammed golf club covers.* More often, though, the three-word pattern prevails.

---

* *Famous Prepositional Phrases*

The prepositional phrases below have been used as titles for songs, television shows, movies, and books. How many do you recognize? Can you think of others?

Above Suspicion	In Living Color
Against the Wind	Of Mice and Men
Around the World in Eighty Days	On Golden Pond
At Long Last Love	On the Waterfront
At the Hop	Over the Rainbow
Behind Closed Doors	Under the Boardwalk
Behind Enemy Lines	Under the Yum Yum Tree
Beneath the Planet of the Apes	Up a Lazy River
Beyond the Sea	Up on the Roof
In Cold Blood	Up the Down Staircase

PRACTICE 7   RECOGNIZING PREPOSITIONAL PHRASES

Cross out the prepositional phrases in each sentence. Underline subjects once and verbs twice.

1. The <u>hum</u> ~~of trucks~~ ~~on the highway~~ <u><u>could be heard</u></u> ~~for miles~~.
2. <u>Two</u> scruffy <u>dogs</u> ~~without collars~~ <u><u>trotted</u></u> ~~beside the road~~.
3. The holly <u>bushes</u> ~~in front of the library~~ <u><u>need</u></u> trimming.
4. The <u>sound</u> ~~of an argument~~ ~~from the neighboring apartment~~ <u><u>kept</u></u> Felice awake ~~until past midnight~~.
5. The sweet, yeasty <u>smell</u> ~~of baking bread~~ <u><u>drifted</u></u> ~~throughout the house~~.

---

* Real-World Writing: Is it okay to end a sentence with a preposition?

How else would you say, "Will you pick me up?" or "I feel left out"?

Sometimes, what seems to be an objection to a preposition at the end of a sentence is really an objection to an awkward or a redundant construction. "Where are you at?" will bring a scowl to any English teacher's face—not because it ends in a preposition, but because it is redundant: "where" and "at" are both doing the same job—indicating location.

But by all means, say "I have nothing to put this in" or "The dog wants to go out." Except in the most formal writing, ending sentences with prepositions is something almost everyone can live with.

REVIEW EXERCISE 1   IDENTIFYING SUBJECTS AND VERBS

Cross out the prepositional phrases in each sentence. Then underline the subject once and the verb twice.

1. ~~To the surprise and delight of her parents~~, Tanya made the dean's list ~~during her first term in college~~.
2. A cold front will move ~~into the Southeast before the weekend~~.
3. ~~After months of complaints from the residents~~, the manager ~~of the apartment complex~~ decided to hire a security guard.
4. The blare ~~of the television~~ gave Damon a headache.
5. The gravity ~~of Jupiter~~, the largest planet ~~in the solar system~~, is more than twice the gravity ~~of Earth~~.
6. The headlines ~~on the front page of the newspaper~~ seemed to contain nothing but bad news.
7. The tart taste ~~of cherries~~ contrasted ~~with the creamy vanilla of the ice cream~~.
8. The last person ~~out of the office~~ should lock the door.
9. The contents ~~of the wastebasket~~ had been scattered ~~across the floor~~.
10. Several members ~~of the class~~ met to study ~~before the test~~.

REVIEW EXERCISE 2   IDENTIFYING SUBJECTS AND VERBS

Cross out the prepositional phrases in each sentence. Then underline the subject once and the verb twice. Some sentences contain more than one subject or more than one verb.

1. Leanne wrote a check, stuffed it in an envelope, and mailed it to the telephone company.
2. The sight of green mold on the white cottage cheese disgusted Arthur.
3. The red light on Marie's answering machine was blinking furiously.
4. The fans in the stadium leaped to their feet and cheered.
5. Citrus fruits like oranges are high in Vitamin C.
6. On the lawn, the children cartwheeled and tumbled.
7. Some of the chemicals in chocolate may reduce the risk of heart disease.
8. A small foreign car in the left lane zipped past Yashika and vanished around a curve.
9. The top shelf of the cabinet contained a few dusty plates and an electric can opener, still in the box.
10. The hands on the clock moved so slowly that they seemed to be standing still.

REVIEW EXERCISE 3   IDENTIFYING SUBJECTS AND VERBS

Cross out the prepositional phrases in each sentence. Then underline the subject once and the verb twice. Some sentences contain more than one subject or more than one verb.

1. The success of the research depended on every member of the team.
2. Again and again, Paul went back to look at the motorcycle on display in the showroom window.
3. Laureen started her car and glanced at the gas gauge.
4. The rhythmic sound of the machinery in the factory was like music to the plant manager.
5. The article in the paper said that the hockey player's broken jaw required surgery.
6. The loss of Kim's job meant financial disaster for her family.
7. Kurt felt no obligation to help anyone.
8. The unfavorable reviews of the movie did not affect its popularity.
9. The sagging roof and boarded windows of the old house suggested that no one lived there.
10. Vickie dislikes her roommate's sloppiness but loves her sense of humor.

REVIEW EXERCISE 4   IDENTIFYING SUBJECTS AND VERBS

Cross out the prepositional phrases and underline the subjects once and the verbs twice in the following paragraph.

[1]The planet Mars has long fascinated its earthbound neighbors. [2]~~In both Hindu and Roman mythology~~, Mars was associated ~~with war~~. [3]~~Writers of science fiction in the twentieth century~~ also created war stories ~~of Martians~~ attacking the people ~~of the earth~~. [4]Now, however, ideas ~~about Mars~~ have taken a more peaceful turn. [5]Scientists now ponder the possibility ~~of colonizing~~ the red planet. [6]The relatively short distance ~~between Mars and Earth~~ makes travel ~~between the two planets~~ a possibility. [7]However, the inhospitable atmosphere and lower surface temperature ~~of Mars~~ pose barriers ~~to colonization~~. [8]Proposed solutions ~~to these problems~~ include underground colonies and seeding the planet ~~with algae~~ to produce oxygen and make the atmosphere more hospitable ~~to humans~~. [9]However, the people ~~of Earth~~ will probably not be calling themselves "Martians" ~~in the near future~~. [10]~~For now~~, Mars will continue to be a fascinating object ~~of study and speculation~~.

11
Subject-Verb Agreement

Plural paired with singular
Can't seem to get along,
And singular with plural
Just doesn't quite belong.

But singular and singular
Will need no referee,
And plural linked to plural
Is in perfect harmony.

The rules for agreement between subjects and verbs sometimes seem complex, but they are based on a simple concept: **a singular subject requires a singular verb, and a plural subject requires a plural verb.**

The Basic Pattern

Most subject-verb agreement problems occur in the present tense. Look at the following conjugation of the present tense verb *dance.* You can see exactly where trouble is likely to occur if you ask the question "Where does the verb change its form?"

	Singular	Plural
First Person	I dance	we dance
Second Person	you dance	you dance
Third Person	he, she, it dances	they dance

As you see, the verb changes its form in the *third person* by adding an *s* to the singular form. Most problems with subject-verb agreement in the present tense occur in the third person.

PRACTICE 1   **CONJUGATING A VERB**

All regular verbs follow the preceding pattern. Using the sample on page 171 as a model, fill in the forms of the verb *inquire* in the spaces provided.

	Singular	Plural
First Person	I inquire	we inquire
Second Person	you inquire	you inquire
Third Person	he, she, it inquires	they inquire

Did you remember to put the *s* on the third-person singular form?

Notice that the third-person verb pattern is exactly the opposite of the pattern seen in nouns. Nouns usually add *-s* or *-es* to become plural. But third-person, present-tense verbs work in exactly the opposite way. It is the third-person **singular** form of the verb that ends in *s*, not the plural form. When you see the verb *walks*, you know that it is singular because it ends in *s*.

Third-person *singular* subjects and verbs usually follow this pattern:

The **dog walks**. (The singular noun does not end in *s*; the singular verb does end in *s*.)

Third person *plural* subjects and verbs usually follow this pattern:

The **dogs walk**. (The plural noun ends in *s*; the plural verb does not end in *s*.)

---

* *Memory Jogger*

If you have trouble with third-person verbs, remember the following verse.

> The Singular *S*
>
> When verbs are in the present tense,
> You never need to guess.
> The singular third-person verb
> Always ends in *s*.

PRACTICE 2   CONJUGATING VERBS

On your own paper, fill in the first-, second-, and third-person forms of the regular verbs *explain, hurl, accommodate, place,* and *decide*. Remember to add the *s* to the third-person singular form.

	Singular	Plural
First Person	I _____	we _____
Second Person	you _____	you _____
Third Person	he, she, it _____	they _____

Now look at the regular verb *press* in the present tense. Here, when the verb already ends in *s*, the third-person singular form also changes, adding *es*. Other verbs that add *es* include those ending in *z, ch,* or *sh*.

	Singular	Plural
First Person	I press	we press
Second Person	you press	you press
Third Person	he, she, it press**es** (Third-person singular also includes any singular noun or pronoun that could be replaced by *he, she,* or *it*.)	they press (Third-person plural also includes any plural noun or pronoun that could be replaced by *they*.)

Notice that third-person subjects include more than just pronouns. Third-person singular subjects also include any noun or pronoun that can be replaced by *he, she,* or *it*. **Samantha, Ms. Green, hedgehog, door, infant, anyone, real estate salesperson, thing,** and **Patrick Henry** are all third person singular. Thus, each requires a present tense verb ending in *s* or *es*.

Third-person plural subjects include any noun or pronoun that can be replaced by *they*. **The Wilsons, several, cars and trucks, beagles, cybercafés,** and **both** are words that could be replaced by **they.** Thus all are third-person plural and require a present tense plural verb, the form that *does not* add *s* or *es*.

The Verb *to be*

Now look at the most common irregular verb, the verb *to be*.

	Singular	Plural
First Person	I am	we are
Second Person	you are	you are
Third Person	he, she, it is	they are

Notice that the pattern still holds: **the third-person singular form of the verb always ends in *s* or *es*.**

Knowing the pattern that present-tense verbs follow should make it a bit easier to apply the basic rule of subject-verb agreement: **A singular subject requires a singular verb, and a plural subject requires a plural verb.**

Examples

✔ Molly calls Tampa every weekend to check on her parents. (singular subject, singular verb)

✔ Thanksgiving is always celebrated on a Thursday. (singular subject, singular verb)

✔ Most people have trouble coping with change. (plural subject, plural verb)

✔ Big dogs make Darien nervous. (plural subject, plural verb)

PRACTICE 3   MAKING SUBJECTS AND VERBS AGREE

Underline the correct verb form in each sentence.

1. Jacob does not understand why the toaster (do, <u>does</u>) not work.
2. With great dignity, the Siamese cat (walk, <u>walks</u>) into the room, her tail high in the air.
3. Cedric (think, <u>thinks</u>) the test is next week.
4. The rains (<u>pour</u>, pours) heavily during March.
5. The dentist (<u>opens</u>, open) her office at 8:00 A.M. daily.

Problems in Subject-Verb Agreement

Prepositional Phrase between Subject and Verb

The subject of a verb is never found in a prepositional phrase. When a prepositional phrase comes between subject and verb, it is easy to make mistakes in subject-verb agreement. Crossing out prepositional phrases will help you avoid errors. (See page 165 for a list of common prepositions.)

Example 1

Consider the following problem in subject-verb agreement:

The members of the public speaking club (gather, gathers) in the student center every Wednesday.

Which verb is correct? Finding the subject without crossing out prepositional phrases, you might look for the subject by asking the question "Who or what *gathers* or *gather?*" It might seem logical to say "The *club* gathers; therefore, *club* is the subject of the sentence and *gathers* is the verb." However, *club* cannot be the subject of the sentence because it already has a job: it is the object of a preposition, and **the subject of a sentence is never found in a prepositional phrase.**

Incorrect solution:

✘   The members of the public speaking **club** **gathers** in the student center every Wednesday.

Correct solution: Cross out prepositional phrases to find the subject.

✔   The **members** ~~of the public speaking club~~ **gather** ~~in the student center on Wednesdays~~.

Example 2

✔   The fast-food **wrappers** ~~in the back seat of Matt's car~~ **reveal** his eating habits over the past few weeks.

The verb agrees with its subject, *wrappers,* not with an object of a preposition.

PRACTICE 4   ELIMINATING PREPOSITIONAL PHRASES

In each of the sentences, cross out prepositional phrases to find the subject of the sentence. Then, underline the subject and double-underline the correct verb.

1. The green Lincoln parked ~~by the azaleas~~ (is, are) large and expensive, much like ~~Uncle Ed's other cars~~.

2. The hungry dogs ~~behind the fence~~ (snap, snaps) greedily ~~at the bowls of moistened food~~.

3. Almost ~~in slow motion~~, a stack ~~of chairs~~ (begin, begins) to tumble ~~to the floor~~.

4. ~~In Denise's dreams~~, a large computer ~~with sharp teeth~~ (start, starts) to chase her ~~around the living room~~.

5. The coaches ~~of the home team~~ (watches, watch) ~~in dismay~~ as the opposing team scores effortlessly.

Other Interrupters between Subject and Verb

Like prepositional phrases, other intervening phrases or clauses have no effect on subject-verb agreement.

Example 1

✔ **James,** the employees' spokesperson, **seems** to seek out confrontation with management.

The verb *seems* agrees with its subject, *James,* and is not affected by the intervening phrase.

Example 2

✔ The **shells** that Grace and Kevin found on the beach yesterday **look** pretty in the jar beside the kitchen window.

The verb *look* agrees with its subject, *shells,* and is not affected by the intervening clause.

PRACTICE 5   WORKING WITH INTERRUPTERS

In the following sentences, underline the subject and double-underline the correct verb

1. The dog, which bears a strange resemblance to its owners, (lives, live) across the street.

2. The two <u>rules</u> that were completely misunderstood by everyone in the company (was, <u>were</u>) scrapped by the ad hoc committee.

3. The <u>hawk</u>, making a third unsuccessful dive at its prey, (<u>cries</u>, cry) out in frustration.

4. The <u>dog</u>, always a little shy and uncertain, (<u>has</u>, have) developed a reluctance to venture far from the house.

5. The <u>plumber</u>, working feverishly to complete the job by sunset, (<u>snaps</u>, snap) the copper pipe into place and (<u>searches</u>, search) for the solder.

Indefinite Pronouns as Subjects

The following **indefinite pronouns** are always singular and require singular verbs.

each	everybody	anyone	anything
either	somebody	everyone	everything
neither	nobody	someone	something
anybody	one	no one	nothing

---

* Memory Jogger

Remember the singular indefinite pronouns more easily by grouping them:

Each, either, neither

All the bodies (anybody, everybody, somebody, nobody)

All the ones (one, everyone, anyone, someone, no one)

All the things (anything, everything, something, nothing)

Examples

✔ Ushi arrived at the airport, but <u>no one</u> <u>was</u> there to meet her.

The subject, *no one,* is singular, as is the verb, *was.*

✔ <u>Each</u> ~~of the lunch bags~~ <u>has been labeled</u> with a child's name.

The singular verb, *has been labeled,* agrees with the singular subject, *each.* The plural object of the preposition, *bags,* does not affect the verb.

PRACTICE 6   MAKING VERBS AGREE WITH INDEFINITE PRONOUNS

In each sentence, cross out the prepositional phrases and underline the correct verb.

1. Everyone ~~in the stalled elevator~~ (<u>was</u>, were) relieved when the lights came on and the elevator started to move.
2. Neither ~~of the cars~~ (<u>has</u>, have) antilock brakes.
3. Each ~~of the cab drivers~~ (<u>has</u>, have) to take a course ~~in customer service and human relations~~.
4. Everything ~~in the house~~ (<u>was</u>, were) sold ~~to the liquidating firm~~.
5. One ~~of the students~~ (<u>has</u>, have) to submit the group project ~~to Professor Sturgis before Tuesday~~.

Subject Following the Verb

In most English sentences, the subject comes before the verb. However, the subject follows the verb in these situations:

1. when the sentence begins with *here* or *there*
2. when the sentence begins with a prepositional phrase that is immediately followed by a verb
3. when the sentence is a question.

Examples

✔ There <u>are</u> only four <u>cars</u> left ~~in the parking lot~~.

The plural subject, *cars*, requires the plural verb, *are*. The word *there* is not the subject of the sentence.

✔ ~~Around Mikayla's neck~~ <u>hangs</u> a slender silver <u>necklace</u>.

The prepositional phrase *around Mikayla's neck* is immediately followed by a verb. Since the subject is never found in a prepositional phrase, it must be somewhere *after* the verb. The singular verb, *hangs*, agrees with the plural subject, *necklace*.

✔ What <u>is</u> the <u>address</u> ~~of the school's new web page~~?

The singular subject, *address*, follows the singular verb, *is*.

✔   Why <u>are</u> those smelly <u>socks</u> ~~in the middle of the kitchen floor~~?

The plural subject, *socks,* follows the plural verb, *are.*

PRACTICE 7   WORKING WITH SUBJECTS THAT FOLLOW VERBS

Cross out the prepositional phrases in each sentence. Then underline the subject and double-underline the correct verb.

1. Printed ~~on the envelope~~ (was, <u>were</u>) detailed <u>instructions</u>.
2. There (come, <u>comes</u>) a <u>time</u> when one realizes that trying to cook a meal is useless ~~without the proper tools and ingredients~~.
3. (<u>Is</u>, Are) there <u>anyone</u> here who can give me a ride home?
4. Here (is, <u>are</u>) the blue <u>forms</u> ~~in triplicate~~ that you asked for.
5. ~~Near the rosebushes~~ (flit, <u>flits</u>) a tiny <u>hummingbird</u>, looking ~~like a fat scarlet bee~~.

Compound Subjects

Compound Subjects Joined by *and*

Because *and* always joins at least two elements (more than one), compound subjects joined by *and* require a plural verb.

Examples

✔ <u>Kelsey</u> *and* <u>Leon</u> <u>plan</u> to open a lawn care business.

✔ <u>Sleeping</u> until ten *and* <u>shopping</u> with her sister <u>are</u> Veronica's weekend pleasures.

✔ Yellow <u>dandelions</u> *and* <u>sprigs</u> of white clover <u>grow</u> on the lawn.

✔ A <u>pair</u> of faded jeans and a white <u>t-shirt</u> <u>were</u> all that Kim could find to wear.

Compound Subjects Joined by *or, either/or,* or *neither/nor*

When a compound subject is joined by *or, either/or,* or *neither/nor,* the verb agrees with the part of the subject closest to it.

Examples

✔   The manager **or** the <u>clerks</u> <u>open</u> the store every morning.

The verb agrees with *clerks,* the part of the subject closest to it. The word *manager* is not considered.

✔   The managers **or** the <u>clerk</u> <u>opens</u> the store every morning.

The verb agrees with *clerk,* the part of the subject closest to it.

✔   The strawberries **or** the <u>banana</u> <u>is</u> enough for my breakfast.

The verb agrees with *banana,* the part of the subject closest to it.

✔   The banana **or** the <u>strawberries</u> <u>are</u> enough for my breakfast.

The verb agrees with *strawberries,* the part of the subject closest to it.

✔   **Either** the CD player **or** the <u>speakers</u> <u>have</u> malfunctioned.

The verb agrees with *speakers,* the part of the subject closest to it.

✔   **Either** the speakers **or** the <u>CD player</u> <u>has</u> malfunctioned.

The verb agrees with *CD player,* the part of the subject closest to it.

PRACTICE 8   MAKING VERBS AGREE WITH COMPOUND SUBJECTS

Cross out the prepositional phrases, then double-underline the verb that agrees with each compound subject. Some subjects are joined by *and,* while others are joined by *or, either/or,* or *neither/nor.*

1.   A tree or the top ~~of the car~~ (<u>is</u>, are) our cat Prudence's first line ~~of defense against dogs~~.
2.   Neither a farmhouse nor grazing cows (seems, <u>seem</u>) out ~~of place in a painting~~ depicting country living.
3.   Books and papers (is, <u>are</u>) scattered ~~across Professor Thomson's desk~~.
4.   Neither papers nor a single volume (litter, <u>litters</u>) Frank's desk.
5.   Bowing so low that they nearly scrape the floor ~~of the stage~~, the actor and the actress (stands, <u>stand</u>) basking ~~in the applause~~.
6.   Ethics and attitude (<u>play</u>, plays) an important role ~~in anyone's success~~.
7.   Harold complained that neither the mousetraps nor the cat (<u>was</u>, were) effective ~~against the mouse~~ that had invaded his house.

8. Neither fish nor turtles (<u>remain</u>, remains) ~~in the area~~ after the last sewage spill fouled the river.

9. The mailboxes and the posts that (<u>hold</u>, holds) them (is, <u>are</u>) ~~in good condition~~.

10. Neither the small country's currency nor its exports (is, <u>are</u>) very stable ~~after the government's fall~~.

REVIEW EXERCISE 1   MAKING SUBJECTS AND VERBS AGREE

Cross out the prepositional phrases, then double-underline the verb that agrees with each compound subject. Some subjects are joined by *and*, while others are joined by *or, either/or,* or *neither/nor.*

1. Each ~~of the cashiers~~ (swear, <u>swears</u>) that the fast-moving light (<u>was</u>, were) a UFO.

2. The cause ~~of the diseases~~ (<u>was</u>, were) the bacteria that (<u>live</u>, lives) ~~in the foul-smelling river near the town~~.

3. Neither ~~of the violations~~ (<u>was</u>, were) serious enough to warrant confiscation ~~of the driver's license~~, so the police officer gave the driver a ticket.

4. When people (<u>accuse</u>, accuses) Samantha ~~of being~~ too outspoken, she says, "I'm a small woman, I need a big mouth."

5. The torpedoes (was, <u>were</u>) sleek-looking gray tubes ~~with bright gold tips~~.

6. The tree and the bush (sways, <u>sway</u>) gently ~~in the May breeze~~.

7. Walking briskly or swimming energetically (<u>is</u>, are) good exercise.

8. Rafael (do, <u>does</u>) not enjoy driving ~~in rush hour traffic~~.

9. Everyone (<u>agrees</u>, agree) that the top salesperson quit the company because ~~of shabby treatment by management~~.

10. The lines ~~at the theater~~ (moves, <u>move</u>) quickly.

REVIEW EXERCISE 2   MAKING SUBJECTS AND VERBS AGREE

Write C in the blank to the left of the sentence if the italicized verb is correct as written. If the verb is incorrect, write the correct present-tense form in the blank. Two of the sentences are correct.

<u>lacks</u>   1. The movie playing at all the theaters *lack* a strong, interesting plot.

<u>were</u>   2. Taking shelter under a tall sycamore *was* a large, hungry bobcat and a plump, nervous weasel.

works **3.** Smiling and looking pleased with the grade report she has in her hands, June says that she *work* hard for her grades.

hangs **4.** Orange with green and gold eyes and a flame-colored tongue, the mask *hang* on the wall over a small table.

flows **5.** The Tiber river *flow* by one of the seven hills of ancient Rome.

claims **6.** Pamela *claim* that all machines should work perfectly all the time.

_C_ **7.** Neither of the party's candidates *believes* that victory is within the party's grasp.

happens **8.** Fly fishing *happen* to be one of Jake's few interests outside of raising cattle.

was **9.** Claiming that he *were* abducted by aliens, Tim turned in his research paper six days late.

_C_ **10.** The consolation prize *was* a copy of a hardback book written by an author no one recognized.

REVIEW EXERCISE 3   MAKING SUBJECTS AND VERBS AGREE

Cross through the two incorrect verb forms in each item. Then write the correct present-tense forms on the lines provided.

1. Jeremy ~~keep~~ the television on while he studies. He swears that the noise and the excitement of the programs ~~does~~ not distract him, but his grades tell a different story.

    Sentence 1: _keeps_   Sentence 2: _do_

2. One of the witnesses ~~state~~ that he can describe the driver of the car that fled the scene of the accident. However, not one witness ~~remember~~ the color or make of the car.

    Sentence 1: _states_   Sentence 2: _remembers_

3. The shipyard ~~build~~ many vessels for the U.S. Navy. Union workers at the shipyard refuse to work overtime because the management of the shipyard ~~refuse~~ to hire additional workers.

    Sentence 1: _builds_   Sentence 2: _refuses_

4. On the side of the road near the bridge ~~stands~~ two new signs. One of the signs ~~say~~ "No Parking"; the other says "No Fishing."

    Sentence 1: _stand_   Sentence 2: _says_

5. When they arrive at the movies, either Catherine or John ~~find~~ good seats in the theater. The person who is not finding a seat ~~stand~~ in line for popcorn.

    Sentence 1: _finds_   Sentence 2: _stands_

REVIEW EXERCISE 4   MAKING SUBJECTS AND VERBS AGREE

Cross through the two incorrect verb forms in each item. Then write the correct present-tense forms on the lines provided.

1. Dust and the grinding noise of the two automobiles finally ~~ceases~~, as they spin together in an unwanted embrace. Seconds later, the drivers emerge from the cars, and accusations ~~begins~~ to fly.

    Sentence 1: _cease_____   Sentence 2: _begin_____

2. The woodpeckers ~~seems~~ to have strong necks and heads. The noisy birds constantly ~~smacks~~ their bills against the hard surface of trees.

    Sentence 1: _seem_____   Sentence 2: _smack_____

3. The sound of the mail truck always ~~bring~~ my neighbor running to her mailbox. I am not so eager; all I ever receive ~~is~~ bills.

    Sentence 1: _brings_____   Sentence 2: _are_____

4. The calendar ~~have~~ blue marks on it, showing the days that the barber will be away from the shop. I can't help but wonder how long the shop will remain in business if the owner ~~are~~ always gone.

    Sentence 1: _has_____   Sentence 2: _is_____

5. Philip ~~admire~~ naval officers and dreams of one day becoming one. He says he will not mind the strenuous training and the responsibility that ~~comes~~ with the job.

    Sentence 1: _admires_____   Sentence 2: _come_____

REVIEW EXERCISE 5   MAKING SUBJECTS AND VERBS AGREE

Underline and correct the ten subject-verb agreement errors in the following paragraph.

[1]Everyone in my neighborhood <u>know</u> the cat that people call "the Midnight Snacker." [2]People say that the family at the end of the block or the man across the street <u>own</u> the cat, but no one seems to be quite sure. [3]On spring nights, when many people <u>leaves</u> a window or door open to catch the breeze, the cat goes into action. [4]He usually <u>wait</u> until late evening when people are likely to be reading or watching TV. [5]Then, he quietly enters a house and <u>head</u> for the kitchen. [6]If any tasty morsel, from pet food to pork chops, <u>attract</u> his attention, he begins eating. [7]Once, I surprised him in my kitchen

eating from the bowl of dry food I usually <u>leaves</u> out for my cats. [8]My neighbor says that she and her husband <u>has</u> stopped leaving the screen door open since she caught the Snacker leaving, carrying a chicken leg he had snagged from a bucket of chicken on the kitchen counter. [9]Everyone in the neighborhood <u>have</u> a story to tell about the thieving cat, and most of them laugh as they tell it. [10]The Midnight Snacker <u>seem</u> to be almost as good at stealing people's hearts as he is at stealing their food.

1.	knows		6.	attracts
2.	owns		7.	leave
3.	leave		8.	have
4.	waits		9.	has
5.	heads		10.	seems

12

Irregular Verbs

1.) I must have (drunk, drank) a quart of water.

2.) The fish (swam, swum) happily in their new tank.

3.) The dog (lay, laid) under the porch, trying to escape the heat.

The verbs you see in the box above are **irregular verbs.** Because they vary in form from regular verbs, they can be puzzling. The answers to the questions in the box are 1.) drunk; 2.) swam; and 3.) lay. This chapter can help eliminate confusion about these and other irregular verbs.

Regular and Irregular Verbs

Regular verbs follow a predictable pattern in the formation of their **principal parts.** Every verb has four **principal parts:** the present tense form, the past tense form, the past participle (used with helping verbs), and the present participle (the *-ing* verb form used with helping verbs). **Regular verbs** add *ed* to form their past tense and past participles. Some examples of regular verbs follow.

Present	Past	Past Participle	Present Participle
talk	talked	(have) talked	(are) talking
use	used	(have) used	(are) using

Present	Past	Past Participle	Present Participle
revise	revised	(have) revised	(are) revising
push	pushed	(have) pushed	(are) pushing

Irregular verbs, on the other hand, follow no predictable pattern in their past and past participle forms. Sometimes a vowel changes: *sing* in the present tense becomes *sang* in the past tense and *sung* in the past participle. Sometimes an *n* or *en* will be added to form the past participle: *take* becomes *taken, know* becomes *known.* Some verbs, such as the verb *set,* do not change at all. Others change completely: *buy* in the present tense becomes *bought* in the past and past participle.

Following are some common irregular verbs and their principal parts. If you are unsure about a verb form, check this list or consult a dictionary for the correct form.

Principal Parts of Common Irregular Verbs

Present	Past	Past Participle	Present Participle
become	became	(have) become	(are) becoming
begin	began	(have) begun	(are) beginning
blow	blew	(have) blown	(are) blowing
break	broke	(have) broken	(are) breaking
bring	brought	(have) brought	(are) bringing
burst	burst	(have) burst	(are) bursting
buy	bought	(have) bought	(are) buying
catch	caught	(have) caught	(are) catching
choose	chose	(have) chosen	(are) choosing
come	came	(have) come	(are) coming
cut	cut	(have) cut	(are) cutting
do	did	(have) done	(are) doing
draw	drew	(have) drawn	(are) drawing
drink	drank	(have) drunk	(are) drinking
drive	drove	(have) driven	(are) driving
eat	ate	(have) eaten	(are) eating
fall	fell	(have) fallen	(are) falling
feel	felt	(have) felt	(are) feeling
fight	fought	(have) fought	(are) fighting

Present	Past	Past Participle	Present Participle
find	found	(have) found	(are) finding
fly	flew	(have) flown	(are) flying
freeze	froze	(have) frozen	(are) freezing
get	got	(have) gotten	(are) getting
give	gave	(have) given	(are) giving
go	went	(have) gone	(are) going
grow	grew	(have) grown	(are) growing
have	had	(have) had	(are) having
hear	heard	(have) heard	(are) hearing
hide	hid	(have) hidden	(are) hiding
hold	held	(have) held	(are) holding
hurt	hurt	(have) hurt	(are) hurting
keep	kept	(have) kept	(are) keeping
know	knew	(have) known	(are) knowing
lay	laid	(have) laid	(are) laying
lead	led	(have) led	(are) leading
leave	left	(have) left	(are) leaving
lie	lay	(have) lain	(are) lying
lend	lent	(have) lent	(are) lending
lose	lost	(have) lost	(are) losing
put	put	(have) put	(are) putting
ride	rode	(have) ridden	(are) riding
rise	rose	(have) risen	(are) rising
run	ran	(have) run	(are) running
see	saw	(have) seen	(are) seeing
sing	sang	(have) sung	(are) singing
speak	spoke	(have) spoken	(are) speaking
steal	stole	(have) stolen	(are) stealing
swim	swam	(have) swum	(are) swimming
take	took	(have) taken	(are) taking
tell	told	(have) told	(are) telling
tear	tore	(have) torn	(are) tearing
think	thought	(have) thought	(are) thinking

Present	Past	Past Participle	Present Participle
throw	threw	(have) thrown	(are) throwing
write	wrote	(have) written	(are) writing
am, are, is (to be)	was, were	(have) been	(are) being

PRACTICE 1 USING IRREGULAR VERBS

Fill in the blank with the correct form of the verb shown to the left of each question. For help, consult the preceding list of irregular verbs.

(become)   1. Nicki has __become__ a soccer fan since her son started playing.

(break)   2. The expensive sunglasses that Randall bought were __broken__ when they were accidentally knocked off the hotel balcony.

(drink)   3. The dog, chained in the hot sun, had long ago __drunk__ the water in his bowl.

(eat)   4. Natalie did not __eat__; instead, she ran errands on her lunch break.

(go)   5. Alvin's birthday had come and __gone__ without any acknowledgment from his family.

(lead)   6. The mother duck __led__ her ducklings toward the calm water of the lake.

(lend)   7. My brother __lent__ me his car, warning me to put gas in it before I returned it.

(run)   8. Shameka __ran__ across the parking lot toward the post office door, hoping to reach it before the clerk locked it for the day.

(see)   9. Armand waved excitedly when he __saw__ his son step off the plane.

(swim)   10. After she had __swum__, Vivian opened her picnic basket.

Puzzling Pairs

Some irregular verbs are easily confused with other words. The following section will help you make the right choice between *lie* and *lay* and *sit* and *set*.

Lay and *Lie*

Lay and *lie* are often confused, partly because their forms overlap. The present tense form of *lay* and the past tense form of *lie* are both the same: *lay*. Look at the following chart to see the different forms of each verb.

Present	Past	Past Participle	Present Participle
lay (put)	laid	(have) laid	(are) laying
lie (recline)	**lay**	(have) lain	(are) lying

The verb *lay* means *to put* or *place*. It always takes an object; that is, there will always be an answer to the question "Lay what?"

✔ Every day at exactly 9:00 A.M., Carlos *lays* his *newspaper* aside and begins to work.

In the present-tense example above, the present-tense form *lays* is used.

✔ Yesterday, Hayley *laid* her *keys* on the table, but today she cannot find them.

Here, the past tense form *laid* is used.

✔ John *has laid* the *groundwork* for the new project.

With *has*, the past participle *laid* is used.

✔ Workers *are laying* the *sod* in front of the new student center.

The verb *lie* means *to recline*. It does not take an object.

✔ James sometimes *lies* in bed until noon on Saturdays.

✔ The library book *lay* forgotten in the back seat of the car.

✔ Marcia said she *had lain* awake all night, worrying about her job interview.

✔ That trowel *has been lying* in the garden all winter long.

PRACTICE 2   PUZZLING PAIRS—*LAY* AND *LIE*

Underline the correct verb forms in the following sentences.

1. Gently, Leo removed the sleeping puppy from the sofa and (<u>lay</u>, laid) down to watch TV.
2. The instructor (lay, <u>laid</u>) a sheaf of papers on her desk and began to call roll.

3. When Michael is on vacation, he usually just (<u>lies</u>, lays) on the beach or goes fishing in the lake.

4. In spite of the pain in her leg, Jacinta was happy to take her first few steps down the hospital corridor because she had (<u>lain</u>, laid) in bed for too long.

5. Just (lie, <u>lay</u>) the newspaper on the desk when you are through with it.

Sit and Set

The verb s*it* means *to take a seat* or *to be located*. It does not take an object.

✔ The old men *sit* on a bench all morning, watching people pass by.

✔ A stack of newspapers *sat* on the porch, waiting to be recycled.

✔ The old car *had sat* in the underbrush for nearly a decade.

Set means *to put* or *place*. The verb *set* always takes an object; that is, you will always find an answer to the question "Set what?"

       verb   object
✔ Please *set* the *groceries* on the table.

                  verb   object
✔ At the beginning of the term, the professor *set* minimum *goals* for the class.

           verb   object
✔ The sales manager *has* not *set* a *time* for the meeting.

PRACTICE 3   PUZZLING PAIRS—*SIT* AND *SET*

Underline the correct verb forms in the following sentences.

1. Olivia's feet hurt, so she (<u>sat</u>, set) down for a few minutes.

2. Alton had (sat, <u>set</u>) his packages down for just a moment; now they were gone.

3. Before adjourning the meeting, Romonda (sat, <u>set</u>) a date and time for the next one.

4. Jermaine had (<u>sat</u>, set) in class for so long that his back began to hurt.

5. Let's (<u>sit</u>, set) on the porch and watch the sun set.

REVIEW EXERCISE 1   USING IRREGULAR VERBS

Fill in the blank with the correct form of the verb shown to the left of each question. For help, consult the list of irregular verbs in this chapter.

(lay)   1. Bernice __laid__ the meat cleaver on the counter and wiped her hands on her apron.

(burst)   2. Andrew had high hopes of a lucrative job, a large corner office, and a company expense account, but his bubble __burst__ after the first few interviews.

(fly)   3. Gracie tried to toss the pizza dough like the chef on TV, but the dough __flew__ out of her hands and landed in a shapeless mass on the dirty kitchen floor.

(put)   4. Ahmed knew he had __put__ the tickets to the game in a safe place; he just could not remember where.

(hurt)   5. The negative publicity __hurt__ the actor's reputation but enhanced his career.

(begin)   6. After the movie __began__, Hank decided he wanted a big tub of buttered popcorn.

(leave)   7. "As you depart, please don't __leave__ coats and umbrellas unless they are expensive, tasteful, and in my size," said the tour guide.

(buy)   8. Carla could not remember if she had __bought__ gas the day before.

(fight)   9. The two office mates __fought__ constantly over the setting of the thermostat.

(throw)   10. Ruby looked for the newspaper, but someone had already __thrown__ it away.

REVIEW EXERCISE 2   USING IRREGULAR VERBS

Fill in the blank with the correct form of the verb shown to the left of each question. For help, consult the list of irregular verbs in this chapter.

(catch)   1. When the young T-ball player __caught__ the ball, he looked astonished, then dropped it.

(fall)   2. Paramedics were called because someone had __fallen__ down the steps of the science building.

(give)   3. Miko said that she had __given__ her brother all of her old textbooks.

(hear)   4. Charles __heard__ a rumor that class would be canceled, so he decided not to bother going.

(hide)   5. The secret message was __hidden__ in a computer file that looked like a photograph of a leopard drinking at a watering hole.

(lay)   6. Leann __laid__ her checkbook aside, wondering where she would get the money to pay this month's bills.

(break)   7. The speaker claimed to have __broken__ a record for reading the highest number of words per minute, but he had no proof.

(go)   8. Thomas said that the power had __gone__ out for nearly an hour.

(do)   9. Keisha has __done__ this procedure many times; she can show you how.

(find)   10. Yesterday, our math instructor gave us a bonus problem and awarded an extra ten points to the person who __found__ the answer first.

REVIEW EXERCISE 3   USING IRREGULAR VERBS

Fill in the blank with the correct form of the verb shown to the left of each question. For help, consult the list of irregular verbs in this chapter.

(freeze)   1. The ground had __frozen__, and digging the hole was nearly impossible.

(choose)   2. Robert __chose__ a tempting-looking item from the appetizer tray, then realized that it was a piece of sushi.

(come)   3. The vacuum cleaner salesman saw a curtain twitch in the front window, but no one __came__ to the door.

(cut)   4. As the barber __cut__ Drew's hair, the shoulder-length locks that had been his trademark fell to the floor in a heap.

(grow)   5. Chantra __grew__ more tomatoes than she could possibly use.

(draw)   6. On his notebook, Naisu had __drawn__ a sad-looking ostrich with a drooping head and a large, round body.

(take)   7. At the beginning of the class period, Mr. Simmons __took__ a few minutes to explain the history of the computer.

(have)   8. Ayesha __had__ every reason to be angry, but she remained polite and gracious.

(know)   9. No one __knew__ how long the meeting would last, but the thick sheaf of papers in front of the chairperson was an ominous sign.

(write)   10. At the airport, Paul __wrote__ a few lines on a post card and mailed it to his brother.

REVIEW EXERCISE 4   USING IRREGULAR VERBS

Fill in the blank with the correct form of the verb shown to the left of each question. For help, consult the list of irregular verbs in this chapter.

(speak)   1. Everyone began to eat, and for a few moments, no one __spoke__ a word.

(tear)   2. Rajiv __tore__ a page from his notebook, scrawled something on it, and passed it across the aisle to Eric.

(sing)   3. Corinne had never __sung__ the song before, but she hummed along with everyone else.

(lose)   4. Has anyone found the keys that I __lost__ yesterday?

(keep)   5. When Harry lived in England, he __kept__ pigeons as a hobby.

(hold)   6. The new father __held__ the baby as if she might break.

(rise)   7. Alphonse quickly __rose__ from his chair to open the door for a woman carrying several large boxes.

(feel)   8. Every Saturday, Bridget's neighbor __felt__ the need to tune his motorcycle's engine at 6:00 A.M.

(blow)   9. During the hurricane, the wind __blew__ the roof off Lamont's storage shed.

(lie)   10. Gerard had __lain__ in bed all morning but still did not feel rested.

REVIEW EXERCISE 5   USING IRREGULAR VERBS

Fill in the blanks in the following paragraph with the correct form of the verb shown. For help, consult the list of irregular verbs in this chapter.

Holly and four of her coworkers (sit) [1] __sat__ at the lunch table and looked at their ruined food. The prankster who (eat) [2] __ate__ people's lunches had been at it again, for the fourth day in a row. Someone had (take) [3] __taken__ a bite out of Holly's sandwich, then put it back. An apple in another worker's lunch had been (eat) [4] __eaten__, and another had a bite (take) [5] __taken__ out of each of the three cookies she had brought. Another coworker looked in her Thermos and (see) [6] __saw__ that the thief had (drink) [7] __drunk__ her iced tea. "If I (think) [8] __thought__ someone was hungry, I would gladly share,"

said Holly, "but this person is just malicious."
The workers (think) [9] _thought_ about it and decided
to fight back. The next day, everyone (bring)
[10] _brought_ two lunches. The first set of lunches,
the real ones, were (hide) [11] _hidden_ in their
desk drawers. A second set of lunches was (put)
[12] _put_ in the refrigerator that (sit) [13] _sat_
in the small kitchen beside the lunch room.
Innocent-looking brown lunch bags (hold) [14] _held_
tuna sandwiches with hot sauce, specially baked
cookies with no sugar and hot pepper on the top,
and tea and coffee laced with vinegar. One of
Holly's coworkers had (bring) [15] _brought_ cat food
sandwiches; another had mixed mayonnaise with
chocolate syrup to resemble pudding. The lunches
(hold) [16] _held_ nothing poisonous, but none of
the food was appetizing. When lunchtime (come)
[17] _came_, the coworkers looked inside the bags and
(burst) [18] _burst_ out laughing. The prankster had
(take) [19] _taken_ a bite or sip of something in each
lunch bag. "I believe our prankster has (steal)
[20] _stolen_ for the last time," said Holly.

13

Verb Tenses

Verb Tenses

Verb tenses give the English language its sense of time, its sense of *when* events occur. The following timeline shows nine verb tenses, and the chart following the timeline briefly explains how each tense is used.

Verb Tense Timeline

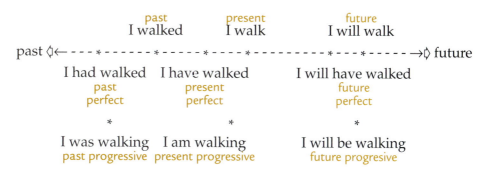

Verb Tense Chart

◊◊◊	Furthest in the past; happened before another past action.	*past perfect* *had* + *-ed* verb (past participle)	I *had walked* up the stairs, and I was out of breath.
◊◊	In the past; happened before now.	*past* *-ed* verb form (past)	I *walked* all the way around the nature trail.
◊◊	In progress during a past time.	*past progressive* was, were + *-ing* verb	I *was walking* around the trail when I saw her.
◊•	In the past but extending to the present.	*present perfect* *have* or *has* + *-ed* (past participle) verb form	I *have walked* every day for the last month. He *has walked* a mile already.
•	Happens regularly or often, or is happening now.	*present* base verb form or base verb + *-s*	I *walk* at least five miles a week. She *walks* quickly.
•	Happening now.	*present progressive* am, are, is + *-ing* verb	I *am walking* as fast as I can.
◊	Happens in the future but before another future event.	*future perfect* *will have* + *-ed* (past participle) verb form	By the time you join me on the track, I *will have walked* at least two miles.
◊◊	Happens at some time in the future.	*future* *will* + base verb	I *will walk* with you tomorrow if we both have time.
◊◊	In progress at a future time.	*future progressive* will be + *-ing* verb	I *will be walking* with you tomorrow at noon.

In English, verbs change form to show the tense of the verb, that is, to show whether the action happens in the present, past, or future.

The Simple Tenses: Present, Past, and Future

The simple tenses are past tense, present tense, and future tense. These tenses are probably the most familiar.

Present Tense

Present tense verbs show customary action or current state of being.

Present Tense of the Verb *to walk*

	Singular	Plural
First Person	I walk	we walk
Second Person	you walk	you walk
Third Person	he, she, it walks	they walk

Examples

✔ Elena **takes** her lunch break at noon every day.

✔ I **rely** on my cellular phone in case of an emergency.

Past Tense

Past tense verbs show past action. Regular verbs form their past tense by adding *ed*.

Past Tense of the Verb *to walk*

	Singular	Plural
First Person	I walked	we walked
Second Person	you walked	you walked
Third Person	he, she, it walked	they walked

Examples

✔ Jason **attended** a technical college last year.

✔ A giant fireball **appeared** in the evening sky and **streaked** toward earth.

Future Tense

Future tense verbs show planned or future action. They are formed by using *will* with the base form of the verb.

Future Tense of the Verb *to walk*

	Singular	Plural
First Person	I will walk	we will walk
Second Person	you will walk	you will walk
Third Person	he, she, it will walk	they will walk

Examples

✔ I **will call** you at your office tomorrow.

✔ Tomorrow **will be** partly cloudy with a chance of rain.

PRACTICE 1   IDENTIFYING VERB TENSES

Underline the verbs in each of the following sentences. In the blank to the left, tell whether the verb is present, past, or future tense.

Present **1.** The weather <u>is</u> not always predictable.

Past   **2.** With his overpowering fastball, the rookie pitcher quickly <u>overcame</u> his fear of batters.

Past   **3.** The large cargo jet <u>rumbled</u> down the long runway.

Future   **4.** For a baseball player, spring <u>will</u> always <u>be</u> a season of expectation and excitement.

Present **5.** During a tornado, the barometric pressure <u>drops</u> dramatically.

The Perfect Tenses: Present Perfect, Past Perfect, and Future Perfect

The **perfect tenses** also show present, past, and future action, but they are different in form from the simple tenses.

Present Perfect Tense

Present perfect tense (has or have + past participle verb form) shows past action that often extends into the present.

Present Perfect Tense of the Verb *to walk*

	Singular	Plural
First Person	I have walked	we have walked
Second Person	you have walked	you have walked
Third Person	he, she, it has walked	they have walked

Examples

✔ Maria *has gone* to the mall.

The sentence implies that Maria is still at the mall.

✔ We *have reviewed* your application and will call you soon.

The sentence suggests that the review is over, but the application process is ongoing.

Past Perfect Tense

Verbs in the *past perfect tense* show a past action that happened before another, more recent past action. Past perfect tense is formed by adding *had* to the past participle verb form.

Past Perfect Tense of the Verb *to walk*

	Singular	Plural
First Person	I had walked	we had walked
Second Person	you had walked	you had walked
Third Person	he, she, it had walked	they had walked

Examples

✔ The detectives *had searched* the scene several times, but yesterday they found the evidence they needed.

✔ We invited Stanley to go to lunch with us, but he *had* already *eaten*.

Future Perfect Tense

Future perfect tense (will have + past participle verb form) shows an action that will have been completed by the time another future action occurs.

Future Perfect Tense of the Verb *to walk*

	Singular	Plural
First Person	I will have walked	we will have walked
Second Person	you will have walked	you will have walked
Third Person	he, she, it will have walked	they will have walked

Examples

✔ By sundown, *we will have driven* five hundred miles.

The drive will be completed by the time another future event—sunset—takes place.

✔ By the time you return, I *will have finished* the entire job.

PRACTICE 2   IDENTIFYING PERFECT TENSES

Underline the verbs in each of the following sentences. In the blank to the left, tell whether the verb is present perfect, past perfect, or future perfect tense.

Present Perfect **1.** Rain has fallen in the countryside for the last eight days.

Future Perfect **2.** By morning, I will have written eight pages in my journal.

Past Perfect **3.** Harry had talked to the coach several times about the lengthy practice sessions.

Past Perfect **4.** Penelope had applied for the teaching position last fall, but she did not receive a job offer until yesterday.

Present Perfect **5.** Luis has embraced the philosophy of live and let live.

The Progressive Tenses: Present, Past, and Future Progressive

The **progressive tenses** usually show ongoing action in the present, past, or future: *am working, were expecting, will be traveling.* Progressive tenses use the present, past, or future form of the verb *to be* plus the -ing form of the verb (the present participle).

Present Progressive

The present progressive tense uses a present-tense form of the verb *to be* along with the *-ing* form of the verb. The verb *work* is shown here in the present progressive tense.

	Singular	Plural
First Person	I am working	we are working
Second Person	you are working	you are working
Third Person	he, she, it is working	they are working

Present Progressive to Describe Ongoing Action

In the examples that follow, present progressive is used to describe ongoing action in the present.

Examples

✔ Olivia is thinking about changing jobs. (She is considering the idea now.)

✔ Jake is working on his master's degree in engineering. (He is working on the degree now.)

Present Progressive to Describe Future Action

The present progressive tense also shows action that will take place in the future. When present progressive tense is used to indicate future action, there will usually be a clue in the sentence, the paragraph, or the situation to show that the action is a future one.

Examples

✔ Karen *is taking* her vacation next month. (*Next month* indicates that the action will happen in the future.)

✔ Robert *is hosting* a dinner for his friends on Friday night.

Which words indicate that the dinner will be in the future?

Past Progressive

The past progressive tense uses a past-tense form of the verb *to be* along with the *-ing* form of the verb. The verb *work* is shown here in the past progressive tense.

	Singular	Plural
First Person	I was working	we were working
Second Person	you were working	you were working
Third Person	he, she, it was working	they were working

Examples

✔ The sky *was becoming* cloudy

✔ The humidity and the heat *were beginning* to make Lars uncomfortable.

Future Progressive

	Singular	Plural
First Person	I will be working	we will be working
Second Person	you will be working	you will be working
Third Person	he, she, it will be working	they will be working

Examples

✔ The bus *will be arriving* in Albuquerque at noon.

✔ Don't call after ten; I *will be sleeping*.

PRACTICE 3   IDENTIFYING PROGRESSIVE TENSES

Underline the verbs in each of the following sentences. In the blank to the left, tell whether the verb is present progressive, past progressive, or future progressive tense.

<u>Future Progressive</u>   **1.** The bus <u>will be leaving</u> the school's main parking lot promptly at 7:00 A.M.

<u>Present Progressive</u>   **2.** The lost hikers <u>are firing</u> flares, hoping for a quick rescue.

<u>Past Progressive</u>   **3.** The small green frog <u>was hopping</u> from plant to plant.

<u>Past Progressive</u>   **4.** Two enormous dogs <u>were barking</u> at the frightened burglar.

<u>Present Progressive</u>   **5.** Old Mossy, too weary to even chase a squirrel, <u>is napping</u> under a tall chestnut tree.

Avoiding Unnecessary Tense Shifts

Writers and speakers of English shift between tenses as easily and smoothly as drivers shift from one gear to another. A writer discussing something that is happening now may want to refer to the past for an example, or look to the future to predict what will happen. These tense shifts are necessary and logical. Following are some examples of logical and necessary tense shifts.

Necessary shifts:

✔ Harold *is* here today, but he *will be* on vacation next week.

    present   future

✔ I *have looked* over your offer, and I *am considering* it carefully.

    present perfect   present

✔ By tomorrow, Marcia *will have finished* the book that she *started* yesterday.

    future perfect   past

However, unnecessary shifts are illogical and should be avoided. The most common error in verb tense is an unnecessary shift from past tense to present tense. It is easy for writers to become so caught up in the past event that they are describing that it becomes, at least temporarily, a part of "the now." Unnecessary shifts from present to past, although not quite as common, are also errors that should be avoided. Look at the following examples:

Unnecessary shift from past to present:

       past tense   present tense

✗ Renata *planned* to study for her test last night, but she *falls* asleep with the book in her hand.

Unnecessary shift corrected:

       past tense   past tense

✔ Renata *planned* to study for her test last night, but she *fell* asleep with the book in her hand.

Unnecessary shift from past to present:

       past tense   present tense

✗ When Jason *arrived* at his house, he *notices* the front door standing open.

Unnecessary shift corrected:

       past tense   past tense

✔ When Jason *arrived* at his house, he *noticed* the front door standing open.

Unnecessary shift from present to past:

       present tense   past tense

✗ Kerry *walks* almost every day and *tried* to walk at least a mile each day.

Unnecessary shift corrected:

       present tense   present tense

✔ Kerry *walks* almost every day and *tries* to walk at least a mile each day.

PRACTICE 4   IDENTIFYING NECESSARY AND UNNECESSARY TENSE SHIFTS

In the blank provided, underline the verbs and identify the tense shifts in each of the following sentences as *necessary* or *unnecessary*.

<u>Unnecessary</u> **1.** Martha expertly <u>fixed</u> the hole in the kitchen wall while her husband <u>watches</u>.

<u>Necessary</u> **2.** John <u>has finished</u> the evening cabinet-making course, and he <u>hopes</u> to make a large cabinet for his stereo.

<u>Unnecessary</u> **3.** The haunting sound of an owl's cry <u>echoes</u> throughout the forest as the campers <u>paused</u> to listen.

<u>Necessary</u>   **4.** Francine <u>walks</u> her Irish setter, Rufus, every day, but someone else <u>will walk</u> him today since Francine is out of town.

<u>Unnecessary</u>   **5.** The judge <u>heard</u> the closing arguments and then <u>gives</u> the jury its final instructions.

PRACTICE 5   USING VERB TENSES

In each sentence, underline the correct verb tense.

1. Rudy arrived at work half an hour late and (finds, <u>found</u>) his boss waiting for him at the door.

2. Harold felt full and uncomfortable from the four slices of pizza he (eats, <u>ate</u>) an hour ago.

3. Charlene complains every day about the temperature in the office, but no one ever (<u>listens</u>, listened).

4. When her doorbell rang, Alicia (looks, <u>looked</u>) out the window and saw a short, well-dressed man carrying a large vacuum cleaner.

5. The convenience store sells bread but (<u>stocks</u>, stocked) only one brand.

PRACTICE 6   CORRECTING TENSE SHIFTS

In each sentence, cross out the incorrect verb and correct the unnecessary shift from past to present or from present to past.

1. Florence made a big pot of baked beans with molasses and ~~takes~~ it to the family reunion.

   <u>took</u>

2. The college library opens every weekday at 8:00 A.M. and ~~closed~~ at midnight.

   <u>closes</u>

3. Barry's insomnia began after he ~~starts~~ watching *Chiller Thriller Theater* every night on television.

   <u>started</u>

4. The light changed from red to green, and the impatient driver behind Bernice ~~honks~~ his horn loudly.

   <u>honked</u>

5. The audience was caught up in the tension of the play, but just at the crucial moment, someone's beeper ~~goes~~ off.

   <u>went</u>

REVIEW EXERCISE 1   IDENTIFYING VERB TENSES

In the blank to the left, identify the tense of the italicized verb.

_Past_____ **1.** Construction on the new bridge *halted* yesterday.

_Future_____ **2.** The inspectors *will return* tomorrow.

_Past Perfect_____ **3.** I *had helped* my neighbor with his sickly lawn.

_Future Perfect_____ **4.** I *will have walked* three miles to the nearest gas station by noon.

_Present Progressive___ **5.** Incidentally, your shirt *is missing* a button.

_Past_____ **6.** The expensive bottle of sparkling water *tasted* flat and bitter.

_Future Progressive____ **7.** For maximum effect, the fire baton twirlers *will be performing* after dark.

_Present Perfect_____ **8.** Helen *has added* her friend's name to her e-mail address book.

_Past_____ **9.** Using one of Henny Youngman's books, Hogan *demonstrated* the art of telling one-liners.

_Present_____ **10.** Please *remove* all the books from the top shelf.

REVIEW EXERCISE 2   IDENTIFYING VERB TENSES

In the blank following each sentence, identify the tense of each italicized verb.

1. As the sun *sets,* John *will finish* painting his house.

   _Present   Future_____

2. I *will think* about attending the reunion only if you *are planning* to go.

   _Future   Present Progressive_____

3. I *recognize* your right to enjoy the great outdoors, but I *reject* your insistence on dragging me with you into the wilderness.

   _Present   Present_____

4. As the ship *pulled* up alongside the dock, the onlookers *cheered.*

   _Past   Past_____

5. Talking to her father, Jasmine *discovered* that the olive tree *bears* edible fruit only after a very long period of careful cultivation.

   _Past   Present_____

REVIEW EXERCISE 3   CORRECTING TENSE SHIFTS

In the blank following each sentence, correct the unnecessary shift in verb tense.

1. Joaquin *met* his parents at the airport when they *arrive* yesterday morning.

    arrived

2. As the storm *broke*, the sun's rays *chase* the clouds from the sky.

    chased

3. The experiment *was* not *working*, so the scientist *decides* to scrap the entire project.

    decided

4. The aroma from the restaurant *enticed* the passersby and *draws* them inside.

    drew

5. To accommodate the customer, the store *remained* opened ten minutes longer, but the customer *decides* not to buy anything.

    decided

REVIEW EXERCISE 4   CORRECTING TENSE SHIFTS

In the blank following each sentence, correct the unnecessary shift in verb tense.

1. The International Student Association held its first meeting on September 5, and a reception *follows* in the Walker Room on the second floor of the Student Center.

    followed

2. The building shown in the photograph housed the city's animal shelter until it *is* torn down last year.

    was

3. Yesterday morning, Carlos washed and waxed his truck, and then it *rains* that afternoon.

    rained

4. A stack of books sat on a table along with a sign that read "Free—please take one." Ursula *stops* to look, then tucked one of the books into her bag.

    stopped

5. The dishwasher made a low gurgling sound, and soapy water *begins* to gush onto the floor.

    began

REVIEW EXERCISE 5   USING VERB TENSES

Use the present, past, or future tense of the verb in parentheses to fill each blank following the paragraph.

> To ancient Greeks, the mythological character Pandora [1](represent) human curiosity. According to legend, the gods [2](give) Pandora gifts such as beauty and the power of persuasion. They also [3](present) her with a beautiful treasure chest and [4](tell) her, "Whatever happens, [5](do) not open this box." Every day, Pandora [6](look) at the beautiful box and [7](wonder) what was inside. At first, she [8](satisfy) her curiosity with thoughts such as "Maybe I [9](open) it tomorrow." Finally, she [10](give) in to the curiosity that [11](consume) her. "I [12](take) just a peek, and then I [13](shut) it," she told herself. With trembling hands, she [14](open) the box slightly. But that was enough. Out of the box [15](fly) all the troubles of humankind: misery, worry, hunger, poverty, sickness, and death. One fluttering, bright creature [16](remain) in the box: hope. To this day, hope [17](sustain) humanity when these troubles arise. Today, people [18](use) the expression "to open a Pandora's box" when they [19](mean) that investigating a situation may bring trouble. The expression [20](mean) roughly the same thing as "opening a can of worms," but it is much more elegantly phrased.

1. represented
2. gave
3. presented
4. told
5. do
6. looked
7. wondered
8. satisfied
9. will open
10. gave
11. consumed
12. will take
13. will shut
14. opened
15. flew
16. remained
17. sustains
18. use
19. mean
20. means

14

Coordination and Subordination

Chain Letter

Dear Friend,

This is a chain letter. It is composed of a chain of simple sentences. Each sentence has one subject and one verb. Each sentence conveys one idea. Each idea is expressed in the same way. The writer has fallen into a pattern. This pattern becomes monotonous to the reader. The reader wants to scream.

If you break the chain, you will have good luck. Your writing will flow more smoothly, and your readers will not scream. In this paragraph, for instance, the chain of simple sentences has been broken using techniques that you will learn in this chapter. Break the chain and set your writing free!

Sincerely,

One Who Wishes You Well

Writing Effective Sentences

When you learned to write, you started by expressing one idea per sentence. Now, your ideas are more complex. Your sentence structure, too, should become more sophisticated to handle more complex ideas. If you are holding on to the habit of expressing yourself in a chain of one-idea sentences, this chapter will give you the tools of **coordination** and **subordination** that will help you to break the chain forever.

Connecting Ideas Through Coordination

Often, ideas expressed in short, simple sentences can be joined to make a more effective sentence. One way to connect sentences is called *coordination.* Coordination can be done in two ways: by using a comma and a FANBOYS conjunction, or by using a semicolon and a joining word.

Comma and FANBOYS

FANBOYS conjunctions, more commonly called *coordinating* conjunctions, are used with a comma to connect two independent clauses. Remember that a **clause** is a grammatical unit that contains a subject and a verb and that an **independent clause** can stand alone as a sentence. The nonsense word FANBOYS stands for all seven coordinating conjunctions: for, and, nor, but, or, yet, so.

This is the pattern used when a FANBOYS conjunction is used with a comma to connect two independent clauses. The comma goes before the FANBOYS conjunction.

Independent clause, and independent clause.

Examples

Marcus scanned the crowded cafeteria. (independent clause)

He did not see his friend Hannah. (independent clause)

The preceding two independent clauses can be connected with a FANBOYS and a comma:

Marcus scanned the crowded cafeteria, but he did not see his friend Hannah.

PRACTICE 1   CONNECTING SENTENCES WITH FANBOYS

Connect each of the following sentence pairs with a comma and a FANBOYS.

1. In the darkened theater, a cell phone began to ring.
    Someone quickly silenced it.

In the darkened theater, a cell phone began to ring, but someone quickly si-
lenced it.

2. David's girlfriend tells him that he is lazy.
    David says he's just an expert at conserving energy.

    David's girlfriend tells him that he is lazy, but David says he's just an expert at
    conserving energy.

3. The parking lot was crowded.
    The library was packed with students studying for finals.

    The parking lot was crowded, and the library was packed with students study-
    ing for finals.

4. Patricia loves her morning cup of coffee from the coffee shop.
    Rising coffee prices are not about to make her give it up.

    Patricia loves her morning cup of coffee from the coffee shop, and rising coffee
    prices are not about to make her give it up.

5. Alisha may live with her parents until the end of the term.
    She may find a roommate and rent an apartment.

    Alisha may live with her parents until the end of the term, or she may find a
    roommate and rent an apartment.

Semicolon and Joining Word

Another method of coordination is using a semicolon and a joining word.
As with a comma and FANBOYS conjunction, a complete sentence (an independent clause) will appear on both sides of the semicolon.

Independent clause; therefore, independent clause.

Examples

✔   Mary thought she would have extra money left over at the end of the
    month.

✔   She did not anticipate having to buy a new battery for her car.

The two separate sentences can be combined with a semicolon and a
joining word.

✔ Mary thought she would have extra money left over at the end of the month; **however,** she did not anticipate having to buy a new battery for her car.

The joining words also function as *transitional expressions,* underscoring the relationship between the two clauses. A list of joining words commonly used with semicolons follows.

Joining Words Used with a Semicolon

accordingly	furthermore	meanwhile
also	however	nevertheless
as a result	in addition	of course
besides	in fact	on the other hand
finally	instead	therefore

PRACTICE 2   CONNECTING SENTENCES WITH A SEMICOLON AND JOINING WORD

Connect each of the following sentence pairs with a semicolon, a joining word from the preceding list, and a comma.

1. Sunny knew she needed to study for the test.
    She resisted the temptation to go out for pizza with her friends.

    Sunny knew she needed to study for the test; therefore, she resisted the temptation to go out for pizza with her friends.

2. Tony agreed to help Felicia move.
    He did not realize she had so much furniture.

    Tony agreed to help Felicia move; however, he did not realize she had so much furniture.

3. The woman who sat next to Bart on the plane insisted on telling him her life's story.
    He pretended to go to sleep to avoid her chatter.

    The woman who sat next to Bart on the plane insisted on telling him her life's story; finally, he pretended to go to sleep to avoid her chatter.

4. Rain came down in torrents.
    Catherine could barely see to drive.

    Rain came down in torrents; as a result, Catherine could barely see to drive.

5. Julie tried desperately to start her stalled car.
   The driver behind her began to honk the horn noisily.

   Julie tried desperately to start her stalled car; meanwhile, the driver behind her
   began to honk the horn noisily.

Connecting Ideas Through Subordination

Another way of connecting ideas is through **subordination.** Placing a **dependent word** such as *because, although, if, when,* or *after* in front of an independent clause makes it a **dependent** or **subordinate** clause, one that can no longer stand on its own as a sentence. It must be connected to another idea that is stated as a complete sentence. It will then *depend on* the sentence it is attached to and can no longer be separated from it. Two examples are shown here using the dependent word *because.*

Example 1

Rashida had no time to sit down for breakfast.

She picked up a banana and a granola bar and walked out the door.

If the dependent clause acts as an introductory clause, a comma follows it.

Because <u>dependent clause</u>, <u>independent clause</u>.

✔ **Because** Rashida had no time to sit down for breakfast, she picked up a banana and a granola bar and walked out the door.

Example 2

Cars were backed up for miles on the interstate.

A tractor-trailer truck had turned over, blocking two lanes.

<u>Independent clause</u> because <u>dependent clause</u>.

✔ Cars were backed up for miles on the interstate **because** a tractor-trailer truck had turned over, blocking two lanes.

A list of dependent words is shown next.

Dependent Words

after	even though	what
although	if	whatever
as	once	when
as if	since	whenever
as long	so that	where
as soon as	that	wherever
as though	though	which
because	unless	while
before	until	who

PRACTICE 3   CONNECTING SENTENCES WITH DEPENDENT WORDS

Choosing from the preceding list of dependent words, connect each sentence pair using the following pattern:

Dependent word <u>dependent clause</u>, <u>independent clause</u>.

The first one is done for you.

1. Kyla said she could not afford to go to school.
   Her friend told her she could not afford not to.

   When Kyla said she could not afford to go to school, her friend told her she
   could not afford not to.

2. Movies and televison have romanticized the pioneers' journey west.
   Pioneers traveled for four to six months in a small wagon with limited food and no baths.

   Though movies and televison have romanticized the pioneers' journey west, pioneers
   traveled for four to six months in a small wagon with limited food and no baths.

3. Johannes Gutenburg invented the printing press in the fifteenth century.
   He provided a way for books to be widely distributed in large numbers.

   When Johannes Gutenburg invented the printing press in the fifteenth century,
   he provided a way for books to be widely distributed in large numbers.

4. The forecast called for snow.

   The grocery store was crowded with people stocking up on food.

   Because the forecast called for snow, the grocery store was crowded with peo-

   ple stocking up on food.

5. Ken sat on an outdoor bench eating his lunch.

   A stray dog looked at him hopefully.

   As Ken sat on an outdoor bench eating his lunch, a stray dog looked at him

   hopefully.

PRACTICE 4   CONNECTING SENTENCES WITH DEPENDENT WORDS

Choosing from the preceding list of dependent words, connect each sentence pair using the following pattern:

Independent clause dependent word dependent clause.

The first one is done for you.

1. State troopers were patrolling the highways.

   Heavy traffic was expected on the holiday weekend.

   State troopers were patrolling the highways because heavy traffic was expected

   on the holiday weekend.

2. Lucia had just fallen asleep.

   The telephone rang, startling her out of a dream.

   Lucia had just fallen asleep when the telephone rang, startling her out of a

   dream.

3. Glover gripped the steering wheel in frustration.

   Traffic on the interstate ground to a complete stop.

   Glover gripped the steering wheel in frustration as traffic on the interstate

   ground to a complete stop.

4. Brett's muscles were sore and tired.

   He had spent an entire day doing construction work.

   Brett's muscles were sore and tired because he had spent an entire day doing

   construction work.

5. Amelia enjoyed her nieces and nephews.

She did not think she was ready to have children.

Amelia enjoyed her nieces and nephews even though she did not think she was

ready to have children.

Creating Emphasis Through Subordination

Dependent words also act as transitional words, showing the relationship between the ideas. Using dependent clauses helps to downplay one idea while emphasizing another. Usually, the idea expressed in the independent clause is of greater importance, while the idea in the dependent clause is of lesser importance.

Examples

✔ Although the work is dangerous, the job pays well.
emphasis on the pay

✔ Although the job pays well, the work is dangerous.
emphasis on the danger

✔ A cheer went up from the crowd as the home team scored the winning run.
emphasis on the cheer

✔ The home team scored the winning run as a cheer went up from the crowd.
emphasis on the run

PRACTICE 5   USING DEPENDENT WORDS TO EMPHASIZE IDEAS

Choosing from the preceding list of dependent words, connect each sentence pair. The idea that is given less emphasis should be introduced by a dependent word. The first one is done for you.

1. Teresa needed the money.

She agreed to work a second shift.   ✔ *Emphasize this idea.*

Because Teresa needed the money, she agreed to work a second shift.

2. The entire day stretched invitingly ahead of Jenna.
   She had no idea what she wanted to do. ✔ *Emphasize this idea.*

   Though the entire day stretched invitingly ahead of Jenna, she had no idea

   what she wanted to do.

3. Lin Yao was excited by the trip. ✔ *Emphasize this idea.*
   She had never traveled by train.

   Lin Yao was excited by the trip because she had never traveled by train.

4. The bananas were soft and speckled with brown. ✔ *Emphasize this idea.*
   Cameron had just bought them yesterday.

   The bananas were soft and speckled with brown although Cameron had just

   bought them yesterday.

5. Anna went to the video store to rent a movie.
   She could not find anything she wanted. ✔ *Emphasize this idea.*

   Although Anna went to the video store to rent a movie, she could not find any-

   thing she wanted.

REVIEW EXERCISE 1   CONNECTING SENTENCES USING COORDINATION

Connect each sentence pair using *coordination.* Use a comma and a FANBOYS *or* a
semicolon, a joining word, and a comma.

1. Rahim popped a compact disc into his computer.
   He listened to his favorite music as he wrote his research paper.

   Rahim popped a compact disc into his computer, and he listened to his

   favorite music as he wrote his research paper.

2. Horace had expected that traffic would be heavy in Atlanta.
   He had not bargained for the drivers who were speeding, weaving in and out
   of traffic, and following an inch from his bumper.

   Horace had expected that traffic would be heavy in Atlanta, yet he had not

   bargained for the drivers who were speeding, weaving in and out of traffic, and

   following an inch from his bumper.

3. Economists tried to account for the sudden improvement in the economy. Politicians scrambled to take credit.

Economists tried to account for the sudden improvement in the economy, and

politicians scrambled to take credit.

4. Piano keys used to be made of ivory from elephant tusks. They are now made of plastic.

Piano keys used to be made of ivory from elephant tusks; however, they are

now made of plastic.

5. People used to have to wait for a daily paper or for the six o'clock news program for a news update. News is now available 24 hours a day in the Internet and on television.

People used to have to wait for a daily paper or for the six o'clock news pro-

gram for a news update, but news is now available 24 hours a day in the Inter-

net and on television.

REVIEW EXERCISE 2   CONNECTING SENTENCES USING SUBORDINATION

Connect the two sentences using *subordination*.

1. Tina does her grocery shopping after most people have gone to bed. The store is never crowded late at night.

Tina does her grocery shopping after most people have gone to bed because

the store is never crowded late at night.

2. Kim's children were bored. She took them to the miniature golf course on Saturday morning.

Since Kim's children were bored, she took them to the miniature golf course on

Saturday morning.

3. Sanjay carefully removed the casserole dish from the oven. It slipped from his fingers and shattered on the floor.

As Sanjay carefully removed the casserole dish from the oven, it slipped from

his fingers and shattered on the floor.

4. Nick had always wanted to try carpentry.

    He signed up for a woodworking class.

    Since Nick had always wanted to try carpentry, he signed up for a woodwork-

    ing class.

5. The applicant seemed charming and capable at the job interview.

    She proved to be undependable and careless.

    Though the applicant seemed charming and capable at the job interview, she

    proved to be undependable and careless.

**REVIEW EXERCISE 3   CONNECTING SENTENCES USING COORDINATION
                        OR SUBORDINATION**

Connect each sentence pair using *coordination* or *subordination.*

1. A little stress can enhance a person's ability to perform a task.

    Too much stress can impair performance.

    A little stress can enhance a person's ability to perform a task; however, too

    much stress can impair performance.

2. Most people go through life with the name their parents gave them.

    In Hong Kong, some people drop their given names and go by exotic names
    such as Komix, Zeus, Boogie, or Maverick.

    Most people go through life with the name their parents gave them, yet in

    Hong Kong, some people drop their given names and go by exotic names such

    as Komix, Zeus, Boogie, or Maverick.

3. The coffee was brewing.

    The pleasant aroma filled the kitchen.

    The coffee was brewing, and the pleasant aroma filled the kitchen.

4. Arlene came to work after a two-week vacation.

    She had 147 e-mail messages waiting for her.

    When Arlene came to work after a two-week vacation, she had 147 e-mail mes-

    sages waiting for her.

5. Laney had trouble concentrating on her work.

   The room was too hot and muggy.

   > Laney had trouble concentrating on her work because the room was too hot
   >
   > and muggy.

REVIEW EXERCISE 4   CONNECTING SENTENCES USING COORDINATION OR SUBORDINATION

Connect each sentence pair using *coordination* or *subordination*.

1. The line at the box office stretched around the theater.

   People shivered in the cold and waited for the line to move.

   > The line at the box office stretched around the theater, and people shivered in
   >
   > the cold and waited for the line to move.

2. The wild cactus grew large and began to flower.

   The carefully planted azaleas withered and died.

   > The wild cactus grew large and began to flower; however, the carefully planted
   >
   > azaleas withered and died.

3. Melva answered the phone and listened impatiently.

   Her cereal grew soggy on the kitchen table.

   > Melva answered the phone and listened impatiently as her cereal grew soggy on
   >
   > the kitchen table.

4. The cat ran quickly away from the tree.

   An offended bluebird followed, screeching and flapping.

   > As the cat ran quickly away from the tree, an offended bluebird followed,
   >
   > screeching and flapping.

5. Lightning heats the air that surrounds it to more that 50,000 degrees Fahrenheit.

   The superheated air rapidly expands, causing the sonic boom that we call thunder.

Lightning heats the air that surrounds it to more that 50,000 degrees Fahren-

heit, and the superheated air rapidly expands, causing the sonic boom that we

call thunder.

**REVIEW EXERCISE 5   CONNECTING SENTENCES USING COORDINATION
OR SUBORDINATION**

There are twenty sentences in the paragraph. Connect the sentences in this paragraph using *coordination* and *subordination,* so that you have no more than ten sentences when you are through. Be sure to use both techniques.

[1]My cousin Rodrigo has a very busy life. [2]He
recently decided to find ways of saving time.
[3]He makes coffee every morning to start the day.
[4]He does not sit and drink it while reading a
newspaper, as many people do. [5]Instead, he carefully
pours it in a plastic mug. [6]Then he drinks it while
he is showering, to save time. [7]As he sits in class,
he reads the assigned work in the textbook. [8]A tape
recorder on his desk records the professor's
lecture. [9]He drives to work after class. [10]He plays
back the tape and listens to the lecture. [11]At work,
he tries to remember the key points of the lecture.
[12]He sells stereo equipment and compact disks.
[13]Sometimes he gets odd looks from his customers.
[14]He tells them that the Romans were able to build
the Colosseum because they invented concrete or
informs them that flatworms are composed of three
basic cell layers. [15]He breaks for lunch at work.
[16]He saves time by eating a lunch brought from home
and studying during his lunch break. [17]At home, he
studies, lays out all his clothes, and makes his
lunch for the next day. [18]He goes to sleep and
starts the whole routine over the next morning.
[19]Rodrigo may make efficient use of his time. [20]He
leads a stressful life.

[1]My cousin Rodrigo has a very busy life, so he recently decided to find ways of

saving time. [2]He makes coffee every morning to start the day, but he does not

sit and drink it while reading a newspaper, as many people do. [3]Instead, he carefully pours it in a plastic mug, and then he drinks it while he is showering, to save time. [4]As he sits in class, he reads the assigned work in the textbook while a tape recorder on his desk records the professor's lecture. [5]He drives to work after class while he plays back the tape and listens to the lecture. [6]At work, he tries to remember the key points of the lecture while he sells stereo equipment and compact disks. [7]Sometimes he gets odd looks from his customers when he tells them that the Romans were able to build the Colosseum because they invented concrete or informs them that flatworms are composed of three basic cell layers. [8]When he breaks for lunch at work, he saves time by eating a lunch brought from home and studying during his lunch break. [9]At home, he studies, lays out all his clothes, and makes his lunch for the next day; then he goes to sleep and starts the whole routine over the next morning.

[10]Rodrigo may make efficient use of his time; however, he leads a stressful life.

15

Writing Concise Sentences

> "I have made this letter longer than usual because I lack the time to make it short."
>
> —Blaise Pascal, *Lettres Provinciales* [1656–1657], no. 16

Making Sentences Concise

Blaise Pascal was a seventeenth-century mathematician. The quotation in the box above, however, shows that Pascal knew a bit about writing, too. As Pascal's words suggest, expressing ideas concisely is likely to take time and effort. The result—an idea expressed simply and straightforwardly—is worth the effort. Conciseness is one of the cornerstones of good writing.

Two ways to make sentences concise are to combine short and simple sentences and to use verbal phrases to convey ideas. Look first at the following examples of short, simple sentences combined for more concise expression of ideas.

Example 1

✗ I bought a CD. It was a used CD. It was called *Polka Party*. I found it at a yard sale. It only cost me a quarter. I thought it would be a good gag gift. I plan to give it to my friend. My friend's name is Jason. (Eight sentences, forty-nine words.)

✔ At a yard sale, I bought a used CD called *Polka Party* for a quarter. I thought it would make a good gag gift for my friend Jason. (Two sentences, twenty-eight words.)

The second of these examples represents a "savings" of twenty-one words and six sentences. No information has been left out, and the information is more logically connected.

Example 2

✗ Keshia approached the front desk of the library. She was carefully balancing a stack of books in front of her. She had twelve books in all. She set the books on the counter. Two of them slid off and landed on the floor. They landed in front of the librarian. (Six sentences, fifty words.)

✔ Keshia approached the front desk of the library, carefully balancing a stack of twelve books. As she set the books on the counter, two slid off and landed on the floor in front of the librarian. (Two sentences, thirty-six words.)

PRACTICE 1   WRITING CONCISE SENTENCES

In each of the following numbered items, combine the four ideas into one concise sentence. Make sure that the sentence expresses the idea fully in as few words as possible.

1. Perry started his car.
   The car was a Toyota.
   The Toyota was blue.
   Perry backed out of the driveway.

   Perry started his blue Toyota and backed out of the driveway.

2. Stadium officials reported attendance.
   They reported attendance at baseball games.
   Attendance at the stadium had increased.
   It had increased for the fourth year in a row.

   For the fourth year in a row, stadium officials reported increased attendance at baseball games.

3. Wade wrote a note.
   He wrote it on the cover of his notebook.

He wrote it to remind himself of a history test.

The history test was on Tuesday.

Wade wrote a note on the cover of his notebook to remind himself of a history

test on Tuesday.

4. Rhonda felt a pain.

The pain was sudden.

It was severe.

It was in her right side.

Rhonda felt a sudden, severe pain in her right side.

5. There was a poster hanging on the wall.

The wall was in the classroom.

The poster was faded.

The poster showed the Eiffel Tower.

On the classroom wall hung a faded poster of the Eiffel Tower.

Using Verbal Phrases

Verbal phrases can make your writing more concise by helping you to combine ideas. They can help you strengthen your ability to write varied, interesting sentences. A verbal phrase is a word group that begins with an -*ing* verb (the present participle) or an -*ed/-en* verb (the past participle). Often, a verbal phrase can be used instead of an entire sentence.

-*ing* Verbal Phrases

Sometimes, an idea expressed in two sentences can be compressed by converting one of the sentences into an -*ing* phrase. Look at the following examples:

The children rode the roller coaster. They screamed with delight.

One of these past-tense sentences can be changed to an -*ing* modifier.

✔ *Riding the roller coaster,* the children screamed with delight.

LaShana gazed at the moon. She wished she had a telescope.

One of these past-tense sentences can be changed to an *-ing* modifier.

✔   *Gazing at the moon,* LaShana wished she had a telescope.

PRACTICE 2   USING *-ING* PHRASES

In each of the following sentence pairs, convert one of the sentences to an *-ing* verbal phrase and combine the two sentences into a single sentence.

1.   The blue van sped past at a high rate of speed.
      It swerved dangerously on the wet pavement.

      Swerving dangerously on the wet pavement, the blue van sped past at a high

      rate of speed.

2.   Vishal took a peppermint disk from the candy jar.
      He unwrapped it and popped it in his mouth.

      Taking a peppermint disk from the candy jar, Vishal unwrapped it and popped

      it in his mouth.

3.   Cathy opened the tool box.
      She pulled out a pair of pliers.

      Opening the tool box, Cathy pulled out a pair of pliers.

4.   Ari picked up the remote control.
      He turned on the television.

      Picking up the remote control, Ari turned on the television.

5.   My neighbors keep me awake.
      They argue and yell in the middle of the night.

      My neighbors argue and yell in the middle of the night, keeping me awake.

-ed/-en Verbal Phrases

Sometimes, an idea expressed in two sentences can be compressed by converting one of the sentences into an *-ed/-en* phrase. Make *-ed/-en* phrases from *passive-voice constructions*—*is, are, was,* or *were* plus the *-ed/-en* verb form. Look at the following examples:

The student was disappointed by her grade.

She withdrew from the class.

✔ *Disappointed by her grade,* the student withdrew from the class.

The apple trees were beaten by the storm.

They dropped ripe, red fruit onto the ground.

✔ *Beaten by the storm,* the apple trees dropped ripe, red fruit onto the ground.

PRACTICE 3   USING *-ED/-EN* PHRASES

In each of the following sentence pairs, convert one of the sentences to an *-ed/-en* verbal phrase to make one sentence.

1. Katrina was captivated by the tiny, yellow puppy.
    She decided to take him home.

    Captivated by the tiny, yellow puppy, Katrina decided to take him home.

2. The pie was baked to a golden brown.
    It had a flaky crust and a tasty, sweet filling.

    Baked to a golden brown, the pie had a flaky crust and a tasty, sweet filling.

3. The photograph was yellowed and cracked around the edges.
    It showed Corinne's great-grandparents on their wedding day.

    Yellowed and cracked around the edges, the photograph showed Corinne's

    great-grandparents on their wedding day.

4. The flag was hung from a pole on the front porch.
    It snapped and fluttered in the strong breeze.

    Hung from a pole on the front porch, the flag snapped and fluttered in the

    strong breeze.

5. Lavarius was invited to serve as a summer intern at the local newspaper.
    He abandoned his plans to work at the Fin and Feather restaurant.

    Invited to serve as a summer intern at the local newspaper, Lavarius aban-

    doned his plans to work at the Fin and Feather restaurant.

REVIEW EXERCISE 1   WRITING CONCISE SENTENCES

In each of the following numbered items, combine the four ideas into one concise sentence. Make sure that the sentence expresses the idea fully but uses as few words as possible.

1. There was an article in the newspaper.

   The newspaper was called the *Daily Sun.*

   The article was about the spread of a virus.

   The virus was called the West Nile virus.

   There was an article in the *Daily Sun* about the spread of the West Nile virus.

2. It was midnight.

   Gavin heard music.

   The music was coming from the apartment next door.

   The music was loud.

   At midnight, Gavin heard loud music coming from the apartment next door.

3. The workers stopped.

   They stopped at noon.

   They stopped for lunch.

   They stopped when a whistle blew.

   When the noon whistle blew, the workers stopped for lunch.

4. The paint was on the house.

   The paint was faded.

   The paint was peeled.

   It was in that condition from exposure to the sun.

   The house's paint was faded and peeled from exposure to the sun.

5. Sara ate dinner.

   She ate quickly.

   She ate a hamburger.

   The hamburger was dry and tasteless.

   Sara quickly ate the dry and tasteless hamburger for dinner.

REVIEW EXERCISE 2   USING *-ING* PHRASES

Join each sentence pair by converting one of the sentences to an *-ing* verbal phrase.

1. Nancy popped her soft drink open with a satisfying snap.
   She realized that she was very thirsty.

   Realizing that she was very thirsty, Nancy popped her soft drink open with a
   satisfying snap.

2. The shoppers were walking through the huge new superstore.
   They looked like tourists on their first visit to a big city.

   Walking through the huge new superstore, the shoppers looked like tourists on
   their first visit to a big city,

3. Roberto lay in a hammock stretched between two trees.
   He was reading a best-selling novel.

   Reading a best-selling novel, Roberto lay in a hammock stretched between two
   trees.

4. Alisa checked her e-mail every five minutes.
   She was expecting an important message from her friend Karen.

   Expecting an important message from her friend Karen, Alisa checked her
   e-mail every five minutes.

5. Brandon made a disgusted face.
   He poured his cold, rancid coffee down the drain.

   Pouring his cold, rancid coffee down the drain, Brandon made a disgusted
   face.

REVIEW EXERCISE 3   USING *-ED/-EN* PHRASES

Join each sentence pair by converting one of the sentences to an *-ed* verbal phrase.

1. The macaroni and cheese was heated in the microwave.
   It bubbled and steamed as Robert spooned it onto a plate.

   Heated in the microwave, the macaroni and cheese bubbled and steamed as
   Robert spooned it onto a plate.

2. Frieda was consumed by ambition.
   She reported the misdeeds of her fellow workers to gain favor with management.

   Consumed by ambition, Frieda reported the misdeeds of her fellow workers to
   gain favor with management.

3. The cheap radio was tuned to a country music station.
   It sounded tinny and unpleasant.

   Tuned to a country music station, the cheap radio sounded tinny and

   unpleasant.

4. Michael was puzzled by the tapping sound coming from his roof.
   He went outside to investigate.

   Puzzled by the tapping sound coming from his roof, Michael went outside to

   investigate.

5. The poodle was clipped and bathed by the groomer.
   The poodle strutted proudly at the end of his leash.

   Clipped and bathed by the groomer, the poodle strutted proudly at the end of

   his leash.

REVIEW EXERCISE 4   USING *-ED/-EN* AND *-ING* PHRASES

Join each sentence pair by converting one of the sentences to an *-ed/-en* or *-ing* verbal phrase.

1. Emily's books and notes were scattered all over the room.
   They provided ample evidence that she had been studying.

   Scattered all over the room, Emily's books and notes provided ample evidence

   that she had been studying.

2. Derek parked in the mall's huge parking lot.
   He hoped he could find his car when he finished shopping.

   Parking in the mall's huge parking lot, Derek hoped he could find his car when

   he finished shopping.

3. Carlena was dressed in a sunflower costume.
   She danced on stage with another child who was dressed as a ladybug.

   Dressed in a sunflower costume, Carlena danced on stage with another child

   who was dressed as a ladybug.

4. Ernie worked even harder than before.
   He was motivated by his supervisor's words of praise.

   Motivated by his supervisor's words of praise, Ernie worked even harder than

   before.

5. Ashley was astonished at the high price of gas.
    She filled her tank anyway.

    Astonished at the high price of gas, Ashley filled her tank anyway.

    _____

REVIEW EXERCISE 5   COMBINING SENTENCES

Rewrite the following paragraph by combining sentences, using *-ed/-en* verbal phrases and using *-ing* verbal phrases. Each numbered group of sentences will reduce to one sentence.

[1]Sisyphus was a character in Greek mythology. He was a king. He displeased the gods. [2]The gods decided to punish Sisyphus. They sentenced him to spend the afterlife pushing a huge rock up a hill. [3]Sisyphus would push the rock. He would push it up a hill. It would roll back down. It would roll all the way to the bottom. [4]Sisyphus would descend to the bottom of the hill. He would begin to push the rock uphill again. [5]Sisyphus was doomed to spend eternity performing the same task over and over again. He is a symbol of frustration and perseverance.

[1]A character in Greek mythology, King Sisyphus displeased the gods. [2]Deciding to punish Sisyphus, the gods sentenced him to spend the afterlife pushing a huge rock up a hill. [3]Sisyphus would push the rock up a hill, but it would roll back down all the way to the bottom. [4]Descending to the bottom of the hill, Sisyphus would begin to push the rock uphill again. [5]Doomed to spend eternity performing the same task over and over again, Sisyphus is a symbol of frustration and perseverance.

16

Run-on Sentences

"Hi. How are you?"

"I'm doing fine now but you should have seen me two months ago I broke my leg and had to wear a cast and let me tell you that was so uncomfortable I had all kinds of itches that I just couldn't scratch Monday I finally got that cast off and things are going just fine now thank you and how are you?"

What Is a Run-on Sentence?

A **run-on sentence** is not just one sentence, but two or more sentences, run together without punctuation, like the sentences in the box above. Reading a run-on sentence is like listening to a person speaking so quickly that the words pour out in a breathless jumble. You may understand the general idea, but you may lose track of where one thought ends and the next begins. The following sentence is a run-on.

✗   Someone close by was popping gum Jonathan could not concentrate on his work.

By examining the sentence, you can probably figure out where the first thought ends and the second begins—between *gum* and *Jonathan*. Grammatically, too, you can figure out why the thoughts should be separate. Each thought has both a subject and a verb, and each is an **independent**

clause, a clause that can stand alone as a sentence or can be combined with other clauses in specific patterns.

Another type of run-on is called a **comma splice** because two independent clauses are spliced, or joined, with a comma. The following sentence is a comma splice.

✗   Someone close by was popping gum, Jonathan could not concentrate on his work.

The sentence can be corrected in a variety of ways. Here are two of them:

✔   Someone close by was popping gum, so Jonathan could not concentrate on his work.

✔   Because someone close by was popping gum, Jonathan could not concentrate on his work.

The first step toward writing paragraphs and essays that are free of run-on sentences is to learn to recognize run-ons and comma splices. When you see a sentence that you believe is a run-on, test it. Read the first part. Is it a sentence that could stand alone? If your answer is "yes," read the second part, asking the same question. If your answer is again "yes," the sentence is probably a run-on.

Example

The bookstore was crowded, Burton had to stand in line for several minutes.

The first part of the sentence could stand alone.

The bookstore was crowded, Burton had to stand in line for several minutes.

The second part of the sentence could stand alone.

The sentence in the example is a comma splice, since each half of the sentence could stand alone.

PRACTICE 1   IDENTIFYING RUN-ONS AND COMMA SPLICES

In each sentence, underline the spot where the run-on or comma splice occurs. Mark *RO* in the blank to the left of the sentence if the sentence is a run-on, *CS* if it is a comma splice.

RO   **1.** In a souvenir shop, Anna bought a crystalline <u>bear she</u> placed it on her desk next to her printer.

CS   **2.** The batter grinned and lifted his bat high above his <u>shoulders, he</u> had seen the sweat running down the rookie pitcher's face.

CS   **3.** Simone's cat hopped on the counter and tipped over an open box of cat <u>food, then</u> he munched contentedly on the brown nuggets that had spilled across the counter.

CS   **4.** The committee members hungrily ate three dozen doughnuts in less than five <u>minutes, the</u> chair made a mental note not to schedule meetings at noon.

CS   **5.** Jason rushed to the office supply store to buy an ink <u>cartridge, his</u> printer had run out of ink while he was printing a paper for his English class.

Correcting Run-ons

Five methods of correcting run-ons are presented in the following sections. The first three methods are simple; the final two are more complex. Learning all five methods will give you more than just ways to correct run-ons; it will give you a variety of sentence patterns and transitional words to use in your writing.

Method 1: Period and Capital Letter

Correcting with a period and capital letter is the easiest method to use. The hard part is knowing when and how often to use it. Short, single-clause sentences can emphasize ideas by setting them apart. However, too many short sentences can make your writing seem choppy and disconnected.

> **Pattern 1:** <u>Independent clause</u>. <u>Independent clause</u>.

Put a period between the two sentences. Use a capital letter to begin the new sentence.

Example

✗ Julie pumped a few gallons of gas into her car she could not afford to fill the tank.

✔ Julie pumped a few gallons of gas into her car. She could not afford to fill the tank.

PRACTICE 2   CORRECTING RUN-ONS WITH A PERIOD AND A CAPITAL LETTER

In each sentence, underline the spot where each run-on or comma splice occurs. Write *RO* in the blank to the left of the sentence if it is a run-on, *CS* if it is a comma splice. Then correct each sentence using a period and a capital letter.

__RO__ **1.** In the Navy, Francis received training as an electronics <u>technician he</u> hoped to open his own shop once his discharge was complete.

In the Navy, Francis received training as an electronics technician. He

hoped to open his own shop once his discharge was complete.

__RO__ **2.** Rain spilled into the gutter from the roof and gushed from a spout at the base of the <u>house the</u> bush directly in front of the gutter grew lush and green.

Rain spilled into the gutter from the roof and gushed from a spout at the

base of the house. The bush directly in front of the gutter grew lush and

green.

__CS__ **3.** After he heard one of his professors say that carrots increase brain power, John bought three pounds of raw <u>carrots, he</u> had a crucial math test Tuesday.

After he heard one of his professors say that carrots increase brain power,

John bought three pounds of raw carrots. He had a crucial math test

Tuesday.

__RO__ **4.** Miguel had never tried sushi <u>before he</u> dipped a piece in the sauce and took a small, tentative bite.

Miguel had never tried sushi before. He dipped a piece in the sauce and

took a small, tentative bite.

__CS__ **5.** Pam's new kitten nestled against her during the drive home from the animal <u>shelter, the</u> kitten's tiny pink nose and worried expression melted Pam's heart.

Pam's new kitten nestled against her during the drive home from the ani-

mal shelter. The kitten's tiny pink nose and worried expression melted

Pam's heart.

Method 2: Comma and FANBOYS Conjunction

Coordinating conjunctions, or FANBOYS conjunctions, are among the most useful and powerful connecting words in the English language. If you can remember the nonsense word FANBOYS, you can remember the seven coordinating conjunctions: **for, and, nor, but, or, yet, so.**

Pattern 2: Independent clause, and independent clause.

When a FANBOYS conjunction is used with a comma to separate two clauses, the comma goes before the FANBOYS conjunction.

Example

✗ Gavin had not eaten lunch, he put a bowl of ramen noodles in the microwave.

✔ Gavin had not eaten lunch, **so** he put a bowl of ramen noodles in the microwave.

* FANBOYS Conjunctions						
for	and	nor	but	or	yet	so

PRACTICE 3   **CORRECTING RUN-ONS WITH A COMMA AND FANBOYS**

In each sentence, underline the spot where each run-on or comma splice occurs. Write *RO* in the blank to the left of the sentence if it is a run-on, *CS* if it is a comma splice. Correct each run-on or comma splice by using a comma and a FANBOYS conjunction.

Answers may vary.

<u>RO</u>   **1.** Jack stared in astonishment at the empty cereal <u>box he</u> wondered which of his roommates shared his craving for corn flakes.

Jack stared in astonishment at the empty cereal box, and he wondered

which of his roommates shared his craving for corn flakes.

<u>CS</u>   **2.** The defendant insisted that he had lost the receipt for the twelve televisions in the back of his <u>van, the</u> jury did not believe his story.

The defendant insisted that he had lost the receipt for the twelve televi-

sions in the back of his van, but the jury did not believe his story.

<u>RO</u>   **3.** Tyler took a cabinetmaking class during the <u>weekends he</u> did not have the time to devote to his hobby during the week.

> Tyler took a cabinetmaking class during the weekends, for he did not have
>
> the time to devote to his hobby during the week.

<u>CS</u>   **4.** The rocket lifted majestically off the launch <u>pad, people</u> closest to the gantry felt the earth shake beneath their feet.

> The rocket lifted majestically off the launch pad, and people closest to the
>
> gantry felt the earth shake beneath their feet.

<u>CS</u>   **5.** Bruce was an impatient Internet <u>surfer, he</u> claimed his service provider was so slow that the images on his monitor changed only with the seasons.

> Bruce was an impatient Internet surfer, and he claimed his service provider
>
> was so slow that the images on his monitor changed only with the seasons.

Method 3: Semicolon

Using a semicolon to join clauses works best with ideas that are closely connected and need no transitional word to explain the connection between them. The semicolon, as used here, is the grammatical equivalent of a period; however, the first letter of the clause after the semicolon is **not** capitalized.

Pattern 3: <u>Independent clause</u>; <u>independent clause</u>.

The semicolon goes between the two clauses.

Example

✗ The bus stopped at the corner Maria hurried to catch it.

✔ The bus stopped at the corner; Maria hurried to catch it.

PRACTICE 4   CORRECTING RUN-ONS WITH A SEMICOLON

In each sentence, underline the spot where each run-on or comma splice occurs. Write *RO* in the blank to the left of the sentence if it is a run-on, *CS* if it is a comma splice. Then correct the sentences using a semicolon alone.

<u>CS</u>   **1.** A blue moon is not really blue at <u>all, "blue</u> moon" is a name given to the second full moon in any month.

A blue moon is not really blue at all; "blue moon" is a name given to the

second full moon in any month.

RO   2. Lifting the sandwich to his mouth, Jake took another bite out of the multilayered <u>masterpiece he</u> did not discover the mustard stains on his shirt until he walked into his math class.

Lifting the sandwich to his mouth, Jake took another bite out of the mul-

tilayered masterpiece; he did not discover the mustard stains on his shirt

until he walked into his math class.

RO   3. Martha paid the <u>rent she</u> did not have enough left over for books and food.

Martha paid the rent; she did not have enough left over for books and

food.

CS   4. The kite flew higher until it agitated a nesting <u>hawk, the</u> bird screeched, lifted into the air, and attacked the paper intruder, tearing it to shreds.

The kite flew higher until it agitated a nesting hawk; the bird screeched,

lifted into the air, and attacked the paper intruder, tearing it to shreds.

CS   5. Jake wasn't interested in the book's <u>content, what</u> drew his attention was its beautiful leather binding and gold-edged pages.

Jake wasn't interested in the book's content; what drew his attention was

its beautiful leather binding and gold-edged pages.

Method 4: Semicolon and Joining Word

A run-on sentence may also be corrected with a type of joining word called a *conjunctive adverb.* These joining words also function as *transitional expressions,* underscoring the relationship between the two clauses.

Pattern 4: <u>Independent clause</u>; therefore, <u>independent clause</u>.

A semicolon precedes the joining word, and a comma follows it. Exceptions: with the words *thus* and *then,* the comma is often omitted.

Example

✗ In 1900, the life expectancy for women in the United States was 48, it had risen to 79 a century later.

✔ In 1900, the life expectancy for women in the United States was 48; **however,** it had risen to 79 a century later.

Joining Words and Phrases Used with a Semicolon

accordingly	furthermore	nevertheless
also	however	of course
as a result	in addition	on the other hand
besides	in fact	similarly
finally	instead	then
for example	meanwhile	therefore
for instance	moreover	thus

PRACTICE 5   CORRECTING RUN-ONS WITH A SEMICOLON AND A JOINING WORD

In each sentence, underline the spot where each run-on or comma splice occurs. Write *RO* in the blank to the left of the sentence if it is a run-on, *CS* if it is a comma splice. Then correct the sentence using a semicolon and an appropriate joining word.

Answers may vary.

__CS__ **1.** Milo was poor, his poverty did not stand in the way of his ambition.

   Milo was poor; however, his poverty did not stand in the way of his ambition.

__RO__ **2.** Snakes are often killed because they are feared most of them are harmless and afraid of people.

   Snakes are often killed because they are feared; in fact, most of them are harmless and afraid of people.

__CS__ **3.** The skies opened, and the rain fell as if a monsoon had entered the area, I had not brought an umbrella with me.

   The skies opened, and the rain fell as if a monsoon had entered the area; however, I had not brought an umbrella with me.

RO **4.** Shonda searched her apartment for the source of a foul <u>odor she</u> found a dead mouse that her cat had placed in one of her shoes.

> Shonda searched her apartment for the source of a foul odor; finally, she
>
> found a dead mouse that her cat had placed in one of her shoes.
>
> _____

RO **5.** As the lights dimmed in the movie theater, enormous speakers mounted on the walls began to <u>vibrate Jamie</u> pulled two earplugs out of her pocket and stuffed them in her ears.

> As the lights dimmed in the movie theater, enormous speakers mounted
>
> on the walls began to vibrate; as a result, Jamie pulled two earplugs out
>
> of her pocket and stuffed them in her ears.

Method 5: Dependent Word

Placing a dependent word in front of an independent clause makes it a dependent clause, a clause that can no longer stand on its own as a sentence. It now *depends on* the sentence it is attached to and can no longer be separated from it.

Two sentence patterns using a dependent clause are shown next.

Pattern 5a: When <u>dependent clause,</u> <u>independent clause</u>.

When the dependent clause acts as an introductory clause, a comma follows it.

Example

✗ Vernon finally finished his phone call and returned to his coffee it had gotten cold.

✔ When Vernon finally finished his phone call and returned to his coffee, it had gotten cold.

Pattern 5b: <u>Independent clause</u> when <u>dependent clause</u>.

✔ Vernon thought no one was watching **when** he poured his cold coffee into the potted plant beside his desk.

Dependent Words

after	as if	as though
although	as long as	because
as	as soon as	before

even though	though	whenever
if	unless	where
once	until	wherever
since	what	which
so that	whatever	while
that	when	who

PRACTICE 6   CORRECTING RUN-ONS WITH A DEPENDENT WORD

In each sentence, underline the spot where each run-on or comma splice occurs. Write *RO* in the blank to the left of the sentence if it is a run-on, *CS* if it is a comma splice. Correct each using a dependent word.

Answers may vary.

RO   **1.** Toads are <u>useful they</u> consume slugs and insects in large quantities, keeping them from infesting gardens and homes.

Toads are useful because they consume slugs and insects in large quanti-

ties, keeping them from infesting gardens and homes.

CS   **2.** Time zones were created in <u>1884, railroads</u> needed a standardized way to publish schedules.

Time zones were created in 1884 because railroads needed a standardized

way to publish schedules.

RO   **3.** Antonio visited the electronics <u>store he</u> noticed that the DVD player he wanted was on sale.

Antonio visited the electronics store after he noticed that the DVD player

he wanted was on sale.

RO   **4.** Jamesha's car had 150,000 miles on <u>it she</u> decided it was time to trade it in.

Since Jamesha's car had 150,000 miles on it, she decided it was time to

trade it in.

RO   **5.** A warning appeared on Emilio's computer <u>screen his</u> antivirus program had found a virus in his incoming mail.

A warning appeared on Emilio's computer screen because his antivirus

program had found a virus in his incoming mail.

Five Ways to Correct Run-on Sentences

Method 1: Period and Capital Letter

Pattern: <u>Independent clause</u>. <u>Independent clause</u>.

Method 2: Comma and FANBOYS Conjunction

Pattern: <u>Independent clause</u>, and <u>independent clause</u>.

A comma goes before the FANBOYS conjunction in this pattern.

FANBOYS Conjunctions

for	and	nor	but	or	yet	so

Method 3: Semicolon

Pattern: <u>Independent clause</u>; <u>independent clause</u>.

Method 4: Semicolon and Joining Word

Pattern: <u>Independent clause</u>; therefore, <u>independent clause</u>.

A semicolon goes before the joining word and a comma follows it.
With the words *thus* and *then*, the comma is often omitted.

Joining Words Used with a Semicolon

also	however	of course
as a result	in addition	on the other hand
besides	in fact	then
finally	instead	therefore
for example	meanwhile	thus

Method 5: Dependent Word

Pattern 1: Although <u>dependent clause</u>, <u>independent clause</u>.

When a dependent word begins the sentence, a comma is used between the dependent and independent clause.

Pattern 2: <u>Independent clause</u> when <u>dependent clause</u>.

When the dependent clause ends the sentence, a dependent word separates the clauses.

Dependent Words

although	because	that	whenever
as	before	though	where
as if	if	unless	wherever
as long as	once	until	which
as soon as	since	whatever	while
as though	so that	when	who

REVIEW EXERCISE 1   CORRECTING RUN-ON SENTENCES

In each sentence, underline the spot where each run-on or comma splice occurs. Then correct the ten run-on sentences, using each of the five methods at least once.

1. An earthquake in Missouri in 1811 was the most powerful ever felt in the United <u>States it</u> actually changed the course of the Mississippi River.

   An earthquake in Missouri in 1811 was the most powerful ever felt in the United

   States; in fact, it actually changed the course of the Mississippi River.

2. John spilled molasses onto his computer <u>keyboard he</u> decided that having a computer in his kitchen might not have been his brightest idea.

   After John spilled molasses onto his computer keyboard, he decided that having

   a computer in his kitchen might not have been his brightest idea.

3. Latrell walked down the snowy <u>path she</u> left deep footprints in the pristine snow.

   Latrell walked down the snowy path. She left deep footprints in the pristine

   snow.

4. A Venus' flytrap is a carnivorous <u>plant it</u> traps live insects and extracts nutrients as it digests them.

   A Venus' flytrap is a carnivorous plant, and it traps live insects and extracts

   nutrients as it digests them.

5. The delivery truck backed into the <u>driveway it</u> crushed a plastic pull toy that had been left out by a child.

   As the delivery truck backed into the driveway, it crushed a plastic pull toy that

   had been left out by a child.

6. Rosa looked hungrily at the juicy cheeseburger in front of <u>her she</u> had not eaten since breakfast.

   Rosa looked hungrily at the juicy cheeseburger in front of her, for she had not

   eaten since breakfast.

7. Earth Day was first celebrated in <u>1970 it</u> is a celebration of the environment and its preservation.

   Earth Day was first celebrated in 1970. It is a celebration of the environment

   and its preservation.

8. The electric eel is really a <u>fish it</u> produces enough electricity to light a small neon bulb.

   The electric eel is really a fish; it produces enough electricity to light a small

   neon bulb.

9. Jill pulled the muscles in her back as she lifted a heavy <u>box for</u> days afterward she could not stand up straight.

   Jill pulled the muscles in her back as she lifted a heavy box; for days afterward

   she could not stand up straight.

10. The egg that Brian was about to break into the frying pan slipped out of his <u>hand, then</u> it rolled off the kitchen counter and broke on the floor.

   The egg that Brian was about to break into the frying pan slipped out of his hand;

   then it rolled off the kitchen counter and broke on the floor.

REVIEW EXERCISE 2   CORRECTING RUN-ON SENTENCES

In each sentence, underline the spot where each run-on or comma splice occurs. Then correct the ten run-on sentences, using each of the five methods at least once.

1. Raul and Bonita signed the papers to buy their first <u>home, they</u> took their family out for a celebration dinner.

   After Raul and Bonita signed the papers to buy their first home, they took their

   family out for a celebration dinner.

2. Over the years, dust and grime had collected in the corners of the <u>room scrubbing</u> the grime away required a good deal of elbow grease.

   Over the years, dust and grime had collected in the corners of the room; as a

   result, scrubbing the grime away required a good deal of elbow grease.

3. The kitten arched its back as it looked into a <u>mirror it</u> relaxed after it realized that the image posed no threat.

   The kitten arched its back as it looked into a mirror, but it relaxed after it real-

   ized that the image posed no threat.

4. The coffee had been sitting on the warming plate for almost four <u>hours, Raj</u> made a face as he tasted it.

   The coffee had been sitting on the warming plate for almost four hours; Raj

   made a face as he tasted it.

5. Sandra never does any shopping on <u>weekends she</u> says the stores are too crowded.

   Sandra never does any shopping on weekends, for she says the stores are too

   crowded.

6. Ron looked at his <u>watch he</u> wondered whether he had time to grab a bite to eat before class.

   As Ron looked at his watch, he wondered whether he had time to grab a bite

   to eat before class.

7. The line at the prescription drug counter was unusually <u>long clearly</u>, flu season had arrived.

   The line at the prescription drug counter was unusually long; clearly, flu season

   had arrived.

8. Under the porch, a cactus grew in the sandy <u>soil eventually</u> a white flower bloomed on its spiny, green surface.

   Under the porch, a cactus grew in the sandy soil. Eventually a white flower

   bloomed on its spiny, green surface.

9. The speed limit on the highway was <u>55, Jennifer</u> was driving at least 70.

   The speed limit on the highway was 55; however, Jennifer was driving at least

   70.

10. Shoppers huddled under the awning outside the grocery store, waiting for the rain to <u>stop a</u> bald man stepped into the downpour, remarking that the rain could not mess up his hair.

    Shoppers huddled under the awning outside the grocery store, waiting for the

    rain to stop. A bald man stepped into the downpour, remarking that the rain

    could not mess up his hair.

REVIEW EXERCISE 3   CORRECTING RUN-ON SENTENCES

In the following exercise, underline the spot where each run-on or comma splice occurs. Then correct the two run-ons in each sentence group.

1. From the north, a huge flock of birds came in <u>sight they</u> filled the sky, calling to one another as they flew. The birds flew <u>southward it</u> took several minutes for the entire flock to pass overhead.

   From the north, a huge flock of birds came in sight; they filled the sky, calling

   to one another as they flew. The birds flew southward, and it took several min-

   utes for the entire flock to pass overhead

2. A dry pond is only a minor problem to a fish known as the walking <u>fish it</u> can "walk" on its fins and tail to another habitat. The walking fish has a special chamber over its gills that allows it to absorb oxygen from the <u>air it</u> can remain out of water for a few days as it searches for a new pond.

   A dry pond is only a minor problem to a fish known as the walking fish, for it

   can "walk" on its fins and tail to another habitat. The walking fish has a special

   chamber over its gills that allows it to absorb oxygen from the air; in fact, it can

   remain out of water for a few days as it searches for a new pond.

3. The laundry piled up for two <u>weeks finally</u> Eric decided to go to the laundromat. He was down to his last pair of <u>jeans his</u> room was beginning to smell like old socks.

   The laundry piled up for two weeks; finally, Eric decided to go to the laundro-

   mat. He was down to his last pair of jeans, and his room was beginning to

   smell like old socks.

4. Neal was <u>hungry he</u> ordered a large pizza with five toppings. He remembered he was on a <u>diet he</u> ordered a large diet soft drink, too.

   Since Neal was hungry, he ordered a large pizza with five toppings. He remem-

   bered he was on a diet, so he ordered a large diet soft drink, too.

5. In Europe and Japan, where gasoline is heavily taxed, many people do not drive to <u>work they</u> ride a bicycle. In large cities, roads are often <u>congested a bike</u> trip may actually take less time than the same trip by car.

   In Europe and Japan, where gasoline is heavily taxed, many people do not drive

   to work; they ride a bicycle. In large cities, roads are often congested, and a

   bike trip may actually take less time than the same trip by car.

REVIEW EXERCISE 4   CORRECTING RUN-ON SENTENCES

In the following exercise, underline the spot where each run-on or comma splice occurs. Then correct the two run-ons in each sentence group.

1. Radar and sonar are two methods of detecting unseen <u>objects they</u> work differently. Radar sends radio waves through the air to locate <u>objects sonar</u> bounces sound waves off underwater objects to determine their size and location.

   Radar and sonar are two methods of detecting unseen objects; however, they

   work differently. Radar sends radio waves through the air to locate objects.

   Sonar bounces sound waves off underwater objects to determine their size and

   location.

2. Gary enjoys talking to people in <u>person he</u> hates making telephone calls. Once, he drove five miles to the dentist's office to make an <u>appointment he</u> could easily have picked up the telephone and made the appointment in less than five minutes.

   Gary enjoys talking to people in person, but he hates making telephone calls.

   Once, he drove five miles to the dentist's office to make an appointment when

   he could easily have picked up the telephone and made the appointment in less

   than five minutes.

3. The landscape gardener Lancelot Brown was more commonly known as <u>"Capability" his</u> work was well known in the eighteenth century and endures to this day. Fussy and formal French gardens were popular at the <u>time Capability</u> Brown replaced them with rolling landscapes that were beautiful and easy to maintain.

   The landscape gardener Lancelot Brown was more commonly known as

   "Capability." His work was well known in the eighteenth century and endures

   to this day. Fussy and formal French gardens were popular at the time; however,

   Capability Brown replaced them with rolling landscapes that were beautiful and

   easy to maintain.

4. Sidney tried to remove the oil spots on his driveway with kitty <u>litter he</u> put litter over the spots and let it stand overnight. He swept away the litter the next <u>morning the</u> spots were lighter but still visible.

Sidney tried to remove the oil spots on his driveway with kitty litter; he put litter over the spots and let it stand overnight. When he swept away the litter the next morning, the spots were lighter but still visible.

5. Three empty cola cans sat on the concrete beside the <u>bench someone</u> had forgotten to throw them away. Janice picked them up and tossed them into the blue recycling receptacle a few yards <u>away then</u> she returned to the bench to read her book.

Three empty cola cans sat on the concrete beside the bench; someone had forgotten to throw them away. Janice picked them up and tossed them into the blue recycling receptacle a few yards away, and then she returned to the bench to read her book.

REVIEW EXERCISE 5   CORRECTING RUN-ON SENTENCES

In the following paragraph, underline the spot where each run-on or comma splice occurs. Then correct the ten run-on sentences or comma splices, using the five methods presented in this chapter. Try to use each method at least once.

[1]The Empire State Building is a famous New York landmark and tourist <u>attraction it</u> was built in 1931 during the Great Depression. [2]During this difficult economic time, few businesses rented space in the <u>building for</u> a while it was jokingly called the "Empty State Building." [3]Once the tallest building in the world, it has 103 stories and stands more than a quarter of a mile <u>high on</u> a clear day, five states are visible from the building's observatories: New York, Connecticut, Pennsylvania, New Jersey, and Massachusetts. [4]The building functions as a working office <u>building it</u> also hosts over three million tourists each year. [5]Visitors stream to the <u>observatories they</u> see breathtaking views of New York City. [6]Central Park and the Statue of Liberty can be seen from the

building, Ellis Island, a historic entry point for immigrants, is visible also. [7]Tourists and New Yorkers alike enjoy seeing the lights on the Empire State Building the lights change colors for many holidays and observances, including Christmas, Hanukkah, St. Patrick's Day, Valentine's Day, Breast Cancer Awareness Day, Earth Day, and several national holidays. [8]Even Americans who have never seen the Empire State Building in person have probably seen it at the movies the building has been featured in dozens of films. [9]King Kong climbed the Empire State Building with the movie's heroine in his clutches Cary Grant waited for Deborah Kerr on the observation deck in *An Affair to Remember*. [10]The Empire State Building stands as a New York landmark it is a source of pride for all Americans.

[1]The Empire State Building is a famous New York landmark and tourist attraction. It was built in 1931 during the Great Depression. [2]During this difficult economic time, few businesses rented space in the building, and for a while, it was jokingly called the "Empty State Building." [3]Once the tallest building in the world, it has 103 stories and stands more than a quarter of a mile high. On a clear day, five states are visible from the building's observatories: New York, Connecticut, Pennsylvania, New Jersey, and Massachusetts. [4]The building functions as a working office building, and it also hosts over three million tourists each year. [5]Visitors stream to the observatories where they see breathtaking views of New York City. [6]Central Park and the Statue of Liberty can be seen from the building; additionally, Ellis Island, a historic entry point for immigrants, is visible also. [7]Tourists and New Yorkers alike enjoy seeing the lights on the Empire State Building, for the lights change colors for many holidays and observances, including Christmas, Hanukkah, St. Patrick's Day, Valentine's Day, Breast Cancer Awareness Day, Earth Day, and several national holidays. [8]Even Americans who have never seen the Empire State Building in person have probably seen it at

the movies. The building has been featured in dozens of films. [9]King Kong climbed the Empire State Building with the movie's heroine in his clutches, and Cary Grant waited for Deborah Kerr on the observation deck in *An Affair to Remember*. [10]The Empire State Building stands as a New York landmark; it is a source of pride for all Americans.

17

Sentence Fragments

To whoever finds this—

I know I am dying. But the secret of my family's treasure shall not die with me. I pass it on to you now.

Here are specific directions to reach it. It is buried in the Oza on a piece of land deeded to me by my grandfather. Take Rout en turn left, walk four paces, and dig beside the old well.

But beware the curse. If you do not it means certain death.

Good luck—you will need it.

Whoever finds the preceding letter is likely to be frustrated because it is only a fragment. Important elements are missing. Readers are similarly frustrated by **sentence fragments** because they leave out important elements of a sentence.

What Is a Sentence Fragment?

Look at the following examples:

✗ Bethany picked up the newspaper from the floor. <u>And took it outside to the recycling bin.</u>

✗ <u>When interest rates are high</u>. More people put off purchasing cars and homes.

The underlined word groups are **sentence fragments**—*pieces* of sentences that cannot stand alone. A **sentence fragment** is an incomplete sentence. It may be a dependent clause that cannot stand on its own, or it may lack a subject, a verb, or both. If you read a fragment by itself, without the other sentences that surround it, you will usually recognize that it does not express a complete thought. It is only a part, or fragment, of a sentence.

Dependent Clause Fragments

✗ **Because** <u>Jorge had forgotten to bring a book with him to the laundromat</u>. He had nothing to do but watch his clothes tumbling in the dryer.

✗ Amelia answered the ringing telephone. **Although** <u>she was already late for work</u>.

Each of the preceding underlined fragments is a **dependent clause fragment.** A dependent clause fragment always begins with a dependent word. A dependent clause fragment can usually be fixed by attaching it to a complete sentence.

✔ Because Jorge had forgotten to bring a book with him to the laundromat, he had nothing to do but watch his clothes tumbling in the dryer.

✔ Amelia answered the ringing telephone although she was already late for work.

Dropping the dependent word or changing it to another type of transitional expression is an alternative to connecting the fragment to the sentence.

✔ Jorge had forgotten to bring a book with him to the laundromat. He had nothing to do but watch his clothes tumbling in the dryer.

✔ Amelia answered the ringing telephone. She was already late for work.

---

* *Punctuation Pointer*

Use a comma to attach a dependent clause fragment at the beginning of a sentence.

List of Dependent Words

after	how	what
although	if	when
as	once	whenever
as if	since	where
as long as	so that	wherever
as soon as	that	which
because	though	while
before	unless	who
even though	until	whoever

PRACTICE 1   CORRECTING DEPENDENT CLAUSE FRAGMENTS

Correct the dependent clause fragments by attaching them to an independent clause.

Answers may vary slightly.

1. Because he knew he had plenty of time to turn around and tag out the runner. The catcher waited patiently for the baseball to reach him.

    Because he knew he had plenty of time to turn around and tag out the runner,

    the catcher waited patiently for the baseball to reach him.

    _____

2. Camilla threw down her new gel pen. When it leaked all over her hand.

    Camilla threw down her gel pen **when** it leaked all over her hand.

    _____

    _____

3. Since the chef did not believe in watching clocks. He burned some dinners and undercooked others.

<u>**Since** the chef did not believe in watching clocks, he burned some dinners and</u>

<u>undercooked others.</u>

4. After he had emptied the contents of the large red container into his empty
    gas tank. Frank noticed the words "windshield fluid" on the side of the
    container.

    <u>**After** he had emptied the contents of the large red container into his empty gas</u>

    <u>tank, Frank noticed the words "windshield fluid" on the side of the container.</u>

5. Imogene eyed her bowl of freshly made ham salad suspiciously. After she no-
    ticed her cat sitting near the bowl, contentedly licking mayonnaise from his
    whiskers.

    <u>Imogene eyed her bowl of freshly made ham salad suspiciously **after** she</u>

    <u>noticed her cat sitting near the bowl, contentedly licking mayonnaise from his</u>

    <u>whiskers.</u>

Verbal Phrase Fragments (*to*, *-ing*, and *-ed/-en* Fragments)

When a verbal phrase stands alone, not attached to a sentence, it is called
a **verbal phrase fragment.** Verbal phrase fragments may be *to* fragments
(infinitive phrases), or they may be *-ing* or *-ed/-en* fragments (participial
phrases).

✗ Police officers were posted at every exit. <u>**To control** the flow of traffic
   and prevent congestion.</u>

✗ <u>**Smiling** and **carrying** diplomas.</u> The graduates hugged their proud
   parents and relatives.

✗ <u>**Dressed** in flowing black academic robes and mortarboard caps.</u> The
   graduates congratulated one another and exchanged high fives.

Correct verbal phrase fragments by attaching them to a complete
sentence.

✔ Police officers were posted at every exit to control the flow of traffic and prevent congestion.

✔ Smiling and carrying diplomas, the graduates hugged their proud parents and relatives.

✔ Dressed in flowing black academic robes and mortarboard caps, the graduates congratulated one another and exchanged high fives.

Correcting *to* Fragments

Correct *to* fragments by connecting them to a sentence or by adding a subject and verb, as shown in the following examples.

✗ To keep her car running well for years. Kayla changes the oil every 3,000 miles.

✔ To keep her car running well for years, Kayla changes the oil every 3,000 miles.

✗ Every ten years, a census is taken. To record changes in population and to allocate federal funds.

✔ Every ten years, a census is taken to record changes in population and to allocate federal funds.

---

* Punctuation Pointer

A *to* fragment attached to the beginning of a sentence is followed by a comma because it is an introductory phrase. A *to* fragment connected to the end of the sentence needs no comma.

PRACTICE 2   CORRECTING *TO* FRAGMENTS

Underline and correct the *to* fragments in the following exercise.

Answers may vary slightly.

1. <u>To mix the ingredients for her automatic bread machine accurately</u>. Margaret purchased an expensive stainless steel measuring set.

   To mix the ingredients for her automatic bread machine accurately, Margaret

   purchased an expensive stainless steel measuring set.

2. The astronomer adjusted the focus of his telescope carefully. <u>To photograph the comet, which wouldn't visit the region again in his lifetime.</u>

     The astronomer adjusted the focus of his telescope carefully to photograph the comet, which wouldn't visit the region again in his lifetime.

3. <u>To make sure no flies landed on his sandwich.</u> Ralph put a napkin over his plate.

     To make sure no flies landed on his sandwich, Ralph put a napkin over his plate.

4. Avery replaced the oil in his car regularly. <u>To keep the car running efficiently.</u>

     Avery replaced the oil in his car regularly to keep the car running efficiently.

5. <u>To avoid paying sales tax.</u> George buys most of his supplies through the Internet.

     To avoid paying sales tax, George buys most of his supplies through the Internet.

Correcting *-ing* Fragments

To correct an *-ing* fragment, connect it to the rest of the sentence with a comma. You may also correct it by adding a subject and a helping verb.

✘ Walking thought the woods in the summertime. People can easily pick up ticks on their clothing and skin.

✔ Walking thought the woods in the summertime, people can easily pick up ticks on their clothing and skin.

✘ Lizzie's five-year-old raced around the house. Wearing a dishtowel as a cape and pretending he was Superman.

✔ Lizzie's five-year-old raced around the house, wearing a dishtowel as a cape and pretending he was Superman.

---

* Punctuation Pointer

Usually, *-ing* fragments can be connected to the rest of the sentence with a comma.

PRACTICE 3   CORRECTING -*ING* FRAGMENTS

Underline and correct the -*ing* fragments.

Answers may vary slightly.

1. Licking his lips in anticipation. Frank smelled the grilled steaks as he entered the restaurant.

    Licking his lips in anticipation, Frank smelled the grilled steaks as he entered

    the restaurant.

2. Dodging the cars artfully and ignoring the blaring horns. The dog made it safely to the other side of the street.

    Dodging the cars artfully and ignoring the blaring horns, the dog made it safely

    to the other side of the street.

3. The train slowed to a crawl. Rounding a very sharp curve as it headed into the city.

    The train slowed to a crawl, rounding a very sharp curve as it headed into the

    city.

4. Making just enough noise to wake their parents. The children turned on the Saturday morning cartoons.

    Making just enough noise to wake their parents, the children turned on the Sat-

    urday morning cartoons.

5. Performing one of the acrobatic splits that were part of his routine. The singer realized that he had just split his tight costume.

    Performing one of the acrobatic splits that were part of his routine, the singer

    realized that he had just split his tight costume.

Correcting -*ed*/-*en* Fragments

Another kind of fragment begins with an -*ed* or -*en* verb form (the past participle). If the verb is a regular verb, the verb form will end in -*ed*, like the verbs *walked, called,* or *plotted.* If the verb is irregular, then the verb form will end in -*en* or in another irregular ending. *Broken, grown, found, bought,* and *written* are some of these forms. These -*ed* and -*en* forms are called *past participles.* For other examples, see the list of irregular verbs in Chapter 12. This type of fragment can usually be corrected by connecting it to a complete sentence.

✗ Bored by the television show. Mike picked up a book.

✔ Bored by the television show, Mike picked up a book.

✗ People clustered around the car. Driven by the racing legend.

✔ People clustered around the car driven by the racing legend.

✗ On the corner stood Antoine. Drenched by rain and looking miserable.

✔ On the corner stood Antoine, drenched by rain and looking miserable.

---

* Punctuation Pointer

Always connect *-ed/-en* fragments to the *beginning* of a sentence with a comma. An *-ed/-en* fragment connected to the end of a sentence may sometimes require a comma, depending on usage. Those in this exercise will not require a comma. See Chapter 27 for more details on comma usage.

PRACTICE 4   CORRECTING *-ED/-EN* FRAGMENTS

Underline and correct the *-ed/-en* fragments in the following exercise.

Answers may vary slightly.

1. <u>Driven by greed and a love of gambling</u>. Joshua bet on everything from football games to turtle races.

    Driven by greed and a love of gambling, Joshua bet on everything from football

    games to turtle races.

2. <u>Confronted by a better and more experienced player</u>. Monica relied on her wits and a little bit of luck to keep her in the game.

    Confronted by a better and more experienced player, Monica relied on her wits

    and a little bit of luck to keep her in the game.

3. <u>Confused by the noise and the whirling lights</u>. The little girl clung to her mother during their visit to an amusement park.

    Confused by the noise and the whirling lights, the little girl clung to her mother

    during their visit to an amusement park.

4. The veterinarian watched the orphaned baby elephant carefully. <u>Concerned that it might not survive the night</u>.

    The veterinarian watched the orphaned baby elephant carefully, concerned that

    it might not survive the night.

5. <u>Woven into the fabric of the blanket</u>. Gold threads outlined the name of the fan's favorite team.

> Woven into the fabric of the blanket**,** gold threads outlined the name of the
>
> fan's favorite team.

Missing-Subject Fragments

Fragments beginning with a joining word such as *and, or, but,* or *then* followed by a verb are missing-subject fragments. The subject of the verb is usually in a previous sentence. Connect the fragment to the sentence or add a subject to begin a new sentence.

✘ The night-blooming cereus is a cactus whose blooms unfold only after sunset. And last only a single night.

✔ The night-blooming cereus is a cactus whose blooms unfold only after sunset and last only a single night.

✘ Ken took a jar of honey from a shelf. And poured a generous spoonful into his hot tea.

✔ Ken took a jar of honey from a shelf and poured a generous spoonful into his hot tea.

Practice 5   Correcting Missing-Subject Fragments

Underline and correct the missing-subject fragments.

Answers may vary slightly.

1. Trying to reach the grassy safety of the park, the snake slithered quickly across the hot asphalt. <u>And stopped briefly beneath a car to rest in the shade</u>.

> Trying to reach the grassy safety of the park, the snake slithered quickly across
>
> the hot asphalt and stopped briefly beneath a car to rest in the shade.

2. Marco felt embarrassed when one of his coworkers told him that licking self-stick stamps was a wasted effort. <u>And made the stamps useless as well</u>.

> Marco felt embarrassed when one of his coworkers told him that licking self-
>
> stick stamps was a wasted effort and made the stamps useless as well.

3. After cooking tofu hot dogs, Filipo ate two of them. <u>And decided that what they lacked most was flavor</u>.

> After cooking tofu hot dogs, Filipo ate two of them and decided that what they
>
> lacked most was flavor.

4. The carpenter learned to work with both hard and soft wood. <u>And to respect the powerful tools that could help him build a table or easily maim a hand.</u>

> The carpenter learned to work with both hard and soft wood and to respect
>
> the powerful tools that could help him build a table or easily maim a hand.

5. The copier made a metallic grinding noise. <u>And stopped with a shudder, emitting a wisp of orange smoke.</u>

> The copier made a metallic grinding noise and stopped with a shudder, emit-
>
> ting a wisp of orange smoke.

✳ *Real-World Writing: Is it okay to start a sentence with* but?

Yes and no. Grammatically, it is correct to start a sentence with *but* or any other FANBOYS conjunction. But your instructors may discourage the practice, for two reasons.

1. It's an informal technique that should not be used in formal, academic writing. (This text, you may have noticed, takes an informal, conversational approach, addressing you directly and occasionally using a FANBOYS to begin a sentence.)

2. It's addictive. *But* is the strongest contrast word in our language, and it's easy to overuse.

The bottom line: use conjunctions to begin sentences only if your instructor gives the green light, and then use them sparingly.

Example and Exception Fragments

Fragments often occur when a writer decides to add an example or to note an exception. Example fragments often begin with *such as, including, like, for example*, or *for instance*. Exception fragments often begin with *not, except, unless, without*, or *in spite of*. To fix the fragment, connect it to the sentence with which it logically belongs. If the fragment begins with "for example" or "for instance," make the fragment into a separate sentence.

✗ Keiko managed to keep her mind on her project. In spite of constant interruptions by her coworkers.

✔ Keiko managed to keep her mind on her project, in spite of constant interruptions by her coworkers.

✘ In spite of his nervousness about speaking in front of a group. Ed impressed the entire class with his presentation.

✔ In spite of his nervousness about speaking in front of a group, Ed impressed the entire class with his presentation.

✘ Carrie says that there are some foods she simply cannot eat. For example, beef liver and key lime pie.

✔ Carrie says that there are some foods she simply cannot eat. For example, beef liver and key lime pie turn her stomach.

---

* Punctuation Pointer

Usually, you can connect fragments beginning with *such as, including, not,* and *in spite of* with a comma, and fragments beginning with *except, unless, without,* and *like* with no comma. Convert fragments beginning with *for example* and *for instance* into complete sentences.

PRACTICE 6   CORRECTING EXAMPLE AND EXCEPTION FRAGMENTS

Underline and correct the example and exception fragments.

Answers may vary slightly.

1. Jamie never seems to be able to hold a job. <u>In spite of the technical expertise she brings to each position.</u>

   Jamie never seems to be able to hold a job**,** in spite of the technical expertise

   she brings to each position.

2. The top model said that she had flaws in her appearance just like anyone else. <u>For example, a tiny gap between her two front teeth.</u>

   The top model said that she had flaws in her appearance just like anyone else.

   For example, **she had** a tiny gap between her two front teeth.

3. The invitation said that the reunion would be held outside. <u>Unless it rained.</u>

   The invitation said that the reunion would be held outside unless it rained.

4. Amy's diabetes keeps her from eating food she used to love. <u>Such as choco-late chip cookies and cinnamon rolls.</u>

   Amy's diabetes keeps her from eating food she used to love, such as chocolate chip cookies and cinnamon rolls.

5. Jeff has made several improvements to the used car that he bought. <u>Including installing a CD player and buying four new tires.</u>

   Jeff has made several improvements to the used car that he bought, including installing a CD player and buying four new tires.

Prepositional-Phrase Fragments

Prepositional phrases, alone or in series, cannot function as sentences. Correct a prepositional-phrase fragment by connecting it to a sentence with which it logically belongs.

✗ Dylan could not believe that his car had broken down. In the middle of nowhere on a deserted country road.

✔ Dylan could not believe that his car had broken down in the middle of nowhere on a deserted country road.

✗ On the first day of her new job. Leigh was held up by a huge traffic jam and arrived an hour late.

✔ On the first day of her new job, Leigh was held up by a huge traffic jam and arrived an hour late.

---

* Punctuation Pointer

Use a comma behind introductory prepositional phrases. No punctuation is required to connect a prepositional phrase to the end of a sentence.

PRACTICE 7   CORRECTING PREPOSITIONAL-PHRASE FRAGMENTS

Underline and correct each prepositional-phrase fragment.

Answers may vary slightly.

1. <u>In the pencil holder filled with quarters.</u> Jamie found enough change to buy lunch.

<u>In the pencil holder filled with quarters, Jamie found enough change to buy</u>

<u>lunch.</u>

2. The ball bounced off the top of the center field wall. <u>Into the stands above.</u>

    The ball bounced off the top of the center field wall into the stands above.

3. <u>After getting a haircut from the new barber.</u> Frank ran his hand through his hair and discovered a bald patch at the base of his head.

    After getting a haircut from the new barber, Frank ran his hand through his

    hair and discovered a bald patch at the base of his head.

4. <u>Within an inside pocket of an old plaid polyester jacket.</u> Rudy found a twenty-dollar bill.

    Within an inside pocket of an old plaid polyester jacket, Rudy found a twenty-

    dollar bill.

5. No one expected to find the missing keys. <u>Under a sweater on the back seat of the car.</u>

    No one expected to find the missing keys under a sweater on the back seat of

    the car.

REVIEW EXERCISE 1   CORRECTING SENTENCE FRAGMENTS

Underline and correct each fragment in the following exercise.

Answers may vary.

1. <u>Puzzled by the hopping katydid.</u> The kitten watched for several minutes before pouncing on the insect.

    Puzzled by the hopping katydid, the kitten watched for several minutes before

    pouncing on the insect.

2. Fred's sunglasses continued to slip down his nose. <u>Even after he replaced the worn pads.</u>

    Fred's sunglasses continued to slip down his nose, even after he replaced the

    worn pads.

3. <u>Realizing that the long wait was not the fault of the overworked teller.</u> Russell managed to hide his impatience.

    Realizing that the long wait was not the fault of the overworked teller, Russell

    managed to hide his impatience.

4. Franklin decided to walk around the fenced yard that housed two snarling, snapping dogs. <u>Rather than take a shortcut through it.</u>

   Franklin decided to walk around the fenced yard that housed two snarling,

   snapping dogs, rather than take a shortcut through it.

5. <u>With no money and little chance of borrowing any from his brother.</u> Jessup decided that an evening at home with a good book might be profitable.

   With no money and little chance of borrowing any from his brother, Jessup de-

   cided that an evening at home with a good book might be profitable.

6. <u>Wasting little time at the start of fishing season.</u> Jason bought a fishing license and headed toward Lake Sinclair.

   Wasting little time at the start of fishing season, Jason bought a fishing license

   and headed toward Lake Sinclair.

7. Ethelred decided that his job search skills needed refining. <u>After an employment interview ended in a shouting match.</u>

   Ethelred decided that his job search skills needed refining after an employment

   interview ended in a shouting match.

8. <u>After Charlotte turned it on.</u> The computer gave off an acrid odor of burning plastic.

   After Charlotte turned it on, the computer gave off an acrid odor of burning

   plastic.

9. <u>Wondering how to make a sound from the wooden flute.</u> John kept puffing air across the small, circular opening of the silent instrument.

   Wondering how to make a sound from the wooden flute, John kept puffing air

   across the small, circular opening of the silent instrument.

10. The singer sang sad songs of loss and disenchantment. <u>And brought tears to the eyes of nearly everyone in the audience.</u>

    The singer sang sad songs of loss and disenchantment and brought tears to the

    eyes of nearly everyone in the audience.

REVIEW EXERCISE 2   CORRECTING SENTENCE FRAGMENTS

Underline and correct each fragment in the following exercise.

Answers may vary.

1. <u>Cleaning his office two weeks ago.</u> Brian discovered a floppy disc that he thought he had lost.

Cleaning his office two weeks ago, Brian discovered a floppy disc that he thought he had lost.

2. Joanne was horrified. <u>After discovering that her mother had picked up a hitchhiker on her trip to Cape Cod.</u>

   Joanne was horrified after discovering that her mother had picked up a hitch-hiker on her trip to Cape Cod.

3. The new car provided a smooth ride. <u>But hesitated around sharp curves.</u>

   The new car provided a smooth ride but hesitated around sharp curves.

4. <u>With the cell phone next to his ear and his mind on tomorrow's problems.</u> Jeff ran several red lights and two stop signs.

   With the cell phone next to his ear and his mind on tomorrow's problems, Jeff ran several red lights and two stop signs.

5. The police officer pulled over the small sports car. <u>After it changed lanes by gliding smoothly under a large truck.</u>

   The police officer pulled over the small sports car after it changed lanes by gliding smoothly under a large truck.

6. <u>By the time he pulled into his mother's driveway after the long trip.</u> Gerald barely recognized the wilted and battered flowers that he had bought for her before he left.

   By the time he pulled into his mother's driveway after the long trip, Gerald barely recognized the wilted and battered flowers that he had bought for her before he left.

7. Rocky decided he needed a larger dictionary. <u>Because the old one was not heavy enough to keep his office door propped open.</u>

   Rocky decided he needed a larger dictionary because the old one was not heavy enough to keep his office door propped open.

8. <u>Filled with pride and a sense of achievement.</u> Selma told her husband that she had sold a painting at a local art gallery.

   Filled with pride and a sense of achievement, Selma told her husband that she had sold a painting at a local art gallery.

9. Charon has operated the ferry for longer than he can remember. <u>And has never received a single complaint from a passenger.</u>

   Charon has operated the ferry for longer than he can remember and has never received a single complaint from a passenger.

10. Louis did not have a sense of humor. <u>And found the jokes that circulated around the office puzzling and pointless.</u>

   Louis did not have a sense of humor and found the jokes that circulated around the office puzzling and pointless.

REVIEW EXERCISE 3   CORRECTING SENTENCE FRAGMENTS

Underline and correct the two fragments in each of the following numbered items.

Answers may vary.

1. Every summer, Susan boards her four dogs at the veterinarian's office. <u>While she goes on vacation.</u> <u>Trying to save a few dollars this year.</u> She has convinced four of her friends to take care of one dog each.

   Every summer, Susan boards her four dogs at the veterinarian's office while she goes on vacation. Trying to save a few dollars this year, she has convinced four of her friends to take care of one dog each.

2. <u>After he followed the assembly instructions with infinite care.</u> Anton had eight parts left over from his portable radio kit. He shrugged, plugged in his newly assembled radio, and turned it on. <u>But was not surprised when the radio remained silent.</u>

   After he followed the assembly instructions with infinite care, Anton had eight parts left over from his portable radio kit. He shrugged, plugged in his newly assembled radio, and turned it on, but **he** was not surprised when the radio remained silent.

3. <u>Because the job ad promised unlimited financial rewards and little work.</u> Rob applied for the position. He had every qualification required for the job. <u>Except the three thousand dollars to buy the shoddy products that he was supposed to sell.</u>

   Because the job ad promised unlimited financial rewards and little work, Rob applied for the position. He had every qualification required for the job, except the three thousand dollars to buy the shoddy products that he was supposed to sell.

4. Sam's car is over twenty years old. <u>And is beginning to break down monthly.</u> However, he keeps fixing it. <u>Because he dislikes making car payments.</u>

Sam's car is over twenty years old and is beginning to break down monthly.

However, he keeps fixing it because he dislikes making car payments.

_____

_____

5.   Even though she was planning to start her diet. Hazel promised to make brownies for her son's class bake sale. As the smell of dark chocolate permeated the room. Hazel decided that her new diet could be put off an extra day.

Even though she was planning to start her diet, Hazel promised to make

brownies for her son's class bake sale. As the smell of dark chocolate perme-

ated the room, Hazel decided that her new diet could be put off an extra day.

_____

REVIEW EXERCISE 4   CORRECTING SENTENCE FRAGMENTS

Underline and correct the two fragments in each of the following.

Answers may vary.

1.   Carole enrolled in a weekend carpentry course. Because she was interested in making her own computer table and chair. Finding the course interesting and working with wood curiously calming. She discovered she had a flair for making furniture.

Carole enrolled in a weekend carpentry course because she was interested in

making her own computer table and chair. Finding the course interesting and

working with wood curiously calming, she discovered she had a flair for making

furniture.

2.   Placing two full grocery bags on top of his small sports car. Gerald opened the driver's-side door and got in the car. Several seconds later, he watched in the rearview mirror. As a full week's groceries rolled across the parking lot like spilled marbles.

Placing two full grocery bags on top of his small sports car, Gerald opened the

driver's-side door and got in the car. Several seconds later, he watched in the

rearview mirror as a full week's groceries rolled across the parking lot like

spilled marbles.

3.   Mira disliked walking across a sandy beach. Because she hated the idea of accidentally stepping on one of the numerous sand crabs skittering across the sand. At the same time, she loved the feeling of the waves. Washing across her ankles.

Mira disliked walking across a sandy beach because she hated the idea of accidentally stepping on one of the numerous sand crabs skittering across the
sand. At the same time, she loved the feeling of the waves washing across her
ankles.

4. Arching its back in defiance. The small white kitten stood its ground as the
toy car approached. When the car got too close. The kitten finally bolted.

Arching its back in defiance, the small white kitten stood its ground as the toy
car approached. When the car got too close, the kitten finally bolted.

5. Picturing an exotic beach with balmy breezes, palm trees, and a beach with
sugar-colored sand. Jasmine was thoroughly disappointed to discover that
the resort's plants were all plastic. In addition, the beach was filthy. Littered
with empty cans and paper plates.

Picturing an exotic beach with balmy breezes, palm trees, and a beach with
sugar-colored sand, Jasmine was thoroughly disappointed to discover that the
resort's plants were all plastic. In addition, the beach was filthy, littered with
empty cans and paper plates.

REVIEW EXERCISE 5   CORRECTING SENTENCE FRAGMENTS

Underline and correct the ten fragments in this exercise.

Answers may vary.

[1]In high school, every instructor seems to begin
and end class on time. [2]Never starting late or
finishing early. [3]However, in a college classroom.
[4]The time class begins and ends depends on the
instructor. [5]My math instructor, Mr. Lambert, begins
every class on time. [6]But covers only what is on the
syllabus for that day. [7]After that, he dismisses the
class. [8]Whether we have gone the full fifty minutes
or just half an hour. [9]No one in the class ever
complains. [10]About Mr. Lambert's approach.
[11]However, students do grumble about Ms. Claudio,
who seems to believe. [12]That the universe does not
exist beyond her classroom. [13]Five minutes after the

class should have ended. [14]Ms. Claudio is still talking about conjunctions or commas. [15]Finally, there's Dr. Korbatz, who almost always enters our computer science classroom five minutes late. [16]Looking harried and rushed. [17]I don't think he's been to class on time all term. [18]Except perhaps during the first week of class. [19]Perhaps colleges, like high schools, need a system of bells. [20]To remind students and teachers when classes begin and end.

In high school, every instructor seems to begin and end class on time, never starting late or finishing early. However, in a college classroom, the time class begins and ends depends on the instructor. My math instructor, Mr. Lambert, begins every class on time but covers only what is on the syllabus for that day. After that, he dismisses the class, whether we have gone the full fifty minutes or just half an hour. No one in the class ever complains about Mr. Lambert's approach. However, students do grumble about Ms. Claudio, who seems to believe that the universe does not exist beyond her classroom. Five minutes after the class should have ended, Ms. Claudio is still talking about conjunctions or commas. Finally, there's Dr. Korbatz, who almost always enters our computer science classroom five minutes late, looking harried and rushed. I don't think he's been to class on time all term, except perhaps during the first week of class. Perhaps colleges, like high schools, need a system of bells to remind students and teachers when classes begin and end.

18

Pronoun Case

<table>
<tr><td>

The Pronoun

It substitutes for any noun you can name,
Improving coherence and flow,
So it is no wonder that people proclaim
This noun's a pro.

</td></tr>
</table>

No matter what the preceding verse seems to suggest, pronouns are not simply nouns that have turned professional. **Pronouns** are words that stand in for nouns or for other pronouns. They are useful words that keep writers and speakers from tedious repetition of words. However, the rules that govern them are complex, and confusion over pronoun usage is common.

If you have ever hesitated over "Carlton and me" or "Carlton and I" or wondered whether to say "between you and I" or "between you and me," this chapter will help you find the answers. In this chapter, you will learn to use **subject pronouns, object pronouns,** and *-self* **pronouns** correctly.

Subject and Object Pronouns

Personal pronouns take different forms, called **cases,** as they perform different jobs in a sentence. Look at the following example to see how the first-person pronoun *I* changes form as its role in a sentence changes.

✔   When **I** went to the post office to pick up **my** mail, the clerk said there was a package for **me**.

subject form · *possessive form* · *object form*

Subject pronouns (the *subjective case*) include pronouns such as *I, we, you, he, she, it,* and *they.*

✔   Jordan and Chloe were tired because **they** were up until midnight trying to put up the wallpaper.

✔   **We** tried to call you, but your line was busy all evening.

✔   The winners were Bryan and **she**.

Object pronouns (the *objective case*) are pronouns such as *me, us, you, him, her, it,* and *them.*

✔   If you are through with the book, please pass it on to **me**.

✔   The cats are waiting for Hilary to feed **them**.

✔   I looked for the flashlight but could not find **it** in the dark.

Subject Pronouns

In most instances, you probably use the subject form of the pronoun correctly without thinking about it. You probably haven't said "Me went to the park" since you were three. However, using the subject form becomes trickier when a *compound subject* is used. Is it "Tiffany and her went to the concert" or "Tiffany and she went to the concert"? Usually, trying the sentence with the pronoun alone will help you *hear* the correct answer. Without "Tiffany and," the sentence becomes clear. "*She* went to the concert" is correct, not "*Her* went to the concert."

Example

Her and Andrew grew up in the same neighborhood.

Step 1: To determine whether the sentence is correct, try the pronoun alone.

✗   **Her ~~and Andrew~~** grew up in the same neighborhood.

✗   **Her** grew up in the same neighborhood.

Step 2: If the pronoun alone sounds incorrect, try changing the form.

✔ **She** grew up in the same neighborhood.

✔ **She and Andrew** grew up in the same neighborhood. (Corrected sentence.)

PRACTICE 1   USING SUBJECT PRONOUNS IN COMPOUND CONSTRUCTIONS

Underline and correct the errors in each sentence. To determine the correct pronoun form, try the pronoun alone, without the compound element.

1. Kay and me worked for an hour after everyone else went home.

   Kay and **I** worked for an hour after everyone else went home.

2. Early on Saturday, Scott and them packed up the car and drove to the lake.

   Early on Saturday, Scott and **they** packed up the car and drove to the lake.

3. When I saw Andrew the other day, he said that Jamie and him were expecting a baby.

   When I saw Andrew the other day, he said that Jamie and **he** were expecting a baby.

4. You and me have been friends for a long time.

   You and **I** have been friends for a long time.

5. Did Max and her bring a map?

   Did Max and **she** bring a map?

Subject Pronouns after Linking Verbs

"Hello?"

"May I speak to Isabella Ruiz, please?"

"This is she."

"Hello, Isabella, this is Michael Osas from your biology class. I was wondering . . ."

This polite exchange is typical of the way many telephone conversations begin, and it illustrates a rule that many people use in telephone conversations but ignore otherwise.

When a pronoun renames the subject and follows the verb *to be* or any *linking verb*, that pronoun takes the subject form.

Example

✔ The <u>subject</u> The guest of honor   <u>linking verb</u> will be   <u>subject pronoun</u> she.

✔ It is *I*. (not *me*)

✔ I had not seen Jin Yong since grade school, so I was not sure that it was *he*. (not *him*)

✔ If you want to see Ms. Kendall, that is *she* in the red coat. (not *her*)

PRACTICE 2   USING SUBJECT PRONOUNS AFTER LINKING VERBS

Underline the correct pronoun in each sentence.

1. I took Dr. McNair's course in American history, and when I found out that the teacher for world history would also be (<u>he</u>, him), I signed up.
2. The president of the chess club is (<u>she</u>, her).
3. It was (<u>he</u>, him) who told me that the class was canceled.
4. Before she opened the door, Shira asked, "Who is it?" "It is (<u>I</u>, me)," said Warren.
5. If there is anyone who needs a vacation, it is (<u>she</u>, her).

Object Pronouns

Object pronouns are used as objects of verbs and prepositions. Again, problems with object pronouns commonly occur in compound constructions. These problems can usually be resolved by isolating the pronoun. Look at the following example:

The professor agreed to give Grace and I a makeup exam.

Step 1: To determine whether the sentence is correct, try the pronoun alone.

✗ The professor agreed to give ~~Grace and~~ I a makeup exam.

✗ The professor agreed to give I a makeup exam.

Step 2: If the pronoun alone sounds incorrect, try changing the form.

✔ The professor agreed to give me a makeup exam.

✔ The professor agreed to give Grace and me a makeup exam. (Corrected sentence).

Object Pronouns with *between*

Object pronouns always follow the preposition *between*. Thus, it is always correct to write *between you and me, between us and them, between him and her, between Norman and him.*

---

* Grammar Alert!

Pronouns are often misused with *between*. Remember to use the object form: between you and *me, him, her,* or *them.*

✘ Just between you and **I,** I have a job offer. (Incorrect: The subject pronoun *I* cannot be used as the object of the preposition *between*.)

✔ Just between you and **me,** I have a job offer.

✘ The agreement was between Anita and **he.** (The subject pronoun *he* cannot be used as the object of the preposition *between*.)

✔ The agreement was between Anita and **him.**

PRACTICE 3   USING OBJECT PRONOUNS IN COMPOUND CONSTRUCTIONS

Underline the correct pronoun in each sentence.

1. The used bookshop gave Lucinda and (I, <u>me</u>) a good deal on the books we bought.
2. I will tell you a secret if you promise to keep it just between you and (I, <u>me</u>).
3. The small car John rented had barely enough room for (he, <u>him</u>) and his family, much less their luggage.
4. At the movie theater, an employee gave Rita and (I, <u>me</u>) a coupon for free candy.
5. You need to hurry if you want to go with Deante and (I, <u>me</u>).

The -*self* Pronouns—Intensive and Reflexive Pronouns

What's wrong with the following sentence?

✘ Rico and myself went to Hammond's Feed and Seed for a bag of fertilizer.

When you leave out the compound element, the problem is easier to spot:

✗ Myself went to Hammond's Feed and Seed for a bag of fertilizer.

A subject pronoun is needed to correct the sentence.

✔ I went to Hammond's Feed and Seed for a bag of fertilizer.

✔ Rico and I went to Hammond's Feed and Seed for a bag of fertilizer.

---

* Grammar Alert!

The -self pronouns are never used as subjects.

What's wrong with the following sentence?

✗ "Isabella makes her mother and myself very proud," said Mr. Pirbright.

When you leave out the compound element, the problem is easier to spot:

✗ "Isabella makes myself very proud," said Mr. Pirbright.

An object pronoun is needed to correct the sentence.

✔ "Isabella makes her mother and me very proud," said Mr. Pirbright.

Using Intensive Pronouns

Pronouns ending in -self are used in only two ways. The first way is for emphasis, as an *intensive* pronoun.

✔ Jake took the package to the post office *himself*. (That is, he did not send another person to do it.)

✔ The manager *herself* came out to greet us. (She did not send an underling.)

Using Reflexive Pronouns

The second use of *-self* pronouns is to reflect action performed *on* and *by* the word it refers to. When it is used in this way, it is used as a *reflexive* pronoun.

✔ Walter cut *himself* as he trimmed the hedges.

✔ Callie forced *herself* to finish her essay.

---

* Grammar Alert!

Never use *hisself, theirself,* or *theirselves.* They are not words. *Himself* and *themselves* are the proper forms.

PRACTICE 4   USING INTENSIVE AND REFLEXIVE PRONOUNS

Underline the correct pronoun in each sentence.

1. To save the expense of calling a plumber, Maggie decided to fix the leaky sink (her, herself).
2. Leo and (I, me, myself) have agreed to travel together and split the costs.
3. When Roshanda received a bonus at work, she said, "I am going to buy (me, myself) that pair of boots I have been wanting.
4. All of the work was done by Dale and (me, myself).
5. Duncan promised (him, himself) that he would spend more time with his family and less time at work.
6. Just between you and (I, me, myself), I think I will apply for a promotion next year.
7. Travon decided to give (he, him, himself) a few days to think about which job offer to accept.
8. Would you like to go for a walk with (I, me, myself) at lunchtime?
9. Hallie put dinner in the crock pot for (she, her, herself) and her family before she left home.
10. The senator (he, him, himself) wrote a letter on Roy's behalf.

REVIEW EXERCISE 1   CHOOSING CORRECT PRONOUN CASE

Underline the correct pronoun in each sentence.

1. Erica would have been very angry if she had known what her so-called friends were saying about (she, <u>her</u>, herself).
2. My dog and (<u>I</u>, me, myself) go for a long walk every evening, rain or shine.
3. Since Mandy was eating alone, she decided to fix (her, <u>herself</u>) a bowl of hot soup.
4. When the door opened, Phillip and (<u>he</u>, him, himself) walked in, soaked to the skin.
5. Keely asked (she, her, <u>herself</u>) if she really needed a hot fudge sundae, then decided that the answer was "yes."
6. Carlton and (<u>I</u>, myself) agreed to take our nephews trick-or-treating, but to the children's disappointment, we refused to dress up as giant pumpkins.
7. "I'm going to buy (me, <u>myself</u>) a computer so that I won't have to go to the library to use one," said Torrance.
8. Matt and (<u>he</u>, him, himself) decided to replace the rotting boards on the porch.
9. John said that his fiancée and (<u>he</u>, him, himself) first met in a laundromat.
10. Paige said that the car dealership had sold (she, <u>her</u>) and her husband a lemon.

REVIEW EXERCISE 2   CHOOSING CORRECT PRONOUN CASE

Underline the correct pronoun in each sentence.

1. Vernon and (<u>I</u>, me, myself) did not think we were hungry, but we finished off an entire double-cheese pizza.
2. To Jillian and (he, <u>him</u>), there is nothing more important than a tennis game.
3. Janice said that (<u>she</u>, her) and her brother had not seen one another in two years.
4. The cases of soft drinks were heavy, so Corey brought (<u>them</u>, they) in first.
5. Regina reminded (she, <u>herself</u>) that she needed to pick up her children early.
6. Gino never reads the newspaper, but he keeps (he, <u>himself</u>) current by visiting news sites on the Internet.

7. April asked Mr. Williams, her supervisor, to give (<u>her</u>, herself) a raise.

8. "I'm going to buy (me, <u>myself</u>) an umbrella before I get caught in the rain again," said Tracy.

9. The senator (her, <u>herself</u>) shook Theo's hand and wished him well.

10. Violet said that the police officer asked Marty and (she, <u>her</u>) if they had seen anything suspicious.

REVIEW EXERCISE 3   CORRECTING ERRORS IN PRONOUN CASE

Underline and correct the pronoun error in each sentence.

1. James and <u>me</u> will wait for you in front of the theater.

   James and **I** will wait for you in front of the theater.

2. Please send copies of the report to Mr. Mortenson and <u>myself</u>.

   Please send copies of the report to Mr. Mortenson and **me.**

3. "Who is it?" asked Ron. "It is <u>me</u>," said a voice from the other side of the door.

   "Who is it?" said Ron. "It is **I**," said a voice from the other side of the door.

4. Paco showed Shawn and <u>I</u> the old car he was planning to restore.

   Paco showed Shawn and **me** the old car he was planning to restore.

5. <u>Her</u> and her brother look nothing alike.

   She and her brother look nothing alike.

6. Karen and <u>myself</u> ate some delicious seafood when we visited Maine.

   Karen and **I** ate some delicious seafood when we visited Maine.

7. Gary says there is no animosity between Richard and <u>he</u>.

   Gary says there is no animosity between Richard and **him**.

8. It was a long trip, but Allan and <u>me</u> took turns driving.

   It was a long trip, but Allan and **I** took turns driving.

9. Jan said that Darren and <u>her</u> had painted the entire house themselves.

   Jan said that Darren and **she** had painted the entire house themselves.

10. "You and <u>me</u> need to talk," Stuart told his girlfriend.

    "You and **I** need to talk," Stuart told his girlfriend.

REVIEW EXERCISE 4   CORRECTING ERRORS IN PRONOUN CASE

Underline and correct the two pronoun case errors in each sentence.

1. Miguel and <u>myself</u> went to the basketball game with Sandra and <u>she</u>.

    Miguel and **I** went to the basketball game with Sandra and **her**.

    _____

    _____

2. Please give the gift to Aunt Susan and <u>they</u>, and be sure to tell them that it is from <u>myself</u>.

    Please give the gift to Aunt Susan and **them**, and be sure to tell them that it is

    from **me**.

    _____

3. "Can you pick the thief from the lineup?" asked the police officer. "Officer, it was <u>him</u>!" said Andrew, pointing to a tall man. "He pulled a gun on the night manager and <u>I</u>."

    "Can you pick the thief from the lineup?" asked the police officer. "Officer, it

    was **he**!" said Andrew, pointing to a tall man. "He pulled a gun on the night

    manager and **me**."

4. Lena picked up the wedding invitation addressed to her husband and <u>she</u>. "I guess Carl and <u>me</u> should make an effort to go," she said.

    Lena picked up the wedding invitation addressed to her husband and **her**. "I

    guess Carl and **I** should make an effort to go," she said.

    _____

5. "Can you help Simon and <u>I</u> with this tire?" asked Fernando. "<u>Him</u> and I will appreciate it."

    "Can you help Simon and **me** with this tire?" asked Fernando. "**He** and I will

    appreciate it."

    _____

REVIEW EXERCISE 5   CHOOSING CORRECT PRONOUN CASE

Underline the correct pronoun in each sentence of the following paragraph.

¹When Karen first enrolled in college after thirteen years in the workforce, (<u>she</u>, her,

herself) worried that she would never be able to keep up with younger students. [2]They seemed so sure of (they, them, <u>themselves</u>) that Karen thought she was the only one having trouble in her math class. [3]But after the first test, Karen discovered (<u>she</u>, her, herself) was not alone. [4]"Just between you and (<u>me</u>, I), I plan to drop this class," the student next to her whispered. [5]Suddenly, Karen knew what (<u>she</u>, her) had to do. [6]"Don't drop it," she told the student. "You and (<u>I</u>, me) can study together." [7]Soon, (<u>she</u>, her, herself) and several other students were meeting regularly to study after class. [8]After the next test, Karen discovered that (<u>she</u>, her, herself) and the other group members had all made a B or better on the test. [9]"Yes, but can (<u>we</u>, us, ourselves) maintain those high grades?" one of the group members asked. [10]"That's strictly up to (we, <u>us</u>, ourselves)," Karen replied confidently.

19

Pronoun Agreement, Reference, and Point of View

> Abbott: I'm telling you, Who is on first.
> Costello: Well, I'm asking YOU who's on first!
> Abbott: That's the man's name.
> Costello: That's who's name?
> Abbott: Yes.
> Costello: Well, go ahead and tell me.
> Abbott: Who.
> Costello: The guy on first.
> Abbott: Who!
> Costello: The first baseman.
> Abbott: Who is on first!
>
> From Abbott and Costello's "Who's on First?"

Abbott and Costello's classic comedy routine deliberately causes confusion through use of pronouns. Sometimes, writers cause confusion without meaning to through errors in pronoun reference, agreement, and point of view. Each of the following sentences contains a pronoun error. Can you figure out why the pronouns in boldface type are incorrect?

✘ By the time Marcie reached the post office, **they** were closed.

✘ Andrew told Jason that **he** needed to wash **his** car.

✘ "I try hard to get along with my stepmother," said Tracy, "but there is only so much **you** can do."

Here are the answers. The first sentence contains an error in pronoun agreement. The pronoun **they** is plural, but the word it refers to is singular. Here is the corrected sentence:

✔ By the time Marcie reached the post office, **it** was closed.

The second sentence contains an error in pronoun reference. The reader cannot be sure whether "he" refers to Andrew or Jason.

✔ Andrew told Jason, "**I** need to wash **my** car."

The third sentence contains an error in pronoun point of view. The speaker switches from the first person (*I try*) to the second person (*you can do*).

✔ "I try hard to get along with my stepmother," said Tracy, "but there is only so much **I** can do."

Keeping your writing free of errors in pronoun agreement, reference, and point of view helps your reader to move through your work smoothly and without confusion. This chapter will help you to learn the rules of **pronoun agreement, pronoun reference,** and **pronoun point of view.**

Pronoun Agreement

A pronoun must **agree in number** with the word it refers to. In other words, a *singular* pronoun can refer only to a singular noun or pronoun, and a *plural* pronoun can refer only to a plural noun or pronoun.

The word that a pronoun refers to is called its **antecedent.** An antecedent may be a noun such as *desk* or *dream,* a pronoun such as *someone* or *them,* or even a compound construction such as *streets and sidewalks* or *Nicole and Deonte.* Look at the following examples:

Example

antecedent   pronoun
✔ The dog retrieved the **ball** in midair and brought **it** back to Ramon.

In the preceding sentence, the singular pronoun *it* refers to one word in the sentence, the singular word *ball.*

✔   *antecedent*   Teresa bought **flowers** at the farmer's market and took **them** to her mother.   *pronoun*

Here, the plural pronoun *them* refers to the plural antecedent *flowers*.

✔   *antecedent*   Teresa brought **peaches and plums** home from the farmer's market *pronoun* and put **them** in a bowl.

In the preceding sentence, the plural pronoun *them* refers to the compound antecedent *peaches and plums*.

Problems in Pronoun Agreement

Errors in pronoun agreement occur when a singular pronoun is used to refer to a plural word or when a plural pronoun is used to refer to a singular word.

✘   *singular   plural*   Marla went to the ice cream **shop,** but **they** had closed for the day.

✔   *singular singular*   Marla went to the ice cream **shop,** but **it** had closed for the day.

✘   *plural   singular*   Tom was carrying two **bags** of groceries, but when he tripped, **it** flew out of his hands and onto the sidewalk.

✔   *plural   plural*   Tom was carrying two **bags** of groceries, but when he tripped, **they** flew out of his hands and onto the sidewalk.

PRACTICE 1   MAKING PRONOUNS AGREE

Underline the correct pronoun in each sentence.

1.   The pieces of pottery on display were so beautiful that Tiffany spent several minutes looking at (it, them).
2.   As the rain pattered on the roof, Molly was lulled by (its, their) hypnotic rhythm.
3.   Mr. Melton shops at Samson's Clothiers because (it is, they are) locally owned.
4.   The restaurant displayed the menu in (its, their) window; Frieda and Jorge stopped to look.

5. Every piece of furniture in the showroom had a sale sticker attached to (it, them).

Singular Indefinite Pronouns

The following **indefinite pronouns** are always singular.

each	everybody	anyone	anything
either	somebody	everyone	everything
neither	nobody	someone	something
anybody	one	no one	nothing

---

* Memory Jogger

Remember the singular indefinite pronouns more easily by grouping them:

Each, either, neither, all the **bodies,** all the **ones,** all the **things.**

✗   **Somebody** called you, but **they** didn't leave a message.

The plural pronoun *they* does not agree with the singular antecedent *somebody.*

✔   **Somebody** called you, but **he** didn't leave a message.

✗   **Each** of the team members has **their** own particular strength.

The plural pronoun *their* does not agree with the singular antecedent *each.*

✔   **Each** of the team members has **her** own particular strength.

Often, the use of indefinite pronouns raises another problem. In the preceding example, saying *"Each of the team members has her own particular strength"* works only if we know that all team members are female. Words like *everybody, somebody, anyone,* and *everyone* often include both males and females. So the use of indefinite pronouns raises not only the question of pronoun agreement but also the question of **gender fairness.**

Pronouns and Gender Fairness

Gender fairness means using gender-neutral terms such as "server," "police officer," and "firefighter." It means not stereotyping people or professions—Anthony Barron is a nurse, not a "male nurse"; Gina Richardson is a doctor, not a "woman doctor." Naturally, gender fairness also includes avoiding describing women solely in terms of their looks or men solely in terms of their bank accounts. Those requirements are fairly simple. The area of gender fairness and pronouns, however, requires more thought. Using "he or she" or "his or her" is often awkward, and constructions such as "he/she" or "(s)he" are downright ungraceful. How, then, can a writer's language be unbiased, graceful, and grammatically correct, all at the same time? There are several possible solutions. Look at the following sentence:

✘ Nobody has received **their** grades from the last term yet.

The sentence contains an error in pronoun agreement—the singular indefinite pronoun *nobody* does not agree with the plural pronoun *their*. Following are several ways to correct pronoun agreement errors such as this one while remaining gender-fair.

Solution 1: Choose a gender and stay with it throughout a single example or paragraph. Then, in your next example or paragraph, switch to the other gender.

✘ Nobody has received **their** grades from the last term yet.

✔ **Nobody** has received **his** grades from the last term yet.

✔ **Nobody** has received **her** grades from the last term yet.

Solution 2: Use a "his or her" construction. Because this solution is grammatically correct but stylistically awkward, use it when you will not have to repeat the construction.

✘ **Nobody** has received **their** grades from the last term yet.

✔ **Nobody** has received **his or her** grades from the last term yet.

Solution 3: Use plural rather than singular constructions.

✘ **Nobody** has received **their** grades from the last term yet.

✔ **Students** have not received **their** grades from the last term yet.

Solution 4: Remove the pronoun agreement problem by removing the pronoun.

✗ **Nobody** has received **their** grades from the last term yet.

✔ **Nobody** has received grades from the last term yet.

PRACTICE 2 MAKING INDEFINITE PRONOUNS AGREE

Underline and correct the pronoun agreement error in each of the following sentences, using the four solutions listed previously.

Answers will vary

1. Each of the patients in the emergency room sat waiting for their name to be called.

   __**The patients** in the emergency room sat waiting for **their names** to be called.__

   _____

2. Someone had left their umbrella underneath a desk in the first row.

   __Someone had left **an** umbrella underneath a desk in the first row.__

   _____

3. The server came by and asked whether everyone had decided what they wanted to order.

   __The server came by and asked whether everyone had decided what **he or she**__

   __wanted to order.__

4. Almost everyone has had the experience of not being able to find their car in a crowded parking lot.

   __Almost everyone has had the experience of not being able to find **his or her** car__

   __in a crowded parking lot.__

5. Almost no one who witnessed the accident wanted to give their name or talk to reporters.

   __**Few people** who witnessed the accident wanted to give **their names** or talk to__

   __reporters.__

6. Everybody is entitled to their own opinion.

   __Everybody is entitled to **an** opinion.__

   _____

7. Each of the group members cast <u>their</u> vote.

   Each of the group members cast **a** vote.
   _____

8. Whenever one of the cashiers takes <u>their</u> break, the lines in the grocery store get longer.

   Whenever one of the cashiers takes **a** break, the lines in the grocery store get

   longer.

9. When we sat down at the picnic table, we saw that someone had left <u>their</u> wristwatch lying there.

   When we sat down at the picnic table, we saw that someone had left **a** wrist-

   watch lying there.

10. The speaker said that anyone who wants to be successful should define <u>their</u> goals and then pursue them.

    The speaker said that anyone who wants to be successful should define **his or**

    her goals and then pursue them.

Pronoun Reference

If a sentence has problems with **pronoun reference,** then either a pronoun has no antecedent, or it has more than one possible antecedent.

Pronoun Reference Problem: No Antecedent

If a pronoun has no antecedent, then it is a potential source of confusion to your reader. Look at the following examples.

✗ When Emma arrived at the doctor's office, **they** told her that Dr. Ross had been called away on an emergency.

Who are *they?* Replacing the pronoun *they* with a more specific word makes the sentence's meaning clear:

✔ When Emma arrived at the doctor's office, **the receptionist** told her that Dr. Ross had been called away on an emergency.

✗   Because his brother drives a truck for a living, Robert wants to be **one,** too.

What does Robert want to be? A brother? A truck? The word that should logically be the antecedent of *one*—the word *trucker*—appears nowhere in the sentence. The simplest way to correct the problem is to replace the word *one* with a more specific word:

✔   Because his brother drives a truck, Robert wants to be **a trucker,** too.

PRACTICE 3   CORRECTING PROBLEMS IN PRONOUN REFERENCE

Underline and correct the pronoun reference problems in each sentence.

Answers will vary.

1. At the driver's license bureau, the clerk told Ross that <u>it</u> would be mailed to him in two weeks.

    At the driver's license bureau, the clerk told Ross that **a license** would be

    mailed to him in two weeks.

2. When Andrea called her cell phone company about the problems she was having, <u>they</u> told her that her phone probably needed a new battery.

    When Andrea called her cell phone company about the problems she was

    having, **the company representative** told her that her phone probably needed a

    new battery.

3. Pierre's dream is to play professional basketball. Ever since childhood, he has wanted to be <u>one</u>.

    Pierre's dream is to play professional basketball. Ever since childhood, he has

    wanted to be **a professional player.**

4. When Erica applied for a scholarship, <u>he</u> told her that with her grades, her chances of receiving a scholarship were excellent.

    When Erica applied for a scholarship, **her teacher** told her that with her grades,

    her chances of receiving a scholarship were excellent.

5. Gunther watched the needle on his gas tank approach E and kept hoping that there would be <u>one</u> at the next exit.

Gunther watched the needle on his gas tank approach E and kept hoping that

there would be **a gas station** at the next exit.

Pronoun Reference Problem: Two Possible Antecedents

When a pronoun could logically refer to either of two words, it has two possible antecedents.

Examples

✗ The instructor told Edward that **his** work was exceptional.

It is unclear whether Edward or his instructor does exceptional work, since "his" could refer to either.

✔ The instructor said, "Edward, your work is exceptional."

✔ Edward's instructor, Ms. Morrow, told him that his work was exceptional.

✗ Alfonzo had eaten a slice of pizza and drunk a large iced tea, but he still wanted another **one**.

✔ Alfonzo had eaten a slice of pizza and drunk a large iced tea, but he still wanted another slice.

✔ Alfonzo had eaten a slice of pizza and drunk a large iced tea, but he still wanted another glass of tea.

PRACTICE 4 CORRECTING PROBLEMS IN PRONOUN REFERENCE

Underline and correct the pronoun reference problems in each sentence.

Answers will vary.

1. Squirrels played among the colorful leaves as Felicia watched from a bench. As she left, she picked up a bright red <u>one</u> and put it in her pocket.

   Squirrels played among the colorful leaves as Felicia watched from a bench. As

   she left, she picked up a bright red **leaf** and put it in her pocket.

2. Joe told Alvin that <u>he</u> was wrong.

    Joe **said, "Alvin, you were** wrong."
    _____

    _____

3. Carlton put a frozen dinner in the microwave and laundry in the washing machine, then set the timer so he could eat <u>it</u> as soon as the buzzer went off.

    Carlton put a frozen dinner in the microwave and laundry in the washing machine,

    then set the timer so he could eat **the dinner** as soon as the buzzer went off.

4. Annie told her sister that <u>she</u> was a special person.

    Annie **said to** her sister, **"You are a** special person."
    _____

    _____

5. When Allen saw the tiny, intricate carvings lined up on the beautifully polished mahogany table, he said that he would like to have <u>one</u>.

    When Allen saw the tiny, intricate carvings lined up on the beautifully polished

    mahogany table, he said that he would like to have **a carving.**

Pronoun Point of View

It is important to avoid unnecessary shifts in **point of view,** that is, shifts from one **person** to another. The following chart shows common **first, second,** and **third person** pronouns in their singular and plural forms.

Point of View

	Singular	Plural
First person *(the person speaking)*	I	we
Second person *(the person spoken to)*	you	you
Third person *(the person spoken about)*	he, she, it singular indefinite pronouns (everybody, anybody, etc.)	they

Look at the following sentences:

✗ Marcus enjoys going to movies because **you** can escape all **your** problems.

The sentence contains an unnecessary shift in point of view. If Marcus goes to a movie, *he* escapes *his* problems.

✔ Marcus enjoys going to movies because **he** can escape all **his** problems.

✗ I love playing computer games, but they waste **your** time.

✔ I love playing computer games, but they waste time. (Pronoun omitted)

✔ I love playing computer games, but they waste **my** time.

PRACTICE 5   CORRECTING PROBLEMS IN PRONOUN POINT OF VIEW

Underline and correct the point-of-view problems in each sentence.

Answers will vary.

1. Michelle always carries a cell phone and a tire repair kit because <u>you</u> never know what will happen on the road.

   Michelle always carries a cell phone and a tire repair kit because **she** never

   knows what will happen on the road.

2. Sallie said she enjoyed living in the South because <u>you</u> found so many friendly people there.

   Sallie said she enjoyed living in the South because **she** found so many friendly

   people there.

3. I go to yard sales because <u>you</u> can always find something interesting and affordable.

   I go to yard sales because **I** can always find something interesting and afford-

   able.

4. Nathaniel has been trying to find out where <u>you</u> can buy concert tickets in advance.

   Nathaniel has been trying to find out where **to** buy concert tickets in advance.

5. I hate driving home in the late afternoon because the sun is always in <u>your</u> eyes.

   I hate driving home in the late afternoon because the sun is always in **my** eyes.

REVIEW EXERCISE 1   RECOGNIZING PROBLEMS IN AGREEMENT, REFERENCE, AND POINT OF VIEW

Underline the correct alternative in each sentence. Then, in the blank to the left of the sentence, indicate whether the problem is one of **agreement** (singular with singular, plural with plural), **reference** (making sure that the pronoun has a clear antecedent), or **point of view** (making sure there are no shifts in person).

Point of View   1. Claire hates working the second shift because (you, <u>she</u>) has so little time to spend with her family.

Reference   2. When Troy took the employment preference test, (they, <u>the employment counselor</u>) told Troy that he would be suited to work in teaching or accounting.

Agreement   3. Neither of Duane's aunts is sure that (<u>she</u>, they) can fly in for his graduation.

Reference   4. When Olivia checked out her videos, (they, <u>a store clerk</u>) reminded her that she owed a fine on a late video.

Agreement   5. Each member of the Men's Philanthropic Society has said that (they, <u>he</u>) will mentor a child.

Agreement   6. A person who procrastinates too much may find (themselves, <u>herself</u>) in trouble at school, at work, or even at home.

Reference   7. Marlon told his instructor (that he was a poor writer, <u>"I am a poor writer."</u>)

Reference   8. As he looked at the pickle slices and the unbuttered toast on his plate, Arthur said, "(They claim, <u>The author of that new diet book claims</u>) that I will lose five pounds in the first week on the Pickle Diet."

Agreement   9. Giselle is rarely home because, as an activities director on a cruise ship, (they have, <u>she has</u>) to travel most of the year.

Reference   10. Rick went by the pharmacy, but (they, <u>the pharmacist</u>) had not filled his prescription yet.

REVIEW EXERCISE 2   CORRECTING PROBLEMS IN AGREEMENT, REFERENCE, AND POINT OF VIEW

Underline and correct the pronoun agreement, reference, or point of view error in each sentence.

Answers will vary.

1. The newspaper and the aluminum cans were being saved for recycling, but Carlene was not sure where to take <u>it</u>.

    The newspaper and the aluminum cans were being saved for recycling, but

    Carlene was not sure where to take **recyclables.**

2. Lou says that he chose a dog as a pet because, unlike a cat, a dog is <u>your</u> constant companion.

   Lou says that he chose a dog as a pet because, unlike a cat, a dog is **a** constant

   companion.

3. Anyone who thinks that <u>they</u> can fix the problem with my computer is welcome to try.

   Anyone who thinks that **he or she** can fix the problem with my computer is

   welcome to try.

4. Jake says that <u>you</u> can tell if a dog is friendly by watching its body language.

   Jake says that **anyone** can tell if a dog is friendly by watching its body language.

5. When Natasha forgot the combination to her gym locker, <u>they</u> stayed in the locker for a whole week until she finally remembered the combination.

   When Natasha forgot the combination to her gym locker, **her athletic shoes**

   stayed in the locker for a whole week until she finally remembered the combination.

6. Someone had dropped <u>their</u> wallet in the parking lot of the convenience store.

   Someone had dropped her wallet in the parking lot of the convenience store.

7. Each of the men on the soccer team brings <u>their</u> own special talent to the game.

   Each of the men on the soccer team brings **his** own special talent to the game.

8. Tomika told her mother that <u>she</u> needed a haircut.

   Tomika told her mother, **"You need** a haircut.**"**

9. Jason enjoys watching comedies because <u>you</u> can always use a good laugh.

   Jason enjoys watching comedies because **he** can always use a good laugh.

10. Each of the employees had <u>their</u> own locker in the back room.

    Each of the employees had **a** locker in the back room.

REVIEW EXERCISE 3   **CORRECTING PROBLEMS IN AGREEMENT, REFERENCE, AND POINT OF VIEW**

Underline and correct the two errors in pronoun agreement, reference, or point of view in each sentence.

Answers will vary.

1. Every time Harry drives through the gate at work, <u>they</u> ask for his ID, even though <u>you're</u> there every day.

   Every time Harry drives through the gate at work, **the guard asks** for his ID,

   even though **Harry is** there every day.

2. Cassandra kept vitamins up high where her child could not reach <u>it</u> and take an accidental overdose. "<u>They</u> think those animal-shaped vitamins are candy," she said.

   Cassandra kept vitamins up high where her child could not reach **them** and

   take an accidental overdose. "**Children** think those animal-shaped vitamins are

   candy," she said.

3. Someone left <u>their</u> cell phone on a park bench. Maybe <u>they</u> will come back for the phone.

   Someone left **a** cell phone on a park bench. Maybe **he or she** will come back

   for the phone.

4. Someone behind Shelley kept making loud comments about the movie, and <u>this</u> annoyed Shelley. Finally, she reported <u>them</u> to an usher.

   Someone behind Shelley kept making loud comments about the movie, and **the**

   noise annoyed Shelley. Finally, she reported **the person** to an usher.

5. Teresa told Gail that <u>her</u> left rear tire was low and that her wheel cover was loose. "I'll get <u>it</u> fixed right away," said Gail.

   Teresa told Gail, **"Your** left rear tire **is** low, and your wheel cover **is** loose." "I'll

   get **the problems** fixed right away," said Gail.

REVIEW EXERCISE 4   **CORRECTING PROBLEMS IN AGREEMENT, REFERENCE, AND POINT OF VIEW**

Underline and correct the error in pronoun agreement, reference, or point of view in each sentence.

Answers will vary.

1. The milk in April's refrigerator was sour, so she threw <u>it</u> away.

   The milk in April's refrigerator was sour, so she threw **the milk** away.

2. Almost everyone surveyed said <u>their</u> driving skills were above average.

   Almost everyone surveyed said **his or her** driving skills were above average.

3. Griffin told Andrew that <u>he</u> was being promoted to a job with more responsibility and higher pay.

   Griffin told Andrew, **"You** are being promoted to a job with more responsibility and higher pay.**"**

4. When Rhea saw fleas on the puppies, she called the veterinarian to ask how to kill <u>them</u>.

   When Rhea saw fleas on the puppies, she called the veterinarian to ask how to kill **the fleas.**

5. The woman angrily asked the waiter, "How do <u>you</u> get some service in this place?"

   The woman angrily asked the waiter, "How do **I** get some service in this place?"

6. Someone on the elevator had eaten garlic on <u>their</u> lunch break, so Brad held his breath all the way to the eighth floor.

   Someone on the elevator had eaten garlic **at lunch**, so Brad held his breath all the way to the eighth floor.

7. At the restaurant's drive-through window, <u>they</u> gave Joaquin incorrect change.

   At the restaurant's drive-through window, **the clerk** gave Joaquin incorrect change.

8. Priscilla told Dr. Smith that <u>she</u> needed to stop smoking.

    Priscilla told Dr. Smith, **"I need** to stop smoking."

9. Myra carefully covered her fried eggs with catsup and ate <u>it</u> hungrily.

    Myra carefully covered her fried eggs with catsup and ate **them** hungrily.

10. When I asked Javon how his brother was doing after the accident, he said that <u>he</u> was fine.

    When I asked Javon how his brother was doing after the accident, he said, **"My brother** is fine."

REVIEW EXERCISE 5   CORRECTING PROBLEMS IN AGREEMENT, REFERENCE, AND POINT OF VIEW

Underline and correct the error in pronoun agreement, reference, or point of view in each numbered sentence.

Answers will vary.

¹May took her meager breakfast to the cafeteria table and, with a sigh, began to eat <u>them</u>. ²She was getting tired of grapefruit and black coffee and tired of a diet where <u>you</u> could have no sugar and no fats. ³However, she was determined to lose twenty-five pounds before <u>they</u> held the ten-year class reunion in October. ⁴At the table next to hers, <u>he</u> had eggs, sausages, strawberries with thick cream, and a separate, small plate of two doughnuts covered in thick powdered sugar. ⁵As she finished her grapefruit, she noticed that the man was getting up, apparently having finished <u>their</u> meal. ⁶The small plate still held a single powdered sugar doughnut, and May knew that the treat would be discarded when <u>they</u> came to clear the table. ⁷Suddenly, her resolve to diet burst like a bubble; <u>you</u> could starve only for so long. ⁸She rose and took two steps to the next table, and her arm, seeming to take on a life of its own, snaked out to grab <u>it</u>. ⁹She bit into the sweet confection, not

caring about the white powdered sugar that clung to her lips, not caring about the extra pounds or whether she could lose <u>it</u> before the reunion. [10]Then, across the cafeteria, she saw the man from the next table; <u>they</u> had just handed him a glass of milk, and he was returning to enjoy his second doughnut.

---

[1]May took her meager breakfast to the cafeteria table and, with a sigh, began to eat. [2]She was getting tired of grapefruit and black coffee and tired of a diet where **she** could have no sugar and no fats. [3]However, she was determined to lose twenty-five pounds before **her high school class** held its ten-year class reunion in October. [4]At the table next to hers, **a man** had eggs, sausages, strawberries with thick cream, and a separate, small plate of two doughnuts covered in thick powdered sugar. [5]As she finished her grapefruit, she noticed that the man was getting up, apparently having finished **his** meal. [6]The small plate still held a single powdered sugar doughnut, and May knew that the treat would be discarded when **the waiter** came to clear the table. [7]Suddenly, her resolve to diet burst like a bubble; **she** could starve only for so long. [8]She rose and took two steps to the next table, and her arm, seeming to take on a life of its own, snaked out to grab **the doughnut.** [9]She bit into the sweet confection, not caring about the white powdered sugar that clung to her lips, not caring about the extra pounds or whether she could lose **them** before the reunion. [10]Then, across the cafeteria, she saw the man from the next table; **the server** had just handed him a glass of milk, and he was returning to enjoy his second doughnut.

20

Relative Pronouns

Relative pronouns just for you—
Whom, which, that, and who.
Useful when you write or chat,
Who, whom, which, and that.
To help you write without a hitch,
Try that, who, whom, and which.
You'll help your sentences to bloom,
With which, that, who, and whom.

A **relative pronoun** introduces a clause that modifies a noun or pronoun within a sentence. That is, a relative pronoun *relates* information in the clause to the noun or pronoun that is its antecedent. In this chapter, you will learn about the relative pronouns **who, whom, whose, which,** and **that,** and about the punctuation used with relative clauses.

Relative Pronouns

The relative pronouns are *who* (along with its object form *whom* and its possessive form *whose*), *which,* and *that.* Ordinarily, the pronoun *who* refers to people; *which* refers to things, ideas, and creatures other than humans; and *that* refers to things, ideas, creatures, or humans. (Acceptance of the use of *that* to refer to humans is relatively new, and some experts still prefer *who.* Follow your instructor's preference.)

Examples

> The relative clause provides information about the peaches.
> ✔ The peaches *that I bought at the farmer's market* were sweet and delicious.

> The relative clause provides information about Monday's mail.
> ✔ Monday's mail, *which had been delivered that morning*, lay unopened on Tom's desk until late afternoon.

> The relative clause provides information about the woman.
> ✔ The woman *who sat in the back of the room* asked several good questions.

> The relative clause provides information about Eudora Welty.
> ✔ Eudora Welty, *whose short stories are widely anthologized*, worked as a photographer before becoming a writer.

PRACTICE 1   RECOGNIZING RELATIVE CLAUSES

Underline the relative pronoun once and underline the rest of the relative clause twice in each of the following sentences.

1. The person who gave Emil directions must have been mixed up.
2. The puppy that was dropped in front of the restaurant was eventually taken home by one of the cooks.
3. At the end of the program, the chorus sang a rousing song that brought the audience to its feet.
4. I gave my ticket to a bored-looking man who stood at the gate.
5. The discovery of the insect, which was thought to be extinct, greatly excited the scientists.

Who, Whom, or Whose?

Here is brief review of the use of the pronouns *who, whom,* and *whose.*

The Pronoun *Who*

Who is a subject form of the pronoun.

> subject   verb
> ✔ Erin Smith, **who** delivers my mail, has been a mail carrier for ten years.

In the preceding sentence, the pronoun *who* is the subject of the verb *delivers*. One trick to check yourself on the use of *who* or *whom* is to isolate the clause beginning with *who* and see whether *he* (a subject pronoun you are probably comfortable using) will also fit. If *he* will substitute, then *who* is correct:

Step 1: Isolate the "who" clause.

Who delivers my mail

Step 2: Substitute "he" for "who."

~~Who~~ **He** delivers my mail

The substitution works, so *who* is the correct pronoun.

The Pronoun *Whom*

Whom is the object form of the pronoun.

✔ My biological father, whom I did not meet until I was eighteen, keeps in close touch with me now.

In the preceding sentence, the pronoun *whom* is the object of the verb *did meet*. Again, to check yourself on the use of *who* versus *whom*, isolate the clause beginning with *whom* and see whether *him* (an object pronoun you are probably comfortable using) will also fit. If *him* will substitute, then *whom* is correct:

Step 1: Isolate the "whom" clause.

Whom I did not meet until I was eighteen

Step 2: Substitute "him" for "whom."

~~Whom~~ **Him** I did not meet until I was eighteen

With whom, the word order does not always fall into place the first time. Play with the sentence a bit until you can be sure that the object form *him* fits into the sentence.

Him I did not meet until I was eighteen.

I did not meet **him** until I was eighteen.

The substitution works, so *whom* is the correct pronoun.

The Pronoun *Whose*

Whose is the possessive form of the pronoun *who*. Like other forms of *who*, *whose* refers to humans. However, because *which* and *that* have no possessive forms, *whose* also correctly refers to things, ideas, and creatures other than humans.

✔ Elton John, *whose* outrageous costumes were once his trademark, has toned down his wardrobe in recent years.

✔ Online education is an idea *whose* time has come.

✔ The dog, *whose* food and water bowls had apparently been empty for days, was hungry and dehydrated.

PRACTICE 2   USING *WHO*, *WHOM*, AND *WHOSE*

In each of the following sentences, choose the pronoun *who*, *whom*, or *whose* to introduce the relative clause.

1. As its president, the club chose Julia Barrantes, __who__ served as treasurer last year.

2. Lamont Self, __whom__ my family has known for years, is retiring to Florida.

3. Will the person __whose__ red car is parked in the fire lane please park in the lot?

4. Anyone __who__ has ever had pets knows how much responsibility they are.

5. Abraham Lincoln, __whose__ words at Gettysburg have echoed through centuries, did not really scrawl his Gettysburg Address on the back of an envelope.

6. Tanisha is a person __whom__ everyone seems to like.

7. Jonathan, __who__ is attending college on a scholarship, has made his family proud.

8. The antique table, __whose__ surface was scratched and marred by years of use, was nevertheless beautiful.

9. Madame Marie Curie, __who__ discovered radium, died of leukemia possibly brought on by exposure to radiation.

10. Politicians __who__ keep their promises are usually the ones who are reelected.

Essential and Nonessential Clauses

Relative clauses come in two types: *essential* and *nonessential,* also called *restrictive* and *nonrestrictive.* The pronouns *who* and *that* introduce essential clauses, while the pronouns *who* and *which* introduce nonessential clauses.

Essential Clauses

An essential clause provides information that is essential in identifying the word that it modifies. In other words, the writer assumes that without this information, the reader would have no way of identifying the person or thing described.

✔ The detective *who arrested the bank robber* was given a citation for bravery.

In the preceding sentence, the clause *who arrested the bank robber* is essential because it is the only means of identifying the detective, of separating him from all of the other detectives on the force. Another way to explain the use of the clause is to say that it *restricts* the term "detective" so that it refers to only one detective: the one who arrested the bank robber. Both explanations are accurate, and the terms *essential clause* and *restrictive clause* are used interchangeably. Notice that essential clauses are not set off from the rest of the sentence by commas.

✔ The truck that just passed us was going at least eighty.

Nonessential Clauses

Nonessential clauses provide extra information about something or someone who is already identified in some way.

✔ Detective Vasquez, *who arrested the bank robber,* was given a citation for bravery.

In this sentence, the clause *who arrested the bank robber* is nonessential because the detective is already identified by name. Nonessential clauses are separated from the rest of the sentence by commas.

✔ The robber's car, *which was found in a wooded area,* contained most of the money from the robbery.

In this sentence, the clause *which was found in a wooded area* is nonessential because the car is already identified in the sentence as "the robber's car." The location where it was found is not essential in identifying it.

PRACTICE 3   RECOGNIZING ESSENTIAL AND NONESSENTIAL CLAUSES

In the following sentences, label the italicized clauses as *essential* or *nonessential*

essential   1. The soccer game *that we watched last night* was exciting.

essential   2. The dental hygienist *who cleaned Paul's teeth* explained why flossing was important.

nonessential   3. Drew Carey, *whose acting abilities are well known,* is also a writer.

nonessential   4. Harry's flight, *which was delayed by bad weather,* arrived six hours late.

nonessential   5. The concrete, *which had been poured an hour ago,* was still wet.

essential   6. All symptoms of the flu *that Hope had last week* are gone.

essential   7. The person *who won the lottery jackpot* has only one more day to claim it.

nonessential   8. My uncle, *who came to the United States with only $100 to his name,* is now wealthy.

essential   9. People *who gain excess weight* often have trouble losing it.

nonessential 10. The old grandfather clock, *which kept perfect time for fifty years,* now seems to be broken.

Punctuation of Relative Clauses

Punctuating Essential Clauses

Essential clauses are not set off by commas.

✔ The artist *whose work is displayed in the library* is a graduate of this college.

✔ The person *who wins the race* will receive a cash prize as well as a trophy.

Relative clauses beginning with *that* are always essential and are not set off by commas.

✔ The colors in the Hawaiian shirt *that Trevor is wearing* hurt my eyes.

✔ Did anyone take the slide *that was in my microscope?*

Punctuating Nonessential Clauses

Nonessential clauses are set off by commas. If the clause interrupts the sentence, place a comma before and after the clause. If the clause concludes the sentence, introduce the clause with a comma, and end the sentence with a period.

✔ Many states have prohibited drivers from using cell phones, *which distract drivers and cause accidents.*

✔ Sea anemones, *which may be red, pink, or yellow,* grow abundantly in coastal waters.

✔ The longest inaugural address was delivered by President William Henry Harrison, *who spoke for almost two hours in a snowstorm.*

PRACTICE 4   PUNCTUATING RELATIVE CLAUSES

Underline the relative clause in each sentence below. Then add commas to the sentences that contain nonessential clauses. Leave the sentences with essential clauses as they are, writing "essential" on the line provided.

1. The library book <u>that Marisa requested</u> had already been checked out.

   essential

   _____

2. *War and Peace* <u>which Marisa had requested from the library</u> had already been checked out.

   War and Peace, which Marisa had requested from the library, had already been

   checked out.

3. People <u>who suffer from arthritis</u> often report more pain during rainy weather.

   essential

   _____

4. Carlotta <u>who suffers from arthritis</u> says she can always tell when a storm is coming.

    Carlotta, who suffers from arthritis, says she can always tell when a storm is

    coming.

5. The shirt <u>that Ross had planned to wear</u> had a big ink stain on the pocket.

    essential

6. The person <u>who hit Pilar's car</u> had no insurance.

    essential

7. Elena's allergies <u>which keep her indoors during pollen season</u> seem to be getting worse.

    Elena's allergies, which keep her indoors during pollen season, seem to be get-

    ting worse.

8. The advertisement <u>which showed sizzling hamburgers on a grill</u> made Kelvin's mouth water.

    The advertisement, which showed sizzling hamburgers on a grill, made Kelvin's

    mouth water.

9. Katherine <u>who usually lets her answering machine screen her calls</u> picked up my call on the first ring.

    Katherine, who usually lets her answering machine screen her calls, picked up

    my call on the first ring.

10. Ronald vowed to lose the ten pounds <u>that he has gained</u> since he began school.

    essential

REVIEW EXERCISE 1   RECOGNIZING RELATIVE CLAUSES

Underline the relative pronoun once, and underline the rest of the relative clause twice in each sentence.

1. The information <u>that</u> <u>you asked for</u> has been extremely hard to find.

2. William Shakespeare, <u>whose</u> <u>works are universally admired</u>, supposedly began his career in the theater as a valet parking attendant for wealthy theatergoers' horses.

3. The police officer <u>who interviewed the suspect</u> failed to ask several key questions.

4. The car <u>that Eduardo bought</u> had only 12,000 miles on it.

5. The sofa, <u>which was extremely large</u>, would not fit through the front door.

REVIEW EXERCISE 2   RECOGNIZING ESSENTIAL AND NONESSENTIAL CLAUSES

Underline the relative clauses in the following sentences. Write *E* in the blank beside sentences containing essential relative clauses, and write *N* in the blank beside those containing nonessential relative clauses.

<u>E</u>   1. The old car lumbered off, heavily burdened by the twelve suitcases <u>that Marcie had brought along for the trip</u>.

<u>N</u>   2. Jewelry, <u>which was worn long before clothing became customary</u>, is one of the earliest forms of adornment.

<u>N</u>   3. Mr. Smith, <u>who lived quietly next door to my grandmother for years</u>, was arrested yesterday for forgery.

<u>N</u>   4. The workers, <u>whose tired faces and slumped shoulders revealed their exhaustion</u>, finally went home at 9:00 P.M.

<u>E</u>   5. On the table lay the videotape <u>that Sandra had rented for the weekend</u>.

<u>N</u>   6. Low tire pressure, <u>which puts more of the tire surface in contact with the road</u>, can cause excessive heat buildup and even a blowout.

<u>E</u>   7. The forms <u>that Ronald signed before surgery</u> were more intimidating than the procedure itself.

<u>N</u>   8. Martha, <u>who had studied all night</u>, overslept and almost missed the test.

<u>E</u>   9. People <u>who saw the crash</u> gave differing accounts of the accident.

<u>E</u> 10. Contrary to popular belief, the water <u>that we drink</u> is safer and more pure than it was fifty years ago.

REVIEW EXERCISE 3   PUNCTUATING ESSENTIAL AND NONESSENTIAL CLAUSES

Underline the relative clause in each sentence below. Then add commas to the sentences that contain nonessential clauses. Leave the sentences with essential clauses as they are, writing "essential" on the line provided.

1. Amy's high school ring <u>which she had worn since she was a teenager</u> was somehow lost during her vacation.

Amy's high school ring, which she had worn since she was a teenager, was

somehow lost during her vacation.

2. Hazel <u>who has a television in every room of her house</u> says that she is going to read more books and watch less TV.

   Hazel, who has a television in every room of her house, says that she is going to

   read more books and watch less TV.

3. The person <u>who answered the phone</u> was obviously annoyed.

   essential

4. Tom the Termite Terminator <u>who had promised to be at the Joneses' house at 9:00 a.m.</u> had not shown up by noon.

   Tom the Termite Terminator, who had promised to be at the Joneses' house at

   9:00 a.m., had not shown up by noon.

5. The site <u>that Nancy found on the Internet</u> gave her more information about Attention Deficit Disorder than any of the articles she had read.

   essential

6. The contract <u>that Tom signed</u> prohibited him from taking on a second job.

   essential

7. Brendan <u>who is a fast runner</u> plans to try out for the track team.

   Brendan, who is a fast runner, plans to try out for the track team.

8. Sara's biology professor <u>whose teaching methods are unconventional</u> often takes the entire class outside to examine plant and insect life on the campus.

   Sara's biology professor, whose teaching methods are unconventional, often

   takes the entire class outside to examine plant and insect life on the campus.

9. The old clay pot <u>which had filled with rainwater</u> now harbored mosquito eggs.

   The old clay pot, which had filled with rainwater, now harbored mosquito

   eggs.

10. The secrecy <u>that surrounded the recent change in management</u> had everyone curious and a little worried.

    essential

REVIEW EXERCISE 4   PUNCTUATING ESSENTIAL AND NONESSENTIAL CLAUSES

Underline the relative clause in each sentence below. Then add commas to the sentences that contain nonessential clauses. Leave the sentences with essential clauses as they are, writing "essential" on the line provided.

1. The cat <u>that was sitting on the porch railing</u> looked fat and contented.

    essential

2. The philodendron <u>which Ralph had forgotten to water</u> died a slow death on the front porch.

    The philodendron, which Ralph had forgotten to water, died a slow death on

    the front porch.

3. The review <u>that appeared in yesterday's paper</u> was not favorable.

    essential

4. Rosie <u>who was the editor of the college newspaper</u> seemed to be the center of attention wherever she went.

    Rosie, who was the editor of the college newspaper, seemed to be the center of

    attention wherever she went.

5. The new chair <u>which was ergonomically designed</u> did not look like any chair Vickie had ever seen.

    The new chair, which was ergonomically designed, did not look like any chair

    Vickie had ever seen.

6. The assignment asked us to describe the person <u>whom we most admired</u>.

    essential

7. My supervisor <u>whom I have always admired</u> is leaving her job to return to school.

    My supervisor, whom I have always admired, is leaving her job to return to

    school.

8. John's old Toyota <u>which used to run well</u> is in the shop again.

    John's old Toyota, which used to run well, is in the shop again.

9. The firefighters <u>who answered the call</u> extinguished the blaze quickly and efficiently.

essential

_____

10. Keiko <u>who has been in the United States for just five years</u> speaks excellent English.

Keiko, who has been in the United States for just five years, speaks excellent

English.

REVIEW EXERCISE 5   USING RELATIVE PRONOUNS

Provide the correct relative pronoun to fill each of the blanks.

[1]Answering an advertisement ___that___ I saw in the paper, I recently interviewed for a job as a computer technician. [2]When I arrived for the interview, ___which___ had been scheduled for ten o'clock, three other applicants were also waiting to be interviewed. [3]I was amazed when I saw these applicants, ___who___ had not even bothered to dress appropriately for the interview. [4]One young man, ___who___ had obviously just tumbled out of bed, had uncombed hair and sleepy eyes. [5]He wore wrinkled and torn jeans ___that___ had not seen the inside of a washer for several weeks. [6]Another applicant had her hair tied back neatly and wore a crisp white blouse, but she wore torn jeans and white athletic shoes ___that___ did not seem appropriate for an interview. [7]There was another female applicant, ___whom___ I might have found attractive if I had met her at a nightclub. [8]She wore a leather skirt

___that___ hugged her body and earrings that dangled to her shoulders. [9]I felt almost too conventional wearing a pressed white shirt, dark pants, and a conservative striped tie, ___which___ I had bought just for the occasion. [10]However, I have always heard that the person ___who___ dresses for the job is the one most likely to be hired.

21

Adjectives, Adverbs, and Articles

> Verbs supply the muscle
> That helps a sentence go,
> And prepositions are the veins
> That help control its flow.
>
> Nouns and pronouns are the bones
> That make it stand upright.
> Conjunctions are the sinews
> That help its parts unite.
>
> But adjectives and adverbs
> Are the flesh upon the bone.
> They give each sentence its own face
> And make its meaning known.

Nouns are the bones of a sentence, and verbs are the muscle that moves them, but **adjectives** and **adverbs** provide the flesh and the cartilage, the color and the texture. Without adjectives and adverbs, you could convey only the basics—what happened and to whom. You could not show *how* and *why*, *how many*, and *what kind*. This chapter provides a brief overview of adjectives and adverbs. It also reviews three useful words called **articles**—*a*, *an*, and *the*.

Adjectives

Adjectives are words that give information about nouns or pronouns. They answer the questions "What kind?" "How many?" and "Which one?" Usually, adjectives within a sentence come before the noun or pronoun they modify *(Virgil wiped his* hot, sweaty *face with a* terrycloth *towel)* or after a verb that *links* them to the noun or pronoun *(Virgil's face was* hot *and* sweaty).

Examples

- ✔ A **steaming** cup of coffee sat on the counter.
- ✔ The computer was **old** and **slow**.
- ✔ Nicole looked **puzzled**.
- ✔ Rick is **optimistic** and **cheerful**.

PRACTICE 1   IDENTIFYING ADJECTIVES AND THE WORDS THEY MODIFY

Underline the two adjectives in each sentence, and draw an arrow connecting each of the adjectives with the word it modifies.

1. Tuesday was chilly and rainy.
2. A flashy billboard towered above the tall pines.
3. Ingrid's only ambition was to own a profitable business.
4. The photograph was faded and cracked.
5. A pair of wet mittens lay on the top step of the porch.

Positive, Comparative, and Superlative Adjective Forms

Each adjective has three forms.

1. The **positive** form is the base form of the adjective. It is used to describe something, but not to compare it with anything else.
   - ✔ The laboratory was **spotless**.
   - ✔ The pizza looks **good.**
   - ✔ Benita drives a **battered** truck.

2. The **comparative** form is used to compare two things, or to compare one thing with a group of similar items.
   - ✔ Ira's salary is **higher** than mine.

✔ Melissa believes that her opinions are **better** than anyone else's.

✔ That horror movie was no **more violent** than any of the others I have seen.

✔ The new surgical technique is **less invasive** than the older methods.

3. The **superlative** form is used to compare one thing with all others in its group.

✔ Courtney does her **best** work in the mornings.

✔ Calculus is George's **least favorite** course.

✔ Since his company was paying for his meal, Vernon ordered the **most expensive** item on the menu.

✔ The thunderclap was the **loudest** that Gavin had ever heard.

Adjective Forms Chart

	Positive	Comparative	Superlative
One syllable		add -er	add -est
	cold	colder	coldest
	smart	smarter	smartest
Two syllables ending in y		change y to i, add -er	change y to i, add -est
	lazy	lazier	laziest
	busy	busier	busiest
Most words of two or more syllables		use more or less	use most or least
	helpful	more helpful	most helpful
	anxious	more anxious	most anxious
	informative	more informative	most informative
	impatient	more impatient	most impatient
	impressive	less impressive	least impressive
Irregular adjectives	good	better	best
	bad	worse	worst

PRACTICE 2   USING ADJECTIVE FORMS

Fill in the comparative and superlative forms of each adjective. Use the Adjective Forms Chart as your guide.

Positive	Comparative	Superlative
1. pale	paler	palest
2. loud	louder	loudest
3. stuffy	stuffier	stuffiest
4. petty	pettier	pettiest
5. majestic	more majestic	most majestic
6. vital	more vital	most vital
7. congenial	more congenial	most congenial
8. violent	more violent	most violent
9. good	better	best
10. bad	worse	worst

---

* Grammar Alert!

Be sure to use *more* and *most* only in combination with base (positive) adjective forms, not with *-er* or *-est* forms. "More significant" is correct, but "more happier" or "most best" is not.

PRACTICE 3   USING ADJECTIVE FORMS

In each of the following sentences, decide whether the positive, comparative, or superlative form is needed. Then convert the adjective in parentheses to the proper form, using the "Adjective Forms Chart" as your guide.

(careful)   1. Vishal is a ___careful___ and meticulous worker.

(large)   2. The avalanche was the ___largest___ in nearly half a century.

(attentive)   3. Marissa was afraid her children would misbehave at the concert, but they were quieter and ___more attentive___ than usual.

(small)   4. Raises for hourly employees were even ___smaller___ than last year's.

(impatient)   **5.** Grady was the type of person who fumed at traffic lights and in grocery lines, so the two-hour wait at the tax office made him even _more impatient_ than usual.

(clean)   **6.** When Kim returned to her hometown, everything seemed different. The shops and houses seemed neater, and the streets looked _____cleaner_____ than she remembered.

(ugly)   **7.** "No offense, Honey, but that has to be the _____ugliest_____ hat on the planet," George told his wife.

(young)   **8.** The _____youngest_____ of the four children was Amy.

(old)   **9.** Pilar was a year _____older_____ than her brother, a fact that he never let her forget.

(good)   **10.** Ed still keeps in touch with Manny, the _____best_____ friend he has ever had.

Adverbs

Adverbs give information about verbs (walked *gracefully*), adjectives (*extremely* hot), or other adverbs (*very* professionally). Often, but not always, adverbs are -*ly* forms of the adjective. *Successful* becomes *successfully*, *bad* becomes *badly*, *weird* becomes *weirdly*. The easiest way to tell an adverb from an adjective is to see what question the word answers. An **adjective** tells *how many, what kind,* or *which one*. An **adverb** tells *how, when,* or *to what degree*.

Examples

✔ Kamal looked **inquisitively** at the man in the purple hat. (how)

✔ The program was **unusually** long. (to what degree)

✔ Kim looked **regretfully** toward the candy store, then decided to stick to her diet. (how)

✔ The job starts **tomorrow.** (when)

PRACTICE 4   IDENTIFYING ADVERBS

Underline the adverb in each sentence, and draw an arrow to the word it modifies.

1. The music played <u>loudly</u>.
2. Edward looked <u>unhappily</u> at the dent in his car.

3.   The balloon floated <u>lazily</u> toward the clouds.
4.   The headache remedy worked <u>quickly</u>.
5.   Andrea arrived late for work <u>yesterday</u>.

Adverb Forms Chart

	Positive	Comparative	Superlative
Adverb ending in -*ly*		use *more*	use *most*
	strangely	more strangely	most strangely
	mildly	more mildly	most mildly
	suddenly	more suddenly	most suddenly
	reliably	more reliably	most reliably
Irregular adverbs	well	better	best
	badly	worse	worst

---

* Memory Jogger

Adjectives tell **how many, what kind,** or **which one. Adverbs** tell **how, when,** or **to what degree.**

PRACTICE 5   USING AND IDENTIFYING ADJECTIVES AND ADVERBS

In each of the following phrases, underline the correct word. Decide whether the word tells **how many, what kind, which one, how, when,** or **to what degree,** and write your response in the first blank. In the second blank, write the part of speech—**adjective** or **adverb.** The first one is done for you.

1.   ate (noisy, <u>noisily</u>)

The word tells <u>how</u> and is an <u>adverb</u>.

2.   a (<u>careful</u>, carefully) accountant

The word tells <u>what kind</u> and is an <u>adjective</u>.

3.   walked (quick, <u>quickly</u>)

The word tells <u>how</u> and is an <u>adverb</u>.

4.   a (<u>slow</u>, slowly) process

The word tells <u>what kind</u> and is an <u>adjective</u>.

5.   an (<u>easy</u>, easily) test

The word tells <u>what kind</u> and is an <u>adjective</u>.

6. passed the test (easy, <u>easily</u>)

   The word tells <u>how</u> and is an <u>adverb</u>.

7. (<u>numerous</u>, numerously) reasons

   The word tells <u>how many</u> and is an <u>adjective</u>.

8. (swift, <u>swiftly</u>) agreed

   The word tells <u>how</u> and is an <u>adverb</u>.

9. (<u>rational</u>, rationally) behavior

   The word tells <u>what kind</u> and is an <u>adjective</u>.

10. behaved (rational, <u>rationally</u>)

   The word tells <u>how</u> and is an <u>adverb</u>.

PRACTICE 6   USING ADJECTIVES AND ADVERBS

In each sentence, underline the correct word.

1. It was winter, and the trees were (<u>bare</u>, barely).
2. Carl put on his turn signal, pulled into the parking lot, and brought the van (smooth, <u>smoothly</u>) to a stop.
3. The black and white dog limped (painful, <u>painfully</u>) to the side of the road.
4. The emergency room doctor trained herself to speak (calm, <u>calmly</u>) even in the most urgent situations.
5. Rodrigo decided to stop for a (<u>quick</u>, quickly) bite to eat.
6. Because she was not feeling well, it was not a (<u>good</u>, well) day for Carlotta to take a test.
7. The twenty-page instruction book that accompanied the machine was not (<u>helpful</u>, helpfully) in the least.
8. The paramedic pounded (loud, <u>loudly</u>) on the locked door and shouted, "Can you hear me?"
9. For no apparent reason, the man in the yellow beret (angry, <u>angrily</u>) shook his fist at a flock of birds flying high overhead.
10. Using a pair of tweezers, the nurse (quick, <u>quickly</u>) extracted a rough wooden splinter from the little boy's finger.

Puzzling Pairs

Certain adjective and adverb pairs are confused more often than others. The next section explains the differences between the pairs *good* and *well*, *bad* and *badly*, and *worse* and *worst*.

Puzzling Pairs: *Good* and *Well, Bad* and *Badly*

Good is an adjective that tells *what kind; well* is an adverb that tells *how.*
Look at the following examples.

✔   Even a *good* mechanic may need some time to diagnose automobile
problems. (tells *what kind of* mechanic)

✔   Andrew and his brother work *well* together. (tells *how* they work)

---

* Grammar Alert!

Well can be an **adjective** when it refers to health, as in "He is not a *well*
man" or "I am not feeling *well.*"

✔   Anita worried at first that she would be a *bad* supervisor, but experience has given her confidence. (tells *what kind of* supervisor)

✔   Sandra played the piano so *badly* that even her parents had to admit
she would never be a musician. (tells *how* Sandra played)

PRACTICE 7   PUZZLING PAIRS: USING *GOOD* AND *WELL, BAD* AND *BADLY*

In each sentence, choose *good* or *well, bad* or *badly.*

1.   Shontae was offered a (good, well) job that pays (good, well).
2.   Because it was (bad, badly) designed, the chair did not hold up (good, well).
3.   Simone is such a (bad, badly) driver that she scares me even on her (good,
well) days.
4.   "If you don't buy (good, well) meat and produce, you can't expect a dish to
turn out (good, well)," said the cooking instructor.
5.   Though he knew he was a (good, well) actor, Damon was so nervous that he
performed (bad, badly) on the play's opening night.

Puzzling Pairs: *Worse* and *Worst*

Worse and *worst* are both adjectives, but they are often confused. *Worse* is
the comparative form, the form you use to compare one thing with another or one set of things with another set. *Worst* is the superlative form,
used to compare one thing with all or many others in its class.

✔ The meteorologist predicted the *worst* snowstorm in years.

Here, the snowstorm is being compared with many others in its class.

✔ The second batch of cookies turned out even *worse* than the first.

Here, a single batch of cookies (one set of things) is being compared with another batch.

✔ When it comes to any problem with his health, Don always imagines the *worst*.

Don is imagining the worst health problem, as compared with all others.

✔ Melina's second test grade was *worse* than her first.

One grade is being compared with a single other grade.

PRACTICE 8   PUZZLING PAIRS: USING *WORSE* AND *WORST*

Underline the correct word in each sentence.

1. The reviewer said that the sequel to the movie was even (<u>worse</u>, worst) than the original.
2. The night security officer's job required long hours of isolation and was probably the (worse, <u>worst</u>) possible career choice for an outgoing person like Erin.
3. Jarvis was sorry he had agreed to judge the "Cooking with Marshmallows" contest; the sticky, sweet entries were the (worse, <u>worst</u>) dishes he had ever tasted.
4. Instead of getting better, Alvin's cold became (<u>worse</u>, worst).
5. Meteorologists say that the snowstorm is the (worse, <u>worst</u>) in years.

Articles

The **articles** in the English language are *a, an,* and *the.* Articles are small, easy-to-overlook words, but they are so often used that it is important to use them correctly. When a writer uses the word *pen,* for example, an article can reveal whether the writer is talking about a specific pen (**the** pen) or a single, unspecified pen (**a** pen).

Using *A* and *An*

The most common mistake people make with articles stems from uncertainty over when to use *a* and when to use *an*. Here are the rules:

Use *a* before a **consonant sound**—that is, before any word that *sounds* as if it begins with anything other than *a, e, i, o,* or *u.*

> *a* **b**ear
>
> *a* **p**esky insect
>
> *a* **y**oung child
>
> *a* **u**seful idea ("Useful" begins with the *sound* of the consonant **y**—the "yoo" sound. Therefore, the article *a* is used.)

Use *an* before a **vowel sound**, that is, before any word that *sounds* as if it begins with *a, e, i, o,* or *u.*

> *an* **u**mbrella
>
> *an* **a**partment building
>
> *an* **o**melet
>
> *an* **h**onor ("Honor" begins a consonant, but the sound is a vowel sound: the *ah* sound often associated with the vowels **o** and **a**. Therefore, the article *an* is used.)

PRACTICE 9   USING *A* AND *AN*

Put *a* in front of words that begin with a consonant sound. Put *an* in front of words that begin with a vowel sound.

1. _a_ cough drop
2. _an_ eggplant
3. _a_ hard-boiled egg
4. _a_ budget
5. _an_ orderly procession
6. _an_ apple
7. _an_ honest person
8. _a_ yawn
9. _a_ union representative
10. _an_ untarnished reputation

11. _a_ strawberry
12. _a_ utility knife
13. _an_ unfriendly dog
14. _a_ pessimist
15. _an_ impulsive comment
16. _an_ authoritative source
17. _a_ comedy
18. _a_ hurricane
19. _an_ overflow valve
20. _an_ alligator

REVIEW EXERCISE 1   USING *A* AND *AN*

Underline the correct articles (*a* or *an*) in each of the sentences.

1. In today's newspaper, Art read (a, <u>an</u>) article about (<u>a</u>, an) recent archaeological discovery.
2. Gail saved the big box that her computer came in, knowing that she would find (<u>a</u>, an) use for it at (<u>a</u>, an) later time.
3. Barney was (a, <u>an</u>) accountant, but he admitted that he had (<u>a</u>, an) problem keeping his checkbook balanced.
4. Because Monday was (<u>a</u>, an) holiday, the employees of the bank enjoyed (<u>a</u>, an) three-day weekend.
5. The news of her father's illness was (a, <u>an</u>) unhappy surprise to Martha, but she knew that he was (<u>a</u>, an) survivor.

REVIEW EXERCISE 2   USING ADJECTIVE FORMS

In each of the following sentences, decide whether the positive, comparative, or superlative form is needed. Then convert the adjective in parentheses to the proper form. Use the "Adjective Forms Chart" in this chapter as your guide.

(bad)   1. The ___worst___ aspect of Jorge's job is that he has to work almost every weekend.

(careful) 2. Alfreda thought she was a careful driver, but after receiving a speeding ticket, she vowed to be even _more careful_ in the future.

(good)   3. The doctor told Tom that the new medication was the ___best___ on the market as well as being the least expensive.

(heavy)   4. Studies have shown that traffic is much ___heavier___ on interstate highways than it was five years ago.

(sunny)   5. The weather report said that this week would be ___sunnier___ than last week.

(good)   6. Alissa was not satisfied with merely being good at what she did; in fact, she strove to be the ___best___ at everything she did.

(good)   7. The book was good, but the movie was even ___better___.

(strong)   8. The odor, an unpleasant, sulfurous smell, became even ___stronger___ as the explorers moved deeper into the cave.

(old)   9. Clarissa said that being ___older___ than her sister had helped her to accept responsibility at an early age.

(hard)   10. Mike expected the class to be easy, but it was the ___hardest___ class he had ever taken.

REVIEW EXERCISE 3   USING ADJECTIVES AND ADVERBS

Underline the correct modifier in each of the sentences.

1. Unlike many artists, Bernard made enough money to support himself and his family; however, his parents worried, asking him when he was going to get a (<u>real</u>, really) job.

2. In desperation, the actor in the monster suit popped off his purple, snarling head and said to the screaming children, "See? I'm not (real, <u>really</u>) a monster."

3. The rabbit bounded (quick, <u>quickly</u>) into the underbrush as the cat approached.

4. "I'll pencil you in," said the executive's secretary, "but I will have to cancel your appointment if something (<u>more important</u>, most important) comes up.

5. Quincy showed us the puppies; each was (<u>cuter</u>, more cuter) than the last.

6. Without stopping or even slowing, the train moved (rapid, <u>rapidly</u>) past the passengers waiting on the platform.

7. The dog moved so (quick, <u>quickly</u>), straining eagerly at her leash, that Matthew had to run to keep up.

8. The police officer said she was (<u>grateful</u>, gratefully) for quiet nights when nothing much happened.

9. The clerk in the shoe store seemed calm and (<u>cheerful</u>, cheerfully) even though the store was crowded with customers.

10. The old man looked crabby and out of sorts, but when he saw Valerie and Max, he smiled (cheerful, <u>cheerfully</u>).

REVIEW EXERCISE 4   USING ADJECTIVES AND ADVERBS

Underline the correct modifier in each of the sentences.

1. Cheryl thinks (quick, <u>quickly</u>), but she speaks (slow, <u>slowly</u>) and deliberately.

2. Looking at a list of (recent, <u>recently</u>) released movies, James decided that there was nothing (<u>better</u>, best) than staying home and reading a good book.

3. Jakesha says that she did not do (good, <u>well</u>) on the last test, but she still had the (better, <u>best</u>) grade in the class.

4. The veterinarian said that Lucky was hurt (bad, <u>badly</u>) but that his injuries could have been much (<u>worse</u>, worst).

5. Gary said that his paycheck seems to be growing (<u>smaller</u>, smallest) as his bills get (<u>larger</u>, largest).

REVIEW EXERCISE 5   USING ADJECTIVES, ADVERBS, AND ARTICLES

Underline the correct adjective, adverb, or article in each numbered pair.

     Greek mythology tells of [1](a, <u>an</u>) evil king named Tantalus who displeased the gods by revealing their secrets to mortals and by cooking and serving his own son at a banquet. For his [2](<u>bad</u>, badly) behavior, the gods sentenced him to [3](a, <u>an</u>) appropriate punishment. He was placed in a [4](<u>beautiful</u>, beautifully) lake of clear water, with boughs of ripe fruit hanging over him. However, when he bent to drink, the lake [5](quick, <u>quickly</u>) dried up around him, leaving only mud. When he reached for the [6](<u>good</u>, well) fruit that seemed just within his grasp, the wind blew the branches out of reach. Tantalus must have been the [7](more, <u>most</u>) tormented of all the souls in Hades. It is [8](<u>bad</u>, badly) enough to be deprived of what one wants and needs, but to see it just out of reach must be even [9](<u>worse</u>, worst). The legacy of Tantalus is the word that comes from his name, [10](<u>a</u>, an) word that means "to teasingly withhold, just out of reach."

22

Misplaced and Dangling Modifiers

Although dangling and misplaced modifiers probably won't ruin your next romance, they may confuse your readers. That's reason enough to learn what they are and how to avoid them.

Look at the following sentences:

✗ **Hanging upside down from a tree,** Sarita saw a small brown bat.

✔ Sarita saw a small brown bat **hanging upside down from a tree.**

The words in bold type are **modifiers.** A **modifier** is a word, phrase, or clause that gives information about another word. In the preceding sentences, the placement of the phrase **hanging upside down from a tree** makes a great deal of difference. It is easy to imagine a bat hanging upside down from a tree, but the idea of Sarita hanging from a tree does not seem logical.

Although they are not always as obvious as the problem in this example, problems with modifiers are always problems in logic. If you approach this chapter—and your writing in general—with the idea that good writing should above all *make sense,* you will have an easier time spotting and correcting misplaced and dangling modifiers.

Misplaced Modifiers

Look at the following sentence:

✗ Covered in marinara sauce and sprinkled lightly with Romano cheese, Frank enjoyed spaghetti.

Do you see what is not logical about the sentence? Of course. Frank is not covered in marinara sauce and sprinkled lightly with Romano cheese. The spaghetti is. This type of modifier problem is called a **misplaced modifier.** The modifier *covered in marinara sauce and sprinkled lightly with Romano cheese* is misplaced to modify *Frank* instead of *spaghetti.* To fix a misplaced modifier, remember this principle: **a modifier should be placed as close as possible to the word it modifies.**

✔ Frank enjoyed spaghetti covered in marinara sauce and sprinkled lightly with Romano cheese.

Examples

✗ The car was road tested by the mechanic that had just had a tune-up.

The sentence seems to suggest that the mechanic had a tune-up. Putting the modifier *that had just had a tune-up* closer to the word it modifies makes the meaning clear.

✔ The car that had just had a tune-up was road tested by the mechanic.

Reconstructing the sentence is also a possibility.

✔ The mechanic road tested the car that had just had a tune-up.

✗ Stark and filled with angles, Paco said he did not like the abstract painting.

The sentence is worded as though Paco, not the painting, is stark and filled with angles.

✔ Paco said he did not like the abstract painting, which was stark and filled with angles.

✘ Old and battered, Glenda finally threw her calculator into the trash can.

   Is Glenda old and battered, or is it her calculator?

✔ Glenda finally threw her old and battered calculator into the trash can.

✔ Because her calculator was old and battered, Glenda finally threw it into the trash can.

PRACTICE 1   CORRECTING MISPLACED MODIFIERS

Correct the misplaced modifiers in the following sentences.

Answers may vary.

1. Brad found two abandoned puppies driving along the highway.

    Driving along the highway, Brad found two abandoned puppies.

    _____

2. Floating belly-up in the fish tank, Leonardo was afraid that his new angelfish was dead.

    Leonardo was afraid that his new angelfish, **floating belly-up in the fish tank,**

    was dead.

3. The customer complained to the server who had just found a fly in his soup.

    The customer **who had just found a fly in his soup** complained to the server.

    _____

4. Lakeisha set the resumé and letters of recommendation on the table that she planned to mail to her prospective employer.

    On the table, Lakeisha set the resumé and letters of recommendation that she

    planned to mail to her prospective employer.

5. From a bench near the playground, a woman kept a close eye on her toddler who was reading the *Wall Street Journal*.

    From a bench near the playground, a woman **who was reading the *Wall Street***

    Journal kept a close eye on her toddler.

Dangling Modifiers

Unlike a misplaced modifier, which needs to be moved closer to the word it modifies, a dangling modifier has no word modify. Look at the following sentence:

✗   After sitting in front of the computer for two hours, Brian's head hurt.

The phrase *after sitting in front of the computer for two hours* has no word in the sentence to modify. Since a modifier needs a noun or pronoun to modify, the word *Brian's* will not work. The *'s* attached to it makes it a modifier itself—it acts as an adjective to modify the word *head. Head* is a noun, but Brian's head did not sit in front of the computer for two hours—at least not without the rest of him. Therefore, the sentence needs to be fixed in one of two ways. The easiest way to fix a dangling modifier is to give it a word to modify. Place the word immediately after the dangling modifier.

✔   After sitting in front of the computer for two hours, **Brian** had a headache.

The sentence may also be reconstructed.

✔   After Brian sat in front of the computer for two hours, his head hurt.
✔   After Brian sat in front of the computer for two hours, he had a headache.

Here is another example:

✗   Sitting in class, Antoinette's cell phone rang.

Obviously, it is Antoinette who is sitting in class, not her cell phone. The easiest way to fix the sentence is to put the word *Antoinette* (not the possessive form *Antoinette's*) immediately after the modifier.

✔   Sitting in class, Antoinette heard her cell phone ring.

But it is also permissible to reconstruct the sentence entirely.

✔   Antoinette's cell phone rang as she sat in class.

✔ As Antoinette sat in class, her cell phone rang.

Look at this example:

✗ By working cheerfully and conscientiously, an employer will be impressed.

It is not the employer who works cheerfully and conscientiously, but the employee trying to make a good impression. The sentence can be fixed by indicating, immediately after the modifier, who is working cheerfully.

✔ By working cheerfully and conscientiously, a worker can make a good impression.

The sentence can also be reworked entirely.

✔ Cheerful, conscientious workers are likely to impress their employers.

Here is another example:

✗ Bored and restless, the minutes seemed to crawl.

Who was bored and restless? (If the sentence does not say, the decision is yours.)

✔ Bored and restless, **Andre** felt the minutes crawl.

PRACTICE 2   CORRECTING DANGLING MODIFIERS

Underline and correct the dangling modifiers in the following sentences.

Answers may vary.

1. Hurrying down the steps, a huge stack of books fell from Jerome's hands.
   A huge stack of books fell from Jerome's hands **as he hurried down the steps.**

2. Swayed by the salesperson's smooth pitch, Arlene's resolve weakened.
   Arlene's resolve weakened **as the salesperson's smooth pitch swayed her.**

3. <u>Embarrassed by the attention</u>, a bright red blush crept up Roy's neck and onto his cheeks.

Because he was embarrassed by the attention, a bright red blush crept up

Roy's neck and onto his cheeks.

4. <u>By planning projects carefully</u>, a last-minute rush can be avoided.

By planning projects carefully, **Jason can avoid a last-minute rush.**

5. <u>Dressed in a green satin ball gown</u>, Brandy's father proudly led her onto the dance floor.

Dressed in a green satin ball gown, **Brandy was led onto the dance floor by her**

proud father.

REVIEW EXERCISE 1   CORRECTING MISPLACED AND DANGLING MODIFIERS

Rewrite the sentences to correct the italicized misplaced or dangling modifiers.

Answers may vary.

1. *Clinging to a tall tree and munching on a piece of bark,* Denise watched the koala with fascination.

With fascination, Denise watched the koala, **which was clinging to a tall tree**

and munching on a piece of bark.

2. *Creaky and unreliable,* Mr. Smith complained to the building's manager about the elevator.

Mr. Smith complained to the building's manager about the **creaky and un-**

reliable elevator.

3. *Singing a popular Broadway show tune,* Dan's luggage was packed into the trunk.

Singing a popular Broadway show tune, **Dan packed luggage** into the trunk.

4. *Barely able to speak,* the award was accepted gratefully.

Barely able to speak, **the teacher gratefully accepted the award.**

5. *Hanging in front of the hardware store,* Marcus was attracted by an advertising banner.

Hanging in front of the hardware store, **the advertising banner attracted**

Marcus.

6. *Taking a big bite out of my hamburger,* the server asked whether I needed anything else.

   As I took a big bite out of my hamburger, the server asked whether I needed

   anything else.

7. *With a pounding headache,* the math homework seemed impossible to Lee.

   The math homework seemed impossible to Lee**, who had a pounding**

   headache.

8. Andrea tried to feed the dog *talking on the telephone.*

   Talking on the telephone, Andrea tried to feed the dog.

9. Al walked through the snow toward the mailbox *wearing heavy boots.*

   Wearing heavy boots, Al walked through the snow toward the mailbox.

10. *By spending more time with his family,* a closer relationship was established with his children.

    By spending more time with his family, **John established a closer relationship**

    with his children.

REVIEW EXERCISE 2   CORRECTING MISPLACED AND DANGLING MODIFIERS

Correct the dangling and misplaced modifiers in the following sentences.

Answers may vary.

1. Frozen solid and covered with snow, Kendra looked at the birdbath.

   Kendra looked at the birdbath, **frozen solid and covered with snow.**

2. Holding a sign that read "Will work for food," the well-dressed woman gave five dollars to a homeless man.

   The well-dressed woman gave five dollars to a homeless man **holding a sign**

   that read "Will work for food."

3. Filthy and flea-bitten, Doris gave the stray kitten a bath.

   Doris gave the **filthy, flea-bitten** stray kitten a bath.

4. Waxed and buffed, Daniel nearly slipped on the floor.

Daniel nearly slipped on the **waxed and buffed** floor.

5. Pickled in brandy, the members of the Garden Club enjoyed the peaches.

The members of the Garden Club enjoyed the peaches **pickled in brandy.**

6. Ben bought hot dogs for the children with mustard on them.

Ben bought hot dogs **with mustard on them** for the children.

7. By advertising in the newspaper, Andrew's car was sold within a week.

By advertising in the newspaper, **Andrew sold his car within a week.**

8. The red truck was driven by a tall man with four huge tires.

The red truck **with four huge tires** was driven by a tall man.

9. Giving off a foul odor whenever the wind came from the east, the citizens complained that the landfill was too close to residential areas.

The landfill gave off a foul odor whenever the wind came from the east, **and**

the citizens complained that the landfill was too close to residential areas.

10. Sanded and refinished, the worker looked with pride at the floor.

The worker looked with pride at the **sanded and refinished** floor.

REVIEW EXERCISE 3   CORRECTING MISPLACED AND DANGLING MODIFIERS

Underline and correct the two misplaced or dangling modifiers in each sentence group.

Answers may vary.

1. Thirty pizzas were brought into the student center at 5:00 P.M. by a delivery person <u>covered with pepperoni and dripping with cheese.</u> <u>Hungry and eager for a treat</u>, every last crumb was devoured by 6:00 P.M.

Thirty pizzas, **covered with pepperoni and dripping with cheese,** were brought

into the student center at 5:00 P.M. by a delivery person. Hungry and eager for

a treat, **the students devoured every last crumb by 6:00 P.M.**

2. Cathy saw a striped tiger <u>visiting Safari Land on vacation</u>. <u>With a striped face and body and a long, graceful tail</u>, Cathy thought the tiger was beautiful.

   Visiting Safari Land while on vacation, Cathy saw a striped tiger. Cathy

   thought the tiger, **with its striped face and body and long, graceful tail,** was

   beautiful.

3. Mitchell went to see the doctor <u>with a bad cold and a sore throat</u>. <u>After describing his symptoms</u>, the doctor prescribed medication, fluids, and plenty of rest.

   With a bad cold and a sore throat, Mitchell went to see the doctor. **After**

   Mitchell described his symptoms, the doctor prescribed medication, fluids,

   and plenty of rest.

4. <u>Furry and cute</u>, Andrew was captivated by the little puppy in the pet store window. As he went in to buy it, he rationalized that the puppy would be good for his children <u>with floppy ears and big eyes</u>.

   The **furry and cute** little puppy in the pet store window captivated Andrew. As

   he went in to buy it, he rationalized that the puppy **with floppy ears and big**

   eyes would be good for his children.

5. <u>Filled with air and tied off at the bottom</u>, the balloon artist created objects from ordinary balloons. <u>With great skill</u>, a few colorful balloons were transformed into a hat.

   The balloon artist created objects from ordinary balloons, **which were filled**

   with air and tied off at the bottom. With great skill, **the artist transformed a**

   few colorful balloons into a hat.

REVIEW EXERCISE 4   CORRECTING MISPLACED AND DANGLING MODIFIERS

Find and correct the misplaced and dangling modifiers in the following paragraph. Write your corrected sentences in the blanks provided.

Answers may vary.

   [1]Dirty and filled with old paint cans and forgotten garden implements, Griffin decided to clean the storage shed. [2]Determined to clean it at last, everything in the shed was removed. [3]Coughing at the dust, a broom was used to sweep dirt from the floor and cobwebs from the walls. [4]Squinting through dirty windows, a bottle of ammonia cleaner was needed to finish the cleaning. [5]Griffin then

sorted through old paint cans, bent lawn chairs, and rusty tools with gloves on. [6]Useless and unusable, Griffin put most of the items in a junk pile to haul away later. [7]Tired from his efforts, the only task that remained was to put back all of the usable items and arrange them neatly on shelves. [8]Finally, surveying his clean shed with pride, the result had been worth the effort.

---

[1]Griffin decided to clean the storage shed **because it was dirty and filled with old paint cans and forgotten garden implements.** [2]**Determined to clean it at last, Griffin** removed everything in the shed. [3]**Coughing at the dust, he** used a broom to sweep dirt from the floor and cobwebs from the walls. [4]**Squinting through dirty windows, Griffin** needed a bottle of ammonia cleaner to finish the cleaning. [5]**With gloves on,** Griffin then sorted through old paint cans, bent lawn chairs, and rusty tools. [6]Griffin put most of the **useless and unusable** items in a junk pile to haul away later. [7]The only task that remained was to put back all of the usable items and arrange them neatly on shelves **even though he was tired from his efforts.** [8]Finally, **Griffin surveyed his clean shed with pride** and realized that the result had been worth the effort.

23

Parallel Structure

Choose the best answer to complete each sequence.

1. **a, b, c,** _____   a. **t** b. **z** c. **d**

2. ↘, ↗↗, ↘, ↗↗, _____   a. ↗ b. ↗↗ c. ↘

3. 20, 40, 60, _____   a. 10 b. 120 c. 80

4. ▶,◼, _____   a. • b. ☐ c. ▣

If you chose *c* each time, you are correct. Your mind was responding to the patterns you saw developing in each sequence. Patterns are pleasing to the human mind, and that is why parallel structure works.

In any famous speech, such as Abraham Lincoln's Gettysburg Address or Martin Luther King, Jr.'s, "I Have a Dream," you will hear the regular, memorable rhythm of **parallel structure**—parallel words, parallel phrases, and parallel clauses. You will see it in good writing, too, lending elegance to ordinary sentences. Once you are used to seeing parallel structure, anything else will seem awkward. Look at the following lists to see examples of nonparallel and parallel structure.

✘ Nonparallel:

worrying about meeting expenses

to hold down two jobs

trying to pay bills on time

The phrase "to hold down two jobs" is not parallel with the *-ing* constructions of the other two phrases.

✔ **Parallel:**

worrying about meeting expenses

holding down two jobs

trying to pay bills on time

The phrases in the revised list have the same structure; that is, they are **parallel.**

✘ **Nonparallel:**

bright green

pale yellow

with a dull gray hue

✔ **Parallel:**

bright green

pale yellow

dull gray

✘ **Nonparallel:**

read two chapters in her sociology book

reviewed her notes for English class

working on a project for a health sciences class

✔ **Parallel:**

read two chapters in her sociology book

reviewed her notes for English class

worked on a project for a health sciences class

PRACTICE 1   USING PARALLEL STRUCTURE

Each of the following lists contains one item that is not parallel. Cross out the nonparallel item and reword it to make it parallel with the other items. Then write the reworded version on the line provided.

Answers will vary.

1. stopped for gas
   ~~buying stamps at the post office~~
   made a deposit at the bank
   <u>bought stamps at the post office</u>

2. friendly
   ~~was a very intelligent person~~
   funny
   <u>intelligent</u>

3. ~~watching the sun rise~~
   to swim in the lake
   to eat freshly caught fish
   <u>to watch the sun rise</u>

4. polished floors
   ~~windows that gleam~~
   newly painted walls
   <u>gleaming windows</u>

5. sitting on the patio
   grilling hamburgers
   ~~to swat at mosquitoes~~
   <u>swatting at mosquitoes</u>

In sentences, items given equal emphasis should be parallel in structure whenever possible. These items include words, phrases, or clauses in pairs or lists. Look at the following examples of nonparallel and parallel structure within sentences.

✗ The technician **tested** the battery and then **was checking** the connections.

✔ The technician **tested** the battery and then **checked** the connections.

✗ The dog **was looking** both ways, **waited** for a car to pass, and **crossed** the street.

✔ The dog **looked** both ways, **waited** for a car to pass, and **crossed** the street.

✗ The manager said he wanted to hire someone who was **courteous, dependable,** and **who was also hardworking.**

✔ The manager said he wanted to hire someone who was **courteous, dependable,** and **hardworking.**

PRACTICE 2   USING PARALLEL STRUCTURE

Each of the following sentences contains one item that is not parallel. Cross out the nonparallel item and reword it to make it parallel with the other items. Then write the reworded version on the line provided.

Answers will vary.

1. Watching football, reading, and ~~to work on his car~~ are my brother's favorite pastimes.

   Watching football, reading, and **working on his car** are my brother's favorite

   pastimes.

2. Alberto found a parking space, parked his car, and ~~was heading for class~~.

   Alberto found a parking space, parked his car, and **headed for class.**

3. The chef chopped the garlic, ~~was grating the cheese~~, and sliced the tomatoes.

   The chef chopped the garlic, **grated the cheese,** and sliced the tomatoes.

4. Mrs. Fabian told her doctor that she needed a medicine that was effective, inexpensive, and ~~that did not present any safety concerns~~.

   Mrs. Fabian told her doctor that she needed a medicine that was effective, in-

   expensive, and **safe.**

5. Jason was proud of his old car because he had rebuilt the motor, ~~the upholstery had been replaced~~, and painted the body.

   Jason was proud of his old car because he had rebuilt the motor, **replaced the**

   upholstery, and painted the body.

REVIEW EXERCISE 1   USING PARALLEL STRUCTURE

Each of the following lists contains one item that is not parallel. Cross out the nonparallel item and reword it to make it parallel with the other items. Then write the reworded version on the line provided.

Answers will vary.

1. to rotate the tires
   ~~checking the tread~~
   to monitor the air pressure
   to check the tread

2. shiny
   new
   ~~costing a lot of money~~
   expensive

3. ~~with warmth from the sun~~
   nourished by the soil
   watered by the rain
   warmed by the sun

4. outstanding references
   a complete resumé
   ~~grades that were good~~
   good grades

5. that he had been speeding
   ~~running a red light~~
   that he had been intoxicated

   that he had run a red light

6. diving toward the ground
   flapping its wings
   ~~caws loudly~~

   cawing loudly

7. worn sneakers
   a ragged T-shirt
   ~~jeans with patches on them~~

   patched jeans

8. pine trees
   oak trees
   ~~trees in the aspen family~~

   aspen trees

9. happy
   wealthy
   ~~having good health~~

   healthy

10. turn on the computer
    bring up the Internet browser
    ~~you'll be typing in the website address~~

    type in the website address

REVIEW EXERCISE 2   USING PARALLEL STRUCTURE

In each of the following sentences, the italicized items should be parallel. Cross out the nonparallel item and reword it to make it parallel with the other items. Then write the reworded version on the line provided.

Answers will vary.

1. By the time Friday evening came, all that Tybolt felt like doing was *staying at home, ordering a pizza,* and ~~to rent a video~~.

   By the time Friday evening came, all that Tybolt felt like doing was *staying at home, ordering a pizza,* and **renting a video.**

2. Many people own dogs because they want *companionship,* and ~~the dog also provides protection~~.

   Many people own dogs because they want *companionship* and **protection.**

3. Halogen bulbs *burn brighter,* ~~are greater in cost~~, and *last longer* than regular incandescent bulbs.

   Halogen bulbs *burn brighter,* **cost more,** and *last longer* than regular incandescent bulbs.

4. The salesman was *polite,* ~~had the quality of patience~~, and *persuasive.*

   The salesman was *polite,* **patient,** and *persuasive.*

5. *Roller-skating servers, old-fashioned jukeboxes, ~~and booths that are cozy~~* are the hallmarks of Bob's Deco Diner.

   Roller-skating servers, old-fashioned jukeboxes, **and cozy booths** are the hallmarks of

   Bob's Deco Diner.

6. Before leaving the house, Eric checked to make sure that he *had unplugged the coffeepot* and ~~the lights had been turned off~~.

   Before leaving the house, Eric checked to make sure that he *had unplugged the cof-*

   feepot and **turned off the lights.**

7. Joanie hated working the late shift because she did not enjoy *losing sleep, driving in the dark,* and ~~the walk through a deserted parking lot to her apartment~~.

   Joanie hated working the late shift because she did not enjoy *losing sleep, driving*

   in the dark, and **walking through a deserted parking lot to her apartment.**

8. The boxer's *unfocused expression* and ~~eyes that were glazed~~ told the referee that it was time to stop the fight.

   The boxer's *unfocused expression* and **glazed eyes** told the referee that it was time

   to stop the fight.

9. The construction project was plagued by ~~weather that was bad~~, *cost overruns,* and *labor problems.*

   The construction project was plagued by **bad weather,** *cost overruns,* and *labor*

   problems.

10. *Warm gloves, ~~clothing that is put on in layers~~,* and *waterproof boots* are necessities in cold, wet weather.

    Warm gloves, **layered clothing,** and *waterproof boots* are necessities in cold, wet

    weather.

REVIEW EXERCISE 3   USING PARALLEL STRUCTURE

Each of the following sentences contains one item that is not parallel. Cross out the nonparallel item and reword it to make it parallel with the other items. Then write the reworded version on the line provided.

Answers will vary.

1. A strong breeze and ~~water that was calm~~ made the day perfect for sailing.

   A strong breeze and **calm water** made the day perfect for sailing.

2. Because she had broken a plate, hit her head on a cabinet door, and ~~the frozen pizza had burned~~, Kristen decided to call for pizza delivery.

   Because she had broken a plate, hit her head on a cabinet door, and **burned**

   the frozen pizza, Kristen decided to call for pizza delivery.

3. The apartment had a cramped kitchen, ~~carpet that was worn~~, and peeling paint, but the price was right.

   The apartment had a cramped kitchen, **worn carpet,** and peeling paint, but the

   price was right.

4. The cat entered the closet, climbed a pair of pants, and ~~onto a shelf he settled~~.

   The cat entered the closet, climbed a pair of pants, and **settled onto a shelf.**

   _____

5. With two active toddlers, the young mother realized it would be impossible to sit down, drink a cup of coffee, and ~~reading a magazine~~ undisturbed.

   With two active toddlers, the young mother realized it would be impossible to

   sit down, drink a cup of coffee, and **read a magazine** undisturbed.

6. At Girl Scout camp, Caroline learned how to tie seven different kinds of knots and ~~cooking over a campfire~~.

   At Girl Scout camp, Caroline learned how to tie seven different kinds of knots

   and **to cook** over a campfire.

7. Under the sofa, Ramon found a dusty potato chip, two quarters, and ~~an old pair of sunglasses was also there~~.

   Under the sofa, Ramon found a dusty potato chip, two quarters, and **an old**

   pair of sunglasses.

8. ~~Programs devoted to news~~, science programs, and professional hockey games are all that Brad watches on TV.

   News programs, science programs, and professional hockey games are all that

   Brad watches on TV.

9. Shanell keeps her car running well by changing the oil every three thousand miles and ~~with regular tuneups~~.

   Shanell keeps her car running well by changing the oil every three thousand

   miles and **by having regular tuneups.**

10. Albert's specialty was repairing commercial ovens and ~~restoration of older ovens~~.

    Albert's specialty was repairing commercial ovens and **restoring older ovens.**

    _____

REVIEW EXERCISE 4   USING PARALLEL STRUCTURE

Each of the sentences in the following paragraph contains one item that is not parallel. Cross out the nonparallel item and reword it to make it parallel with the other items. Then write the reworded version on the lines provided.

Answers will vary.

[1]Everyone experiences stress, regardless of gender, race, or ~~what age the person is~~. [2]*Eustress* (from the Greek root *eu* meaning *good* or *well*) is stress in response to a positive event such as going on vacation, ~~to win the lottery~~, or receiving a job promotion. [3]Even positive events bring stress in the form of the need to act and ~~making decisions~~. [4]Eustress is relatively easy to deal with: the decision whether to buy a Mercedes or ~~leasing a BMW~~ with lottery winnings may be tough, but most people can handle it. [5]*Distress,* stress in response to negative events, is more serious and ~~causing more harm~~. [6]This type of stress is often in response to traumatic events such as the loss of a job, ~~a family member dying~~, or the end of a romance. [7]Such stress can cause a person to feel anger, ~~having nightmares~~, or to gain or lose weight, among other responses. [8]As if the stress itself is not bad enough, chronic stress is also said to contribute to illnesses such as heart disease, ~~becoming depressed~~, and cancer. [9]But for most people, after a period of adjustment, stress and its symptoms fade and ~~are seen to disappear~~. [10]Most stress is a normal response to the changes, good and ~~also the ones that are bad~~, in people's lives.

[1]Everyone experiences stress, regardless of gender, race, or **age**. [2]*Eustress* (from the Greek root *eu* meaning *good* or *well*) is stress in response to a positive event such as going on vacation, **winning the lottery,** or receiving a job promotion. [3]Even positive events bring stress in the form of the need to act and **to make decisions**. [4]Eustress is relatively easy to deal with: the decision whether to buy a Mercedes or **to lease a BMW** with lottery winnings may be tough, but most

people can handle it. [5]*Distress,* stress in response to negative events, is more serious and **causes more harm.** [6]This type of stress is often in response to traumatic events such as the loss of a job, **the death of a family member,** or the end of a romance. [7]Such stress can cause a person to feel anger, **to have nightmares,** or to gain or lose weight, among other responses. [8]As if the stress itself is not bad enough, chronic stress is also said to contribute to illnesses such as heart disease, **depression,** and cancer. [9]But for most people, after a period of adjustment, stress and its symptoms fade and **disappear.** [10]Most stress is a normal response to the changes, good and **bad,** in people's lives.

24

Capital Letters

DuDe,

dId The ConCERt LAst nIghT reALLy Rock, oR WhaT?

E-Mail U LaTeR,

JOSh

Among some young computer users, mixed-case messages are common. Although mixed case may be fun to experiment with, it is so difficult to read that it almost makes a reader appreciate rules of capitalization. This chapter reviews the fundamentals of capitalization and introduces many of the fine points.

Capitalization of a Word That Begins a Sentence

Capitalize the first word of a sentence or direct quotation.

✔ Anita found a black widow spider near the garage door.

✔ On the other side of the lake, volunteers began planting a botanical garden.

✔ "Where did I put that map?" the bus driver asked impatiently.

Capitalization of Words Referring to Individuals

Capitalize people's names and the pronoun "I."

✔ May I read that report after you have finished with it?

✔ Ms. Burton handed an extra copy of the environmental impact report to Hari.

Capitalize a word that designates a family relationship if it is used in place of a name.

Family designations are capitalized if they are used as direct substitutes for names. To make sure that the word is used as a name, try substituting a name for the word. It will sound natural.

✔ I asked Grandma if she needed an extra set of snowshoes.

✔ I asked ~~Grandma~~ Judith Graham if she needed an extra set of snowshoes.

Try your own substitution in the next sentence. If substituting a name for "Dad" sounds natural, the capitalization is correct.

✔ As I was growing up, Dad always told me that a mind is a terrible thing to waste.

When family designations such as "father," "mother," or "great-uncle Elmo" are preceded by a possessive pronoun (*my, her, his, their*), a possessive noun (*Theo's, Pat's*), or an article (*a, an,* or *the*), they are not capitalized. For additional proof, try directly substituting a name for the family designation. It will sound awkward.

✔ I asked my grandma if she needed an extra set of snowshoes.

✗ I asked my ~~grandma~~ Judith Graham if she needed an extra set of snowshoes.

In this sentence, substituting a name does not work. The phrase "my Judith Graham" sounds awkward.

Try substituting a name for "dad" in this sentence, making sure to leave the pronoun "my" in the sentence. If the name does not sound natural, then the lower-case "dad" is correct.

✔ As I was growing up, my dad always told me that a mind is a terrible thing to waste.

Do not capitalize professional titles unless they are used immediately before a name.

✔ Vasanta Patel is the doctor on duty in the hospital's emergency room.

✔ The patient with the broken leg was treated by Dr. Vasanta Patel.

✔ Brian Tobler is my economics professor.

✔ I am taking microeconomics with Professor Brian Tobler.

PRACTICE 1   CAPITALIZING WORDS REFERRING TO INDIVIDUALS

Underline and correct the capitalization mistake in each sentence below.

1. My <u>Mother</u> has always been afraid to travel by air.

   My **mother** has always been afraid to travel by air.
   _____

2. The biology instructor, <u>professor</u> Smith, specializes in mosquito research.

   The biology instructor, **Professor** Smith, specializes in mosquito research.
   _____

3. My brother took <u>dad</u> on a week-long fishing trip last year.

   My brother took **Dad** on a week-long fishing trip last year.
   _____

4. On the advice of his <u>Doctor</u>, my cousin is giving up all contact sports.

   On the advice of his **doctor**, my cousin is giving up all contact sports.
   _____

5. My grandma voted for <u>senator</u> Krantz because of his pledge to reduce taxes for senior citizens.

   My grandma voted for **Senator** Krantz because of his pledge to reduce taxes for

   senior citizens.

Capitalization of Words Referring to Groups

Capitalize words that refer to specific religions, geographic locations, races, and nationalities.

✔ People of many races attend school with me. I have classmates who are Asian, Caucasian, African American, Latino, and Native American.

✔ Though Pramesh is originally from India, he considers himself a New Yorker. He drives an American car, enjoys Italian food, and collects Mexican glassware.

✔ Ahmed was brought up Baptist but converted to Islam when he was twenty-six.

Capitalize specific names of organizations, businesses, and government agencies.

✔ Carlos belongs to the Association of Information Technology Students and the Organization of Latin American Students.

✔ Leanne works for Microsoft, and her husband works for First National Bank.

✔ After Jenna finished her degree in finance, she went to work for the Internal Revenue Service.

Do not capitalize nonspecific or generic organization names.

✔ Madeleine attends church and is also a member of the choir.

✔ As an executive in a large corporation, Reese often travels.

✔ When Blanca finishes college, she wants to work for the government.

PRACTICE 2   CAPITALIZING WORDS REFERRING TO GROUPS AND PLACE NAMES

Underline and correct the capitalization mistake in each sentence.

1. Hal decided to join the <u>stargazers' club</u> after he visited the planetarium.

   <u>Hal decided to join the **Stargazers' Club** after he visited the planetarium.</u>

2. Sandra has attended First Baptist Church since she was a small child, and she is now director of the <u>Choir</u>.

> Sandra has attended First Baptist Church since she was a small child, and she is now director of the **choir**.

3. When the new highway was planned across sacred Ocmulgee burial mounds, <u>native american</u> groups protested.

> When the new highway was planned across sacred Ocmulgee burial mounds, **Native American** groups protested.

4. When Antoine saw that the envelope was from the <u>internal revenue service</u>, he was sure his tax refund had arrived.

> When Antoine saw that the envelope was from the **Internal Revenue Service**, he was sure his tax refund had arrived.

5. After any major disaster, the <u>american red cross</u> is on the scene to provide aid to those affected.

> After any major disaster, the **American Red Cross** is on the scene to provide aid to those affected.

Capitalization of Words Referring to Time and Place

Capitalize months of the year, days of the week, and names of holidays.

✔ Thanksgiving is always celebrated on the last Thursday in November.

✔ February holidays include Valentine's Day and Presidents' Day.

Do not capitalize the names of the four seasons.

✔ Eduardo wants to take one last summer trip before his children go back to school in the fall.

Capitalize *specific* place names.

✔ On her trip to Seattle, Kacey visited the Seattle Aquarium and Woodland Park Zoo.

✔ She also visited Pike Place Market, famous for its fish, produce, restaurants, and crafts.

✔ While Eric attended Norfolk Technical & Community College, he worked part-time at Papa John's Pizza.

✔ The shoplifter ran out of the Kwik-Stop Food Mart and down Third Street.

Do not capitalize *general, nonspecific* place names.

✔ On her trip to Seattle, Kacey visited the aquarium and the zoo.

✔ She also shopped at a large farmer's market.

✔ While Eric attended college, he worked for a pizza place.

✔ The shoplifter ran out of the convenience store and down the street.

Do not capitalize compass points unless they refer to a specific geographical area.

✔ The car traveled south on the interstate before turning west toward the mountains.

✔ Having lived in New Orleans all her life, Lin found it hard to adjust to the mountains of Northern California.

PRACTICE 3   CAPITALIZING WORDS REFERRING TO TIME AND PLACE

Underline and correct the capitalization mistake in each sentence.

1. Lorena drove east on the interstate, headed for her new home in <u>kentucky</u>.

   Lorena drove east on the interstate, headed for her new home in **Kentucky**.

2. On <u>veteran's day</u>, Duncan always feels proud that he served his country in the military.

   On **Veteran's Day**, Duncan always feels proud that he served his country in the military.

3. Kim will meet us at the aquarium on <u>tuesday</u>.

   Kim will meet us at the aquarium on **Tuesday**.

4. Every <u>Winter</u>, Natalie fantasizes about moving to the South and staying warm all year.

> Every **winter**, Natalie fantasizes about moving to the South and staying warm
>
> all year.

5. The movie *Fargo* is set in snowy <u>north</u> Dakota.

> The movie *Fargo* is set in snowy **North** Dakota.

Capitalization of Words Referring to Things and Activities

Do not capitalize subjects studied in school unless they are part of a *specific* course title.

✔ Olan is taking chemistry, German, and psychology this term.

✔ Olan is taking Chemistry 1101, German 1102, and Psychology 2208 this term.

✔ Olan is taking Principles of Chemistry, Intermediate German, and Psychology of Development this term.

Capitalize titles of novels, short stories, poems, newspapers, magazines, articles, works of art, television shows, movies, songs, and other musical works.

There are exceptions to many rules in English, and this rule has more exceptions than most. Some newspapers and journals capitalize only the first word in the title of an article. Some writers, like e. e. cummings, do not follow the conventional rules of capitalization. When you write about an article, a poem, or any other piece of writing, preserve the title as it was published.

When writing the name of a newspaper, do not capitalize or italicize the word *the*. Though newspaper titles are almost always prefaced by *the* (**the** *Daily Rag*, **the** *Podunk Fishwrapper*) and though the word *the* often appears on the newspaper's masthead, modern usage treats that initial *the* as just another word in the sentence, not as part of the title. Therefore, write "the *Atlanta Journal-Constitution*" or "the *Wall Street Journal*," not "*The Atlanta Journal-Constitution*" or "*The Wall Street Journal*."

Otherwise, follow these rules: Capitalize the first word of a title. Do not capitalize articles (a, an, the) or short prepositions (to, of, from, and other prepositions) unless they are the first word in a title. Capitalize all other words.

✔ Kenji read an article in *Astronomy* called "Build a Backyard Observatory."

✔ Melanie's literature class read Henrik Ibsen's play *A Doll's House.*

✔ Carlotta wrote her paper on "I Sit and Sew," a poem by Alice Dunbar-Nelson.

✔ Myra tried to keep the children busy by teaching them to sing a slightly modified song that she called "Ninety-Nine Bottles of Milk on the Wall."

For consumer products, capitalize the brand name but not the general product name. Often, the general product name is omitted.

✔ At the college bookstore, Roger bought a Marks-A-Lot highlighter, a roll of Scotch tape, a Sanford pen, and a Top Flight notebook.

✔ A Ford Explorer broke down in front of the drive-through at Taco Bell.

Capitalize some common abbreviations.

Abbreviations of organizations, corporations, and professional designations are capitalized. Some examples include NBC, AFL-CIO, FBI, NAACP, CIA, UPS, CPA, M.D. Ph.D., and D.D.S. The disease AIDS (Acquired Immune Deficiency Syndrome) is always written in all capitals.

PRACTICE 4   CAPITALIZING WORDS REFERRING TO THINGS AND ACTIVITIES

Underline and correct the capitalization mistake in each sentence.

1. For its grand finale, the choral group sang "America the <u>beautiful</u>."

    For its grand finale, the choral group sang "America the **Beautiful**."

    _____

2. Jason buys <u>purina</u> cat food because his cat refuses to eat any other brand.

    Jason buys **Purina** cat food because his cat refuses to eat any other brand.

    _____

3. The yellowed copy of the <u>*new york times*</u> was dated December 7, 1941.

    The yellowed copy of the ***New York Times*** was dated December 7, 1941.

    _____

4. At her tenth <u>High School</u> reunion, Elise was maliciously thrilled to see that Monica, who had stolen her boyfriend in the tenth grade, had gained twenty-five pounds.

At her tenth **high school** reunion, Elise was maliciously thrilled to see that Monica,

who had stolen her boyfriend in the tenth grade, had gained twenty-five pounds.

5. Jillian read a magazine article called "<u>how to start your own small business</u>."

Jillian read a magazine article called "**How to Start Your Own Small Business**."

REVIEW EXERCISE 1 CORRECTING ERRORS IN CAPITALIZATION

Underline and correct the two capitalization mistakes in each sentence.

1. Caught in traffic on <u>bedford avenue</u>, Lucas watched helplessly as huge chunks of hail damaged the pristine hood of his new <u>volkswagen beetle</u>.

Caught in traffic on **Bedford Avenue**, Lucas watched helplessly as huge chunks

of hail damaged the pristine hood of his new **Volkswagen Beetle**.

2. Garrett bought a <u>thanksgiving</u> turkey in early <u>november</u> and stored it in his freezer.

Garrett bought a **Thanksgiving** turkey in early **November** and stored it in his

freezer.

3. Folding her copy of the *arizona republic*, Victoria took a final sip of her <u>tropicana</u> orange juice and headed out the door.

Folding her copy of the ***Arizona Republic***, Victoria took a final sip of her

Tropicana orange juice and headed out the door.

4. Arnold bought four big cans of <u>folger's</u> coffee on sale at <u>wal-mart</u>.

Arnold bought four big cans of **Folger's** coffee on sale at **Wal-Mart**.

5. In the <u>Library</u>, Clara found a fascinating old book called *plain speaking: oral biographies of harry s. truman*.

In the **library**, Clara found a fascinating old book called ***Plain Speaking: Oral***

Biographies of Harry S. Truman.

REVIEW EXERCISE 2 CORRECTING ERRORS IN CAPITALIZATION

Underline and correct the two capitalization mistakes in each sentence.

1. On <u>june</u> 27, Amelia celebrated her twenty-first birthday at a <u>french</u> restaurant called Bonjour.

    On **June** 27, Amelia celebrated her twenty-first birthday at a **French** restaurant called Bonjour.

2. Even after almost a lifetime in Kansas, <u>grandpa</u> misses the <u>blue ridge</u> mountains of West Virginia.

    Even after almost a lifetime in Kansas, **Grandpa** misses the **Blue Ridge** mountains of West Virginia.

3. In <u>hershey</u>, Pennsylvania, there is a Chocolate Avenue and a <u>cocoa avenue</u>.

    In **Hershey**, Pennsylvania, there is a Chocolate Avenue and a **Cocoa Avenue**.

4. Alan opened a can of Del Monte <u>Peaches</u> to eat with his Quaker <u>Oatmeal</u>.

    Alan opened a can of Del Monte **peaches** to eat with his Quaker **oatmeal**.

5. After an hour of reading <u>*understanding physics*</u>, Herschel was ready to close his textbook and turn on a rerun of <u>*the three stooges*</u>.

    After an hour of reading ***Understanding Physics***, Herschel was ready to close his textbook and turn on a rerun of ***The Three Stooges***.

REVIEW EXERCISE 3   CORRECTING ERRORS IN CAPITALIZATION

Underline and correct the two capitalization mistakes in each sentence.

1. The <u>toyota's</u> bumper sticker read, "<u>honk if you hate noise pollution</u>."

    The **Toyota's** bumper sticker read, "**Honk If You Hate Noise Pollution**."

2. As my <u>Grandmother</u> began to carve the Christmas ham, it slipped off the platter and shot into <u>uncle</u> Harry's lap.

    As my **grandmother** began to carve the Christmas ham, it slipped off the platter and shot into **Uncle** Harry's lap.

3. The headline in <u>*The Orlando Sentinel*</u> read, "<u>baby thrown from burning apartment, caught by firefighters</u>."

    The headline in the ***Orlando Sentinel*** read, "**Baby Thrown from Burning Apartment, Caught by Firefighters**."

4. Valerie is originally from the <u>midwest</u>, but now she considers herself a <u>new yorker</u>.

> Valerie is originally from the **Midwest**, but now she considers herself a **New**
>
> **Yorker**.

5. The <u>Doctor</u> prescribed pills for my <u>Father's</u> heart condition, but Dad refuses to take them.

> The **doctor** prescribed pills for my **father's** heart condition, but Dad refuses to
>
> take them.

REVIEW EXERCISE 4   CORRECTING ERRORS IN CAPITALIZATION

Underline and correct the twenty capitalization errors in the following paragraph.

[1]My friend <u>kelly</u> can never go to lunch with me because she has to watch her favorite show, *the young and the restless*. [2]Maybe I am in the minority, but I think that <u>Soap Operas</u>, originally sponsored by <u>Detergents</u> such as <u>tide</u>, are silly and unrealistic. [3]They always feature beautiful people named Alden, Nikki, or Simone who live in cities with romantic names like <u>genoa city</u> or <u>port charles</u>. [4]<u>there</u> is never an average-looking <u>herbert</u> from Pawtucket. [5]The<u>se characters</u> lie, cheat, and steal while drinking dom perignon and eating caviar in chauffeur-driven <u>cadillac</u> limousines. [6]They may be doctors or <u>Lawyers</u> or have copies of *business week* on their coffee tables, but they never seem to do any actual work. [7]Soap opera characters also spend weeks in <u>Hospitals</u> or in exotic clinics in the <u>bahamas</u> recovering from car crashes or from diseases such as <u>Amnesia</u>. [8]Characters have also been known to return from the dead long after the <u>Memorial Service</u> is over and the last notes of "<u>amazing grace</u>" have faded away. [9]Kelly says that after a week of watching *one life to live*, I would be addicted, but <u>i</u> believe I will stay addicted to reality.

[1]My friend **Kelly** can never go to lunch with me because she has to watch her favorite show, ***The Young and the Restless***. [2]Maybe I am in the minority, but I think that **soap operas**, originally sponsored by **detergents** such as **Tide**, are silly and unrealistic. [3]They always feature beautiful people named Alden, Nikki, or Simone who live in cities with romantic names like **Genoa City** or **Port Charles**. [4]**There** is never an average-looking **Herbert** from Pawtucket. [5]These characters lie, cheat, and steal while drinking **Dom Perignon** and eating caviar in chauffeur-driven **Cadillac** limousines. [6]They may be doctors or **lawyers** or have copies of ***Business Week*** on their coffee tables, but they never seem to do any actual work. [7]Soap opera characters also spend weeks in **hospitals** or in exotic clinics in the **Bahamas** recovering from car crashes or from diseases such as **amnesia.** [8]Characters have also been known to return from the dead long after the **memorial service** is over and the last notes of "**Amazing Grace**" have faded away. [9]Kelly says that after a week of watching ***One Life to Live***, I would be addicted, but I believe **I** will stay addicted to reality.

25

Words Commonly Confused

```
Hi, Emily—
I wanted too send you an e-mail to let
you no I finally finished my paper. I
took your advise and used the spelling
checker on the computer. I think I made
less errors. I won't loose any points
for spelling, so I bet I'll make a A!
                              Keith
P.S. I ran this through the spelling
checker, to. Can you tell?
```

Poor Keith. Although his e-mail has no misspelled words, it contains several errors involving words that are commonly confused. This chapter will help you to avoid the kinds of errors that Keith has made—errors that a spelling checker will not catch.

Read the following words listed in pairs or groups, making sure you understand the differences in their meanings. Then complete the exercises at the end of this chapter.

Words Commonly Confused

a, an   The article *a* is used before consonant sounds. The article *an* is used before vowel sounds.

Thus you would write **a** dance, **a** rotten banana, and **a** potato chip; but **an** ice storm, **an** otter, **an** eggplant. Remember, though, that your choice of *a* or *an* is based on the consonant or vowel *sound* at the beginning of the next word. Some words, such as those beginning with a silent *h* or with a *u* that is pronounced like *y*, require careful treatment: **an** honest person, but **a** hat; **an** uncle, but **a** used car.

✔ For breakfast, Ann ate **an** egg, **an** English muffin, **a** small bowl of grits, and **a** cup of coffee.

✔ The fan said it had been **an** honor to meet the famous actor.

accept, except   To *accept* is to *take* or *believe;* the word *except* means *but* or *with the exception of.*

✔ The instructor said that she would **accept** nothing **except** our very best work.

advice, advise   *Advice* is a noun; one gives advice or asks for it. *Advise* is the verb form; one person may *advise* another.

✔ During her pregnancy, Jenna has received **advice** from almost everyone she knows. Even strangers **advise** her about health, childbirth, and nutrition.

affect, effect   *Affect* is the verb form. It means to *cause a change or variation. Effect* is the noun form. It means *outcome* or *result.*

✔ Today's industrial pollution will **affect** the environment for decades to come.

✔ The **effect** of smoking on the lungs is well documented.

all right, ~~alright~~   *All right* is absolutely the only correct spelling. It is never all right to write "alright."

✔ The toaster was not working this morning, but it seems to be **all right** now.

a lot, ~~alot~~, allot   *A lot* is always written as two words when you mean *much* or *many,* but it's preferable to use a word such as *much, many, several,* or a specific amount instead of *a lot.* The word *allot* (never *alot*) means to *allow* or *set aside for a special purpose: Belle allotted $25.00 for impulse purchases at the mall.*

✔ **acceptable**   **A lot** of people believe that the number thirteen is unlucky.

✔ **better**   **Many** people believe that the number thirteen is unlucky.

among, between *Among* is used with three or more persons or things; *between* is used with two.

✔ The instructor walked **among** the students, passing out graded papers.

✔ The dog sat **between** Mia and her date.

breath, breathe *Breath* is the noun form: a person can take a breath or be out of breath. *Breathe* is the verb form: someone may *breathe* heavily after exercising.

✔ Trevor took a deep **breath** and began his presentation.

✔ A person who is hyperventilating is often told to **breathe** into a paper bag.

by, buy *By* means *beside* or *through*. *Buy* means to *purchase*.

✔ Claire went **by** the post office, but she forgot to **buy** stamps.

fewer, less Use *fewer* when writing about things you count; use *less* when writing about things you measure. Specifically, if you can put a number in front of a word (five dollars), use *fewer*. If you cannot put a number in front of a word (~~five~~ money), use *less*. You would write *fewer* rocks but *less* sand, *fewer* cookies but *less* flour.

✔ I earn **less** money than Olivia does, but I also have **fewer** responsibilities.

good, well *Good* is an adjective that answers the question "What kind?" *Well* is an adverb that answers the question "How?" or "In what manner?" Therefore, a person writes a *good* essay. (*Good* answers the question "What kind of essay?") But he writes it *well*. (*Well* answers the question "How did he write it?")

✔ Rico is not a **good** athlete, but he does almost everything else **well**.

himself, ~~hisself~~ The word is always *himself*, never *hisself*.

✔ Herman helped **himself** to more turkey and potatoes.

its, it's If you mean *it is* or *it has*, use *it's* (with the apostrophe). To indicate possession, use *its*.

✔ Be careful with the flashlight; **it's** the only one I have.

✔ "**It's** been too long since we have gotten together," said Jessica.

✔   The spider spun **its** web in a dark corner of the garage.

knew, new   *Knew* is the past tense of *know; new* means *not old*.

✔   Sam **knew** that he would need a **new** microwave.

know, no   *Know* means to *understand; no* means *not any* or the opposite of *yes*.

✔   Does anyone **know** why there is an Optimist Club but **no** club for pessimists?

loose, lose   *Loose* is the opposite of *tight; lose* is the opposite of *find*.

✔   The doorknob rattles because it is **loose.**

✔   No one likes to **lose** money.

past, passed   *Past* (an adjective) means *beyond* or *before now. Past* (a noun) means *a previous time. Passed* (a verb) means *went by*.

✔   Gretchen's interest in history and her hobby of collecting antiques stem from her fascination with the **past.**

✔   Blowing his horn and gesturing rudely, the driver in the blue truck **passed** Tim.

peace, piece   *Peace* means *calm* or *tranquility; piece* means a *part*.

✔   Scott hoped that he would find **peace** living on a small **piece** of land out in the country among the pines.

plain, plane   *Plain* means *clear* or *simple*. A *plane* is a form of air transportation, a carpenter's tool, or a geometric surface.

✔   Rita's attire was so **plain** and her appearance so ordinary that no one on the **plane** suspected that she was a federal agent working to protect the passengers and crew.

principal, principle   *Principal* means *chief* (principal reason) or a *person in charge of a school* (principal of West River High). A *principle* is a *policy*, a *moral stand*, or a *rule*.

✔   Willingness to stand by their **principles** is the **principal** reason that whistleblowers report an employer's illegal activities.

✔ The elementary school **principal** said that faculty members try to instill moral **principles** in students through a curriculum that focuses on ethics.

quit, quite, quiet   To *quit* is to *stop*. *Quite* means *very*, and *quiet* is the opposite of *loud*.

✔ It was so **quiet** in the house that for a moment, Adam was not **quite** certain that his children were there.

✔ June wanted to **quit** her job while she attended school, but her family could not survive without her salary.

regardless, ~~irregardless~~   Regardless of the number of times you may have seen it, *irregardless* is not a word. The word is *regardless*.

✔ Avery plans to make the trip **regardless** of the weather.

themselves, ~~themself~~, ~~theirself~~, ~~theirselves~~   The word is always *themselves*.

✔ Anna and Tyrone were proud that they had built their business by **themselves,** without financial help from their family.

then, than   *Then* is used to show time or cause and effect; *than* is used to compare.

✔ The dentist's office offered Charlene an appointment next month, but she could not wait until **then**.

✔ If petroleum emissions continue to erode the ozone layer, **then** global warming is likely to result.

✔ The bank's new building is much more modern **than** the old one, but it is not nearly as beautiful.

there, their, they're   *There* is used to mean *in that place* (Put it over *there*) or to start a sentence or clause (*There* are some disadvantages to airbags). *Their* means *belonging to them*, and *they're* means *they are*.

✔ Chincoteague Island is known for the wild horses that live **there**.

✔ **There** seems to be a television station for everything; music, sports, food, decorating, and even shopping are available at the flick of a remote control.

✔ Joel took his dogs to the veterinarian for **their** annual vaccinations.

✔ "Save me some peanut butter cookies; **they're** my favorite," said William.

through, threw   *Through* means *within, between,* or *finished. Threw* is the past tense of *throw.*

✔ Jamarcus came **through** the front door and **threw** a stack of papers on the table. "I'm **through** with my research," he announced.

two, too, to   *Two* refers to the number 2; *too* means *also* or indicates an excessive amount, as in the phrase *too much.* Any other use requires *to.*

✔ "I need **two** heads to hold all the information I have to learn," said Duane.

✔ There is an old saying that **too** many cooks spoil the broth.

✔ Tonya stopped on the way home **to** buy gas.

weather, whether, rather   *Weather* includes *natural phenomena* such as temperature, rainfall, and wind velocity. *Whether* indicates the *existence of two possibilities* and is often paired with *or not. Rather* indicates a *preference.*

✔ Lately, the **weather** seems to be getting colder.

✔ Kim did not know **whether** to apply to an out-of-state school or to attend college near her home.

✔ I would **rather** read than watch television.

where, were   *Where* rhymes with *air* and refers to *place. Were* rhymes with *fur* and is a past tense form of *to be.*

✔ When Doug did not see you, he asked **where** you **were**.

REVIEW EXERCISE 1   USING WORDS COMMONLY CONFUSED

Refer to the explanations in this chapter to choose the correct word in the following sentences. Underline the correct choice.

1. Almost everyone agrees that getting (a, <u>an</u>) education is (<u>quite</u>, quiet) important in today's world.

2. When the exam ended, Lucinda was not sure (rather, <u>whether</u>) she had (past, <u>passed</u>) it or not.

3. Austin went (threw, <u>through</u>) his trunk carefully, but he could not find the flashlight that he (<u>knew</u>, new) he had put there.

4. Haley promised to (<u>buy</u>, by) her lunch for her friends (<u>regardless</u>, irregardless) of the cost.

5. Rico blamed (<u>himself</u>, hisself) for being (<u>too</u>, to, two) stubborn to admit that he was wrong.

REVIEW EXERCISE 2   USING WORDS COMMONLY CONFUSED

Refer to the explanations in this chapter to choose the correct word in the following sentences. Underline the correct choice.

1. Kesha said, "I would like to (loose, <u>lose</u>) weight, but I don't want all the clothes I just bought to become too (<u>loose</u>, lose).

2. Dwight ate a (peace, <u>piece</u>) of the birthday cake and said that it was (<u>good</u>, well).

3. Sandra plays the piano (good, <u>well</u>); (its, <u>it's</u>) evident that she has been practicing.

4. Laurie could not (except, <u>accept</u>) her mother's (<u>advice</u>, advise) to stay away from serious relationships until she finished school.

5. After Edward (<u>threw</u>, through) the ball a few times, it became (<u>plain</u>, plane) that his injury would force him to sit out the game.

REVIEW EXERCISE 3   CORRECTING ERRORS IN WORDS COMMONLY CONFUSED

Underline and correct the two word-choice errors in each of the following numbered items.

1. At the animal shelter, Heather found it <u>quiet</u> difficult to choose <u>among</u> a white kitten and one with tabby spots.

   At the animal shelter, Heather found it **quite** difficult to choose **between** a

   white kitten and one with tabby spots.

2. My sister is older <u>then</u> I am, but I am <u>alot</u> more mature.

   My sister is older **than** I am, but I am **a lot** more mature.

3. "I don't swim very <u>good</u>," said Mike, "so I'm not sure <u>weather</u> I should go whitewater rafting or not."

   "I don't swim very **well**," said Mike, "so I'm not sure **whether** I should go

   whitewater rafting or not."

4. The workers were proud of <u>theirselves</u> when they exceeded the production goals set <u>buy</u> management.

   The workers were proud of **themselves** when they exceeded the production

   goals set **by** management.

5. Hiro was so <u>effected</u> by the smog that she could hardly <u>breath</u>.

   Hiro was so **affected** by the smog that she could hardly **breathe**.

REVIEW EXERCISE 4   CORRECTING ERRORS IN WORDS COMMONLY CONFUSED

Underline and correct the two word-choice errors in each numbered item.

1. The school <u>principle</u> said that the new curriculum was based on sound educational <u>principals</u>.

   The school **principal** said that the new curriculum was based on sound educa-

   tional **principles**.

2. Annie's car was in <u>it's</u> parking space behind the office, but all four of its tires <u>where</u> missing.

   Annie's car was in **its** parking space behind the office, but all four of its tires

   were missing.

3. Courtney was not <u>quiet</u> sure <u>weather</u> she would be able to visit her parents during winter vacation.

   Courtney was not **quite** sure **whether** she would be able to visit her parents

   during winter vacation.

4. Brian <u>through</u> a log onto the fire, <u>than</u> jumped back as sparks flew out into the room.

   Brian **threw** a log onto the fire, **then** jumped back as sparks flew out into the

   room.

5. "On this test, it is <u>alright</u> to use your books and notes," said the instructor, "and when you are <u>threw</u> with the test, please leave quietly."

"On this test, it is **all right** to use your books and notes," said the instructor,

"and when you are **through** with the test, please leave quietly."

REVIEW EXERCISE 5   CORRECTING ERRORS IN WORDS COMMONLY CONFUSED

Underline the ten word-choice errors in the following paragraph. Then rewrite the corrected version on the lines provided.

[1]Some employers offer exotic perks in order to induce prospective employees to <u>except</u> a job. [2]At an interview, a candidate may be offered a <u>knew</u> laptop computer or told that the company provides a nap room for employees. [3]In addition, an employer may offer <u>a</u> on-site health club, massage therapy, or a recreation room. [4]Many candidates may be tempted <u>too</u> join the company by descriptions of employee get-togethers or lunches catered as employees work. [5]However, the best <u>advise</u> is to ask what employers expect in return for these extras. [6]The <u>principal</u> that there is no free lunch is especially true in modern business. [7]In return for these perks, employees are often expected to work extra hours and give up <u>there</u> weekends to get the job done. [8]They may <u>loose</u> personal or family time as they attend special training sessions in their off hours. [9]Job candidates may welcome such a working environment, or they may prefer <u>too</u> keep work and leisure separate. [10]In any case, it always pays to find out just how much that free laptop or other perks will <u>effect</u> an employer's expectations.

[1]Some employers offer exotic perks in order to induce prospective employ-ees to **accept** a job. [2]At an interview, a candidate may be offered a **new** laptop computer or told that the company provides a nap room for employees. [3]In addition, an employer may offer **an** on-site health club, massage therapy, or a recreation room. [4]Many candidates may be tempted **to** join the company by descriptions of employee get-togethers or lunches catered as employees work. [5]However, the best **advice** is to ask what employers expect in return for these

extras. [6]The **principle** that there is no free lunch is especially true in modern business. [7]In return for these perks, employees are often expected to work extra hours and give up **their** weekends to get the job done. [8]They may **lose** personal or family time as they attend special training sessions in their off hours. [9]Job candidates may welcome such a working environment, or they may prefer **to** keep work and leisure separate. [10]In any case, it always pays to find out just how much that free laptop or other perks will **affect** an employer's expectations.

26

Word Choice

Mary is interviewing for the job of her dreams. When she meets the interviewer, what should she say?

    a. What's up, dude! Like, got any jobs, man?
    b. Permit me to take the necessary step of introducing myself to you.
    c. Good afternoon. I'm Mary Smith.
    d. If you're looking for the cream of the crop, it's as plain as the nose on your face that I am a cut above the rest.

If you answered *c* to the question in the box above, you have shown good judgment in word choice. But when you write, word choice is not always clear-cut. This chapter will help you to fine-tune your judgment and to recognize categories of word choice that are generally not appropriate for college writing: **slang, clichés,** and **wordiness.**

Slang

People enjoy using **slang** because it is informal, up-to-the-minute, and fun. Just as a common language forms a bond among those who speak it, slang reinforces the bond within the groups that use it. Yet the very things that make slang appealing in conversation make it unsuitable for writing to a broad audience. Writing requires a common language and is usually more formal than conversation. In addition, no writer wants to use words that may be out of date by the time an audience reads them. Slang expressions such as *the bee's knees, hunky-dory,* and *groovy* may have sounded up-to-the-minute decades ago, but now they are relics of another time.

Group Exercise 1   Discussing Slang Terms

Form small groups. Try to include members of both sexes, of different ages, and with varied backgrounds. Once you have formed your group, each member should write down five slang terms and then share the list with other group members. Are some of the terms different? (The more diverse the group, the more likely that it will generate a variety of slang.) Are there any slang expressions that not all group members are familiar with? What conclusions can the group draw about the use of slang? Choose one spokesperson to report the group's findings, along with a few of the most interesting slang terms, to the class.

PRACTICE 1   ELIMINATING SLANG

Replace the italicized slang expressions in each sentence with more traditional word choices. The first one is done for you.

Answers will vary.

1. Jiro thought that he looked *cool* wearing a new pair of reflective wraparound *shades.*

   fashionable

   sunglasses

2. Sam said, "Let's go to the coffee shop, and I'll treat you to *some grub.* I have *deep pockets* today."

   breakfast

   money

3. Amber had *maxed out her plastic,* so she felt *poor as a church mouse* at the mall.

   charged the limit on her credit card

   poor

4. Frank said, "My mother was *tripping* last night because I told her she was *phat* compared to my friends' moms. She just can't take a compliment."

   upset

   wonderful

5. Kevin is so *clueless* that he paid full price at the dealership for his new *ride.*

inexperienced *or* naive

car

Clichés

While slang is fresh and new, **clichés** are expressions used so often for so long that they have become worn out. The cliché "burn the midnight oil," for instance, is a relic of a time when working until midnight meant lighting an oil lamp. Because they are easy to remember and widely used, clichés may often be the first expressions that come to mind. It takes a deliberate effort to recognize them and eliminate them from your writing.

Look at the following list of clichés. Can you think of others?

light as a feather	raining cats and dogs	apple of my eye
once in a blue moon	dead as a doornail	flat as a pancake
sick as a dog	pretty as a picture	at the drop of a hat
cream of the crop	live and let live	as good as gold
as old as Methuselah	in the lap of luxury	easy as pie

PRACTICE 2   ELIMINATING CLICHÉS

Rewrite each sentence to eliminate the two italicized clichés. The first one is done for you.

Answers will vary.

1. The stereo cost *an arm and a leg*, but Derrick decided to *bite the bullet*.

    The stereo **was expensive**, but Derrick decided to **buy it**.

    _____

2. As she walked onstage, Quina looked *as cool as a cucumber*, but inside, she was *shaking like a leaf*.

    As she walked onstage, Quina looked **calm**, but inside, she was **nervous**.

    _____

3. Getting money from my parents used to be *like taking candy from a baby*, but now it's *an uphill battle*.

    Getting money from my parents used to be **easy**, but now it's **difficult**.

    _____

4. After her bout with the flu, Karina said she was feeling *fit as a fiddle*, but she looked like *death warmed over*.

    After her bout with the flu, Karina said she was feeling **fine**, but she looked
    very ill.

5. My next-door neighbor dreams of *living in the lap of luxury,* but he *has his head in the clouds.*

    My next-door neighbor dreams of **living a life of wealth**, but he **is unrealistic**.

Wordiness

Wordiness sometimes happens when writers do not take the time to be concise. The shortest and simplest way of expressing an idea is usually the best way.

Wordy Expressions

The words and phrases in the following list contribute to wordiness and can usually be omitted:

totally	usually ~~totally~~ unnecessary
basically	~~basically~~ performs no function in most sentences
very	can ~~very~~ often be omitted
definitely	is ~~definitely~~ a space-waster
in my opinion	usually weakens a sentence ~~in my opinion~~
the fact is that	~~The fact is that~~ facts, like opinions, can usually be stated without preamble.

The phrases that follow are wordy and can usually be shortened and strengthened.

Wordy	Concise
at the present time	now, today
due to the fact that	because, since
long in length	long

Wordy	Concise
in today's society	today
in point of fact	in fact
for the reason that	because, since

✘ Due to the fact that I am basically broke at this point in time, I plan to ask my parents to float me a small loan.

✔ Because I am broke, I plan to ask my parents for a small loan.

✘ On the occasion of my twenty-first birthday, my friends hosted a party in my honor which came as a completely unexpected surprise to me.

✔ On my twenty-first birthday, my friends hosted a surprise party for me.

PRACTICE 3   ELIMINATING WORDINESS

Each sentence contains two italicized wordy expressions. Rewrite the sentences to eliminate wordiness.

Answers will vary.

1. The package was *large in size* and *blue in color*.

    The package was **large and blue.**

2. The speaker said that he was *basically* appalled at the erosion of morality *in today's society*.

    The speaker said that he was appalled at the **current** erosion of morality.

3. *It goes without saying that* this company appreciates the work that its employees do *each and every day*.

    This company appreciates the work that its employees do.

4. *In my opinion, I think* that paying *cash money* is preferable to using a credit card.

    I think that paying **cash** is preferable to using a credit card.

5. Albert is *honest in character* and *totally and completely* committed to his family.

    Albert is **honest** and committed to his family.

It Is and *There Is*

Wordiness often occurs in constructions beginning with "it is" or "there is." Sentences that start with "It is" or "There is (are, was, were, had been . . .)" can often be shortened and strengthened.

✘ It was evident that there were too many people crowded onto the elevator.

✔ Too many people were crowded onto the elevator.

✘ There is a feeling among the members of the class that the instructor is showing favoritism.

✔ Many class members believe the instructor is showing favoritism.

PRACTICE 4   ELIMINATING WORDINESS

Rewrite each sentence to eliminate wordiness.

Answers will vary.

1. It is my opinion that we should take no action at the present time.

    We should not act yet.

2. There are many people who believe that UFOs regularly visit the planet Earth.

    Many people believe that UFOs regularly visit Earth.

3. It is important to note that safety has always been the company's first priority.

    Safety has always been the company's first priority.

4. There was much discussion among the family members about where the family reunion should be held.

    The family members discussed where to hold the reunion.

5. It is the hope of every student currently enrolled in this college that he or she will one day graduate.

    Every student enrolled in this college hopes to graduate one day.

REVIEW EXERCISE 1   RECOGNIZING AND ELIMINATING SLANG, CLICHÉS, AND WORDINESS

In the blank to the left of each sentence, indicate whether the italicized expressions are slang (S), clichés (C), or wordy expressions (W). Then rewrite or omit the italicized expression to eliminate the problem in word choice.

Answers will vary.

S 1. Andrew *went ballistic* when he found out that the class he needs to graduate will not be offered until fall.

    was enraged

__C__ **2.** When her son is *as quiet as a mouse,* Anita always checks to see what mischief he is up to.

quiet

__W__ **3.** *Basically,* the Internet has made the world a smaller place.

Omit italicized expression.

__W__ **4.** The envelope was *large in size* and required extra postage.

large

__C__ **5.** Marisa is *as happy as a clam* at her new job.

happy

__S__ **6.** Adam said he had *aced* the chemistry test.

done well on, made an A on

__W__ **7.** The company has no plans for expansion *at the present time.*

now (or omit italicized expression)

__S__ **8.** Sandra could not eat dinner because she had *scarfed* chips and cookies an hour before.

gorged on

__C__ **9.** Hank plans to work full time and attend school full time. I think he *has lost his marbles.*

is crazy

__W__ **10.** *In point of fact,* no one has applied for the job.

Omit italicized expression.

REVIEW EXERCISE 2   RECOGNIZING AND ELIMINATING SLANG, CLICHÉS, AND WORDINESS

Underline and correct the two word choice problems in each sentence.

Answers will vary.

1. The tire was <u>as flat as a flitter</u>, and it took all the <u>elbow grease</u> I could muster to change it.

flat

effort

2. Caroline was <u>basically</u> upset with herself for having <u>bombed</u> the history test.

omit

failed

3. In the final analysis, each and every person makes an important contribution.

   omit

   Every

4. The mall is only a stone's throw from here. I'll show you; I know this town like the back of my hand.

   a short distance

   well

5. Anna never liked her old job; she felt like a square peg in a round hole. She was pleased as punch when the company transferred her to a new position.

   out of place

   pleased

REVIEW EXERCISE 3   RECOGNIZING AND ELIMINATING SLANG, CLICHÉS, AND WORDINESS

Underline the two problems in word choice in each sentence; then rewrite the sentences to eliminate word choice problems.

Answers will vary.

1. The herbal tea was pale orange in color and deliciously minty in taste.

   The **pale orange** herbal tea tasted deliciously **minty**.

2. Janine used to be afraid of her own shadow, but now she has come out of her shell.

   Janine used to be **timid**, but now she **is more outgoing**.

3. Arnold was steamed due to the fact that his car would not start.

   Arnold was **angry because** his car would not start.

4. Basically, Jim's idea is as sound as a dollar.

   Jim's idea is **sound**.

5. Bert found that keeping his nose to the grindstone led to total and complete exhaustion.

   Bert found that **working too hard** led to **exhaustion**.

REVIEW EXERCISE 4   RECOGNIZING AND ELIMINATING SLANG, CLICHÉS, AND WORDINESS

Rewrite the following letter to eliminate problems in word choice.

Answers will vary.

Dear Juliet,

[1]I am clueless about why you have not answered your door or returned my calls. [2]Maybe your phone is not working, and your doorbell is as dead as a doornail. [3]However, I am certain beyond a shadow of a doubt that you did not mean it when you told me to get out of your life forever.

[4]Basically, ever since we met at that party, you have been the only one for me. [5]The many other women who pursue me don't amount to a hill of beans. [6]It is not my fault that women think I am da bomb.

[7]I know that you were also majorly ticked off that I charged your birthday present to your credit card. [8]However, the fact is that I fully intend to pay you back eventually.

[9]You have given me the cold shoulder lately, but I forgive you. [10]I hope you will always consider me your main squeeze.

Love,

Romeo

Dear Juliet,

[1]I do not understand why you have not answered your door or returned my calls. [2]Maybe your phone and doorbell are not working. [3]However, I am certain that you did not mean it when you told me to get out of your life forever.

[4]Ever since we met at that party, you have been the only one for me. [5]The many other women who pursue me are not important. [6]It is not my fault that women think I am irresistible.

[7]I know that you were also angry that I charged your birthday present to your credit card. [8]However, I fully intend to pay you back eventually.

[9]You have ignored me lately, but I forgive you. [10]I hope you will always consider me your only love.

Love,

Romeo

27
Commas

There are so many comma rules that, in desperation, people often resort to makeshift rules like the ones above. Unfortunately, these blanket statements don't always work. When it comes to commas, rules—and exceptions—abound. The rules laid out in this chapter will help you cope with the complexities of comma usage.

Commas to Set Off Introductory Words, Phrases, and Clauses

Commas should be used after an introductory word, phrase, or clause.

Examples

✔ Instead, Beth decided to study veterinary medicine.

✔ After a long pause, the old man began to speak.

✔ When Andrea smelled popcorn, she remembered that she had not eaten all day.

PRACTICE 1   USING COMMAS AFTER INTRODUCTORY ELEMENTS

Rewrite the following sentences, inserting commas after introductory words, phrases, and clauses.

1. Cautiously the firefighters picked their way through the rubble.

   Cautiously, the firefighters picked their way through the rubble.

   _____

2. To Robert's annoyance the telephone rang again.

   To Robert's annoyance, the telephone rang again.

   _____

3. By the time her classified ad appeared in the paper Lisa had already sold her car.

   By the time her classified ad appeared in the paper, Lisa had already sold her

   car.

4. Sipping from a bottle of water the runner told a reporter that she had run her best race ever.

   Sipping from a bottle of water, the runner told a reporter that she had run her

   best race ever.

5. When Teresa first enrolled in the tennis class she did not even know how to hold a racket.

   When Teresa first enrolled in the tennis class, she did not even know how to

   hold a racket.

Commas to Join Three or More Items in a Series

When a series of three or more words, phrases, or clauses is connected with *and, or,* or *nor,* place a comma after each item except the last one. The final comma will come before *and, or,* or *nor.*

> ## ✳ *Real-World Writing*
>
> In journalism, it is becoming customary to omit the comma before *and, or,* or *nor.* Academic usage is more traditional and favors keeping the final comma.

Examples

✔ Nursing, information technology, and business administration are the college's three most popular majors.

✔ The dog has been digging under the rosebushes, around the zinnias, and in the neighbor's flowerbed.

✔ The career counselor asked Alison what her interests were, where her talents lay, and what her dream job would be.

If only two items appear in the series, no comma is used.

✔ The only two classes Quinton plans to take during the summer term are drafting and mathematics.

✔ The weather channel reported wildfires in California and an earthquake in Japan.

✔ The corporate consultant was hired to examine how workers approached their jobs and how effective they were in doing them.

PRACTICE 2   USING COMMAS TO JOIN ITEMS IN A SERIES

Rewrite the following sentences, inserting commas to join words, phrases, and clauses in a series of three or more. One sentence has only two items in the series and does not require a comma.

1. Jason loaded detergent fabric softener and bleach into his laundry basket.

    Jason loaded detergent, fabric softener, and bleach into his laundry basket.

    _____

2. According to a survey of employers, June July and August are the most popular months for vacations.

According to a survey of employers, June, July, and August are the most popu-

lar months for vacations.

3. Pollen animal dander and dust make Eric sneeze.

   Pollen, animal dander, and dust make Eric sneeze.

4. Shannon carefully cut the wallpaper to size applied it to the wall and watched as it slowly curled back down toward the floor.

   Shannon carefully cut the wallpaper to size, applied it to the wall, and watched

   as it slowly curled back down toward the floor.

5. Kerry said that there was no time left for work once she answered her e-mail and returned her telephone messages.

   This sentence does not require a comma.

Commas to Join Independent Clauses

Use a comma before the FANBOYS conjunctions *for, and, nor, but, or, yet,* and *so* to join independent clauses. Recall that an independent clause has a subject and a verb, and can stand alone as a complete sentence.

✔ Vishal was not sure how to get to the convention center, so he took a map and left an hour early.

✔ The pain in Teresa's head intensified, but she kept working anyway.

✔ A bank of clouds slid in from the west, and soon fat droplets of rain began to fall.

Do not use a comma if the FANBOYS connects a verb to a verb rather than a clause to a clause. That is, do not use a comma unless there is a complete sentence on both sides of the FANBOYS.

    subject   verb   verb

✔ Cassie popped the diskette into her computer and sighed with annoyance.

✔ The refrigerator makes horrible noises but keeps on running.

✔ Rafael will fix his old car or replace it.

PRACTICE 3   USING COMMAS WITH FANBOYS

Place commas before FANBOYS conjunctions that join two independent clauses. One sentence contains a compound verb, not two clauses, and does not need a comma.

1. The "For Sale" sign on the house was nearly covered by weeds and vandals had broken the tall windows at the front of the house.

   The "For Sale" sign on the house was nearly covered by weeds, and vandals had

   broken the tall windows at the front of the house.

2. Hal put a pat of butter on each pancake and carefully poured syrup over the entire stack.

   This sentence does not require a comma.

3. Althea checked her hair in the mirror but she did not notice the piece of spinach between her teeth.

   Althea checked her hair in the mirror, but she did not notice the piece of

   spinach between her teeth.

4. Flag etiquette specifies that the American flag should be taken down at sunset but it may be flown all night if it is properly illuminated.

   Flag etiquette specifies that the American flag should be taken down at sunset,

   but it may be flown all night if it is properly illuminated.

5. We have two choices but neither of them is very appealing.

   We have two choices, but neither of them is very appealing.

Commas around Interrupters

An **interrupter** is a word, phrase, or clause inserted between subject and verb to give more information about some element within the sentence. An interrupter is not essential to the meaning of the sentence; that is, it is not necessary in identifying the word that it follows.

✔ Joan's car, an old Nissan, was parked near the building.

The car in the sentence is already identified as *Joan's car*. The modifier *an old Nissan* gives more information, but if it were removed from the sentence, the sentence would still make sense.

✔ The Burger King bag, crumpled and stuffed under a bench, held the remains of someone's lunch.

The modifier *crumpled and stuffed under a bench* is nonessential because the bag is already identified as a Burger King bag.

PRACTICE 4   USING COMMAS AROUND INTERRUPTERS

Rewrite the following sentences, inserting commas around interrupters.

1. Joel's car a ten-year-old Ford had over one hundred thousand miles on its odometer.

   Joel's car, a ten-year-old Ford, had over one hundred thousand miles on its

   odometer.

2. Dr. Hopper the podiatrist Jessy saw last week said that high heels were the worst shoes anyone could wear.

   Dr. Hopper, the podiatrist Jessy saw last week, said that high heels were the

   worst shoes anyone could wear.

3. The coffee shop the only restaurant open after midnight was a gathering place for night-shift workers.

   The coffee shop, the only restaurant open after midnight, was a gathering

   place for night-shift workers.

4. A loaf of rye bread forgotten in the cabinet for weeks was covered in bright green mold.

   A loaf of rye bread, forgotten in the cabinet for weeks, was covered in bright

   green mold.

5. The jogging path a popular place for runners and walkers stretches through the woods and beside the lake on its two-mile course.

   The jogging path, a popular place for runners and walkers, stretches through

   the woods and beside the lake on its two-mile course.

Punctuating Essential and Nonessential Modifiers

Not all phrases that come between subject and verb require commas. Some phrases and clauses, called *essential modifiers*, are not set off by commas. Essential modifiers include all clauses beginning with *that* and any other phrase or clause that is essential in identifying the subject. Essential modifiers are also known as *restrictive modifiers* because they restrict the meaning of the subject. See Chapter 20, "Relative Pronouns," for additional information on this topic.

✔ The forty dollars that I took from the ATM on Friday did not last long.

Like all clauses beginning with "that," the clause "that I took from the ATM on Friday" is essential. It restricts the discussion to the forty dollars taken from the ATM on Friday. Because the clause is an essential modifier, no commas are used.

✔ The woman with red hair is Tom's fiancée.

In this sentence, the phrase "with red hair" is essential. Of all the women present, the phrase restricts the one being discussed to just one: the woman with red hair. Because the phrase is an essential modifier, no commas are used.

✔ The person who robbed the First National Bank is still at large.

The clause "who robbed the First National Bank" is essential. It restricts the discussion to just one person: the one who robbed the First National Bank. Because the clause is an essential modifier, no commas are used.

The following examples show nonessential modifiers, also called nonrestrictive modifiers. These modifiers are not absolutely essential in restricting the meaning of the subject. Commas are used to set off these interrupters from the rest of the sentence.

✔ Kate, wearing a red dress and high heels, appeared in the doorway.

Here, the phrase "wearing a red dress and high heels" is nonessential because the subject has already been identified as Kate. "Wearing a red dress and high heels" gives us more information about her, but it is not essential to identifying her. Out of all people who could appear in the doorway, the possibilities have already been restricted to "Kate." Since the clause is nonessential, commas are necessary.

✔ Hawthorn T. Berry, who owns a landscaping business, told me that slow-growing grasses are best for people who hate to mow lawns.

Even though knowing that Hawthorne T. Berry is a landscaper might add to his credibility, the clause "who owns a landscaping business" is nonessential because, out of a universe full of people, the subject has already been restricted to just one: Hawthorn T. Berry. With nonessential clauses, commas are used.

PRACTICE 5　USING COMMAS AROUND NONESSENTIAL INTERRUPTERS

Five of the following sentences contain nonessential interrupters. Rewrite those sentences, placing commas around nonessential interrupters. Five sentences contain essential interrupters which do not require commas. Write "essential" on the line below each of those sentences.

1.　The song that just played on the radio is Bryan's favorite.

essential

2.　The woman who just walked through the door is Todd's attorney.

essential

3.　The mechanic who fixes my car is retiring.

essential

4.　Jeff Loomis who fixes my car is retiring.

Jeff Loomis, who fixes my car, is retiring.

5.　Shonda Bartholomew who sits by the door made an A on the last test.

Shonda Bartholomew, who sits by the door, made an A on the last test.

6.　A small puppy with brown spots looked longingly out of the pet store window.

essential

7.　Boozoo Chavis who played the accordion was one of the originators of Zydeco music.

Boozoo Chavis, who played the accordion, was one of the originators of Zydeco music.

8.　Mr. Smith wearing a green tie greeted customers at the door.

Mr. Smith, wearing a green tie, greeted customers at the door.

9. The figures that were put into the database yesterday will need to be redone.

essential

10. Hurricane Mitch which killed more than nine thousand people was classified as a Category 5 hurricane.

Hurricane Mitch, which killed more than nine thousand people, was classified

as a Category 5 hurricane.

Commas with Direct Quotations

A **direct quotation** is an exact repetition of the words that someone speaks or thinks. When a comma is used with a direct quotation, it is always placed in front of the quotation mark.

1. When a direct quotation is followed by a **dialogue tag** such as "he said," a comma goes after the quoted words and **in front of the quotation mark.**

    ✔ "What I need most right now is a nap," said Kitt.

2. When a dialogue tag leads into a direct quotation, a comma goes after the tag and **in front of the quotation mark.**

    ✔ Edward asked, "Are you through with the sports section of the paper?"

3. When a sentence is written as a split quotation, commas are placed **in front of the quotation marks.**

    ✔ "If the school board were doing its job," the woman told the reporter, "we would not be standing out here with picket signs."

PRACTICE 6   USING COMMAS WITH DIRECT QUOTATIONS

Rewrite the following sentences, inserting commas to set off direct quotations.

1. Glenn asked "Can you tell me how to get to the bookstore?"

    Glenn asked, "Can you tell me how to get to the bookstore?"

2. "I started voice lessons last year" said Alisa "and my singing has really improved."

"I started voice lessons last year," said Alisa, "and my singing has really improved."

3. "I am a walking disaster" said Alex, picking up the books he had dropped.

"I am a walking disaster," said Alex, picking up the books he had dropped.

4. "Not only is our new quarterback ambidextrous" joked the football coach "but he can also throw with either hand."

"Not only is our new quarterback ambidextrous," joked the football coach,

"but he can also throw with either hand."

5. "I wish I could remember where I parked my car" said Ashley.

"I wish I could remember where I parked my car," said Ashley.

Commas in Names and Dates

When a professional title follows a name, it is set off with commas.

✔ The check was made out to Gregory Makin, M.D.

✔ John Ramirez, D.D.S., has announced his retirement.

When you write the month, day, and year, a comma goes between the day and year.

✔ The 19th Amendment, which gave women the right to vote, was ratified on August 26, 1920.

When you write just the month and year, no comma is used.

✔ Alexander Graham Bell was granted a patent for the telephone in March 1876.

PRACTICE 7   USING COMMAS IN NAMES AND DATES

Rewrite the following sentences, inserting commas as needed. One sentence needs no comma.

1. While tearing up a floor to remodel his house, Howard found an old letter dated April 13 1922.

   While tearing up a floor to remodel his house, Howard found an old letter

   dated April 13, 1922.

2. Katherine Peavy D.V.M. examined the kittens and pronounced them healthy.

   Katherine Peavy, D.V.M., examined the kittens and pronounced them healthy.

3. The flyer nailed to the telephone pole said that the missing woman had last been seen in December 2003.

   The sentence does not need a comma.

4. The nameplate on the office door said Khalil Oldham C.P.A.

   The nameplate on the office door said Khalil Oldham, C.P.A.

5. Eugenia Mize M.D. has been our family doctor since we moved to the city.

   Eugenia Mize, M.D., has been our family doctor since we moved to the city.

REVIEW EXERCISE 1   USING COMMAS

Rewrite the sentences, inserting commas where they are needed.

1. The radio station held a drawing for concert tickets T-shirts and compact disks.

   The radio station held a drawing for concert tickets, T-shirts, and compact

   disks.

2. Professor Tate who hated tardiness frowned as Daniel walked into the class-room five minutes late.

   Professor Tate, who hated tardiness, frowned as Daniel walked into the class-

   room five minutes late.

3. Bark Avenue a salon for dogs is offering a half-price grooming and shampoo to new clients.

   Bark Avenue, a salon for dogs, is offering a half-price grooming and shampoo

   to new clients.

4. In July 1776 the Declaration of Independence proclaimed the United States a free nation.

    In July 1776, the Declaration of Independence proclaimed the United States a

    free nation.

5. When the doorbell rang the dog began to bark loudly.

    When the doorbell rang, the dog began to bark loudly.

6. The seven continents on Earth are North America South America Europe Asia Africa Australia and Antarctica.

    The seven continents on Earth are North America, South America, Europe,

    Asia, Africa, Australia, and Antarctica.

7. The employment ad promised a job with opportunity for travel but Lauren did not realize that the company was a long-distance trucking firm.

    The employment ad promised a job with opportunity for travel, but Lauren did

    not realize that the company was a long-distance trucking firm.

8. The broken windowpane the open front door and the empty space where her CD player had been told Susan that her house had been burglarized.

    The broken windowpane, the open front door, and the empty space where her

    CD player had been told Susan that her house had been burglarized.

9. "Sorry I'm late" said Patrick "but traffic was terrible."

    "Sorry I'm late," said Patrick, "but traffic was terrible."

10. Elizabeth Suarez my sister's best friend has been accepted to medical school.

    Elizabeth Suarez, my sister's best friend, has been accepted to medical school.

REVIEW EXERCISE 2   USING COMMAS

Rewrite the sentences, inserting commas where they are needed.

1. Ron bought security lights for his house but he complains that they come on whenever his dogs walk through the yard.

    Ron bought security lights for his house, but he complains that they come on

    whenever his dogs walk through the yard.

2. Paula Kasabian M.D. burst through the doors of the emergency room and ran to meet the ambulance.

    Paula Kasabian, M.D., burst through the doors of the emergency room and ran

    to meet the ambulance.

3. Juanita yawning hugely poured coffee into a large mug.

    Juanita, yawning hugely, poured coffee into a large mug.

4. Phillip's friends and relatives armed with noisemakers and wearing funny hats hid quietly in the shadows as they heard the sound of his key in the door.

    Phillip's friends and relatives, armed with noisemakers and wearing funny hats,

    hid quietly in the shadows as they heard the sound of his key in the door.

5. From its position high on the wall a photograph of Great-Aunt Prudence looked sternly down at Erin.

    From its position high on the wall, a photograph of Great-Aunt Prudence

    looked sternly down at Erin.

6. The Smiths' children wearing Halloween costumes and carrying flashlights ran across the lawn to the next house.

    The Smiths' children, wearing Halloween costumes and carrying flashlights, ran

    across the lawn to the next house.

7. Marcie bought magazines paperback books and a basket of fruit to take to her friend in the hospital.

    Marcie bought magazines, paperback books, and a basket of fruit to take to

    her friend in the hospital.

8. The telephone directory had two separate listings for Joseph Rawlins D.D.S.

    The telephone directory had two separate listings for Joseph Rawlins, D.D.S.

9. Just before the sun rose Esther put on her running shoes and headed for the park.

    Just before the sun rose, Esther put on her running shoes and headed for the

    park.

10. Gratefully Julia took the steaming cup of coffee and sank into a comfortable chair.

    Gratefully, Julia took the steaming cup of coffee and sank into a comfortable

    chair.

REVIEW EXERCISE 3   USING COMMAS

Rewrite the sentences, inserting commas where they are needed. Each numbered item contains two problems that can be fixed with the addition of a comma or commas.

1. As Josh pulled the laundry from the washer he noticed dark blue stains covering several pieces of laundry. He said "Oh, no! I left a pen in one of my shirt pockets."

   As Josh pulled the laundry from the washer, he noticed dark blue stains cover-

   ing several pieces of laundry. He said, "Oh, no! I left a pen in one of my shirt

   pockets."

2. It was almost midnight and Alicia had to get up early in the morning. However she was determined not to fall asleep until she heard her daughter's car in the driveway.

   It was almost midnight, and Alicia had to get up early in the morning.

   However, she was determined not to fall asleep until she heard her daughter's

   car in the driveway.

3. A thickening waist thinning hair and a complete lack of interest in MTV told Todd that he was getting old. "I don't mind getting old. It's better than the alternative" he said.

   A thickening waist, thinning hair, and a complete lack of interest in MTV told

   Todd that he was getting old. "I don't mind getting old. It's better than the al-

   ternative," he said.

4. As the students began their exam the classroom was quiet. Suddenly the loud slam of a door somewhere down the hall caused everyone to jump.

   As the students began their exam, the classroom was quiet. Suddenly, the loud

   slam of a door somewhere down the hall caused everyone to jump.

5. The date on the old marriage certificate was June 23 1942. "This belonged to my great-grandparents" said Leland.

   The date on the old marriage certificate was June 23, 1942. "This belonged to

   my great-grandparents," said Leland.

REVIEW EXERCISE 4 USING COMMAS

Rewrite the sentences, inserting commas where they are needed.

1. Unsteadily Maria rolled down the driveway on her new in-line skates. The skates worked perfectly but her feet were not cooperating at all.

   Unsteadily, Maria rolled down the driveway on her new in-line skates. The

   skates worked perfectly, but her feet were not cooperating at all.

2. The lawn mower which had run well for over a decade shuddered once and rolled to a stop. "I think I can fix it " said Newton.

   The lawn mower, which had run well for over a decade, shuddered once and

   rolled to a stop. "I think I can fix it," said Newton.

3. After Shawn rolled his spare change, he had two rolls of quarters a roll of dimes two rolls of nickels and five rolls of pennies. As he counted the rolls he realized he had enough money to last until payday.

   After Shawn rolled his spare change, he had two rolls of quarters, a roll of

   dimes, two rolls of nickels, and five rolls of pennies. As he counted the rolls, he

   realized he had enough money to last until payday.

4. In the trunk of the car were four paperback books a blue jacket and a tire pressure gauge. The inspection sticker on the windshield read July 2004.

   In the trunk of the car were four paperback books, a blue jacket, and a tire

   pressure gauge. The inspection sticker on the windshield read July 2004.

5. Ed who was sleeping peacefully was awakened by a pounding on his door. It was his friend Al who had come to pick him up for a fishing trip they had planned.

   Ed, who was sleeping peacefully, was awakened by a pounding on his door. It

   was his friend Al, who had come to pick him up for a fishing trip they had

   planned.

REVIEW EXERCISE 5   USING COMMAS

Rewrite the paragraph, inserting commas where they are needed. Each sentence contains one comma problem.

[1]During World War II top secret messages were transmitted by a select group of U.S. Marines known as Navajo code talkers. [2]Important information about troop movements was sent through radio transmissions which were relatively easy for the enemy to listen in on. [3]The Japanese army's expert cryptographers could break almost any code but the code used by Navajo code talkers proved to be an exception. [4]Part of the reason for the success of the code was that the Navajo language which existed only in spoken form was known by few outside the Navajo nation. [5]Enemy soldiers listening in on a transmission would probably not recognize the language and they might even believe that the language itself was a code. [6]When American troops had a message to convey it was given to a code talker to convert into code and transmit. [7]A second code talker received the message translated the words into English and decoded the message. [8]The code long held secret worked like this: the first letter of the English equivalent of the Navajo word spelled out the coded message. [9]For example the sound "wol-la-che" meant "ant" in English and therefore stood for the letter A. [10]The Navajo code talkers helped preserve the secrets of U.S. troops and their allies until the signing of a surrender and peace agreement on August 14 1945.

[1]During World War II, top secret messages were transmitted by a select group of U.S. Marines known as Navajo code talkers. [2]Important information about troop movements was sent through radio transmissions, which were relatively easy for the enemy to listen in on. [3]The Japanese army's expert cryptographers could break almost any code, but the code used by Navajo code talkers proved to be an exception. [4]Part of the reason for the success of the code was

that the Navajo language, which existed only in spoken form, was known by few outside the Navajo nation. [5]Enemy soldiers listening in on a transmission would probably not recognize the language, and they might even believe that the language itself was a code. [6]When American troops had a message to convey, it was given to a code talker to convert into code and transmit. [7]A second code talker received the message, translated the words into English, and decoded the message. [8]The code, long held secret, worked like this: the first letter of the English equivalent of the Navajo word spelled out the coded message. [9]For example, the sound "wol-la-che" meant "ant" in English and therefore stood for the letter *A*. [10]The Navajo code talkers helped preserve the secrets of U.S. troops and their allies until the signing of a surrender and peace agreement on August 14, 1945.

28

Other Punctuation

Punctuation marks other than the comma are the focus of this chapter. Some of these punctuation marks, such as the period and the question mark, will be very familiar to you. Others, such as the colon and parentheses, are more exotic and less often used. This chapter will reinforce the familiar marks of punctuation and introduce the less familiar.

End Punctuation: Period, Question Mark, and Exclamation Point

The period, the question mark, and the exclamation point are all forms of **end punctuation;** that is, they signal the end of a sentence.

The Period

The period is used to mark the end of a sentence that makes a statement. It is also used to signal an abbreviation.

1. Use a period at the end of a sentence that makes a statement.
    ✔ The newspaper's classified ad section is one source of employ-
      ment information.
    ✔ The turtle pulled its head under its shell as Jon approached.
2. Use a period to signal an appropriate abbreviation.
    ✔ Dr. Lopez assigned a library research project that is due in two
      weeks.
    ✔ Please tell Mr. Marshall that I cannot wait for him any longer.

Except for abbreviations in courtesy titles, such as *Mr., Ms., Dr.,* or *Rev.*
used before proper names, spell out words in your paragraphs and essays. Most other abbreviations should be reserved for only the most informal usage.

The Question Mark

A question mark is used at the end of a **direct question.**

✔ Who left a box of doughnuts on my desk**?**

✔ Is the yellow Volkswagen yours**?**

No question mark is used with an **indirect question.**

✔ I wonder if there are other solar systems like ours in the universe.

✔ Judge Weeks asked whether anyone objected to postponing the trial.

The Exclamation Point

Exclamation points are used to show extreme excitement or surprise, and
are seldom needed in college writing. Unless you are quoting someone
who has just discovered that the building is on fire, there will be few opportunities to use an exclamation point. Interjections such as "Ouch!" or
"Yikes!" are followed by exclamation points, but they, too, are seldom
needed for college writing. Use exclamation points when you quote someone who is shouting or speaking excitedly. Otherwise, let your words, not
your punctuation, carry the excitement of your essay.

✗ Reginald heard the scream of a fire truck's siren! When he turned onto
  the street where he lived, he saw that the fire truck had stopped in
  front of his house!

✔ Reginald heard the scream of a fire truck's siren. When he turned onto the street where he lived, he saw that the fire truck had stopped in front of his house.

✔ "My dog is inside! Save her!" the man yelled to the firefighters.

PRACTICE 1   USING END PUNCTUATION

Rewrite each sentence, placing a period after an appropriate abbreviation or placing a period or a question mark where needed.

1. Xavier asked, "Why don't relationships come with an instruction book"

   Xavier asked, "Why don't relationships come with an instruction book?"

2. The pills that Dr Angelo prescribed were so large that Marcy could hardly swallow them.

   The pills that Dr. Angelo prescribed were so large that Marcy could hardly swallow them.

3. A large, hairy-looking insect has taken up residence in my mailbox

   A large, hairy-looking insect has taken up residence in my mailbox.

4. Ms Groover loves to wear flamboyant hats and colorful suits.

   Ms. Groover loves to wear flamboyant hats and colorful suits.

5. James drove back to work, eating his lunch at stoplights

   James drove back to work, eating his lunch at stoplights.

The Semicolon

Semicolon to Join Independent Clauses

A semicolon may be used with a transitional expression between independent clauses or alone between independent clauses that are closely related. For a more detailed discussion of this use of the semicolon, see Chapter 14, "Coordination and Subordination," and Chapter 16, "Run-on Sentences."

✔ The campus e-mail server will be down all morning; technicians say it should be working by early afternoon.

✔ Todd always reads the newspaper at breakfast; after that, he is far too busy.

Semicolon to Join Items in a List

Ordinarily, items in a list are joined by commas. However, if the items themselves contain commas, semicolons are used to avoid confusion.

✔ Jean has relatives in Phoenix, Arizona; Brunswick, Georgia; and Louisville, Kentucky.

✔ The new book on veterinary medicine was written by Latrice James, D.V.M.; Carl Nutt, Ph.D.; and G. M. Shepherd, D.V.M.

PRACTICE 2   USING SEMICOLONS

Rewrite the following sentences, using semicolons to join independent clauses or items in a series.

1. The office was quiet on the weekend the security guard made his rounds through dark and quiet halls.

   The office was quiet on the weekend; the security guard made his rounds

   through dark and quiet halls.

2. The customer service representative hid her irritation with her rude customer she smiled and answered politely.

   The customer service representative hid her irritation with her rude customer;

   she smiled and answered politely.

3. Kenneth's three children were born on February 24, 1998 June 20, 2000 and September 26, 2003.

   Kenneth's three children were born on February 24, 1998; June 20, 2000; and

   September 26, 2003.

4. The air quality in the city improved over the last few years however, environ-mental groups say more progress is needed.

   The air quality in the city improved over the last few years; however, environ-

   mental groups say more progress is needed.

   _____

5. At its first meeting, the club elected the following officers: Keiran Williams, President Luciano Hubbard, President-elect Fiona Shoemaker, Treasurer and Allan Gupta, Recorder.

   At its first meeting, the club elected the following officers: Keiran Williams,

   President; Luciano Hubbard, President-elect; Fiona Shoemaker, Treasurer; and

   Allan Gupta, Recorder.

The Colon

The colon is used to introduce a list. The single most important thing to remember when using a colon is that a colon must always follow a complete sentence.

Example 1

✘ In his briefcase, Dewayne carried only: a yellow legal pad, a calcula-tor, and a package of Twinkies.

This usage is incorrect because the colon is not preceded by a complete sentence.

✔ In his briefcase, Dewayne carried only the necessities: a yellow legal pad, a calculator, and a package of Twinkies.

In this corrected sentence, the colon follows a complete sentence. It is also correct—and sometimes simpler—to integrate a list into a sentence with-out using a colon.

Example 2

✔ In his briefcase, Dewayne carried only a yellow legal pad, a calculator, and a package of Twinkies.

PRACTICE 3   LISTING ITEMS WITH AND WITHOUT COLONS

Write each of the following sentences according to directions.

Answers will vary.

1. Write a sentence containing a partial list of the items—at least three—in your backpack or briefcase. Use a colon to introduce the list, and make sure that there is a complete sentence before the colon. Use the second sentence in Example 1 as your model. If you do not carry a backpack or briefcase, use your imagination.

    In my briefcase, I carry only the necessities: a legal pad, a cell phone, and a

    large bag of jellybeans.

2. Rewrite the sentence you wrote for question 1, eliminating the colon. Use the sentence in Example 2 as your model.

    In my briefcase, I carry only a legal pad, a cell phone, and a large bag of jelly-

    beans.

3. Write a sentence listing three things you would bring if you had to spend a year on a deserted island. Use a colon to introduce the list, and make sure that there is a complete sentence before the colon. Use the second sentence in Example 1 as your model.

    If I were stranded for a year on a deserted island, a would bring three important

    items: a large tank of water, a truckload of canned food, and a can opener.

4. Rewrite the sentence you wrote for question 3, eliminating the colon. Use the sentence in Example 2 as your model.

    If I were stranded for a year on a deserted island, I would bring a large tank of

    water, a truckload of canned food, and a can opener.

5. Write a sentence listing at least three courses you will need to take to complete the degree that you are working toward. Use a colon to introduce the list, and make sure that there is a complete sentence before the colon. Use the corrected sentence in Example 1 as your model.

    To complete my degree, I need several courses: History 2112, Math 1121, and

    English 2140.

REVIEW EXERCISE 1   EXPLAINING PUNCTUATION RULES

Look at the boldfaced punctuation in each sentence; then briefly explain the rule that justifies its use. The first one is done for you.

1. The dust on the computer keyboard suggested that no one had used the machine for a long time.

   A period is used to end a sentence that makes a statement.

2. How far can a camel travel without stopping to drink water?

   A question mark is used at the end of a direct question.

3. The old man explained his formula for a long and happy marriage: patience, forgiveness, and liberal use of the words "yes, dear."

   The colon is used to introduce a list.

4. Dr. McClam is booked through the end of September.

   The period is used to signal an abbreviation.

5. Don't move! There's a wasp on your ear!

   Exclamation points are used to show extreme excitement or surprise.

6. The overturned tractor-trailer blocked two lanes; rush-hour traffic ground to a halt.

   A semicolon may be used between independent clauses that are closely related.

7. As the light turned green, the impatient driver behind Harold leaned on the horn and yelled, "Hey! What color are you waiting for?"

   Exclamation points are used to show extreme excitement or surprise.

8. The company had flown Maria to Sidney, Australia; London, England; and Paris, France.

   Ordinarily, items in a list are joined by commas. However, if the items themselves contain commas, semicolons are used to avoid confusion.

9. Though she had a degree and met all the requirements for the job, Elizabeth's most important qualifications were personal: eagerness to learn, absolute desire to succeed, and ability to get along with people.

   The colon is used to introduce a list.

10. Sarah's tennis game has improved; she is hitting shots that would have seemed impossible a month ago.

   A semicolon may be used between independent clauses that are closely related.

   _____

REVIEW EXERCISE 2   USING PUNCTUATION MARKS

Fill the blanks in each sentence with a period, a question mark, an exclamation point, a semicolon, or a colon.

1. Fred says that he eats only three times a day _:_ morning, noon, and night.

2. "Evacuate the building now _!_ " yelled the police officer.

3. The music was so soothing that LaShae nearly fell asleep _._

4. "Why did my laundry turn blue _?_ " Luis wondered.

5. The online course had a high dropout rate _;_ students found it hard to motivate themselves since they never had to attend a class.

6. The bank will close on Thursday, December 24 _;_ Friday, December 25 _;_ and Saturday, December 26.

7. Hiro stopped at the roadside stand for fresh plums and shelled pecans _._

8. "Have you had any previous experience in the field _?_ " asked the interviewer.

9. "We're number one _!_ " yelled the members of the victorious basketball team.

10. The food in this restaurant is good _;_ however, the service is slow.

REVIEW EXERCISE 3   USING PUNCTUATION MARKS

Rewrite each sentence, adding a period, a question mark, an exclamation point, a semicolon, or a colon.

1. From somewhere down the street, the repeated revving of a car engine broke the silence

   From somewhere down the street, the repeated revving of a car engine broke

   the silence.

2. After the attendant had described the five kinds of car washes offered and the price of each, Irene said, "Could you repeat that"

   After the attendant had described the five kinds of car washes offered and the

   price of each, Irene said, "Could you repeat that?"

3. John says he has a photographic memory it's just out of film.

John says he has a photographic memory; it's just out of film.

4. The headline read, "Red Tape Holds Up New Bridge"

The headline read, "Red Tape Holds Up New Bridge."

5. After pulling a twelve-hour shift, Kelvin wanted a hot meal and a shower

After pulling a twelve-hour shift, Kelvin wanted a hot meal and a shower.

6. "Don't jump until we spread the net" the firefighter yelled to the woman in the burning building.

"Don't jump until we spread the net!" the firefighter yelled to the woman in

the burning building.

7. John flipped over the large stone with his toe several bugs scuttled away into the grass.

John flipped over the large stone with his toe; several bugs scuttled away into

the grass.

8. Melissa said she had little chance of winning the award she thought the other contestants' poems were much better than hers.

Melissa said she had little chance of winning the award; she thought the other

contestants' poems were much better than hers.

9. Even before he opened the envelope, Luke knew what it contained it was a birthday card from his parents.

Even before he opened the envelope, Luke knew what it contained; it was a

birthday card from his parents.

10. The scientists were excited by the discovery of fossil dinosaur eggs near the riverbank

The scientists were excited by the discovery of fossil dinosaur eggs near the

riverbank.

REVIEW EXERCISE 4   USING PUNCTUATION MARKS

Fill the blanks in the paragraph with a period, a question mark, an exclamation point, a semicolon, or a colon.

¹When I was young, my mother used to ask in exasperation, "Can't you look where you're going_?_" ²An embarrassing incident last week made me decide I should have paid more attention to her_._ ³It was lunchtime_;_as usual, I was buying lunch from the vendor's cart across the street from the building where I work. ⁴The hot dog vendor, Mr Gianetti, handed me my customary lunchtime fare_:_a wrapped hot dog, a sleeve of onion rings, and a tall cup of cola. ⁵As I took them and started to leave, Mr. Gianetti said, "Don't you want your change_?_" ⁶My hands were full_;_I glanced back over my shoulder to tell him to keep it. ⁷Too late, I saw the woman standing directly in my path_._ ⁸I bumped into her_;_cola splashed down the front of her crisp business suit. ⁹I could only do two things_:_apologize profusely and offer to pay to have her suit cleaned. ¹⁰She accepted my apology, but as I walked away, she could not resist yelling, "Next time, look where you're going_!_"

29

Apostrophes

Freds Fixit Shop
Lawn Mower's
Repaired

The hand-lettered sign above is displayed in the window of a small shop. Fred may fix lawn mowers to perfection, but his sign is in need of apostrophe repair. Can you pinpoint the two apostrophe problems in the sign? One apostrophe is omitted, and the other is unnecessary. This chapter outlines the two main uses of apostrophes: forming contractions and showing possession.

Apostrophes in Contractions

Contractions are informal or conversational shortenings of words: *doesn't* for *does not*, *won't* for *will not*, and *it's* for *it is* or *it has*. Contractions are used in informal writing, but they are generally inappropriate for formal or scholarly writing. You will find contractions in journalistic writing, textbooks, works of fiction, and informal essays. Contractions are considered inappropriate in reports of academic research or in legal documents. Your instructor will specify the level of formality you should use in your essays and other writings.

The rule for forming contractions is as follows:

To form a contraction, replace omitted letters with a single apostrophe. Close the spaces between words.

Examples

couldn't = could not

don't = do not

hasn't = has not

isn't = is not

won't = will not (An irregular contraction: the *ill* in *will* changes to an *o*.)

wouldn't = would not

PRACTICE 1   FORMING CONTRACTIONS

Make a contraction of each expression. Be sure to place an apostrophe where letters are omitted, not in the space between the words.

1. she is   she's
2. I am   I'm
3. would not   wouldn't
4. does not   doesn't
5. he is   he's
6. it is   it's
7. we are   we're
8. I will   I'll
9. they are   they're
10. cannot   can't

PRACTICE 2   CORRECTING ERRORS IN CONTRACTIONS

In each sentence, underline the error. Then supply the missing apostrophe in the contraction and write the contraction in the blank provided.

he's   **1.** Scott says <u>hes</u> going to miss the next two games because of his sprained wrist.

hasn't   **2.** Tomeka <u>hasnt</u> even started on her term paper, and it is due next week.

Isn't   **3.** <u>Isnt</u> that Donnie's car parked over by the theater?

It's   **4.** "<u>Its</u> a good thing that the library is open all night," said Wai-Ling.

I've   **5.** <u>Ive</u> had two of those candy bars since noon.

we're   **6.** "Sorry, <u>were</u> closed," said the clerk to the woman who was knocking on the closed door of the shop.

Haven't   **7.** <u>Havent</u> you ever heard that song before?

couldn't   **8.** Annie <u>couldnt</u> resist peeking at the brightly wrapped packages hidden in the back of the closet.

can't   **9.** Kareem <u>cant</u> tell the difference between the vegetarian burgers and the ones made with beef.

I'll   **10.** "<u>Ill</u> read just one more chapter before I go to sleep," Jasmine promised herself.

Apostrophes to Show Possession

If you could not use apostrophes to show possession, you would have to rely on long, tedious constructions such as "I drove the car of my sister to the house of Elizabeth to study for the test of next week" instead of "I drove my sister's car to Elizabeth's house to study for next week's test."

Making Nouns Possessive

There are two rules for making nouns possessive.

Rule 1: Add an apostrophe and *s* (*'s*) to form the possessives of singular nouns and of plurals that do not end in *s*.

> *** Grammar Alert!**
>
> When a singular word ends in *s*, it is also acceptable to use an apostrophe alone to make it possessive. Thus, you may write *Mr. Jones' job* or *Mr. Jones's job; the boss' office* or *the boss's office.*

Examples

✔ the book that belongs to Eduardo = Eduardo's book

✔ the shell of the turtle = the turtle's shell

✔ the computer belonging to Jonas = Jonas's computer

✔ the work of a week = a week's work

✔ the flower garden belonging to Jennifer = Jennifer's flower garden

✔ the books that belong to the children = the children's books

PRACTICE 3   FORMING POSSESSIVES USING AN APOSTROPHE AND *s*

Practice Rule 1 by converting the ten expressions in the exercise to possessives by using 's.

1. the pages of the newspaper = the newspaper's pages

2. the paws of the dog = the dog's paws

3. the car of Bertram = Bertram's car

4. the career of the actor = the actor's career

5. the calendar for next year = next year's calendar

6. color of the night sky = the night sky's color

7. the left tire of the Chevrolet Blazer = the Chevrolet Blazer's left tire

8. the voices of the children = the children's voices

9. the aroma of the rose = the rose's aroma

10. the speech of the candidate = the candidate's speech

Rule 2: If a plural noun already ends in *s*, add an apostrophe after the *s* to make it possessive.

✔ the cheers of the soccer fans = the soccer fans' cheers

✔ the driveway belonging to the Harrises = the Harrises' driveway

✔ the gleam of the stars = the stars' gleam

PRACTICE 4   FORMING POSSESSIVES USING AN APOSTROPHE ALONE

Practice Rule 2 by converting the ten expressions in the exercise to possessives by using an apostrophe.

1. the soles of the shoes = _the shoes' soles_
2. the buzz of the bees = _the bees' buzz_
3. the endurance of the runners = _the runners' endurance_
4. the uniforms of the athletes = _the athletes' uniforms_
5. the music of the Temptations = _the Temptations' music_
6. the color of the marbles = _the marbles' color_
7. the house of the Millers = _the Millers' house_
8. the new car of the Joneses = _the Joneses' new car_
9. the fur of the dogs = _the dogs' fur_
10. the votes of the committee members = _the committee members' votes_

PRACTICE 5   FORMING POSSESSIVES

Reread Rule 1 and Rule 2. Then convert the ten expressions in the exercise to possessives by adding *'s* or by adding an apostrophe after the *s*.

1. the hum of the air conditioner = _the air conditioner's hum_
2. the beat of the drum = _the drum's beat_
3. the toys of the children = _the children's toys_
4. the part-time job of Carey = _Carey's part-time job_
5. the resale value of the Honda = _the Honda's resale value_
6. the insistence of the boss = _the boss's insistence_
7. the opinions of the men = _the men's opinions_
8. the poetry of Maya Angelou = _Maya Angelou's poetry_
9. the gleam of the traffic lights = _the traffic lights' gleam_
10. the truck of Mr. Moss = _Mr. Moss's truck_

Distinguishing Possessives from Simple Plurals

To use apostrophes correctly, it is important to distinguish between possessives and simple plurals. A plural may be followed by a verb, by a prepositional phrase, or by nothing at all. Words that show possession will end in *s*, like plurals, but will be immediately followed by something that is being possessed, as in *Jamal's five-alarm chili* or the *dentist's office*. Look at the following examples:

Possessive (apostrophe used)	Plural (no apostrophe used)
a newspaper's classified section	newspapers stacked for recycling
a holiday's significance	home for the holidays
Mother's Day	Mothers Against Drunk Driving
king's crown	kings in medieval England
the cats' toys	cats chasing fireflies
the waves' roar	listening to the roar of the waves
the hammer's weight	several hammers in a toolbox

PRACTICE 6   DISTINGUISHING POSSESSIVES FROM PLURALS

In each sentence, decide whether the noun in bold print that ends in *s* is possessive or simply plural. If the noun is possessive, write *possessive* in the blank provided. If the noun is simply a plural, remove the apostrophe and write the corrected plural form in the blank. The first one is done for you.

<u>puppies</u>   **1.** By the side of the road, Diego found two **puppies'** that someone had abandoned.

<u>possessive</u>   **2.** The **school's** fundraiser was a success.

<u>possessive</u>   **3.** The **speaker's** voice was so soothing that Kim nearly fell asleep.

<u>pecans</u>   **4.** Kelly picked up the **pecan's** that had fallen from the tree.

<u>styles</u>   **5.** Our instructor says that people have different **styles'** of learning.

<u>possessive</u>   **6.** The **sofa's** dull brown upholstery depressed Noriko.

<u>possessive</u>   **7.** The **Watsons'** dog is a nuisance to the entire neighborhood.

<u>owls</u>   **8.** Burrowing **owl's** dig underground nests or use a burrow deserted by a prairie dog.

<u>benefits</u>   **9.** Exercise physiologists are beginning to recognize the **benefit's** of exercise for people of all ages.

<u>possessive</u>   **10.** The **women's** department had a sale on woolen gloves.

Possessive Forms of Pronouns

Personal pronouns (*I, we, you, he, she, it,* and *they*) have their own possessive forms that never require an apostrophe. These forms include **my, mine, our, ours, your, yours, his, hers, its, their,** and **theirs.**

The pronoun that is the focus of the most confusion is **its.** Since the possessive form of a pronoun never takes an apostrophe, **its** is the possessive form, meaning "belonging to it." **It's,** the form with the apostrophe, is a contraction of **it is** or **it has.**

✔   The soft drink seems to have lost **its** fizz. (belonging to it)

✔   **It's** a shame to throw away so much food. (it is)

✔   That old pair of shears has outlived **its** usefulness. (belonging to it)

✔   **It's** been a difficult year for Catherine. (it has)

PRACTICE 7   CORRECTING APOSTROPHE ERRORS

Underline and correct the apostrophe error in each of the following sentences.

1. Last week, the Student Government Association held <u>it's</u> first meeting of the academic year.

    Last week, the Student Government Association held **its** first meeting of the

    academic year.

2. The car was old, and <u>it's</u> owner had apparently not washed it in years.

    The car was old, and **its** owner had apparently not washed it in years.

3. Hiroshi is determined to have a successful banking career; <u>its</u> his first priority.

    Hiroshi is determined to have a successful banking career; **it's** his first priority.

4. The wren built <u>it's</u> nest under the eaves of the garage.

    The wren built **its** nest under the eaves of the garage.

5. The package is damaged because <u>its</u> been sitting out in the rain.

    The package is damaged because **it's** been sitting out in the rain.

REVIEW EXERCISE 1   FORMING POSSESSIVES

Convert the ten expressions in the exercise to possessives using 's or '.

1. the sound of the piano = _the piano's sound_

2. the shell of a turtle = _the turtle's shell_

3. the entrance of the restaurant = <u>the restaurant's entrance</u>

4. the pages of the books = <u>the books' pages</u>

5. the mailbox belonging to Mr. Rose = <u>Mr. Rose's mailbox</u>

6. the corona of the sun = <u>the sun's corona</u>

7. work of two hours = <u>two hours' work</u>

8. the evening class of Dr. Yoshida = <u>Dr. Yoshida's evening class</u>

9. the preferences of the customers = <u>the customers' preferences</u>

10. the scent of the pine needles = <u>the pine needles' scent</u>

REVIEW EXERCISE 2   USING APOSTROPHES IN CONTRACTIONS AND POSSESSIVES

In each sentence, an apostrophe has been omitted in a contraction or a possessive form. Underline the error; then, in the blank, write the word with the apostrophe placed correctly.

<u>couldn't</u>   1. Wanda <u>couldnt</u> stand hearing the mindless song over and over.

<u>store's</u>   2. The grocery <u>stores</u> ad featured store brand items at half price.

<u>Jeanell's</u>   3. Two aspirin tablets helped to ease the throbbing in <u>Jeanells</u> temples.

<u>newspaper's</u> 4. The <u>newspapers</u> headline read, "Flashlight company's founder arrested, charged with battery."

<u>water's</u>   5. Quinton stood by the <u>waters</u> edge and cast his line into the pond.

<u>It's</u>   6. "<u>Its</u> always good to see you," Jillian said politely.

<u>table's</u>   7. The <u>tables</u> surface was littered with playing cards, empty soft-drink cans, and half-empty bowls of popcorn and chips.

<u>hospital's</u>   8. The <u>hospitals</u> maze of corridors and interconnected buildings confused even the staff.

<u>Ms. Hall's</u>   9. The secretary asked for <u>Ms. Halls</u> signature on the last page of a thick document.

<u>waitress's</u> 10. The <u>waitress</u> attention was diverted by a loud group in the back of the café.

REVIEW EXERCISE 3   USING APOSTROPHES IN CONTRACTIONS AND POSSESSIVES

In each sentence, two apostrophes have been omitted. Underline the errors; then, in the blank, rewrite the sentences with the apostrophes placed correctly.

1. Roger says that he <u>hasnt</u> eaten all day but <u>doesnt</u> have time for lunch.

   Roger says that he **hasn't** eaten all day but **doesn't** have time for lunch.

2. The <u>hotels</u> elevator creaked to the lobby and discharged its passengers in front of the <u>bellhops</u> station.

   The **hotel's** elevator creaked to the lobby and discharged its passengers in front

   of the **bellhop's** station.

3. The <u>singers</u> voice <u>wasnt</u> strong enough to be heard all over the auditorium.

   The **singer's** voice **wasn't** strong enough to be heard all over the auditorium.

4. The <u>coffees</u> bitterness did not deter Bill, who <u>couldnt</u> keep his eyes open without caffeine.

   The **coffee's** bitterness did not deter Bill, who **couldn't** keep his eyes open with-

   out caffeine.

5. "I've forgotten the <u>books</u> plot, <u>its</u> been so long since I've read it," said Corinne.

   "I've forgotten the **book's** plot, **it's** been so long since I've read it," said

   Corinne.

REVIEW EXERCISE 4   CORRECTING APOSTROPHE ERRORS

Each numbered item contains two apostrophe errors, one omitted apostrophe and one misplaced or unnecessary apostrophe. Underline the errors; then rewrite each sentence with the correct form of each word.

1. <u>Rons</u> car hit one of the orange <u>cone's</u> placed on the road by the highway crew.

   Ron's car hit one of the orange **cones** placed on the road by the highway crew.

2. It took two <u>days</u> work to put the patio in, not counting the time it took to pick up and haul in the <u>brick's</u>.

   It took two **days'** work to put the patio in, not counting the time it took to pick

   up and haul in the **bricks**.

3. Mr. <u>Robeys</u> <u>relative's</u> all visited him in the hospital during his recovery.

   Mr. **Robey's relatives** all visited him in the hospital during his recovery.

4. The <u>cars</u> price was high, but <u>it's</u> performance and safety record were excellent.

   The **car's** price was high, but **its** performance and safety record were excellent.

   _____

5. The <u>refrigerators</u> best feature was <u>it's</u> icemaker.

   The **refrigerator's** best feature was **its** icemaker.

   _____

REVIEW EXERCISE 5   CORRECTING APOSTROPHE ERRORS

Underline and correct the ten apostrophe errors in the following restaurant review, writing your answers in the numbered blanks that follow. Each numbered section of the review contains one error.

[1]Restaurant Review: <u>Eileens</u> Canine Café

[2]Locally, almost everyone <u>know's</u> Eileen Hunter as a friend to animals. [3]<u>Its</u> no surprise that in her latest venture, she has found another way to serve animals. [4]In fact, one might say <u>shes</u> gone to the dogs. [5]<u>Theres</u> no food for humans on Eileen's menu; her specialties are aimed straight at Rover and Fido. [6]I took my own <u>dogs'</u>, Penny and Bert, to try Eileen's fare. [7]Penny had the Chicken <u>Liver's</u> in Gravy and licked her plate clean. [8]For Bert, I ordered <u>Chefs</u> Choice Beef, which was gone in a gulp, and both dogs ate bone-shaped, tartar-control cookies for dessert. [9]The tab came to a little more than twenty dollars, but the look in my two <u>pup's</u> eyes said it was worth every dime. [10]Eileen's Canine Café is sure to be your <u>dogs</u> favorite, too.

1.	Eileen's	6.	dogs
2.	knows	7.	Livers
3.	It's	8.	Chef's
4.	she's	9.	pups'
5.	There's	10.	dog's

30

Quotation Marks, Underlining, and Italics

Quotation marks are visual signals that give a reader information that would otherwise have to be conveyed in words. They are a kind of academic shorthand that says, "Someone else wrote, said, or thought these words" or "These words are the title of a short work." Underlining and italics serve the same purpose. They say, "These words are the title of a long work." Learning to use quotation marks, underlining, and italics adds another dimension to your ability to communicate within the academic world.

Quotation Marks to Signal a Direct Quotation

Quotation marks are used to signal a **direct quotation;** that is, they are placed around the exact words that someone speaks, writes, or thinks. As you look at the examples, notice that when a comma or period comes at the end of a quotation, it is always placed inside the quotation mark.

When a direct question is quoted, the question mark also goes inside the quotation marks.

✔ "I'll take a math course next term," said Alex.

✔ Shanisa said, "I have never been whitewater rafting, but I am willing to give it a try."

✔ The child asked, "Are we there yet?"

✔ "Did you bring the pizza?" asked Kevin.

PRACTICE 1   USING QUOTATION MARKS WITH DIRECT QUOTATIONS

Following the preceding examples, rewrite each sentence, placing quotation marks around the direct quotations.

1. I may be a few minutes late for the meeting, said Gary.

   "I may be a few minutes late for the meeting," said Gary.

2. Could you explain that one more time? Karina asked.

   "Could you explain that one more time?" Karina asked.

3. The bumper sticker said, If it's too loud, you're too old.

   The bumper sticker said, "If it's too loud, you're too old."

4. The meteorologist said, The cold front covering the western half of the United States should linger through the weekend.

   The meteorologist said, "The cold front covering the western half of the United States should linger through the weekend."

5. I had the worst dream last night, said Kelsey.

   "I had the worst dream last night," said Kelsey.

Split Quotations

Some direct quotations are **split quotations.** Following are two rules for splitting quotations.

1. In a split sentence, commas set off the **dialogue tag** (such as "she said") that tells who said, thought, or wrote the quoted words.

   ✔ "When you handle corrosive substances," said the supervisor, "always wear goggles and protective gloves."

2. When the dialogue tag is preceded by a complete sentence and followed by another complete sentence, a comma is placed after the first sentence. Periods are placed after the dialogue tag and after the second sentence.

   ✔ "I have not played the trombone since high school," said Calvin. "I am not even sure I still know how to hold it."

PRACTICE 2 USING QUOTATION MARKS WITH SPLIT QUOTATIONS

Following the preceding examples, rewrite each sentence, placing quotation marks around the direct quotations.

1. The trouble with babies, said Tony, is that they grow up to be teenagers.

   "The trouble with babies," said Tony, "is that they grow up to be teenagers."

   _____

2. The problem with parents, said Tony's teenage daughter, is that they forget they were once teenagers, too.

   "The problem with parents," said Tony's teenage daughter, "is that they forget

   they were once teenagers, too."

3. A bird in the hand, said Grandpa, is safer than one overhead.

   "A bird in the hand," said Grandpa, "is safer than one overhead."

   _____

4. I am tired of picking up my family's clothes, said Rob. Doesn't anyone but me know where the laundry hamper is?

   "I am tired of picking up my family's clothes," said Rob. "Doesn't anyone but

   me know where the laundry hamper is?"

5. I'll have the apple pie, Clara told the server. Oh, and bring me a cup of coffee, too.

   "I'll have the apple pie," Clara told the server. "Oh, and bring me a cup of cof-

   fee, too."

Rewrite each sentence, placing quotation marks around the direct quotations. In addition, add commas or question marks as needed.

1.   I need to stop for something to eat said Arnold.

"I need to stop for something to eat," said Arnold.

2.   I don't know why this Internet page won't load said Renee.

"I don't know why this Internet page won't load," said Renee.

3.   Tapping the microphone, the senator said Is this thing on?

Tapping the microphone, the senator said, "Is this thing on?"

4.   Did you put this milk on your cereal asked Martin. It expired a week ago.

"Did you put this milk on your cereal?" asked Martin. "It expired a week ago."

5.   The boards in these steps are rotted said Sam. I need to replace them this weekend.

"The boards in these steps are rotted," said Sam. "I need to replace them this

weekend."

Direct and Indirect Quotations

As you have seen, a **direct quotation** tells the exact words that someone said, wrote, or thought. It is set off by quotation marks.

✔   Tasha said, "I am going to the gas station."

The preceding example repeats Tasha's exact words with no alteration. Therefore, it is a **direct quotation** that requires quotation marks.

An **indirect quotation,** on the other hand, is a **paraphrase.** It repeats the essence of what a person said, and it may repeat some or all of the words, but it is not a word-for-word quotation. The word *that* is stated or implied before an indirect quotation. Finally, an indirect quotation is not set off by quotation marks.

✔ Tasha said that she was going to the gas station. (The word *that* is stated.)

✔ Tasha said she was going to the gas station. (The word *that* is implied.)

The two preceding examples are **indirect quotations.** They do not repeat Tasha's exact words (Tasha spoke in present tense and did not use the word *she*). The word *that* is stated in the first example and implied in the second. Therefore, no quotation marks are used.

PRACTICE 4   RECOGNIZING DIRECT AND INDIRECT QUOTATIONS

On the line provided, label each quotation direct (*D*) or indirect (*I*).

__D__ **1.** The public speaking instructor said, "Always stop talking before the audience stops listening."

__I__ **2.** Our public speaking instructor says that a speaker should always stop talking before the audience stops listening.

__D__ **3.** The bumper sticker said, "Love: Two vowels, two consonants, two fools."

__I__ **4.** Jennifer said she was having a bad day.

__I__ **5.** The salesperson told Jill that the speakers had a one-year warranty.

__D__ **6.** Herschel said, "Let's stop for gas on the way home."

__I__ **7.** Edie asked whether anyone had phoned.

__D__ **8.** "Do you want this magazine when I am through?" asked Ted.

__I__ **9.** Valerie said it was raining outside.

__D__ **10.** "If you are headed for the doughnut shop," said Armand, "please bring back a cup of coffee for me."

PRACTICE 5   WORKING WITH DIRECT AND INDIRECT QUOTATIONS

On the line provided, label each quotation direct (*D*) or indirect (*I*). Then place quotation marks around direct quotations and leave indirect quotations as they are.

__I__ **1.** Grady promised that he would make his special marinated chicken for the party.

_____

_____

_____

D   2. I'll be back in five minutes, Reba promised.

    "I'll be back in five minutes," Reba promised.

I   3. Erin told her professor that she would miss the next day's class.

D   4. The painting on this slide, said the art instructor, is by the artist Sandro Botticelli.

    "The painting on this slide," said the art instructor, "is by the artist

    Sandro Botticelli."

D   5. Craig said, I hear a strange noise outside.

    Craig said, "I hear a strange noise outside."

D   6. As a picture of a mother bear and her cubs flashed on the screen, the narrator said, The white fur of the polar bear provides camouflage in a snowy environment.

    As a picture of a mother bear and her cubs flashed on the screen, the nar-

    rator said, "The white fur of the polar bear provides camouflage in a

    snowy environment."

I   7. Someone said that power had been knocked out for the entire western half of the city.

D   8. I'll take anything you have left, Bill told the sandwich vendor.

    "I'll take anything you have left," Bill told the sandwich vendor.

__D__ **9.** Have you seen the comics section of the paper? asked Dan.

"Have you seen the comics section of the paper?" asked Dan.

_____

_____

__I__ **10.** The plumber said he could fix the problem in fifteen minutes.

_____

_____

_____

Setting Off Titles with Quotation Marks, Underlining, and Italics

Quotation marks, underlining, and italics act as academic shorthand to signal a title. **Quotation marks** are used around titles of short works or works that are contained within other works.

Using Quotation Marks to Set Off Titles

The following types of titles are set off by quotation marks:

Chapter title (short works contained within a longer work)
"Organizational Patterns" (in *Reading Skills for College Students* by Ophelia H. Hancock)
"The Upper Paleolithic World" (in *Physical Anthropology and Archaeology* by Carol R. Ember et al.)

Essays
"Complexion" (Richard Rodriguez)
"Am I Blue?" (Alice Walker)

---

* *Grammar Alert!*

When you write *about* an essay, place the title of the essay within quotation marks. When you type the title of *your* essay on a cover sheet or at the head of the essay, do not use quotation marks.

Individual episodes of a TV series (short works contained within the longer series)

"The Goldberg Variation" (An episode of *The X-Files*)

"Walking Wounded" (an episode of *Third Watch*)

Song titles (short works, often contained within a longer album of works)

"Man of Constant Sorrow" (Traditional)

"Mean Woman Blues" (C. Demetrius)

Newspaper articles

"Pitching, not hitting, lifts Braves over Padres" (Bill Zack, Morris News Service)

"Jobless claims hit nine-year high" (Martin Crutsinger, Associated Press)

Poems

"My Wicked Wicked Ways" (Sandra Cisneros)

"Reflections on Milkweed" (Peter Blue Cloud)

Short stories

"The Necklace" (Guy de Maupassant)

"To Serve Man" (Damon Knight)

Using Italics or Underlining to Set Off Titles

Underline or italicize the title of a long work, a continuing work (such as a comic strip or television series), or a complete published work such as a pamphlet or brochure.

---

* Grammar Alert!

Italics are used instead of underlining in published materials, and modern word processors have italic capability. However, the MLA (Modern Language Association) recommends underlining for clarity.

Books

The Bonesetter's Daughter or *The Bonesetter's Daughter* (Amy Tan)

Girl with a Pearl Earring or *Girl with a Pearl Earring* (Tracy Chevalier)

Comic strips (a series containing individual daily or weekly strips)

Rex Morgan, M.D. or *Rex Morgan, M.D.* (Woody Wilson and Graham Nolan)

Boondocks or *Boondocks* (Aaron McGruder)

Newspapers

the Washington Post or the *Washington Post*

the Seattle Post-Intelligencer or the *Seattle Post-Intelligencer*

Anthologies (collections) of poetry, essays, or short stories

Shakespeare's Early Tragedies: A Collection of Critical Essays or *Shakespeare's Early Tragedies: A Collection of Critical Essays* (Mark Rose)

Literatures of Asia, Africa and Latin America or *Literatures of Asia, Africa and Latin America* (William Barnstone, Tony Barnstone)

Compact discs

Blue Gardenia or *Blue Gardenia* (Etta James)

New Favorite or *New Favorite* (Alison Kraus)

Television programs

Pop-Up Video or *Pop-Up Video*

Inside the Actors Studio or *Inside the Actors Studio*

Movies

Gattaca or *Gattaca*

The Shawshank Redemption or *The Shawshank Redemption*

PRACTICE 6   USING QUOTATION MARKS AND UNDERLINING WITH TITLES

Rewrite the following sentences, using quotation marks or underlining to set off titles. Five of the sentences contain two titles each; five contain just one title.

1. Breanna wrote herself a note so she would remember to watch The Vikings, tonight's episode of Nova.

   Breanna wrote herself a note so she would remember to watch "The Vikings,"

   tonight's episode of Nova.

2. The class was assigned to read the chapter How a Microprocessor Works in the book How Computers Work.

   The class was assigned to read the chapter "How a Microprocessor Works" in

   the book How Computers Work.

3. Rita's favorite song on the album Love and Theft is called Lonesome Day Blues.

   Rita's favorite song on the album Love and Theft is called "Lonesome Day

   Blues."

4. The class read a poem by Robert Herrick called To the Virgins, to Make Much of Time.

   The class read a poem by Robert Herrick called "To the Virgins, to Make Much

   of Time."

5. The headline in the Wall Street Journal said, Fed reassures nation's banks.

   The headline in the <u>Wall Street Journal</u> said, **"**Fed reassures nation's banks.**"**

6. Some scholars believe that William Shakespeare's play, The Tempest, is based on an actual wreck in Bermuda in 1609.

   Some scholars believe that William Shakespeare's play, <u>The Tempest</u>, is based

   on an actual wreck in Bermuda in 1609.

7. The band played a song called If Love Were Oil, I'd Be a Quart Low.

   The band played a song called **"**If Love Were Oil, I'd Be a Quart Low.**"**

8. Cindy was reading an article in Smithsonian called Where the Gooney Birds Are.

   Cindy was reading an article in <u>Smithsonian</u> called **"**Where the Gooney Birds

   Are.**"**

9. In the back seat, Marty's children broke into yet another chorus of Yes, We Have No Bananas.

   In the back seat, Marty's children broke into yet another chorus of **"**Yes, We

   Have No Bananas.**"**

10. Roshonda said that her favorite comic strip was Jumpstart.

    Roshonda said that her favorite comic strip was <u>Jumpstart</u>.

REVIEW EXERCISE 1   USING QUOTATION MARKS WITH DIRECT QUOTATIONS

Rewrite the following sentences, placing quotation marks around the direct quotations.

1. I think I have lost a button from my shirt, said Rashid.

   "I think I have lost a button from my shirt,**"** said Rashid.

2. John Lennon said, Life is what happens to you while you're busy making other plans.

   John Lennon said, **"**Life is what happens to you while you're busy making other

   plans.**"**

3. I don't know what's wrong with me, said Victoria. I never seem to get any sleep.

   "I don't know what's wrong with me," said Victoria. "I never seem to get any

   sleep."

4. Hand me a napkin, please, said Gordon. I have barbecue sauce all over my chin.

   "Hand me a napkin, please," said Gordon. "I have barbecue sauce all over my

   chin."

5. The car's bumper sticker read, It's the twenty-first century. Where's my flying car?

   The car's bumper sticker read, "It's the twenty-first century. Where's my flying

   car?"

6. The slip of paper in Misty's fortune cookie said, If you come to a fork in the road, take it.

   The slip of paper in Misty's fortune cookie said, "If you come to a fork in the

   road, take it."

7. The room looks much better now that it has been painted, said Daniel.

   "The room looks much better now that it has been painted," said Daniel.

8. The price of gasoline has gone up again, said Kim.

   "The price of gasoline has gone up again," said Kim.

9. Luke looked out the window and said, It looks like we're in for more rain.

   Luke looked out the window and said, "It looks like we're in for more rain."

10. I wish this ladder were a bit steadier, said Elizabeth.

   "I wish this ladder were a bit steadier," said Elizabeth.

REVIEW EXERCISE 2   DIRECT AND INDIRECT QUOTATIONS

Rewrite each of the following sentences that contain direct quotations, placing quotation marks around the quotations. For the six sentences that do not require quotation marks, write "indirect quotation" in the blanks.

1. Ramon said that he had seen a black widow spider in the garage.

   indirect quotation

2. Would you like to learn a new trick? Mark asked his dog.

   "Would you like to learn a new trick?" Mark asked his dog.

3. If he could have talked, Mark's dog might have said that the only trick he wanted to learn was to open the refrigerator.

   indirect quotation

4. As she approached the tunnel, Annabel muttered, Now where did I put my toll?

   As she approached the tunnel, Annabel muttered, "Now where did I put my toll?"

5. Ron swore that he would never ride the Vertical Limit roller coaster again.

   indirect quotation

6. Patrick said he had already finished his paper.

   indirect quotation

7. Latasha said that she had not eaten breakfast.

   indirect quotation

8. Have a doughnut; it will give you energy, said Jason.

   "Have a doughnut; it will give you energy," said Jason.

9. The caller told the 911 operator that a fallen tree was completely blocking the southbound lane of Highway 41.

   indirect quotation

10. I can't believe Derrick is late again, Sarah said, looking at her watch.

    "I can't believe Derrick is late again," Sarah said, looking at her watch.

REVIEW EXERCISE 3   USING QUOTATION MARKS AND UNDERLINING WITH TITLES

Rewrite each sentence, using underlining or quotation marks to set off the titles.

1. Amanda listened to a jazz CD called Flirting with Twilight.

   Amanda listened to a jazz CD called <u>Flirting with Twilight</u>.

2. For the fifth time, Cornelius read his well-worn copy of Harry Potter and the Prisoner of Azkaban.

   For the fifth time, Cornelius read his well-worn copy of <u>Harry Potter and the Prisoner of Azkaban</u>.

3. The textbook for my math class is called Business Mathematics: A Collegiate Approach.

   The textbook for my math class is called <u>Business Mathematics: A Collegiate Approach.</u>

4. The professor told us that we would begin Chapter 4, Basic Statistics and Graphs, next week.

   The professor told us that we would begin Chapter 4, "Basic Statistics and Graphs," next week.

5. As she left for the video store, Winona's husband begged her not to rent The Lord of the Rings again.

   As she left for the video store, Winona's husband begged her not to rent <u>The Lord of the Rings</u> again.

6. Paul swears there is a country song called I'd Rather Have a Bottle in Front of Me Than a Frontal Lobotomy.

   Paul swears there is a country song called "I'd Rather Have a Bottle in Front of Me Than a Frontal Lobotomy."

7. Veronica loves to watch classic movies such as Casablanca and All about Eve.

   Veronica loves to watch classic movies such as <u>Casablanca</u> and <u>All about Eve.</u>

8. Everyone at the Fourth of July concert was invited to stand and sing America the Beautiful.

   Everyone at the Fourth of July concert was invited to stand and sing "America the Beautiful."

9. In a business magazine, Ann read an article called Work Smarter, Not Harder.

   In a business magazine, Ann read an article called "Work Smarter, Not Harder."

10. Javarez read a news story headlined Man found dead in cemetery.

    Javarez read a news story headlined "Man found dead in cemetery."

REVIEW EXERCISE 4 USING QUOTATION MARKS AND UNDERLINING

Rewrite the following sentence groups, placing quotation marks around direct quotations. Use underlining or quotation marks to set off titles. Do not place indirect quotations in quotation marks.

1. Kevin said that he keeps a mental list of his top ten movies. The Shawshank Redemption has been at the top of his list since he first saw it many years ago.

> Kevin said that he keeps a mental list of his top ten movies. <u>The Shawshank Re-</u>
>
> <u>demption</u> has been at the top of his list since he first saw it many years ago.

2. Would you answer the telephone? Marilyn called to her husband. I didn't even hear it ringing, he said.

> "Would you answer the telephone?" Marilyn called to her husband. "I didn't
>
> even hear it ringing," he said.

3. Angelina saved an article called Eat Right, Feel Better from a magazine. The article said that eating the right foods could improve well-being.

> Angelina saved an article called "Eat Right, Feel Better" from a magazine. The
>
> article said that eating the right foods could improve well-being.

4. We care about your call, said the recorded voice on the telephone. If you cared that much, you'd answer, Jo muttered.

> "We care about your call," said the recorded voice on the telephone. "If you
>
> cared that much, you'd answer," Jo muttered.

5. Yesterday, Todd bought a book called The Complete Idiot's Guide to Rock Climbing. I must be an idiot to want to climb rocks, he joked.

> Yesterday, Todd bought a book called <u>The Complete Idiot's Guide to Rock</u>
>
> <u>Climbing.</u> "I must be an idiot to want to climb rocks," he joked.

REVIEW EXERCISE 5   USING QUOTATION MARKS AND UNDERLINING

Rewrite the following paragraph, placing quotation marks around direct quotations. Use underlining or quotation marks to set off titles. Do not place indirect quotations in quotation marks.

> [1]Ever since my cousin Carlton read a book called Smooth Moves to Impress Ladies, I am embarrassed to be seen in public with him. [2]When we went to a club together, he actually walked up to a young woman and said, Do you believe in love at first sight, or should I walk by again? [3]That line must have been from a chapter called World's Lamest Lines. [4]Then he turned to another attractive woman. You look so

sweet, he said, that I'm getting cavities just standing beside you. Needless to say, she did not stand beside him for long. [5]As the band began to play I Will Always Love You, Carlton made another embarrassing move. [6]He walked up to a woman sitting at a table, but instead of simply asking her to dance, he said, Baby, I must be a broom because I would love to sweep you off your feet. [7]She said Sorry, I think I sprained my ankle on the dance floor. [8]Then, Carlton spotted a woman he knows from work. You must be tired, he said to her. You've been running through my mind all day. [9]When she suddenly left, I said, Carlton, can't you see that those stale lines don't work? [10]I am not going anywhere else with my cousin until he reads another book—the one called How to Act Like a Normal Person.

---

[1]Ever since my cousin Carlton read a book called <u>Smooth Moves to Impress Ladies,</u> I am embarrassed to be seen in public with him. [2]When we went to a club together, he actually walked up to a young woman and said, "Do you believe in love at first sight, or should I walk by again?" [3]That line must have been from a chapter called "World's Lamest Lines." [4]Then he turned to another attractive woman. "You look so sweet," he said, "that I'm getting cavities just standing beside you." Needless to say, she did not stand beside him for long. [5]As the band began to play "I Will Always Love You," Carlton made another embarrassing move. [6]He walked up to a woman sitting at a table, but instead of simply asking her to dance, he said, "Baby, I must be a broom because I would love to sweep you off your feet." [7]She said "Sorry, I think I sprained my ankle on the dance floor." [8]Then, Carlton spotted a woman he knows from work. "You must be tired," he said to her. "You've been running through my mind all day." [9]When she suddenly left, I said, "Carlton, can't you see that those stale lines don't work?" [10]I am not going anywhere else with my cousin until he reads another book—the one called <u>How to Act Like a Normal Person.</u>

Part 3

Essential Readings for Writers

A Day Away

Maya Angelou

Maya Angelou describes her practice of taking twenty-four hours away from duties and demands, twenty-four hours that are hers alone.

We often think that our affairs, great or small, must be tended continuously   1
and in detail, or our world will disintegrate, and we will lose our places in the
universe. That is not true, or if it is true, then our situations were so temporary
that they would have collapsed anyway.

Once a year or so I give myself a day away. On the eve of my day of ab-   2
sence, I begin to unwrap the bonds which hold me in harness. I inform house-
mates, my family and close friends that I will not be reachable for twenty-four
hours; then I disengage the telephone. I turn the radio dial to an all-music station, preferably one which plays the soothing golden oldies. I sit for at least an
hour in a very hot tub; then I lay out my clothes in preparation for my morning
escape, and knowing that nothing will disturb me, I sleep the sleep of the just.
In the morning I wake naturally, for I will have set no clock, nor informed my
body timepiece when it should alarm. I dress in comfortable shoes and casual
clothes and leave my house going no place. If I am living in a city, I wander
streets, window-shop, or gaze at buildings. I enter and leave public parks, libraries, the lobbies of skyscrapers, and movie houses. I stay in no place for very
long.

On the getaway day I try for amnesia. I do not want to know my name,   3
where I live, or how many dire responsibilities rest on my shoulders. I detest en-
countering even the closest friend, for then I am reminded of who I am, and the
circumstances of my life, which I want to forget for a while.

Every person needs to take one day away. A day in which one consciously   4
separates the past from the future. Jobs, lovers, family, employers, and friends
can exist one day without any one of us, and if our egos permit us to confess,
they could exist eternally in our absence.

Each person deserves a day away in which no problems are confronted, no   5
solutions searched for. Each of us needs to withdraw from the cares which will
not withdraw from us. We need hours of aimless wandering or spates of time
sitting on park benches, observing the mysterious world of ants and the canopy
of treetops.

If we step away for a time, we are not, as many may think and some will ac-   6
cuse, being irresponsible, but rather we are preparing ourselves to more ably
perform our duties and discharge our obligations.

When I return home, I am always surprised to find some questions I sought   7
to evade had been answered and some entanglements I had hoped to flee had
become unraveled in my absence.

A day away acts as a spring tonic. It can dispel rancor, transform indeci-   8
sion, and renew the spirit.

■ **Building Vocabulary**

For each numbered item, choose the meaning that most closely defines the
underlined word or phrase as it is used in the essay.

1. The word affairs most nearly means
   a. romances
   b. daily activities
   c. rare opportunities
   d. conspiracies

2. The word disintegrate most nearly means
   a. dismiss
   b. improve
   c. fall into place
   d. fall apart

3. The word amnesia most nearly means
   a. association with familiar things and people
   b. total recall
   c. ambrosia
   d. memory loss

4. The phrase discharge our obligations most nearly means
   a. avoid our responsibilities
   b. perform our duties
   c. obligate ourselves
   d. pay our debts

5. The word evade most nearly means
   a. answer
   b. acknowledge
   c. avoid
   d. respond to

■ Understanding the Essay

1. Which statement best expresses the main idea of the essay?
   a. Our responsibilities and relationships are often so pressing that it is beneficial to be irresponsible and to put off our duties, as long as we do it only occasionally.
   b. Taking time off from spouses or significant others serves to remind us that they really could get along without us.
   c. A relaxing bath, a good night's sleep, and a day off are effective ways of coping with stress.
   d. Taking time away from our daily lives can renew our spirits and prepare us for the work ahead.

2. On her day away, the author says that she
   a. decides on one special place to go and spends the day there.
   b. drifts aimlessly from place to place.
   c. stays at home relaxing in a hot bath.
   d. visits a relative in a nearby city.

3. If the author ran into a friend on her day away, she would probably
   a. invite the friend to join her for the day.
   b. have lunch with her friend.
   c. pretend she had amnesia and did not remember the friend.
   d. keep the encounter as brief as possible.

4. According to the passage, who should take a day away?
   a. everyone
   b. people with no other responsibilities
   c. busy executives
   d. only those who won't be missed from their other duties

5. Which is *not* mentioned as one of the benefits of a day away?
   a. Unresolved questions and issues tend to solve themselves.
   b. A day away refreshes and renews the spirit.
   c. It separates the past from the future.
   d. It makes friends, family, and employers realize how necessary you are to them.

■ Writing in the Margins

These questions encourage you to think not just about the essay but about the issues it raises. Your instructor may ask you to write down your answers, to discuss them in groups, or simply to think about them for class discussion.

Answers will vary.

1. Angelou writes that "Jobs, lovers, family, employers, and friends can exist one day without any one of us, and if our egos permit us to confess, they could exist eternally in our absence." Do you believe this statement is true, particularly the last part? If so, why is it so difficult for most of us to admit that fact?

2. The author says that on her day away, she does not set a clock or "inform my body timepiece when it should alarm." What does she mean by "her body timepiece"? Does every person come equipped with one?

TOPICS FOR WRITING

Assignment 1: Your Day Away

In a paragraph or journal entry, describe your ideal day away.

Assignment 2: Nowhere to Hide

Cell phones make it increasingly difficult to get away. People receive calls in grocery stores, malls, and cars; cell phones interrupt even plays, classes, and church services. Are cell phones a blessing or a curse? Write a paragraph taking either side, or, if you wish, write a paragraph discussing both the advantages and the disadvantages of cell phones.

Assignment 3: Solo or No?

One of the features of Angelou's day away is twenty-four hours of solitude. She takes no phone calls and makes herself unavailable to even her family. Some people enjoy solitude and do not mind being alone. Others, however, find it comforting to be in the company of others. What is your tolerance for solitude? Do you enjoy being alone or prefer being around others? Write a paragraph discussing your preference. Give specific examples of times when you prefer being with others or being alone.

Assignment 4: The Pace of Life

In the nineteenth century, the American poet Henry David Thoreau retreated to Walden Pond in Massachusetts to live a simple life. Today, books and magazines lure readers with the promise of simpler, less complicated lives. Does a simple life appeal to you, or would you prefer to lead an exciting and busy life? Write a paragraph describing the ideal pace of life for you—fast, slow, or somewhere in between. Be sure to include supporting examples of daily activities that reflect your choice.

Borrowed History

Snow Anderson

Living in a place that reminds her of her native land, Snow Anderson is finally putting down roots in her adopted country.

"I just can't get enough of her," I told a friend over dinner recently, describing the writer Bailey White. In addition to reading her essays, I had been listening to them on tape while driving.

White is a Southern writer who's lived her entire life in one place. She writes about eccentric relatives, quirky neighbors and places she has known since she was a child.

"Borrowed history," my friend suggested, and I, to my surprise, burst into tears. Borrowing history. It's what I've been doing since my parents immigrated to the United States in December 1966, three weeks before my 11th birthday. It is as if during that transcontinental flight from Belgrade, Yugoslavia, to Chicago, Illinois, my history was erased.

I left behind my eccentric neighbors "Crazy Drina," with her many cats, and her one-legged mother who scared us children with nothing more than her appearance. Gone were my friends, the books from which I learned the Cyrillic alphabet, my uncle who taught me how to tell time and my aunt who sewed clothes for me and my dolls.

I would no longer spend summers in my grandmother's village, where day and night blended into one and meals consisted of what we picked from her orchard. My colorful childhood ceased to exist. Everything in Chicago felt as gray as the color of the fire escape on the apartment building that had become my home. The contrast made me yearn for every familiar street corner on the way from my house to the school in Belgrade, the aroma from the neighborhood bakery, the sound of my aunt's sewing machine, the grain bin and the oil lamp in my grandmother's old house. These images embedded themselves so deeply in my cellular memory that three decades later I still feel a sense of loss.

I love this country with an immigrant's passion, but like everyone who has become an American citizen, I also live with a part of me missing. I search flea markets and antiques stores for objects that other families might have passed down to each other. I display an old, faded quilt my son's great-grandmother made in Kentucky as if it were a priceless treasure. "Mammama," as her family called her, recently passed away at the age of 104. Her grandson and I are divorced, but his Southern roots helped to give me more of a sense of belonging.

I never quite adapted to life in America until 11 years ago when I moved to   7
New Mexico, a simple, rustic place with breathtaking beauty, not unlike my
homeland. Here, in an old adobe house with a wood floor in my bedroom,
stained pine laid simply over dirt, I feel at home. It's not the packed-dirt floor
of my grandmother's house, but in its imperfection it comes close. My house
does have electricity and running water, of course, but it also once had a well
like my grandmother's from which I drew water as a child.

The house was last occupied by a much-loved schoolteacher. When the son   8
of the local gas-station owner delivered my car one day, he asked if I saw a lot
of butterflies on this property. Puzzled, I answered, "Yes, why do you ask?"

"Well, you know, the woman who used to live here was such a sweet old   9
lady. They say butterflies come around to people like that."

My landlady, the old woman's daughter, seems to understand my need for   10
history. She's given me some things that once belonged to her mother. The
granddaughter, who lives in Colorado and visits often, has become a friend.
When we sit in this house where she played as a child or go for walks on land
she knows so intimately, I vicariously gain some more history.

My father doesn't understand my passion for old things. He's always been   11
eager to shed his past. His childhood memories are not as idyllic as mine. He
was 11 when World War II made him head of the household. His home in
Chicago, with its parquet floors, crystal chandeliers, hot tub and fireplaces, is a
monument to the American Dream. He has had to work very hard for his success, but he has also lived a life unencumbered by the economic and spiritual
constraints of communism. In his heart he may sometimes wonder if he made
the right choice coming to America, but to me he is a hero for making that
choice and giving me the life I have today.

It has not been an easy thing, this business of becoming American. But there   12
are times, like when I walk my dog in the country outside Santa Fe, when the
sights and sounds of horses, roosters and donkeys so strongly evoke my childhood that I feel a deep sense of belonging. I've come to realize that by planting
my roots here so firmly, I am no longer borrowing history. I am living and even
creating it. Perhaps someday when I'm gone, someone will ask the person who
lives in this house after me, "Do you see a lot of butterflies on this property?"

■ **Building Vocabulary**

For each numbered item, choose the meaning that most closely defines the
underlined word or phrase as it is used in the essay.

1. The word eccentric most nearly means
   a. odd
   b. cat-loving
   c. friendly
   d. conventional

2. The word vicariously most nearly means
   a. unhappily
   b. vivaciously
   c. enthusiastically
   d. through another person

3. The phrase unencumbered by most nearly means
   a. threatened with
   b. free of
   c. unaware of
   d. burdened by

4. The word constraints most nearly means
   a. freedoms
   b. restraints
   c. choices
   d. pleasures

5. The word evoke most nearly means
   a. call to mind
   b. revoke
   c. understand
   d. eliminate

■ Understanding the Essay

1. As it relates to the essay, "borrowed history" means
   a. the history of a country that is not one's own.
   b. history books borrowed from the public library to learn about one's adopted country.
   c. bits of another's history or culture borrowed to replace one's own lost history.
   d. family history handed down from older relatives.

2. As a child, what was the main difference the author saw between life in the United States and life in Yugoslavia?
   a. Her new home in Chicago was gray and dreary in contrast to her colorful childhood home.
   b. The freedom she found in America was a pleasant contrast to the constraints of communism.

    c. City life in Chicago was much more exciting than her grand-mother's farm.

    d. The crystal chandeliers of her father's new home contrasted sharply with the dirt floors of her former home.

3. Items that reflect the author's borrowed history include all but which of the following?

    a. Bailey White's essays

    (b.) Books from which the author learned the Cyrillic alphabet

    c. Mammama's quilt

    d. The conversations that the author has with her landlady's daughter

4. The author feels a connection to her homeland when she moves to

    a. Chicago.

    (b.) Santa Fe.

    c. Belgrade.

    d. Kentucky.

5. The essay suggests that after her death, the author would like some-one to ask "Do you see a lot of butterflies on this property?" because

    a. butterflies are beautiful and colorful, much like her homeland.

    b. local legend suggests that butterflies like to live near old ladies, and she wants to live to be 100.

    c. in New Mexico, butterflies are rarely seen.

    (d.) she wants to be someone who, like the schoolteacher, was well loved and made a difference in people's lives.

■ **Writing in the Margins**

These questions encourage you to think not just about the essay but about the issues it raises. Your instructor may ask you to write down your answers, to discuss them in groups, or simply to think about them for class discussion.

Answers will vary.

1. Is it important to have a sense of personal and family history, or is the past best forgotten?

2. Explain the following statement from the essay: "I love this country with an immigrant's passion, but like everyone who has become an American citizen, I also live with a part of me missing." Specifically,

what does the author mean by "an immigrant's passion"? What do you think she feels is missing?

3. One saying goes "Home is where you hang your hat." Is the philosophy expressed by this statement compatible with the author's philosophy? If not, how are the two views different?

TOPICS FOR WRITING

Assignment 1: Neighbors

The author describes her eccentric neighbors, "Crazy Drina" and her mother. Describe a neighbor of yours who stands out in your mind for being unusual in some way—unusually kind, unusually grouchy, or just plain unusual.

Assignment 2: Disconnected

The author of "Borrowed History" describes a feeling of disconnection from her homeland. Write about an experience that made you feel disconnected. Perhaps it was a move to another country, or perhaps it was something less dramatic—changing schools, moving away from your parents' home, or starting a new job. In a paragraph, describe those elements of the new situation that made you feel disconnected.

Assignment 3: Borrowed Lives

At one time or another, almost everyone borrows something or enjoys some vicarious experience from another person's life. A person without children may occasionally borrow nieces, nephews, or a friend's children. A person who leads an ordinary life may borrow extraordinary adventures through books or movies. A person who enjoys acting may like the feeling of borrowing someone else's identity for a while. What do you enjoy borrowing from someone else's life? Answer in a paragraph, explaining how you borrow a particular experience and why you enjoy it.

Assignment 4: Your History

Write a paragraph describing an item that reflects your history. It may be a quilt that has been handed down in your family, a photograph album, or an old toy. Describe it and tell how it reveals some part of your family history.

Employment Test

Barbara Ehrenreich

Barbara Ehrenreich, author and social critic, went undercover for several months to live as a low-wage worker. In this excerpt from her book Nickel and Dimed, *Ehrenreich writes about her experiences with employment testing.*

At a suburban Wal-Mart that is advertising a "job fair" I am seated at a table with some balloons attached to it (this is the "fair" part) to wait for Julie. She is flustered, when she shows up after about a ten-minute wait, because, as she explains, she just works on the floor and has never interviewed anyone before. Fortunately for her, the interview consists almost entirely of a four-page "opinion survey," with "no right or wrong answers," Julie assures me, just my own personal opinion in ten degrees from "totally agree" to "totally disagree." As with the Winn-Dixie preemployment test I took in Key West, there are the usual questions about whether a coworker observed stealing should be forgiven or denounced, whether management is to blame if things go wrong, and if it's all right to be late when you have a "good excuse." The only thing that distinguishes this test is its obsession with marijuana, suggesting that it was authored by a serious stoner struggling to adjust to the corporate way of life. Among the propositions I am asked to opine about are, "Some people work better when they're a little bit high," "Everyone tries marijuana," and, bafflingly, "Marijuana is the same as a drink." Hmm, what kind of drink? I want to ask. "The same" how—chemically or morally? Or should I write in something flippant like, "I wouldn't know because I don't drink"? The pay is $6.50, Julie tells me, but can shoot up to $7 pretty fast. She thinks I would be great in the ladies' department, and I tell her I think so too. 1

What these tests tell employers about potential employees is hard to imagine, since the "right" answers should be obvious to anyone who has ever encountered the principle of hierarchy and subordination. Do I work well with others? You bet, but never to the point where I would hesitate to inform on them for the slightest infraction. Am I capable of independent decision making? Oh yes, but I know better than to let this capacity interfere with a slavish obedience to orders. At The Maids, a housecleaning service, I am given something called the "Accutrac personality test," which warns at the beginning that "Accutrac has multiple measures which detect attempts to distort or 'psych out' the questionnaire." Naturally, I "never" find it hard "to stop moods of self-pity," nor do I imagine that others are talking about me behind my back or 2 believe that "management and employees will always be in conflict because they have totally different sets of goals." The real function of these tests, I decide, is to convey information not to the employer but to the potential employee, and the information being conveyed is always: You will have no secrets from us. We don't just want your muscles and that portion of your brain that is directly connected to them, we want your innermost self.

■ Building Vocabulary

For each numbered item, choose the meaning that most closely defines the underlined word or phrase as it is used in the essay.

1. The word flustered most nearly means
   - (a.) rattled and upset
   - b. calm and composed
   - c. angry and belligerent
   - d. cordial and polite

2. The word denounced most nearly means
   - a. forgiven
   - b. counseled
   - (c.) turned in
   - d. announced

3. The word opine most nearly means
   - a. complain
   - b. confess
   - c. agree
   - (d.) give an opinion

4. The word flippant most nearly means
   - a. sincere
   - (b.) sarcastic
   - c. pious
   - d. informative

5. The phrase hierarchy and subordination most nearly means
   - (a.) a system in which some have more power than others
   - b. a system in which everyone has equal rank
   - c. a system in which leaders are elected
   - d. a system run by workers who are also owners

■ Understanding the Essay

1. The author's purpose in writing the essay is
   a. to show that employment tests are all the same.
   b. to uphold the validity of employment tests.
   c. to question the validity of employment tests.
   d. to report a positive experience with employment tests.

2. When the author attends the Wal-Mart job fair, an employment questionnaire is administered by
   a. the Wal-Mart manager that she will work for if she is offered the job.
   b. a Human Resources representative who has been trained in testing.
   c. a computer.
   d. a Wal-Mart employee who has never administered an employment test.

3. Which of the following issues is *not* mentioned as being a part of the employment tests the author has taken?
   a. Attitude toward management
   b. Attitude toward drugs
   c. Attitude toward customers
   d. Attitude toward employee theft

4. The author implies that the test questions on the employment tests she has taken are
   a. easy to see through and easy to answer in a way that will please an employer.
   b. intelligently crafted and hard to "psych out."
   c. only opinion questions with no right or wrong answers.
   d. fair questions that are likely to warn off employees who are not suitable.

5. The author concludes that the real purpose of employment tests is to demonstrate that employers want
   a. a drug-free workplace.
   b. honest workers who can get along well with others.
   c. an employee's innermost self.
   d. workers who will cooperate with management.

■ Writing in the Margins

These questions encourage you to think not just about the essay but about the issues it raises. Your instructor may ask you to write down your answers, to discuss them in groups, or simply to think about them for class discussion.

1. Have you ever taken an employment test? What was it like?

Answers will vary.

2. In paragraph 2, the author says that she works well with others, but "never to the point where I would hesitate to inform on them for the slightest infraction." Should readers take that statement seriously, or is the author making a different point?

Answers will vary slightly but should indicate that the author is making a different point. She is showing the contradictions inherent in the ideal employee's personality—how can a person establish the trust needed to work well with others if she is tattling on them all the time? In addition, she is demonstrating how transparent the test items are and how easy it is to fake out the test.

TOPICS FOR WRITING

Assignment 1: Interview

Anyone who has ever participated in a job interview, an interview for a scholarship, or a similar interview knows that some interviews go well and others go badly. In a paragraph, describe the best or worst interview you have ever been through.

Assignment 2: Is Marijuana the Same as a Drink?

The author is baffled by the employment test item that asks whether marijuana is the same as a drink. Brainstorm on the similarities and differences between marijuana and an alcoholic beverage. Then write a paragraph describing the most important similarities, differences, or both. Your audience for this essay is not an employment tester, but a general adult audience.

Assignment 3: Firing Offenses

If you owned a business, what would it take to make you fire an employee? In a paragraph, describe up to three "firing offenses" that you, as a business owner, would not tolerate and the reasons you would not tolerate them.

Assignment 4: Body and Soul

Ehrenreich believes that employment tests say to a prospective employee, "We don't just want your muscles and that portion of your brain that is directly connected to them, we want your innermost self." Following are some requirements imposed on employees or prospective employees. All are requirements that have been criticized by some as "going too far." Choose one and argue for or against an employer's right to require it.

Preemployment drug screening

Random drug screening of employees

Preemployment credit checks

Preemployment background checks

Preemployment polygraph (lie detector) testing

Broken Windows

Leonard Pitts

Profanity? It's everywhere. It's no big deal anymore—or is it? Leonard Pitts explores the question.

1 I guess it was only a matter of time before Sue Richards said "ass." I mean, everybody else has. Why not her?

2 It's right there in black and white, Page 2, "Fantastic Four No. 38: the Invisible Woman," an offhand reference to "knocking Dr. Doom on his ass."

3 It was too much for a fellow named Marcus Lusk. He wrote Marvel Comics a letter, which the company published last week.

4 "What in the world were you thinking?" he demanded. "This is wrong. Just flat-out wrong."

5 Truth to tell, I can think of several ways to punch holes in Lusk's indignation. I could point out, for instance, that it's unlikely the majority of readers exposed to the offending word were young children. As Jim Welker of Tropic Comics in North Miami Beach points out, comics fans tend to range in age from 17 to 25 years. I could observe, too, that it's only "ass"—hardly the big kahuna in the hierarchy of naughty terms. Finally, I could note that you can hardly watch a TV sitcom or drama these days without some character spouting the same word.

6 Yet for all of that, Lusk's complaint resonates with me, though my discomfort stems from a different place.

7 What bothers me is that I'm not bothered. Or, at least, I wasn't. I read right over the passage in question and it registered only as a <u>lamentable</u> sign of the times. Then I read Lusk's letter, I see that he is indignant, and I begin to wonder why I was not.

8 Media used to set stuff with bad language or suggestive pictures aside, consigning it to hours and locations where young people were unlikely to encounter it. Now it's everywhere. To the point that a comic book heroine talks about knocking the bad guy on his ass.

9 Another barrier is breached, another small crudity seeps into a forbidden place.

10 I wouldn't even mind the <u>intrusion</u> if there was some point to it. Thirty years ago, for instance, this same company bucked the Comics Code Authority—the industry's censoring group—to publish a controversial tale about drug addiction. That was brave.

11 This is . . . lazy.

And if you're thinking, "So what? Comic book character says a bad word. 12
That isn't such a big thing," . . . well, you're right. That's the point.

I'm reminded of the "broken windows" theory of crime prevention. It says 13
that if one window is shattered in a factory and allowed to go unrepaired, people will perceive that no one cares, that this is a lawless place. And it won't be
long before all the windows are shattered and the street becomes one where
prudent people do not walk.

I wonder if something similar isn't true of the tendency of crude material to 14
seep into inappropriate places, if hesitancy to raise a ruckus over small
breaches isn't analogous to leaving the window shattered.

"We are doing our best to balance the demands of a new generation with 15
the expectations of our more traditional readers," went the company's response to Marcus Lusk.

In other words, the lines of propriety are shifting, blurring away to irrele- 16
vance. And you wonder where or whether they'll ever take shape again.

■ **Building Vocabulary**

For each numbered item, choose the meaning that most closely defines the
underlined word or phrase as it is used in the essay.

1. The word lamentable most nearly means
   a. commonplace
   b. regrettable
   c. lighthearted
   d. unmentionable

2. The word intrusion most nearly means
   a. barrier
   b. invasion
   c. horror
   d. word

3. The word prudent most nearly means
   a. level-headed
   b. crude
   c. unscrupulous
   d. destructive

4. The word analogous most nearly means
   a. dissimilar
   b. unrelated
   c. restricted
   d. comparable

5. The word <u>propriety</u> most nearly means
   a. oppression
   b. correctness
   c. property
   d. progress

■ Understanding the Essay

1. What is the main idea of the essay?
   a. Censorship of comic books, like censorship of any other art form, is wrong.
   b. A small impropriety such as a bad word in a comic book can open the door to further inappropriateness.
   c. A popular theory in crime prevention holds that if a window is broken and not fixed, other broken windows will soon follow.
   d. Marcus Lusk, a comic book reader, became upset over a mild profanity in a comic book.

2. The author's first reaction to the word that prompted Marcus Lusk's letter was
   a. outrage.
   b. amusement.
   c. indignation.
   d. indifference.

3. Which argument does *not* support including a profane word in a comic book?
   a. Most comics readers are adults in their late teens or early twenties.
   b. Similar words are heard on prime-time TV.
   c. The first profanity can lead to many more.
   d. The profanity is a relatively mild one.

4. Another way of stating the "broken windows" theory of crime prevention is that
   a. broken windows lure the criminal element to a particular area.
   b. breaking windows is a criminal act, however small, that should be prosecuted to the fullest extent of the law.
   c. neighborhoods with broken windows probably have a high crime rate.
   d. if it appears that people in a particular area do not care about a small crime, more crime will result.

5. What is the relationship between the "broken windows" theory and profanity in comic books?

   a. When the author applies the "broken windows" theory to comic books, he realizes that if enough people do not protest that first profane word in a comic book, more will follow.

   b. When the author applies the "broken windows" theory to comic books, he realizes that one small profanity is not cause for concern.

   c. The author is using the "broken windows" theory as an example of censorship.

   d. The "broken windows" theory is used as a point of contrast to the idea of profanity in comic books.

■ **Writing in the Margins**

These questions encourage you to think not just about the essay but about the issues it raises. Your instructor may ask you to write down your answers, to discuss them in groups, or simply to think about them for class discussion.

Answers will vary.

1. What is your position on profanity? Does it offend you? Do you embrace it as a colorful and emphatic enhancement to your vocabulary? Or is there so much of it around that you barely notice it?

2. Think of some areas where standards of what is right and proper have changed in your lifetime. Do most of the changes you have listed serve to loosen the standards or to tighten them? Are these changes good, bad, or unimportant?

TOPICS FOR WRITING

Assignment 1: #"%&#!

A team of extraterrestrial language experts lands near your home and asks you for guidance. They are interested in the phenomenon known as "cursing" or "profanity," for they do not have such forbidden language on their home planet. They ask you to direct them to three sources where they are likely to hear profanity. In a journal entry or paragraph, describe for the aliens three sources where they can hear profanity and try to explain why profanity is commonly found in those places.

Assignment 2: The "Broken Windows" Theory and You

The "broken windows" theory is a lot like the old expression "Give a person an inch, and he'll take a mile." In other words, if one tiny infraction of the rules is ignored, additional and larger ones will follow. Take the "broken windows" theory, and apply it to a situation in your life: school, relationships, driving, dieting, child rearing, housekeeping, car maintenance—you name it! Write a paragraph giving specific examples of how the "broken windows" theory applies to the area you choose.

Assignment 3: Drawing the Line

Even people who use profanity do not use it everywhere and in every situation. There are still places and situations where most people believe profanity should not be used. In a paragraph discuss three places or situations where you believe profanity is inappropriate, and give your reasons for considering each place or situation inappropriate for the use of profanity.

Assignment 4: Breaking Taboos

Leonard Pitts believes that Marvel Comics was right and brave in breaking the taboos against writing about drug addiction in comics. Have you ever felt right and brave about bringing up a forbidden topic with a friend or family member? Describe your experience in a paragraph.

Confrontation at Register Two

Constance Daley

A confrontation between an old man and a young cashier leads the writer to recall a lesson she learned about responsibility and choice.

The one inevitable thing about a checkout line is you will wait your turn. I was 1 fourth and the man at the register was asked if he wanted paper or plastic and he said he wanted paper. The cashier, thin and wan with dark eyes, handed him a paper bag.

"What's this for?" Then he asked quietly, "Aren't you going to bag my 2 groceries?"

"No, I'm four months pregnant and I don't want to reach across the 3 counter," she said, rather directly. He snapped open the large, two-ply bag, efficiently, stood it on the counter, and started to bag his cans of cat food, one at a time, not advancing toward the end of the counter, so she could start ringing up the next customer.

"Sooo," he said, softly, very slowly, "you are four months pregnant and all 4 of us here on line have to bag our own groceries at a store that prides itself on customer service? Is that what you're saying?"

His voice was low and lyrical, like that of an actor or teacher, but his words 5 came straight from Psychology 101. He continued, "I venture to say you do not know any of us personally and yet you are angry at all of us. Oh, and may I have a refrigerator-bag for this ice cream? It'll melt before I get home."

The girl, no more than 17 years old, was visibly seething, rolling her eyes, 6 pursing her lips, but saying nothing in case a manager should come over to see what was holding up the line. None of us spoke. This man was making sense and I, for one, wanted him to play it out.

Of course, she had problems; of course, she shouldn't have to reach across 7 counters and lift 5-lb. bags of potatoes and gallons of milk, or put up with whatever else she was juggling in her life—but we weren't in it. I believe the manager wasn't in it either, or he would have rearranged the assignments.

"I'm not one to complain about my problems," the gentleman drawled, 8 eyes still down tending to business while hers sparked with silent fury, "but since you complained about yours, let me tell you I come here precisely because the cashier ordinarily bags my groceries. Here, I don't usually have to bend my fingers picking up these little cans and setting off an all day bout with arthritis. Think about it, young lady. We all have problems but they don't belong to anybody else but ourselves. This morning, you made your problem, my problem, and your store is losing a very good customer." He now looked her in the eye. "If your manager asks you why this store lost this customer, you tell him it's because you're four months pregnant. Even I might find humor in that."

She had to keep looking in his direction as he spoke because they do have 9 spot checkers. She had to put his receipt in the bag and, of course, say, "Have a nice day." She did that quietly but not mournfully, not by any means. He answered her, but looked at those of us on line for the first time. "I plan to salvage the rest of the day, young lady, but I have to acknowledge you put a chink in my morning. You try to have a nice day, too, because I'm sure I've put a chink in yours, too." He tipped his hat with gnarled fingers and we nodded back silently.

The girl was visibly relieved when he went out the automatic door instead 10 of into the manager's office, and began ringing up the next customer. She started shoving the groceries into the requested plastic and when the customer reached and said, "I'll get that," the girl held tightly and said nothing. The woman did not protest. We all recognize rage when we see it and it was brewing.

Some of us on that line might have been torn between exactly who was 11 right in that exchange. Not I, though. Although this girl is learning it from an 80-year old, I learned about blame and how to place it squarely from a three-year-old.

I was sitting on the side of young Jack's bed tying his shoe. The laces fairly 12 snapped in my fingers as I formed the loop, wrapped the string, formed the tie, then double knot, dropped the foot lankly, picked up the other one, flung it across my knee and repeated the procedure. He was leaning back on his hands on his unmade bed and said: "Mommy, how come you're always so angry?"

I didn't answer right away. But when I did, I told the truth. He'd know if I 13 didn't—kids have a way of knowing, even if we don't tell them.

"Jack, I'm angry because when I woke up there was a sink full of dirty dishes 14 and I don't like seeing that. And they were dirty because I didn't wash them last night. And, the beds aren't made because I didn't make them and I like the rooms pretty. And I'm angry because I want to take you to the park, but I have to do all that dirty laundry or there'll be nothing to wear tomorrow. I should have been doing it every day. So, I'm angry with myself, not at you. Can you understand that?"

I don't know if he did or not but I understood that morning that if I am 15 angry with myself, I have to deal with it myself and not drag anyone else into it—because nobody else caused my problem.

We hear a lot about choice lately and reflect on the times—the moments, 16 really—when we made bad choices. With the cashier, it was her choosing to be with a man; with me, it was my choosing to go to bed leaving dirty dishes in the sink.

Neither one of us gave a thought to what we'd face tomorrow. And, oh 17 boy, that really made us mad!

■ Building Vocabulary

For each numbered item, choose the meaning that most closely defines the underlined word or phrase as it is used in the essay.

1. The word inevitable most nearly means
    a. lowly
    (b.) certain
    c. unlikely
    d. daily

2. The word lyrical most nearly means
    (a.) musical
    b. trustful
    c. spiteful
    d. enthusiastic

3. The word seething most nearly means
    a. apologetic
    b. hesitant
    c. happy
    (d.) angry

4. The word salvage most nearly means
    a. scrap
    (b.) rescue
    c. complain
    d. shop

5. The word gnarled most nearly means
    (a.) twisted
    b. smooth
    c. strong
    d. flexible

■ Understanding the Essay

1. Which description best expresses the writer's purpose?
    a. To complain about the poor service at a local store
    b. To defend the right of pregnant women not to lift heavy loads
    c. To examine the right of customers to complain about shoddy service
    (d.) To explore the unforeseen implications of some personal decisions

2. The author's sympathies lie
   a. with the pregnant employee.
   b. with the old man.
   c. with the customers waiting in line.
   d. with the store manager.

3. The old man did not want to bag groceries because
   a. it was not his job.
   b. he is a paying customer and deserves better treatment.
   c. his arthritis would flare up.
   d. he is grumpy and looking for something to complain about.

4. The pregnant woman reacts to the old man's remarks with
   a. shame.
   b. rage.
   c. sadness.
   d. cheerfulness.

5. The author says that both she and the cashier have been confronted with the lesson that
   a. old people and little children tell the truth.
   b. if you have burdens and troubles, the best way to handle them is to share the load.
   c. having children is more trouble than it's worth.
   d. other people should not have to suffer because of your troubles.

■ Writing in the Margins

These questions encourage you to think not just about the essay but about the issues it raises. Your instructor may ask you to write down your answers, to discuss them in groups, or simply to think about them for class discussion.

Answers will vary.

1. The writer says, "Some of us on that line might have been torn between exactly who was right in that exchange." Are you torn, or do you see the situation as clear-cut? Explain your views.

2. What if the customer were thirty-three and pregnant? Or what if the roles were reversed, and the cashier were an eighty-year-old man who did not want to bag groceries because of his arthritic hands, and the customer were seventeen years old and four months pregnant? Does age matter in this story, or is it irrelevant?

3. Do you agree with the author's assumption that the cashier's problem became every customer's problem? Is it fair to be burdened by the problems and actions that others generate, or is it just a part of life?

TOPICS FOR WRITING

Assignment 1: Troubles

Do you believe that people's troubles are mostly of their own making? Answer in a paragraph or journal entry.

Assignment 2: Cheerful Service

Employees who work with the public are expected to be unfailingly polite and cheerful, no matter what. Is this a reasonable expectation? Discuss your answer in a paragraph.

Assignment 3: Taking Responsibility

Are you a person who takes responsibility for your choices and actions? If so, what influences helped you become the person you are? Write a paragraph to answer these questions.

Assignment 4: Letting Others Pick Up the Pieces

Write a paragraph describing a time when you (or someone you know) failed to take responsibility and others had to pick up the pieces. How did your actions (or those of the person you are describing) cause trouble for others? Give specific examples.

Walking the Tightrope between Black and White

Cecelie Berry

"Be yourself," the author would like to tell her son. But she knows it's never that simple.

I recognize the sassy swivel of the head, the rhythmic teeth sucking and finger snapping. My son Spenser has come home from kindergarten talking like he's black. Never mind that he is black; somehow his skin color is no longer adequate to express his racial identity. Sometimes, in diverse schools like the one he attends, black children feel pressure to "act" black. My 8-year-old son Sam asks me to tell Spenser not to use "that phony accent" around his friends. "I'll talk to him," I say with a sigh.

"Be yourself" seems insufficient at times like this. I know from my experience with integration that it takes a long time to own your identity. In an all-black elementary school in Cleveland, I carried around a dog-eared copy of "A Little Princess" and listened to Bach on my transistor radio. Nobody paid attention. When my family moved to Shaker Heights, an affluent suburb known for its successfully integrated schools, I encountered the war over who was authentically black. I had hoped that when I raised my own children there wouldn't be any more litmus tests, that a healthy black identity could come in many styles. But the impulse to pigeonhole each other endures.

As I considered what to say to Spenser, I recalled my own struggles over my accent. In seventh grade, I was rehearsing a play after school when a group of black girls passed by. "You talk like a honky," their leader said. "You must think you're white." In the corner of my eye, I could see her bright yellow radio, shaped like a tennis ball, swinging like a mace. A phrase I'd found intriguing flashed through my mind: "The best defense is a good offense." I stepped forward and slapped her hard.

I was suspended for that fight, but I felt I deserved a medal. My true reward came later, when I heard two girls talking about me in the hallway. "I heard she's an oreo," one said. "Don't let her hear you say that," the other replied, "'cause she'll kick your butt!"

I hesitate to tell Spenser to be himself because I know it's not that simple. From integration, I learned that you have to fight for the right to be yourself, and often, your opponents have the same color skin as you. My sons will discover, as I did, that you can feign a black accent, but your loyalty will continue to be tested as long as you allow it.

In high school, I enhanced my reputation as an "oreo" by participating in activities that most black students didn't: advanced-placement classes, the school newspaper and the debate team. Mostly, I enjoyed being different. It put me in a unique position to challenge the casually racist assumptions of my liberal classmates. I remember a question posed by my social-studies teacher, "How many of you grew up addressing your black housekeepers by their first names?" Many students raised their hands. "And how many of you addressed white adults that way?" The hands went down. One girl moaned: "That's not racist. Everybody does that." 6

"We never addressed our housekeeper that way," I said. In the silence that followed, I could feel myself being reassessed. I'd challenged my classmate on the fairness of a privilege she had, like many whites, taken completely for granted. I had defied the unspoken understanding of how blacks in white settings are supposed to be: transparent and accommodating. 7

If black students inflicted upon each other a rigid code of "blackness," liberal whites assumed that the blacks in their midst would not dispute their right-mindedness. Being myself, I found, could be lonely. In high school, I grew weary of walking the tightrope between black and white. 8

By college, I was eating regularly at the controversial "black tables" of Harvard's Freshman Union. I talked black, walked black and dated black men. My boyfriend, an Andover graduate, commented on my transformation by saying that I had never been an oreo; I was really a "closet militant." I laughed at the phrase; it had an element of truth. I had learned that people—black or white—tend to demonize what they don't understand and can't control. So I sometimes hid the anger, ambition and self-confidence that provoked their fear. Integration taught me to have two faces: one that can get along with anybody and one that distrusts everybody. 9

I've seen both sides, now. I've "hung" white and I've "hung" black, and been stereotyped by both groups. I choose integration for my children, not out of idealism, but a pragmatic assessment of what it takes to grow up. When it comes to being yourself—and finding out who that person is—you're on your own. Experimentation is a prerequisite, trying on various accents and dress styles, mandatory. Diversity is the best laboratory for building individuality. 10

I am about to explain this to Spenser, when I see him change, like quicksilver, into someone else. Playfully, he stretches his arm out toward my face, turns his gap-toothed smile in the opposite direction and, in a tone as maddening as it is endearing, he says, "Mom, talk to the hand." 11

■ Building Vocabulary

For each numbered item, choose the meaning that most closely defines the underlined word or phrase as it is used in the essay.

1. The word <u>pigeonhole</u> most nearly means
   a. question.
   b. ignore.
   c. accept.
   d. stereotype.

2. The word <u>feign</u> most nearly means
   a. pretend.
   b. cast aside.
   c. ignore.
   d. reject.

3. The word <u>accommodating</u> most nearly means
   a. agreeable.
   b. hospitable.
   c. unyielding.
   d. resisting.

4. The word <u>demonize</u> most nearly means
   a. to refuse to face reality about something.
   b. to imagine something as powerful and wicked.
   c. to imagine something as weak and ineffective.
   d. to imagine something as better than it is.

5. The word <u>pragmatic</u> most nearly means
   a. vague.
   b. fuzzy.
   c. idealistic.
   d. realistic.

■ Understanding the Essay

1. The main reason that it upsets the author to see her son coming home "talking like he's black" is that
   a. he *is* black.
   b. she never felt pressured to be anyone other than herself.
   c. she had hoped her children would not have to prove themselves as she did when she was in school.
   d. her son's "phony accent" upsets his brother.

2. The one place where the author did not have to prove her black identity was
   a. in an all-black elementary school.
   b. in seventh grade at an integrated school.
   c. at Harvard.
   d. in high school.

3. After slapping the girl who confronted her about her accent, the author felt
   a. ashamed that she had resorted to physical violence.
   b. embarrassed at being suspended.
   c. proud that she had fought for the right to be herself.
   d. worried that the girl and her friends might retaliate.

4. Walking the "tightrope between black and white," the author found all but which of the following to be true?
   a. She had to prove her black identity to be accepted by blacks.
   b. Being herself was a lonely enterprise.
   c. Everyone accepted her as she was.
   d. She had to be accommodating and agreeable to be accepted by whites.

5. The author concludes that experimentation with dress and accents
   a. is a part of growing up and building individuality.
   b. is unnecessary in the modern world.
   c. is something that she will not allow her son Spenser to do.
   d. is a painful result of stereotyping.

■ Writing in the Margins

These questions encourage you to think not just about the essay but about the issues it raises. Your instructor may ask you to write down your answers, to discuss them in groups, or simply to think about them for class discussion.

Answers will vary.

1. Have you ever felt pressured by peers, parents, or others to conform to a certain standard of cultural identity in dress, speech, or behavior? How did you react?

2. The author says, "Diversity is the best laboratory for building individuality." What does she mean? What are some of the reasons that diver-

sity might help build individuality? Are there also roadblocks to building individuality in a diverse culture?

TOPICS FOR WRITING

Assignment 1: Your Personal Tightrope

The author describes walking "a tightrope between black and white." People walk tightropes every day—between black and white, between wrong and right, between friends and family, between work and school, and many other situations. Write a paragraph or journal entry describing a tightrope that you have walked. Make sure to include specific details that convince your reader of the difficulty in walking that tightrope.

Assignment 2: Loyalty Test

The author says, "your loyalty will continue to be tested as long as you allow it." This statement can be applied not only to racial groups but also to other kinds of groups. Has your loyalty to a group ever been questioned? Write a paragraph describing how your loyalty was tested and how you handled the situation.

Assignment 3: Being Yourself

Even though finding oneself involves experimentation and change, there are some things that are so much a part of our being that we could not change them if we had to. What unique qualities, habits, beliefs, or activities are so much a part of you that group pressure could never induce you to give them up? Answer in a paragraph.

Assignment 4: Choosing an Education

The author says that she chose integrated schools for her children, "not out of idealism, but a pragmatic assessment of what it takes to grow up." Do you believe it is better for children to be educated with a diverse population, or is it better for them to be segregated by gender, ability, race, interest, or some other criterion? Write a paragraph describing your choice and your reasons for it.

My Dead Dog May Already Be a Winner!

Lee Coppola

After listing his telephone in his dog's name, Lee Coppola was surprised at how many calls and offers the dog received.

Ever wonder what happens when a pet takes on a persona? Ashley could have told you, if he could have talked. Ashley was the family mutt, an SPCA special, part beagle and part spaniel.

For years, most of them after he died, he also served as the family's representative in the local telephone book. He was picked for the role quite haphazardly one day when I tried to keep my number out of the book to avoid getting business calls at home. When I balked at the $60-a-year fee, the cheery telephone company representative suggested I list the number in one of my children's names.

I was munching on a sandwich at the time and Ashley followed me around the kitchen waiting for a crumb to fall. "Can I put the phone in any name?" I asked the rep as I sidestepped Ashley. "Certainly," she answered, and therein gave birth to 10 years of telephone calls and mail to a dog.

"A remarkable new book about the Coppolas since the Civil War is about to make history—and you, Ashley Coppola, are in it," touted one letter asking Ashley to send $10 right away for "this one-time offer." Ashley received hundreds of pieces of mail, the bulk soliciting his money.

The most ironic pitches for cash were from the SPCA and the Buffalo Zoo, a kind of animal-helping-animal scenario. And we wondered how the chief executive of a local cemetery might react if he knew he was asking a canine to buy a plot to give his family "peace of mind." Or a local lawn service's thoughts about asking a dog who daily messed the grass, "Is your lawn as attractive as it could be?" Then there was the letter offering Ashley "reliable electronic security to protect your home." One of the kids asked if that wasn't Ashley's job.

The kids soon got into the swing of having their dog receive mail and telephone calls. "He's sleeping under the dining-room table," one would tell telemarketers. "He's out in the backyard taking a whiz," was the favorite reply of another. My wife would have nothing of that frivolity, preferring to simply reply, "He's deceased."

But that tack backfired on her one day when our youngest child took an almost pleading call from a survey-company employee looking for Ashley. "I'm

Ashley," the 17-year-old politely replied, taking pity on the caller. He dutifully gave his age and answered a few questions before he realized he was late for an appointment and hurriedly cut short the conversation. "Can I call you again?" the surveyor asked. "OK," our son said as he hung up.

Sure enough, the surveyor called again the next day and asked for Ashley. But this time Mom answered and gave her standard reply. "Oh my God," exclaimed the caller. "I'm so, so sorry." The surveyor's horrified grief puzzled my wife until our son explained how he had been a healthy teenage Ashley the day before. 8

It seemed direct mailers had a tough time figuring out Ashley's sex and marital status. He was named by our daughter at the time she was reading "Gone With the Wind" and was smitten with Ashley Wilkes. "Dear Mr. Coppola," his mail sometimes would begin. More often, though, Ashley's mail came to Mrs. Coppola or, on those politically correct occasions, to Ms. Coppola. 9

Sometimes we worried about our dog's fate. You see, he broke several chain letters urging him to copy and send 20 others or risk some calamity. After all, Ashley was warned, didn't one person die nine days after throwing out the letter? 10

Did I mention credit cards? Ashley paid his bills on time, judging from the $5,000 lines-of-credit for which he "automatically" qualified. Made us wonder about the scrutiny of the nation's credit-card industry. 11

Of course, Ashley was no ordinary dog. He was an Italian dog. How else to explain the solicitation to Mr. Coppola Ashley that came all the way from Altamura, Italy, and sought donations to an orphanage? Then there was the offer to obtain his family's cherished crest, "fashioned hundreds of years ago in Italy," and purchase the Coppola family registry that listed him along with all the other Coppolas in America. 12

Is there some message to all this? Think of the saplings that were sacrificed to try to squeeze money from a canine. Or the time, energy and money that were wasted each time a postage or bulk-mail stamp was affixed to an envelope being sent to a mutt. We did feel sheepish about the deception when the mail came from the self-employed trying to make a buck. We wondered if a local dentist really would have given Ashley a "complete initial consultation, exam and bitewing X-rays for only three dollars." And what might have been the expression on the saleswoman's face if Ashley had shown up for his complimentary Mary Kay facial? 13

Ashley did appreciate, however, the coupon for dog food. 14

■ Building Vocabulary

For each numbered item, choose the meaning that most closely defines the underlined word or phrase as it is used in the essay.

1. The word haphazardly most nearly means
   a. by chance.
   b. through careful planning.

   c. unhappily.

   d. dangerously.

2. The phrase <u>balked at</u> most nearly means

   (a.) refused.

   b. accepted.

   c. paid.

   d. earned.

3. The word <u>soliciting</u> most nearly means

   a. refusing.

   (b.) asking for.

   c. adding to.

   d. stealing.

4. The word <u>frivolity</u> most nearly means

   a. deception.

   b. lying.

   (c.) foolishness.

   d. reply.

5. The word <u>saplings</u> most nearly means

   a. foolish people.

   b. units of energy.

   c. units of time.

   (d.) young trees.

■ Understanding the Essay

1. The author decides to put his home telephone in his dog's name because

   a. he thinks it will be funny.

   b. he is tired of receiving so many calls from telemarketers.

   (c.) the charge for an unlisted number is too expensive.

   d. the dog is popular and receives many calls.

2. What type of mail does the author *not* say that Ashley receives?

   a. Credit card offers

   b. Chain letters

   (c.) Bills

   d. An offer for discounted dental work

3. When telephone calls came for Ashley, the author's children typically
   a. gave humorous answers.
   b. offered to take a message.
   c. said that Ashley was dead.
   d. pretended to be Ashley.

4. The surveyor who believes that the author's seventeen-year-old son has just died is the victim of
   a. a cruel prank by the author's son.
   b. a deliberate and tasteless joke.
   c. an unintentional misunderstanding.
   d. revenge on the part of a family who has been tormented by telemarketers for too long.

5. Though the essay is humorous, the author makes a serious point. What is that point?
   a. Soliciting people chosen from the phone book can waste time, money, and environmental resources.
   b. Telemarketing is usually a scam and constitutes invasion of privacy.
   c. Credit card companies should use more caution in offering preapproved credit cards.
   d. A telephone can be listed in any name, even a dog's.

■ Writing in the Margins

These questions encourage you to think not just about the essay but about the issues it raises. Your instructor may ask you to write down your answers, to discuss them in groups, or simply to think about them for class discussion.

Answers will vary.

1. What conclusions would you draw from the fact that Ashley, a dead dog, received preapproved credit card offers?

2. Telemarketers interrupt people's lives, their meals, and their time at home. For that reason, some people feel no obligation to be polite, and they hang up on the telemarketers or make rude comments. On the other hand, telemarketers are people with feelings, and they, like most people, are trying to make a living. You decide: should simple human decency compel people to be polite to telemarketers, or is rudeness permitted?

TOPICS FOR WRITING

Assignment 1: Pets and People

Even if most of them do not receive mail and telephone calls, pets are a part of the family for many people. What are some of the reasons people keep pets? Answer in a paragraph, using specific examples to show why people keep pets.

Assignment 2: Putting Telemarketers on Hold

Write a paragraph describing the best ways to handle unwanted calls from telemarketers.

Assignment 3: Where Credit Is Due

Like many Americans, Ashley the dog received credit card offers. Unlike many Americans, Ashley never ran up too much credit card debt. Why do so many people charge too much on credit cards? Answer in a paragraph.

Assignment 4: Rude and Crude

Telemarketers are not the only ones who have to deal with rude behavior. A recent survey shows that most people say rudeness is on the increase. What are some of the reasons that rudeness is increasing in our society? Answer in a paragraph.

Imprisoned by Ex-Convict Status

Walter Scanlon

Walter Scanlon served his time, paid his debt to society, and turned his life around. He believes it's time he was freed from the stigma of ex-convict status.

Thirty years ago I decided to drastically turn my life around. With a state-issued olive suit on my back, a high-school equivalency diploma and $40 travel money in my pocket, I became an ex-convict. I had done my time—almost five years in all—and now had the opportunity to redeem myself. I felt almost optimistic. As the huge outer gate of New York state's Clinton Prison slammed behind me, the discharge officer bid me farewell: "Get your act together," he bellowed with a mix of sincerity and humor. "I don't want to see you back here any time soon." A Department of Corrections van sat rumbling at the prison's checkpoint—my ride to the Greyhound bus depot. 1

As we pulled away, the towering walls, razor wire and iron gates of the prison grew even more awesome, and the looming gun towers more ominous. It was a bright early autumn morning, my thirty-second birthday was days away, and the last ten years of my life had been spent in and out of men's shelters, hospitals and prisons. I wanted to make it this time. 2

Alcohol and other drugs had been my failing. Realizing I would need help, I sought an organization of other recovering addicts. Within a few days I landed a job in a metal-plating factory and rented a tiny furnished room. On the urging of a new friend who had a similar past, I soon took my first college course. My first grade was a disappointing C, but before long I was scoring A's and B's. I also got better jobs, eventually landing a counseling job in a substance-abuse treatment program. On job applications, I left questions about past arrests and convictions blank. I'd read that this would probably go unnoticed and, if it didn't, it would be better to discuss such matters in person. Time passed and, in a few short years, I completed college. I went on to get my master's degree and, using my graduate thesis as its foundation, I wrote a book on drugs in the workplace. 3

Today I live a full life, enjoying what most people enjoy: movies, books, theater, good food and good friends. My significant other is a South Asian woman and her diverse circle of friends has enriched my life. My annual income as a substance-abuse specialist is adequate, my standing in the community solid and my commitment to continued recovery is permanent. 4

All of these qualities notwithstanding, I remain, irrevocably, an ex-convict.   5
Although the years have removed all but hazy memories of addiction, hospital-
izations, street living and prison, I secretly carry the baggage of a former offender. As my qualifications for higher-level positions grew, so, too, did the
potential for a more detailed scrutiny of my past. Opportunities for better jobs
that colleagues took for granted were not so available to me. On virtually every
job application, the question continued to haunt me: "Have you ever been convicted of a felony or misdemeanor or denied bond in any state?" Staring
blankly at the application, I would often wonder, will this nightmare ever end?
For minorities, who have a higher rate of incarceration, the nightmare is even
more likely to occur.

To the average person, the ex-convict is an individual of questionable char-   6
acter. And without the experience of meeting a rehabilitated offender, there is
little chance that this image will change. It is reinforced by the fact that the only
thing usually newsworthy about an ex-convict is bad news—another arrest.

Yet the real news is that many former offenders are, like me, rehabilitated   7
members of society. No one would guess at our pasts. We don't deserve kudos
for not committing crimes, but our failings should not supersede decades of
personal growth and responsible citizenship. Unfortunately, that's often what
happens.

Under employment discrimination laws, hiring decisions cannot be made   8
on the basis of age, sex or the color of a person's skin. A job applicant does not
have to reveal a disability or medical condition, including former drug dependence. Employability is based on the ability to perform the essential function of
the job. Yet the former offender, whose past may be directly related to substance abuse, is expected to reveal his transgression.

No one is born an ex-convict; the title is earned and the individual must ac-   9
cept responsibility. Yet wouldn't it be nice if there were an ex-ex-con status? It
would feel good not to panic at the sight of a job application and that dreaded
question: "Have you ever been convicted of a felony or misdemeanor or denied
bond in any state?" This question, without exclusionary criteria (i.e., within the
last ten years), serves no one's interest. To those of us who have paid our debt
to society, it's a form of discrimination that undermines our efforts to continue
to rebuild our lives.

■ Building Vocabulary

For each numbered item, choose the meaning that most closely defines the
underlined word or phrase as it is used in the essay.

1. The word irrevocably most nearly means
   a. gladly
   b. irrelevantly
   c. temporarily
   (d.) permanently

2. The word scrutiny most nearly means

 (a.) inspection
 b. history
 c. dismissal
 d. cover-up

3. The word kudos most nearly means

 a. jobs
 (b.) praise
 c. criticism
 d. blame

4. The word supersede most nearly means

 (a.) overshadow
 b. record
 c. excuse
 d. maximize

5. The word transgression most nearly means

 a. translation
 (b.) wrongdoing
 c. virtue
 d. disability

■ Understanding the Essay

1. The author implies that the crimes that put him in prison

 a. were committed by someone else.
 (b.) were related to alcohol and drugs.
 c. were nonviolent.
 d. were "victimless crimes."

2. Since his release from prison, the author

 a. has been unable to find a job.
 b. has been in and out of substance-abuse programs.
 c. has been forced to accept minimum-wage jobs where interviewers don't ask too many questions.
 (d.) has earned multiple college degrees and written a book.

3. On job applications, how does the author say that he handled questions about past arrests and convictions?

(a.) He left the questions blank.

b. He lied.

c. He told the truth.

d. He made an appointment to discuss his prison sentence with the interviewer.

4. On employment applications, people can be asked about

a. former drug or alcohol abuse.

(b.) former arrests and convictions.

c. medical problems.

d. all of the above.

5. Which statement most accurately reflects the author's views on revealing ex-convict status to employers?

a. Ex-convicts should never be required to reveal their status to employers.

b. Ex-convicts should accept responsibility, including the responsibility of reporting their ex-convict status.

(c.) Some limitations, such as a time limitation or the ability to earn "ex-ex-convict status," would be reasonable.

d. If ex-convicts have to reveal their status, then people with disabilities, medical conditions, or former drug dependence should have to reveal theirs too.

■ Writing in the Margins

These questions encourage you to think not just about the essay but about the issues it raises. Your instructor may ask you to write down your answers, to discuss them in groups, or simply to think about them for class discussion.

Answers will vary.

1. List the pros and cons of granting "ex-ex-convict" status after a ten-year probationary period. Considering the pros and the cons, do you believe the idea is a good one?

2. Scanlon refers to questions regarding conviction of a crime as discrimination, pointing out that no applicant can be asked about drug dependence, disability, or any medical condition. Is asking about previous convictions discrimination against ex-convicts who are trying to rehabilitate themselves, or is it reasonable?

TOPICS FOR WRITING

Assignment 1: Hiring Ex-Convicts

Suppose you are an employer about to hire a job candidate. He has the right qualifications, excellent references, and a pleasing personality. When you ask him
about the one answer he has left blank on your employment questionnaire, he
confesses that he was in prison ten years ago. What can he say to you, if anything,
to convince you to hire him anyway? Answer in a paragraph or journal entry.

Assignment 2: Rehabilitation or Punishment?

Prisons are supposed to rehabilitate and to punish, but studies show that prisons
do little to rehabilitate criminals. Should prisons do more to rehabilitate convicts,
or should they mainly exist to punish lawbreakers and keep them off the streets?

Assignment 3: Making a Fair Policy

Suppose you were asked to come up with a plan for giving deserving ex-convicts
"ex-ex-convict" status. What plan would you devise that would be fair both to ex-
convicts who wanted to rehabilitate themselves and to employers who wanted to
hire reliable employees? Write a paragraph outlining your plan. Include any requirements you wish to impose, such as length of time out of prison, education,
or drug testing.

Assignment 4: Changes in the Justice System

If you could make one change in the American system of justice, what would it
be, and why? Answer in a paragraph.

Down-Covered Dinosaur

Michael D. Lemonick and Andrea Dorfman

Is T-Rex Tweety Bird's great-great-great-great-grandpa? Paleontologists are discovering surprising connections between dinosaurs and birds.

The once radical notion that birds descended from dinosaurs—or may even be dinosaurs, the only living branch of the family that ruled the earth eons ago—has got stronger and stronger since paleontologists first started taking it seriously a couple of decades ago. Remarkable similarities in bone structure between dinos and birds were the first clue. Then came evidence, thanks to a series of astonishing discoveries in China's Liaoning province over the past five years, that some dinosaurs may have borne feathers. But a few scientists still argued that the link was weak; the bone similarities could be a coincidence, they said. And maybe those primitive structures visible in some fossils were feathers—but maybe not. You had to use your imagination to see them. 1

Not anymore. A spectacularly preserved fossil of a juvenile dinosaur, announced by a team of paleontologists from the Chinese Academy of Geological Sciences and New York City's American Museum of Natural History in the latest issue of *Nature,* is about as good a missing link as anyone could want. "It has things that are undeniably feathers," exults Richard Prum, of the University of Kansas Natural History Museum, an expert on the evolution of feathers. "But it is clearly a small, vicious theropod similar to the velociraptors that chased the kids around the kitchen in *Jurassic Park.*" 2

In fact, this duck-size relative of Tyrannosaurus rex, dating from 124 million to 147 million years ago, has no fewer than three different types of feathers. The head sports a thick, fuzzy mat of short, hollow fibers ("like a butch cut," says Prum), while the shoulders and torso have plumelike "sprays" of extremely thin fibers up to two inches long. The backs of its arms and legs, meanwhile, are draped in multiple filaments arranged in a classic herringbone pattern around a central stem. Even the tail is covered with feathers, with a fan, or tuft, at the end. "It doesn't look anything like what most people think dinosaurs look like," explains the American Museum's Mark Norell, one of the team's co-leaders. "When this thing was alive, it looked like a Persian cat with feathers." 3

The find helps cement the dinosaur-bird connection, but it also casts new light on the mystery of why nature invented feathers in the first place. For the better part of a century, biologists have assumed that these specialized structures evolved for flight, but that's clearly not true. "The feathers on these dinosaurs aren't flight-worthy, and the animals couldn't fly," says paleontologist Kevin Padian, of the University of California, Berkeley. "They're too big, and 4 they don't have wings." So what was the original purpose of feathers? Nobody knows for sure; they might have been useful for keeping dinos dry, distracting predators or attracting mates, as peacocks do today.

But many biologists suspect that feathers originally arose to keep dinosaurs warm. The bone structure of dinosaurs shows that, unlike modern reptiles, they grew as fast as birds and mammals—which <u>dovetails</u> with a growing body of evidence that dinos were, in fact, warm-blooded. Says Padian: "They must have had a high basal metabolic rate to grow that fast. And I wouldn't be surprised if they had some sort of skin covering for insulation when they were small." Says Norell: "Even baby tyrannosaurs probably looked like this one."   5

At the rate feathered dinosaurs are turning up, it shouldn't take long to solidify scientists' understanding of precisely how and why feathers first arose and when the first birdlike creature realized they were useful for flight. Meanwhile, kids had better get used to the idea that T. Rex may have started life looking an awful lot like Tweety Bird.   6

■ Building Vocabulary

For each numbered item, choose the meaning that most closely defines the underlined word or phrase as it is used in the essay.

1. The word <u>radical</u> most nearly means
   a. ordinary
   b. fundamental
   c. accepted
   d. revolutionary

2. The word <u>paleontologists</u> most nearly means
   a. scientists who study fossils
   b. people who collect rocks
   c. biologists who study living creatures
   d. feathery dinosaurs that roamed the earth in ancient times

3. The word <u>cement</u> most nearly means
   a. solidify
   b. concrete
   c. confuse
   d. invent

4. The word <u>specialized</u> most nearly means
   a. confined only to dinosaurs
   b. extraordinary and outstanding
   c. designed for a specific purpose
   d. preferred over others

5. The word <u>dovetails</u> most nearly means
   a. tails of small, pigeonlike birds
   b. fits in
   c. disagrees
   d. method of joining used in carpentry

■ Understanding the Essay

1. Which description best expresses the writer's purpose?
   a. To catalog all of the different types of fossil remains of dinosaurs that have been found.
   b. To prove without a doubt that birds are direct descendants of dinosaurs.
   c. To examine the reason that feathers evolved.
   d. To describe a recent find and show how it changes our view of dinosaurs.

2. The connection between dinosaurs and birds was first suspected because of similarities in
   a. fossil remains.
   b. feathers.
   c. bone structure.
   d. wings.

3. The juvenile dinosaur bones described in the passage probably belonged to
   a. Tyrannosaurus Rex.
   b. a small, vicious theropod.
   c. a velociraptor.
   d. a Persian cat.

4. According to the passage, the original purpose of feathers on dinosaurs was probably *not*
   a. to allow flight.
   b. to keep dinosaurs dry.
   c. to provide warmth.
   d. to attract mates.

5. The author implies that in the future, research regarding feathered dinosaurs

a. is unlikely to find any serious support in the scientific community.

b. will help scientists to understand how feathers arose and became useful for flight.

c. will help to prove that dinosaurs flew.

d. will help scientists re-create the dinosaur from DNA preserved in amber and will enable the creation of an actual Jurassic Park.

■ **Writing in the Margins**

These questions encourage you to think not just about the essay but about the issues it raises. Your instructor may ask you to write down your answers, to discuss them in groups, or simply to think about them for class discussion.

Answers will vary.

1. Does this article suggest that our scientific knowledge of the world is fixed and unchanging, or is it open to revision? Explain

2. One of the issues raised in this essay is the question of why feathers first arose on living creatures. The assumption behind the question seems to be that features arise because they have some use. What are some possible functions of certain human characteristics, such as bodies with exposed skin rather than fur or feathers? Of long, slender fingers rather than short, toelike appendages? Of long hair on the head? Of beards on men, but not on women?

TOPICS FOR WRITING

Assignment 1: A Trip in the Wayback Machine

Imagine that you have taken a trip in a time machine, back to the time when dinosaurs lived. The room you are sitting in, the walls around you, all melt into nothingness, and you are left in the world of the dinosaur, some 130 million years ago. In a paragraph or journal entry, describe that world. What does it look like? What sounds do you hear? Sniff the air, and describe what you smell. Try to reproduce for your reader the sights, sounds, and smells of the prehistoric era when dinosaurs walked the earth.

Assignment 2: Dino Mania

From the PBS show *Barney* to the movie *Jurassic Park*, children seem to be crazy about dinosaurs. Write a paragraph describing the reasons that dinosaurs appeal to children.

Assignment 3: Under Revision

In part, the article describes how the scientific world's view of dinosaurs has changed. Most academic fields—science, history, literature, and medicine—are constantly under revision. Are your ideas, too, under revision? In a paragraph, discuss how an idea of yours has changed since you began college (or since you graduated from high school, or since some other important milestone).

Assignment 4: Science and You

The term "science" can cover a lot of territory. It can refer to paleontology, the study of fossil remains, as in this article. It can refer to astronomy and exploration of space, medicine, or even computer science. Although science often deals with theory, it also makes practical contributions to our lives: new machines are developed to do the work we need done, new medicines cure diseases, and new advances in surgery and dentistry help us live longer, healthier lives. Write a paragraph discussing one important scientific discovery or invention and the reason that it is important to you.

From the Welfare Rolls, a Mother's View

Elyzabeth Joy Stagg

A single mother writes about the lessons she has learned while on welfare.

1   I am a single mother of a three-year-old girl, and I'm expecting a son in November. My children have different fathers. I am a welfare mom, a burden to society. I live off your tax dollars.

2   I first went on welfare when I was pregnant with my daughter, after I lost my job and a house fire took nearly everything I owned. I was living in a hotel paid for by the Red Cross with no possessions, no job and no boyfriend.

3   Since then, I've gotten temp jobs that pay enough to let me get off welfare, but when they end, I find myself struggling again. For the last several months I scoured the classifieds and sent out resumes to find a job that would coincide with day care and pregnancy. I ended up serving food part-time at a bar for minimum wage. I tried to supplement that income as best I could, even directing plays and giving swing-dance lessons, but somehow I never seemed to get ahead. Now, due to complications with my pregnancy, I can't work at all and depend totally on welfare.

4   Being on welfare has taught me a lot. I've learned to go to the grocery store when it's the least busy, so I don't get annoyed looks from the people behind me in line when I pay with coupons and food stamps. I've learned that when I meet with a caseworker periodically, I should get to the welfare office forty-five minutes before it opens, or I'll be waiting all day.

5   The biggest lesson I've learned from being on welfare is that most people assume I don't want to work. When I list my job skills for the caseworkers, they can't seem to understand why I don't have a job. To them, and the rest of society, I am just one of the seven million people on welfare who survive off less than 1 percent of the federal budget.

6   But I'm more than just a statistic. I graduated in the top 10 percent of my high-school class. I'm studying nursing at my community college. I've played the flute since I was five. My parents have been married thirty years. I can type more than eighty words a minute. I'm bilingual. I know half a dozen computer programs inside and out. I'm twenty-four years old.

7   Now that I'm unable to work, I live off the $265 a month I receive from TANF (Temporary Assistance to Needy Families), which doesn't even cover my

rent. My utility bills get paid when I receive final disconnect notices and I can take the bills to a community agency for financial assistance. At the end of the month, when my daughter asks for an ice-cream cone I sometimes don't have the extra $2 to buy it for her.

I don't spend my money on anything I don't absolutely need. I borrow 8
videos from the library. I take my daughter to garage sales to look for clothes. I've never bought an alcoholic drink or a cigarette in my life. I don't buy expensive steaks or junk food. I drive a small car that leaks when it rains.

I don't have the kind of relationship I want with either of my kids' fathers. 9
Both men are more than 10 years older than I. They've been unable to keep their promises to help me in whatever way I needed. My daughter's father comes in and out of our lives. When he's gone, we miss him. The father of the new baby and I broke up in May because we choose to live different lifestyles. I doubt he will participate in the baby's life when it is born.

I acknowledge that it was my having unprotected sex, and getting pregnant, 10
that caused my situation. I don't regret becoming a mom, but I do regret the difficulties I've gone through as a result. My life isn't anything I'd hoped it would be. I find myself constantly having to make choices that force me to compromise what I really want. Do I struggle for a few more years to finish college, or do I work for little money the rest of my life?

My parents tell me I should give the new baby up for adoption. They won- 11
der how I will possibly manage with two kids. I don't wonder. I'll do it because I have to and, more important, because I want to. They're my children, and I wouldn't leave them for anything. It boggles my mind that there are so many parents out there who are not taking responsibility for their kids.

My daughter and my unborn child have forced me to grow up and taught 12
me more about life than any other experience I can possibly think of. They've taught me patience, compromise, love and that being a mom is a blessing. Although parenthood is often a struggle, I wouldn't trade it for anything.

I'm grateful for the help that welfare has given me in the past. It subsidized 13
my day care so I could go back to work and helped me return to school. I will continue to accept public assistance, but only until I can get back on my feet and make it on my own. I want more for my life. I want more for my children.

■ **Building Vocabulary**

For each numbered item, choose the meaning that most closely defines the underlined word or phrase as it is used in the essay.

1. The word scoured most nearly means
   a. scrubbed
   b. searched
   c. soured
   d. ignored

2. The word <u>supplement</u> most nearly means
   - (a.) add to
   - b. spend
   - c. earn
   - d. receive

3. The word <u>compromise</u> most nearly means
   - (a.) settle for
   - b. promise
   - c. agree to
   - d. put at risk

4. The phrase <u>boggles my mind</u> most nearly means
   - (a.) stuns me
   - b. pleases me
   - c. occurs to me
   - d. eludes me

5. The word <u>subsidized</u> most nearly means
   - a. dismissed
   - b. synchronized
   - c. sympathized
   - (d.) funded

■ Understanding the Essay

1. Which of the following is *not* one of the author's purposes in writing the essay?
   - a. To demonstrate that life on welfare is not easy.
   - b. To contradict the stereotype that welfare recipients are lazy and do not want to work.
   - (c.) To convince the reader that she is a burden to society.
   - d. To express her commitment to her children.

2. At the time the essay was written, the author was totally dependent on welfare because
   - a. her house and possessions had burned.
   - (b.) she had complications in her pregnancy.
   - c. she had grown comfortable on welfare.
   - d. she could not work out a schedule that would allow her to put her child in day care.

3. The statistic that "seven million people on welfare . . . survive on less that one percent of the federal budget" seems to suggest that
   a. the author is not a statistic.
   b. a large percentage of the federal budget is spent on welfare.
   c. no one seems to understand why the author does not have a job.
   (d.) a relatively small part of the federal budget is allocated to welfare.

4. The author states that she regrets
   a. having had unprotected sex.
   b. having had children.
   c. that having children has forced her to grow up too fast.
   (d.) the difficulties that having children has brought.

5. The author's parents have advised her to
   (a.) give up her unborn child for adoption.
   b. move back home with them.
   c. earn a college degree.
   d. take a job, even a minimum wage job, if it meant staying off welfare.

■ **Writing in the Margins**

These questions encourage you to think not just about the essay but about the issues it raises. Your instructor may ask you to write down your answers, to discuss them in groups, or simply to think about them for class discussion.

Answers will vary.

1. Based on the information in the essay, what are the advantages and disadvantages of living on welfare? Are there more advantages or more disadvantages?

2. Do you believe that people (both men and women) have a responsibility to postpone parenthood until they can afford it, or are children a responsibility that society should willingly take on?

TOPICS FOR WRITING

Assignment 1: Advice

The author outlines her possible choices in this way: "Do I struggle for a few more years to finish college, or do I work for little money the rest of my life?" She also mentions her parents' advice to give her unborn child up for adoption. If you were in a position to give the author (or someone in her situation) your best advice, what would your advice be? Write a paragraph or journal entry giving that advice.

Assignment 2: Responsibilities of an Absent Parent

The author writes that her daughter's father "comes in and out of our lives" and that the father of her unborn child will probably not participate in his child's life. When a child is in the custody of one parent, what responsibilities should the absent parent have?

Assignment 3: Safety Net

Financial experts advise that everyone should have the equivalent of six months' living expenses as a safety net in case of unexpected unemployment. However, the truth is that many Americans are just one paycheck away from financial disaster. Although not everyone has a financial safety net equivalent to six months' salary, some people have other safety nets in place. These informal safety nets may include family and friends who can be relied on for temporary help, other skills that can serve as alternate methods of earning money, or an ability to shift into "thrift mode" and live on very little. Some also rely on government safety nets such as unemployment or welfare. What are your safety nets? In a paragraph, describe the safety nets you have in place now in case of financial disaster, or alternatively, describe the safety nets you intend to set up for yourself when you are settled in your future career.

Assignment 4: Money, Money, Money

The writer of the essay you have just read would have had fewer problems and fewer tough decisions if she had only had enough money. Although money can't buy happiness, the lack of money can certainly lead to misery. Read the following quotations about money, and choose one as the basis for your paragraph.

The topic sentence of your paragraph should incorporate the quotation and should look something like this:

> I agree/disagree with the writer who said, "Money can't buy happiness."

> I agree/disagree with Publilius Syrus, who said, "A good reputation is more valuable than money."

Note the punctuation and the use of quotation marks. For an explanation of comma use before the word *who,* see Chapter 20, "Relative Pronouns." For an explanation of the use of quotation marks, see Chapter 30, "Quotation Marks."

- Money can't buy happiness. *Anonymous*
- A good reputation is more valuable than money. *Publilius Syrus*

- The love of money is the root of all evil.   *New Testament, I Timothy 6:10*
- Lack of money is the root of all evil.   *George Bernard Shaw*
- Money talks . . . but all mine ever says is good-bye.   *Anonymous*
- What's money? A man is a success if he gets up in the morning and goes to bed at night and in between does what he wants to do.   *Bob Dylan*

Acknowledgments

Maya Angelou, "A Day Away" from *Wouldn't Take Nothing for My Journey Now* by Maya Angelou, copyright © 1993 by Maya Angelou. Used by permission of Random House, Inc.

Snow Anderson, "Borrowed History" from *Newsweek*, February 28, 2000. All rights reserved. Reprinted by permission.

Barbara Ehrenreich, "Employment Test," excerpt from "Scrubbing in Maine" from *Nickel and Dimed: On (Not) Getting By in America* by Barbara Ehrenreich, © 2001 by Barbara Ehrenreich. Reprinted by permission of Henry Holt and Company, LLC.

Leonard Pitts Jr., "Broken Windows: Crudity in Language" from *The Miami Herald*, February 15, 2001. Reprinted with the permission of *The Miami Herald* via The Copyright Clearance Center.

Constance Daley, "Confrontation at Register Two" (original title, "Don't Blame Me!") from a collection of columns published in *Skyline to Shoreline*, initially appearing in *The American Reporter* and reprinted in *Golden Isle Weekend*. Reprinted with the permission of the author.

Cecelie Berry, "Walking the Tightrope between Black and White" from *Newsweek*, February 7, 2000. All rights reserved. Reprinted by permission.

Lee Coppola, "My Dead Dog May Already Be a Winner!" from *Newsweek*, July 5, 1999. All rights reserved. Reprinted by permission.

Walter Scanlon, "Imprisoned by Ex-Convict Status" (original title, "It's Time I Shed My Ex-Convict Status") from *Newsweek*, February 21, 2000. All rights reserved. Reprinted by permission.

Michael D. Lemonick and Andrea Dorfman, "Down-Covered Dinosaur" from *Time*, May 7, 2001. © 2001 TIME Inc. Reprinted by permission.

Elyzabeth Joy Stagg, "From the Welfare Rolls, a Mother's View" from *Newsweek*, August 23, 1999. All rights reserved. Reprinted by permission.

Paul Raeburn, Julie Forster, Dean Foust, and Diane Brady, "Why We're So Fat" from *Business Week*, October 21, 2002. Copyright © 2002 by *Business Week*.

Cara DiMarco, excerpt from "Healthy and Dysfunctional Relationships" from *Moving Through Life Transitions with Power and Purpose, 2/e,* by Cara DiMarco, © 2000. Reprinted by permission of Pearson Education, Inc., Upper Saddle River, NJ.

Index

Instructor's Guide

This Instructor's Guide includes icebreakers, suggestions for using the book, a discussion of grading and class matters, and model syllabi for ten- and fifteen-week terms. Please take whatever you find useful and make it your own.

Beginnings

The following icebreaker strategies can be used during the first week of class to introduce students to one another and to the writing process.

Icebreaker 1: Introductions

Setting aside time for introductions during the first class session allows students to get to know one another and to speak out publicly during the first class session, paving the way for class participation as the term progresses.

Encourage students to talk about their major, their families, their future careers, and generally anything they want to divulge as they introduce themselves. To break the ice and model an introduction, you might go first. One of this textbook's authors always tells students how scared she was on her first day as a twenty-eight-year-old first-year student, how college helped her find her true calling in life, and how fortunate she feels to be teaching them. When you ask for volunteers to speak, the first students to volunteer are usually willing to open up a bit and to reveal personal information. Most others follow suit, but there are always a few students who simply tell their names and majors. But the result is the same. When the introductions are finished, the class is no longer a class of strange faces, but a class of fellow human beings with similar hopes and fears and dreams.

Icebreaker 2: Why Do People Write?

Another effective icebreaker is the question "Why do people write?" Ask students to jot a quick list of reasons that people write. Then have students form groups of three or four and put their ideas together into a list of five reasons.

After five minutes or so, go to each group, asking for one reason that people write. (Groups after the first one can be asked to give a reason that has not been mentioned before.) With no prompting from you, students will come up with excellent reasons every time: recording history, expressing feelings, transmitting information, recording agreements, and on and on. This exercise not only gets students talking to one another about writing but also reinforces the importance of writing in our culture.

Icebreaker 3: What Are the Qualities of Good Writing?

The third icebreaker is similar to the second. Ask students to jot a list of qualities of good writing, and then ask them to form groups to make a list of five qualities of good writing in priority order, from most important to least. Discuss their lists and their priorities, which will probably not be too different from your own. This exercise breaks the ice and brings out what students already know about good writing.

One Approach to the Text

The suggestions for specific chapters and the sample syllabi reflect the approach of one of the authors to the text and to teaching the class. If your approach is different, the text, with its flexible three-part structure, can be easily adapted to your own methods.

Chapter 1, "The Writing Process"

I always use the Writing Assignment, "Writing and You," at the end of Chapter 1 as an in-class exercise. It helps me to learn a little about the students' writing abilities and attitudes toward writing. In the interests of time, we skip the revision step. I never grade or mark this exercise, but I do keep it on file as a baseline sample of students' writing. I also discuss the exercise in class, reading excerpts from different paragraphs so that students can see the variety of attitudes toward writing in the class.

Chapter 2, "Preparing to Write"

In addition to doing individual prewriting exercises at home, students benefit from prewriting as a class. I always have students do two forms of prewriting: a timed freewriting and a brainstorming exercise.

First comes the timed freewriting (usually about five minutes). I challenge my students to write without stopping for the entire five minutes. I watch them as they write, and of course, some people do stop writing, regardless of the instructions. (I have even seen people stop to check dictionaries!) But I do not try to alter their behavior; I simply observe. I then collect the prewriting and hold up (but do not read aloud) samples—long ones, short ones—and describe to them the behavior I observed as they did the exercise. The activity always provides the opportunity to reiterate the uncensored and freewheeling nature of prewriting.

Students also do a brainstorming exercise in class. I let the students suggest a topic. Then I ask for their associations on the topic, reminding them not to censor themselves—even seemingly silly answers have a place in prewriting. I write answers on the board until the flood of suggestions slows to a trickle. Then I ask which ideas seem to be related, which might belong as different points in a single paragraph. If the exercise is going well, we sometimes even try to work out a topic sentence and points of development. The activity serves as an informal bridge to a discussion of topic sentences in Chapter 3.

Journal Writing

I like to use journals for several reasons. Journals allow students to begin writing from day one of the class. They loosen up students' writing muscles and help students become better, less fearful writers. They improve students' ability to get ideas on paper, and they can help students develop a flow, a natural voice in writing.

If you would like to use journals but hesitate because they will add to an already hefty grading load, there are ways to give students the benefit of journals without making your job too much more difficult. Here are some suggestions:

1. Never mark errors in students' journals. Journals are tools for rehearsal and experimentation. An occasional brief, positive comment every other entry or so is enough to keep students encouraged. Let students know that although you will be examining their paragraphs and other compositions carefully, journals are strictly for practice and for writing improvement.

2. Stagger the due dates if you are using journals in several classes.

3. Keep your grading system simple. A system wherein students receive 100 possible points per journal due date works well: if five entries are due, then each entry is worth 20 points.

4. If you arrange your class so that part of the term is "writing-heavy" and part is not, use journals only during the part of the term when students are writing less.

5. One time-saving method that I don't recommend is "selective reading" of journal entries—skipping most and reading at random. I have heard some people say it works for them, but I have always felt that if I require students to write something, I obligate myself to read it. In addition, students often "test" me to see whether I really read all those journals. Some write notes in the middle of a journal entry, asking me direct questions. I answer in the margins. Some make little comments in the middle of an entry: "I enjoy your class." "Thanks," I write. Every time I pass one of those little tests, I convince yet another

student that yes, I'm paying attention and yes, I care about his or her writing.

A model journal assignment handout follows.

Your Journal Assignment

Why a Journal?

A journal is a time-honored method for expressing opinions, recording thoughts, and practicing writing. Writing is a skill, and no skill is improved without practice. Journal writing is a relatively painless way to get some of the practice that will make you a better writer.

Guidelines for Journal Writing

Subject Matter: You may write about issues that concern you, react to assigned or unassigned reading selections, and practice specific writing techniques. For a topic list, see Chapter 2 of your textbook. Entries should show evidence of your thoughtful consideration of the topic you choose.

Grading: Your journal is graded twice during the term. Your grades for each journal period will be averaged at the end of the term.

Format: Please do your journals on 8½ × 11 lined looseleaf paper or, if you type your entries, on 8½ × 11 white paper. Journals should be done in ink or on a word processor. Each time you turn in your journal, turn in the entire journal, even the parts that have been graded. Entries should be numbered.

Due Dates: _____

_____

Chapter 3: "Writing a Paragraph: The Topic Sentence"

Chapter 4, "Writing a Paragraph: Support"

Chapter 5, "Writing a Paragraph: Unity and Coherence"

These chapters lead students through the process of writing a paragraph. It's a good idea to provide plenty of feedback as students move through these chapters. For example, the topic sentences that students write for practice in Chapter 3 can be put on the board for discussion by the class. Chapter 4 and 5 exercises may also be discussed in class, and students may be assigned to work in peer review groups to evaluate the paragraphs they are writing.

Chapter 6, "Revising, Proofreading, and Formatting"

The "Checklist for Revision" in the chapter is a good tool to introduce and to use throughout the term.

Chapter 7, "Essays, Essay Exams, and Summary Reports"

This chapter takes students from paragraph to essay. When students write an essay, it is often helpful to schedule time for whole-class feedback for thesis statements and peer-group feedback for the other elements of the essay.

The sections on essay exams and summary reports may be used by some instructors and not by others. In the section on summary reports, paraphrasing and summarizing may need particular emphasis. A field trip to the college library is a good accompaniment to this chapter.

Chapter 8, "Communication Beyond the Classroom: Oral Presentations and E-Mail"

Not only does this chapter allow students practice in different types of writing as they write presentations and e-mail messages, but it also prepares them for the two types of communication they will use most often beyond the English classroom: oral communication and email. Is e-mail something that needs to be taught? I don't even ask that question anymore. I have received too many e-mail messages with no salutation and no signature that read, in all caps, "HEY I JUST WONDERED WHAT THE HOMEWORK WAS FOR TOMORROW."

The Grammar Chapters

In a typical term, it is not possible to address each grammar chapter with students in class. Therefore, most instructors will want to address essential chapters in class. For most instructors, those essential chapters center around sentence structure, verbs, pronouns, and major sentence errors such as sentence fragments and run-ons.

Other chapters that are lower on the priority list can be handled in various ways. Some can be briefly reviewed in class, while easier chapters, such as "Word Choice," "Words Commonly Confused," and "Capital Letters," can often be assigned as independent study chapters. If your students have access to computers, show them how to use the Wordsmith website (www.prenhall.com/arlov). As they complete the chapters, you may wish to have them send website exercises to you.

Some chapters that you do not cover in class you may wish to refer students to on an "as needed" basis. I always make a standing offer to give extra credit for any extra work students wish to do from the textbook or the Wordsmith website (www.prenhall.com/arlov).

The Readings

Good readers make good writers, but many students have never developed the habit of reading for pleasure. Readings can be used in class discussions to point up similarities between professional essays and the kinds of compositions that students are writing. These readings illustrate that unity, coherence, and vivid, specific support are not just meaningless words in a textbook, they are techniques employed by people who earn their living by writing.

Here are some ideas for using readings not assigned for class discussion, or for using readings if you do not use them as a basis for class discussion:

1. If you assign journals, allow students the option of writing about the readings. Journal entries could react to the reading—agreement, disagreement, or discussion—or could answer a question from the "Writing in the Margins" or "Topics for Writing" section.

2. Assign readings as extra-credit projects.

Grading and Class Matters

English teachers traditionally have heavier grading loads than instructors in other disciplines. My math colleagues in particular, often remark that they are glad they "don't have all those papers to grade."

English teachers also traditionally assign a lot of homework. If we graded it all, we would never do anything else.

It is up to each of us to develop a system to make our grading accurate, efficient, and helpful to the student. I share my methods with you here. If you are a new instructor, take heart. I know that the grading load can seem impossible at times. I can still remember my early days as an instructor, when I sat at home all weekend grading papers. Don't worry. It will get better.

Homework

I assign plenty of homework, but I grade much less than I assign. When I take up homework, I reserve the option to grade it or to assign a check indicating that the work was received. If I do not take up the work, I call on students at random or go down the rows, calling on students in turn. Either way, I can usually gauge students' level of preparation.

Calling on Students in Class

Because I know that calling on students in class puts them on the spot and exposes them to possible embarrassment, I have developed a few techniques to make the experience more comfortable for them. One of my favorites is a technique I call "Second Opinion." I establish it early in the term by saying, after a student has given a correct answer to a relatively easy question, "Let's get a second opinion." Everyone looks at me, and I make a joke of it, saying "Well, you'd get a second opinion if the doctor wanted to take your pancreas out. Maybe we should get one before we take this comma out." Then I say, "Of course, I'm not saying Ms. Smith's answer is wrong, just that a second opinion never hurts." Then I ask another student, "Do you agree that we need to take the comma out?" The student says, "Yes," and I say, "Excellent!" or "Great minds think alike," and we move on.

A little later, I ask for a second opinion on another question, and another. Then, along comes a wrong answer, and I ask for a second opinion, immediately taking the focus off the person who answered incorrectly. When I have two conflicting opinions, I say, "Looks like we need a tiebreaker," and ask someone else. Then, we have a discussion of which answer is correct and why. The focus, by then, has turned totally away from the student who has answered incorrectly and is where it belongs—on the question at hand.

Grading Students' Writing

Different instructors have different theories about grading paragraphs and essays. If you have not yet settled on a grading method, here is a synopsis of two methods of grading—the point system and the holistic system. There are many possible variations on each system, and you can easily tailor either system to your needs.

The Point System

One often-heard complaint about the grading of writing is that there is too much subjectivity involved. The point system attempts to eliminate that subjectivity by assigning a point value to various elements of a paragraph. The following example shows a point system that assigns 50 percent of the point value to content and structure and 50 percent to grammar, punctuation, and mechanics.

Example

Elements of the Paragraph, 50%

Topic sentence: 10 points

Support: 25 points

Coherence and Transitional Elements: 5 points

Unity: 5 points

Summary Sentence: 5 points

Grammar, Punctuation, and Mechanics, 50%

Fragments, run-ons, comma splices, and other sentence structure errors: −10 points each

Verb errors and pronoun errors: −5 points each

Errors in spelling, word usage, and mechanics: −2 points each

Maximum points subtracted, 50

The point system, of course, can be manipulated to emphasize the elements that the instructor wishes to stress. I know one instructor who starts out with a system similar to this one but doubles the points off for each grammar error after midterm.

Advantages and Disadvantages of the Point System

The main advantage to a point system is that students perceive it as fair. It is also useful in classes where grammar is the main emphasis. A point system allows paragraphs to be, in essence, exercises in grammatically correct expression.

The point system has disadvantages, too. It can sometimes be *too* objective. It may not adequately reward such elements as style and word choice. The less tangible elements that can sometimes mean the difference between a good paragraph and an excellent one all but disappear under the point system. In addition, the point system can sometimes result in grades so low that students who initially make low grades but improve late in the term have little chance of passing.

The Holistic System

The holistic system of grading is a subjective system that has many permutations. When I was a student, I received some papers that bore no marks except a grade—not very satisfactory in terms of feedback. I received others with a grade followed by a brief comment. My favorite type of feedback, though, entailed comments interspersed throughout the composition, with a brief sentence or two to accompany the grade at the bottom. I knew that the instructor had read my work carefully, and I usually found the comments helpful and encouraging.

It is this method that I use now with my own students. I scan the paragraph and physically check off elements such as topic sentence, summary sentence, and transitional expressions. I make specific comments in the margins beside the body of the paragraph, such as "good transition," "excellent word choice," or "example needed." I also mark errors, particularly major errors.

My comments at the end of the paragraph are general comments. I try to balance praise and criticism in comments such as "A strong topic sentence and summary sentence. Work on providing sharp detail and good examples." I always find something positive to say. Even constructive criticism is hard to take without an encouraging word or two.

Conferences

I try to have at least two conferences with my students during the term. The first is a rough draft conference. I make comments on the draft and give advice on revising the paragraph.

The second conference is an exit conference (and sometimes a paragraph conference as well). It allows me to discuss a student's progress and expected grade. At this conference, depending on the student's standing in class, I can congratulate, encourage, or soften the blow, whichever is appropriate.

Time does not usually permit additional scheduled conferences, but I make myself available during office hours to any student who wants to confer with me about a work in progress.

Using a Weekly Agenda

I have known instructors who could create a ten- or fifteen-week syllabus and stick to it like Velcro for the entire term. For most of us, however, the term-long syllabus is a guideline, not a day-by-day schedule. As a day-by-day guide for my classes, I use a printed weekly agenda.

Before I began using a weekly agenda, I was occasionally guilty of beginning a class with the not-so-professional question "Okay, what were we doing last time?" Now, at the beginning of each week, I pass out to my students an agenda of everything planned for the week, including all assignments. (I give out a term-length syllabus on the first day of class, but I tell students it is tentative and that we will go by our weekly agenda.)

It takes a few minutes each week to sit down and type up the agenda, but it is, in my view, time well spent. After the first term that you use the system, you will have all your weekly agendas stored on your computer, and you can simply go back in and make minor alterations as needed. I have been using agendas for so long that I now have several versions ready to go, with minor modifications, for day classes, night classes, MW classes, TTh classes, and classes in both the regular term and the shortened summer term.

Using a weekly agenda makes my life easier, and I hope it will work for you. The following sample is for Week 2 of an evening class during the summer term.

Sample Weekly Agenda

English   **Week 2, MW Class**   **Arlov**

Monday

Reminder: Journals are due next Monday, June 17

Continue discussion of Chapter 3, "Writing a Paragraph: The Topic Sentence"

Begin discussion of Chapter 4, "Writing a Paragraph: Support"

Begin discussion of Chapter 11, "Subject-Verb Agreement"

In-class peer review and revision of topic sentences.

For Wednesday:

Continue work on journals.

Homework TBA in Chapters 4 and 11 (TBA = to be announced)

Wednesday

Continue discussion of Chapter 4, "Writing a Paragraph: Support"

Review selected homework exercises

Continue discussion of Chapter 11, "Subject-Verb Agreement"

In class: Write a rough draft of your paragraph

For Monday:

Chapter 11, "Subject-Verb Agreement," through Review Exercise 4

Model Syllabi for a Ten-Week Quarter and a Fifteen-Week Semester

Each instructor will adapt *Wordsmith* to his or her own needs. The model syllabi represent possible ways of organizing a ten-week or fifteen-week class using *Wordsmith* as a text. I have included more than I could address in a typical term. If you decide to adopt some modification of this syllabus, it will be easier for you to weed out excess material than to add new items.

The syllabus is arranged by week rather than by day. That way, you can adjust it to meet your needs whether you are teaching a class that meets for several hours once a week or one that meets daily.

A Model Syllabus: Ten-Week Quarter

Assignment for week 1 (given on first day of class):

Begin journals.
Read Chapter 1 "The Writing Process."
Read Chapter 2, "Preparing to Write."

Week 1

- Welcome
- Discussion of syllabus and class expectations
- Journal assignment (handout sheet)
- Introductions
- Icebreaker/Group Activity—Why Do People Write?
- Icebreaker/Group Activity—What Are the Qualities of Good Writing?
- Writing Assignment, Chapter 1, "The Writing Process."
- Brief discussion of the writing process (Chapter 1)
- Chapter 2, "Preparing to Write." Freewriting and brainstorming exercises.
- Brief review of Chapter 9, "Parts of Speech."

- Begin Chapter 10, "Verbs and Subjects." (In class, discuss each section of the chapter and review the first two or three items in each practice. Homework is to read the chapter, complete the practice items, and complete Review Exercises 1 and 2.)

Assignment for week 2:

Continue journals.

Read Chapter 3, "Writing a Paragraph: The Topic Sentence," and do selected exercises (suggested: 1, 2, 3, and 4).

Read "A Day Away" by Maya Angelou.

Chapter 10, "Verbs and Subjects," through Review Exercise 2.

Week 2

- Discussion of Chapter 3, "Writing a Paragraph: The Topic Sentence."

- Discussion of "A Day Away" by Maya Angelou, focusing on topic sentences and main ideas.

- Turn in Exercise 4, Chapter 3—the topic sentences done at home. Selected topic sentences will be put on the board and evaluated by the class.

- In class: Exercises 5 and 6, Chapter 3, "Writing a Paragraph: The Topic Sentence," together as a class.

- Discuss Chapter 10, "Verbs and Subjects," through Review Exercise 2.

- Computer classroom option: Introduce the *Wordsmith* website. In class, complete a multiple choice or pattern match exercise for Chapter 10, using books as a reference. (Note: The exercises on the *Wordsmith* website are meant to be completed using the text as a reference.)

- Begin Chapter 11, "Subject-Verb Agreement." (In class, discuss each section of the chapter and review the first two or three items in each practice. Homework is to read the chapter, complete the practice items, and complete Review Exercises 1 and 2.)

- In class or at home: Writing Assignment 1, 2, or 3 from Chapter 3, "Writing a Paragraph: The Topic Sentence."

Assignment for week 3:

Read Chapter 4, "Writing a Paragraph: Support," selected exercises.

Read "Confrontation at Register Two," by Constance Daley.

Continue working on journals—5 entries due in week 3.

Chapter 11, "Subject-Verb Agreement," through Review Exercise 2.

Week 3

- Turn in journals (first five entries)

- In-class peer review and revision of Writing Assignment 1, 2, or 3 from Chapter 3, "Writing a Paragraph: The Topic Sentence."

- Discuss Chapter 4, "Writing a Paragraph: Support."

- Discuss "Confrontation at Register Two," by Constance Daley, focusing on support.

- Chapter 11, "Subject-Verb Agreement." Discuss selected practices and review exercises.

- Brief review of Chapter 12, "Irregular Verbs." Assign pattern match or multiple choice website assignment (www.prenhall.com/arlov).

- Begin Chapter 13, "Verb Tenses." (In class, discuss each section of the chapter and review the first two or three items in each practice. Homework is to read the chapter, complete the practice items, and complete Review Exercises 1 and 2.)

Assignment for week 4:

Continue journals.

Chapter 13, "Verb Tenses," through Review Exercise 2.

Read "Walking the Tightrope between Black and White" by Cecelie Berry.

Week 4

- Discuss "Walking the Tightrope between Black and White" by Cecelie Berry, focusing on support.

- In-class writing assignment: Writing Assignment 1, 2, or 3 from Chapter 4, "Writing a Paragraph: Support."

- Discuss selected Practices and Review Exercises in Chapter 13, "Verb Tenses."

- Begin Chapter 14, "Coordination and Subordination." (In class, discuss each section of the chapter and review the first two or three items in each practice. Homework is to read the chapter, complete the practice items, and complete Review Exercises 1 and 2.)

- In-class peer review and revision of Writing Assignment 1, 2, or 3 from Chapter 4, "Writing a Paragraph: Support."

Assignment for week 5:

Continue journals.

Read Chapter 5, "Writing a Paragraph: Unity and Coherence," and do selected exercises.

Read "Imprisoned by Ex-Convict Status" by Walter Scanlon.

Chapter 14, "Coordination and Subordination," through Review Exercise 2.

Week 5

- Discuss Chapter 5, "Writing a Paragraph: Unity and Coherence," and review selected exercises.

- Discuss "Imprisoned by Ex-Convict Status" by Walter Scanlon in terms of unity and coherence.

- In-class writing assignment: Writing Assignment 1, 2, or 3 in Chapter 5.

- Discuss Chapter 14, "Coordination and Subordination," through Review Exercise 2.

- Begin Chapter 16, "Run-on Sentences." (In class, discuss each section of the chapter and review the first two or three items in each practice. Homework is to read the chapter, complete the practice items, and complete Review Exercises 1 and 2.)

Assignment for week 6:

Journals due (entries 5–10).

Read Chapter 6, "Revising, Proofreading, and Formatting."

Chapter 16, "Run-on Sentences," through Review Exercise 2.

Week 6

- Journals due (entries 5–10).

- Group proofreading exercise from Chapter 6.

- Proofread, revise, and format the paragraph written last week (Writing Assignment 1, 2, or 3 in Chapter 5, "Writing a Paragraph: Unity and Coherence").

- Discuss selected Practices and Review Exercises in Chapter 16, "Run-on Sentences."

- Begin Chapter 17, "Sentence Fragments." (In class, discuss each section of the chapter and review the first two or three items in each practice. Homework is to read the chapter, complete the practice items, and complete Review Exercises 1 and 2.)

Assignment for week 7:
Read Chapter 7, "Essays, Essay Exams, and Summary Reports."
Chapter 17, "Sentence Fragments," through Review Exercise 2.

Week 7

- Discuss Chapter 7, "Essays, Essay Exams, and Summary Reports." Do selected exercises.

- Field trip to library to choose article for summary report.

- At home: Read and annotate article.

- In class: Outline and draft summary report.

- Peer review of summary reports.

- Review Chapter 17, "Sentence Fragments," through Exercise 2.

- Begin Chapter 18, "Pronoun Case." (In class, discuss each section of the chapter and review the first two or three items in each practice. Homework is to read the chapter, complete the practice items, and complete Review Exercises 1 and 2.)

Assignment for week 8:
In Chapter 8, "Communication Beyond the Classroom: Oral Presentations and E-Mail," read the section on e-mail and do selected exercises.
Chapter 18, "Pronoun Case," through Review Exercise 2.

Week 8

- Discuss selected exercises, Chapter 8, "Communication Beyond the Classroom: Oral Presentations and E-Mail."

- In-class writing assignment: E-mail writing assignment selected from Chapter 8.

- Peer review and in-class revision of e-mail.

- Discuss Chapter 18, "Pronoun Case," through Review Exercise 2.

- Begin Chapter 19, "Pronoun Agreement, Reference, and Point of View." (In class, discuss each section of the chapter and review the first two or three items in each practice. Homework is to read the chapter, complete the practice items, and complete Review Exercises 1 and 2.)

Assignment for week 9:

In Chapter 8, "Communication Beyond the Classroom: Oral Presentations and E-Mail," read the section on oral presentations.

Chapter 19, "Pronoun Agreement, Reference, and Point of View," through Review Exercise 2.

Week 9

- Discuss oral presentations section from Chapter 8, "Communication Beyond the Classroom: Oral Presentations and E-Mail."

- In class or at home: Craft a 2–3 minute presentation. Use assignment 1, 2, or 3 from "Assignments for Prepared Speeches" in Chapter 8, or prepare a presentation based on the summary report written in week 6.

- Discuss Chapter 19, "Pronoun Agreement, Reference, and Point of View," through Review Exercise 2.

- Begin Chapter 27, "Commas." (In class, discuss each section of the chapter and review the first two or three items in each practice. Homework is to read the chapter, complete the practice items, and complete Review Exercises 1 and 2.)

Assignment for week 10:

Chapter 27, "Commas," through Review Exercise 2.

Rehearse and prepare to present oral presentations

Read "Broken Windows" by Leonard Pitts.

Read "From the Welfare Rolls, a Mother's View" by Elyzabeth Joy Stagg.

Week 10

- Oral presentations.
- Discuss "Broken Windows" by Leonard Pitts and "From the Welfare Rolls, a Mother's View" by Elyzabeth Joy Stagg.
- Discuss selected Practices and Review Exercises in Chapter 27, "Commas."
- Final exam: Selected Writing Assignment chosen from the assignments listed after "Broken Windows" by Leonard Pitts or "From the Welfare Rolls, a Mother's View" by Elyzabeth Joy Stagg.

A Model Syllabus: Fifteen-Week Semester

Assignment for week 1 (given on first day of class):
Begin journals.
Read Chapter 1, "The Writing Process."

Week 1

- Welcome
- Discussion of syllabus and class expectations
- Journal assignment (handout sheet)
- Introductions
- Icebreaker/Group Activity—Why Do People Write?
- Icebreaker/Group Activity—What Are the Qualities of Good Writing?
- Writing Assignment, Chapter 1
- Brief discussion of the writing process (Chapter 1)

Assignment for week 2:
Continue journals.
Read Chapter 2, "Preparing to Write."

Week 2

- Chapter 2, "Preparing to Write." Freewriting and brainstorming exercises.
- Brief review of Chapter 9, "Parts of Speech."

- Begin Chapter 10, "Verbs and Subjects." (In class, discuss each section of the chapter and review the first two or three items in each practice. Homework is to read the chapter, complete the practice items, and complete Review Exercises 1 and 2.)

Assignment for week 3:

Continue journals.

Read Chapter 3, "Writing a Paragraph: The Topic Sentence," and do selected exercises (suggested: 1, 2, 3, and 4).

Chapter 10, "Verbs and Subjects," through Review Exercise 2.

Week 3

- Discussion of Chapter 3, "Writing a Paragraph: The Topic Sentence."

- Turn in Exercise 4, Chapter 3—the topic sentences done at home. Selected topic sentences will be put on the board and evaluated by the class.

- In class: Exercises 5 and 6, Chapter 3, "Writing a Paragraph: The Topic Sentence," together as a class.

- Discuss Chapter 10, "Verbs and Subjects," through Review Exercise 2.

- Computer classroom option: Introduce the *Wordsmith* Website. In class, complete a multiple choice or pattern match exercise for Chapter 10, using books as a reference. (Note: The exercises on the *Wordsmith* website are meant to be completed using the text as a reference.)

Assignment for week 4:

Continue journals.

Read "A Day Away" by Maya Angelou.

Week 4

- Discussion of "A Day Away" by Maya Angelou, focusing on topic sentences and main ideas.

- In class: Writing Assignment 1, 2, or 3 from Chapter 3, "Writing a Paragraph: The Topic Sentence."

- Begin Chapter 11, "Subject-Verb Agreement." (In class, discuss each section of the chapter and review the first two or three items in each practice. Homework is to read the chapter, complete the practice items, and complete Review Exercises 1 and 2.)

- In-class peer review and revision of Writing Assignment 1, 2, or 3 from Chapter 3, "Writing a Paragraph: The Topic Sentence."

Assignment for week 5:

Continue working on journals—5 entries due in week 5.

Read Chapter 4, "Writing a Paragraph: Support," selected exercises.

Read "Confrontation at Register Two" by Constance Daley.

Chapter 11, "Subject-Verb Agreement," through Review Exercise 2.

Week 5

- Turn in journals (first five entries).
- Discuss Chapter 4, "Writing a Paragraph: Support."
- Discuss "Confrontation at Register Two" by Constance Daley, focusing on support.
- Chapter 11, "Subject-Verb Agreement." Discuss selected practices and review exercises.
- Brief review of Chapter 12, "Irregular Verbs." Assign pattern match or multiple choice website assignment (www.prenhall.com/arlov).
- Begin Chapter 13, "Verb Tenses." (In class, discuss each section of the chapter and review the first two or three items in each practice. Homework is to read the chapter, complete the practice items, and complete Review Exercises 1 and 2.)

Assignment for week 6:

Continue journals.

Chapter 13, "Verb Tenses," through Review Exercise 2.

Read "Walking the Tightrope between Black and White" by Cecelie Berry.

Week 6

- Discuss "Walking the Tightrope between Black and White" by Cecelie Berry, focusing on support.
- In-class writing assignment: Writing Assignment 1, 2, or 3 from Chapter 4, "Writing a Paragraph: Support."

- Discuss selected Practices and Review Exercises in Chapter 13, "Verb Tenses."

- Begin Chapter 14, "Coordination and Subordination." (In class, discuss each section of the chapter and review the first two or three items in each practice. Homework is to read the chapter, complete the practice items, and complete Review Exercises 1 and 2.)

Assignment for week 7:

Continue journals.

Read Chapter 5, "Writing a Paragraph: Unity and Coherence," and do selected exercises.

Read "Imprisoned by Ex-Convict Status" by Walter Scanlon.

Chapter 14, "Coordination and Subordination," through Review Exercise 2.

Week 7

- Discuss Chapter 5, "Writing a Paragraph: Unity and Coherence," and review selected exercises.

- Discuss "Imprisoned by Ex-Convict Status" by Walter Scanlon in terms of unity and coherence.

- In-class writing assignment: Writing Assignment 1, 2, or 3 in Chapter 5.

- Discuss Chapter 14, "Coordination and Subordination," through Review Exercise 2.

- Begin Chapter 16, "Run-on Sentences." (In class, discuss each section of the chapter and review the first two or three items in each practice. Homework is to read the chapter, complete the practice items, and complete Review Exercises 1 and 2.)

Assignment for week 8:

Continue journals.

Read Chapter 6, "Revising, Proofreading, and Formatting."

Chapter 16, "Run-on Sentences," through Review Exercise 2.

Week 8

- Group Proofreading Exercise from Chapter 6.

- Proofread, revise, and format the Writing Assignment already completed in Week 6 or Week 7 (Writing Assignment 1, 2, or 3 from Chapter 4, "Writing a Paragraph: Support" or Writing Assignment 1, 2, or 3 in Chapter 5, "Writing a Paragraph: Unity and Coherence").

- Discuss selected Practices and Review Exercises in Chapter 16, "Run-on Sentences."

- Begin Chapter 17, "Sentence Fragments." (In class, discuss each section of the chapter and review the first two or three items in each practice. Homework is to read the chapter, complete the practice items, and complete Review Exercises 1 and 2.)

Assignment for week 9:

Continue journals. Entries 5–10 are due in week 9.

Read Chapter 7, "Essays, Essay Exams, and Summary Reports."

Chapter 17, "Sentence Fragments," through Review Exercise 2.

Week 9

- Discuss Chapter 7, "Essays, Essay Exams, and Summary Reports." Do selected exercises.

- Field trip to library to choose article for Summary Report.

- At home: Read and annotate article; outline and draft summary report.

- Review Chapter 17, "Sentence Fragments," through Exercise 2.

- Begin Chapter 18, "Pronoun Case." (In class, discuss each section of the chapter and review the first two or three items in each practice. Homework is to read the chapter, complete the practice items, and complete Review Exercises 1 and 2.)

Assignment for week 10:

Finish draft of summary report.

Chapter 18, "Pronoun Case," through Review Exercise 2.

Week 10

- Peer review and revision of summary report.

- Discuss Chapter 18, "Pronoun Case," through Review Exercise 2.

- Begin Chapter 19, "Pronoun Agreement, Reference, and Point of View." (In class, discuss each section of the chapter and review the first two or three items in each practice. Homework is to read the chapter, complete the practice items, and complete Review Exercises 1 and 2.)

Assignment for week 11:

In Chapter 8, "Communication Beyond the Classroom: Oral Presentations and E-Mail," read the section on e-mail, and do selected exercises.

Chapter 19, "Pronoun Agreement, Reference, and Point of View," through Review Exercise 2.

Week 11

- Discuss selected exercises, Chapter 8, "Communication Beyond the Classroom: Oral Presentations and E-Mail."

- In-class writing assignment: E-mail writing assignment selected from Chapter 8.

- Peer review and in-class revision of e-mail.

- Discuss Chapter 19, "Pronoun Agreement, Reference, and Point of View," through Review Exercise 2.

- Begin Chapter 20, "Relative Pronouns." (In class, discuss each section of the chapter and review the first two or three items in each practice. Homework is to read the chapter, complete the practice items, and complete Review Exercises 1 and 2.)

Assignment for week 12:

In Chapter 8, "Communication Beyond the Classroom: Oral Presentations and E-Mail," read the section on oral presentations.

Chapter 20, "Relative Pronouns," through Review Exercise 2.

Week 12

- Discuss oral presentations section from Chapter 8, "Communication Beyond the Classroom: Oral Presentations and E-Mail."

- In class or at home: Craft a 2–3 minute presentation. Use assignment 1, 2, or 3 from "Assignments for Prepared Speeches" in Chapter 8, or prepare a presentation based on the summary report written in weeks 9 and 10.

- Discuss Chapter 20, "Relative Pronouns," through Review Exercise 2.

- Begin Chapter 27, "Commas." (In class, discuss each section of the chapter and review the first two or three items in each practice. Homework is to read the chapter, complete the practice items, and complete Review Exercises 1 and 2.)

Assignment for week 13:

Chapter 27, "Commas," through Review Exercise 2.

Rehearse and prepare to present oral presentations.

Week 13

- Oral presentations.

- Discuss selected Practices and Review Exercises in Chapter 27, "Commas."

- Begin Chapter 28, "Other Punctuation." (In class, discuss each section of the chapter and review the first two or three items in each practice. Homework is to read the chapter, complete the practice items, and complete Review Exercises 1 and 2.)

Assignment for week 14:

Chapter 28, "Other Punctuation" through Review Exercise 2.

Read "Broken Windows" by Leonard Pitts.

Read "My Dead Dog May Already Be a Winner!" by Lee Coppola.

Week 14

- Discuss "Broken Windows" by Leonard Pitts and "My Dead Dog May Already Be a Winner!" by Lee Coppola.

- Selected Writing Assignment chosen from the assignments listed after "Broken Windows" and "My Dead Dog May Already Be a Winner!"

- Discuss selected Practices and Review Exercises in Chapter 28, "Other Punctuation."

- Begin Chapter 30, "Quotation Marks, Underlining, and Italics." (In class, discuss each section of the chapter and review the first two or three items in each practice. Homework is to read the chapter, complete the practice items, and complete Review Exercises 1 and 2.)

Assignment for week 15:

Chapter 30, "Quotation Marks, Underlining, and Italics," through Review Exercise 2.

Read "Employment Test" by Barbara Ehrenreich or "From the Welfare Rolls, a Mother's View," by Elyzabeth Joy Stagg.

Week 15

- Student conferences.

- Discuss selected Practices and Review Exercises in Chapter 30, "Quotation Marks, Underlining, and Italics."

- Discuss "Employment Test" by Barbara Ehrenreich or "From the Welfare Rolls, a Mother's View" by Elyzabeth Joy Stagg.

- Final exam: Selected Writing Assignment chosen from the assignments listed after "Employment Test" by Barbara Ehrenreich or "From the Welfare Rolls, a Mother's View" by Elyzabeth Joy Stagg.